EXTRAORDINARY ORIGAMI

20 Projects from Contemporary **North American Masters**

Edited by MARC KIRSCHENBAUM

FOX CHAPEL PUBLISHING

Extraordinary Origami is an original work, first published in North America in 2018 by Fox Chapel Publishing Company, Inc., 903 Square Street, Mount Joy, PA 17552.

ISBN 978-1-56523-949-4

Library of Congress Cataloging-in-Publication Data

Names: Kirschenbaum, Marc, editor.
Title: Extraordinary origami / edited by Marc Kirschenbaum.
Other titles: Origami grandi maestri americani
Description: Mount Joy : Fox Chapel Publishing, [2018] | Translation of:
Origami grandi maestri americani.
Identifiers: LCCN 2018028297 | ISBN 9781565239494 (pbk.)
Subjects: LCSH: Origami. | Paper work.
Classification: LCC TT872.5 .O75 2018 | DDC 736/.982--dc23
LC record available at https://lccn.loc.gov/2018028297

Printed in Singapore
First printing

Credits

Text and diagrams

Sy Chen
Neal Elias
Paul Frasco
Beth Johnson
Jason Ku
Robert J. Lang
Bernie Peyton
Jeremy Shafer
Stephen Weiss
Patricia Crawford
Peter Engel
Gay Merrill Gross
Marc Kirschenbaum
Michael LaFosse
Bob Neale
Fred Rohm
John Szinger
Wensdy Whitehead

Photography

Araldo De Luca

Video

Marc Kirschenbaum

This book would not have been possible without the contributions of the artists involved. Everyone was able to contribute stunning examples of their work.

Hideo Komatsu provided the excellent illustrations for the pieces by Peter Engel.

Some of the artists are deceased, so valuable assistance was provided by the following people to aid with permissions and sourcing materials: Mick Guy, JC Nolan, Sam Randlett, Laura Rozenberg, David Shall, and Dave Venables.

Contents

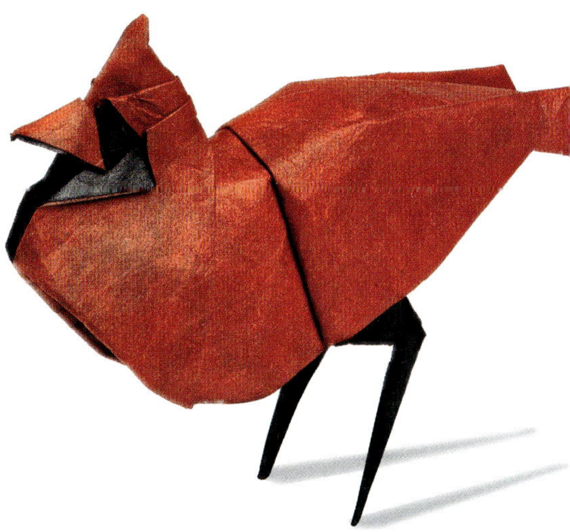

Introduction

America might conjure up things like baseball and apple pie, but origami? Yes, it is true that decorative paper folding has roots in Japan, but as an art form origami grew rapidly in the West. The USA in particular was a catalyst for the exchange of origami ideas and development, and is the home of some of the most prominent origami masters in the world. In the 1950s Lillian Oppenheimer of New York City traveled around the world connecting origami artists who had been working independently. The subsequent exchange of ideas certainly helped push the sophistication and polish that origami was experiencing. An origami center was founded in 1958, and in 1980 this spawned off into a full-fledged organization known today as OrigamiUSA, largely from the efforts of fellow New Yorker Michael Shall. Alice Gray, an entomologist at the American Museum of Natural History, provided the organization a home base in the museum. Gray, a respected origami artist herself, also created diagrams for now classic origami pieces, and became the editor of the organization's magazine.

This book showcases the works of eighteen origami artists, some who were prominent back in the early days of this paper-folding renaissance, as well as a few people who are relatively new to the art. As you can see from their biographies, these are all very accomplished artists. There is certainly a tremendous amount of paper-folding talent in America.

An exciting part of this showcase is how varied the approaches are, and there is certainly a wide variety of subjects tackled. You can recreate their masterworks through the clear instructions. There are also links to see videos of the pieces being folded. Throughout the course of these projects, there are plenty of folds to keep fingers busy for hours. Enjoy!

Symbols and Terminology

Types of Folds

Valley fold

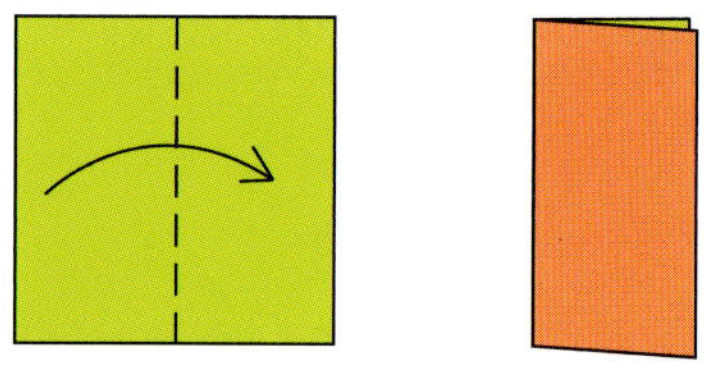

Mountain fold

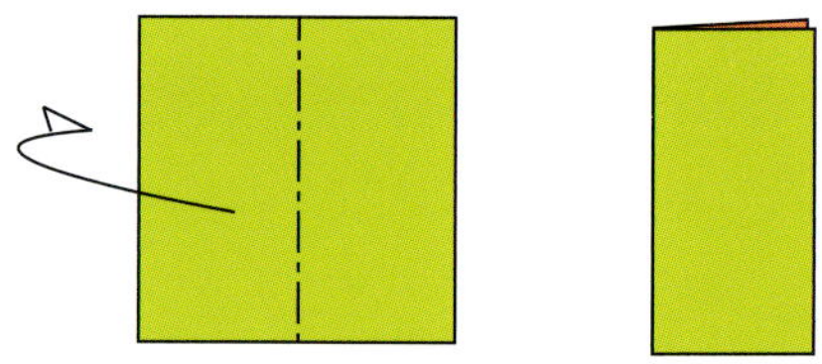

Crease line

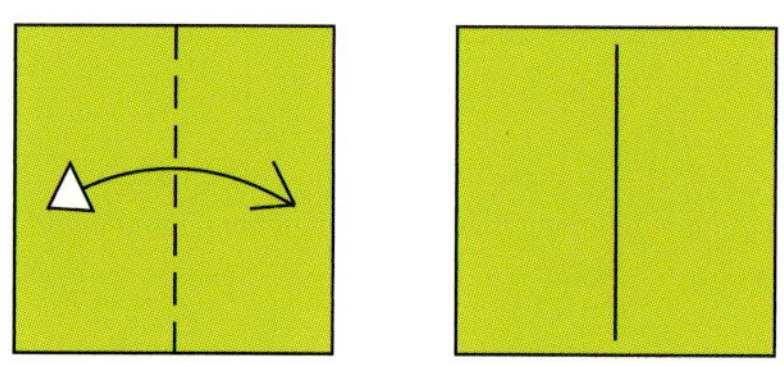

Hidden/X-ray line

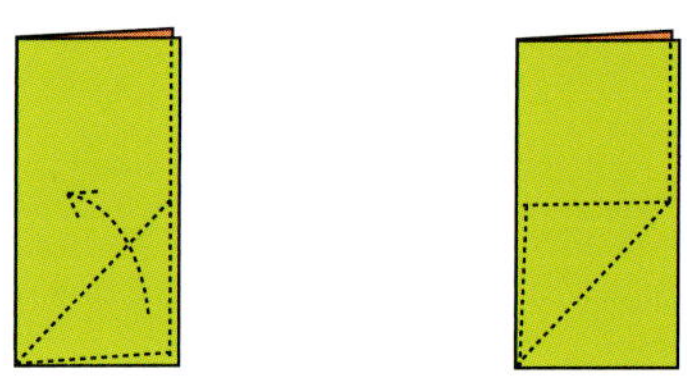

Arrows

Fold forward

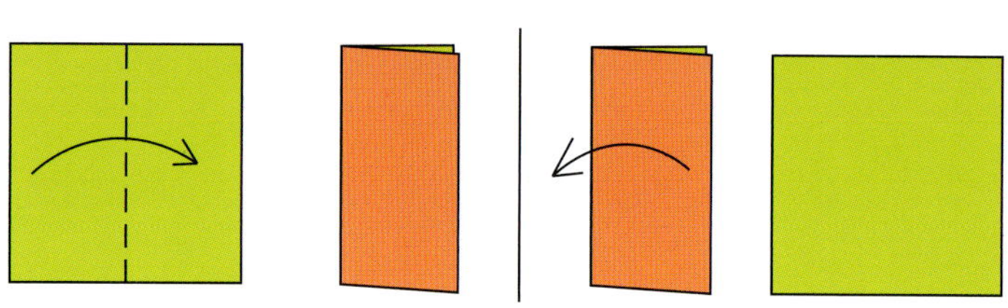

Fold behind

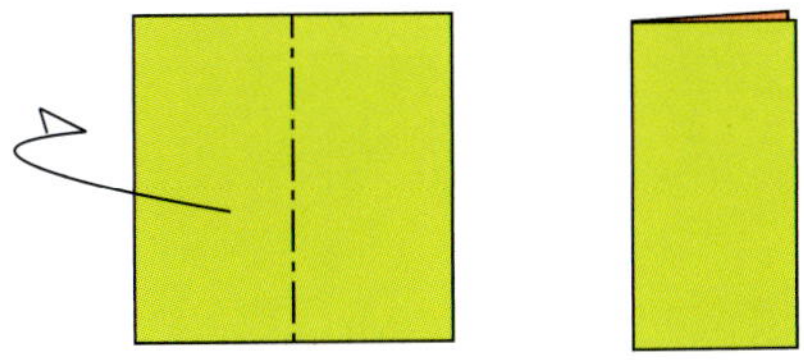

Fold and unfold

Sink/Reverse/Push in/
Closed Sink

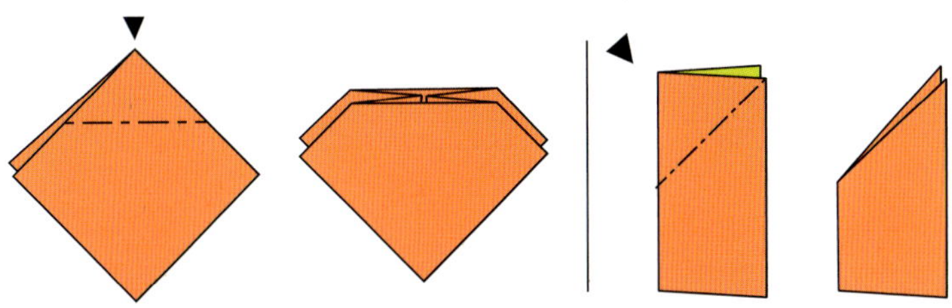

Turn over

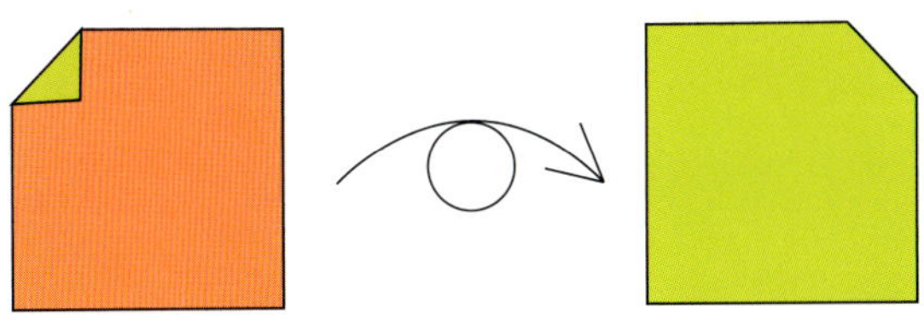

Turn 90 degrees, half
turn, etc.

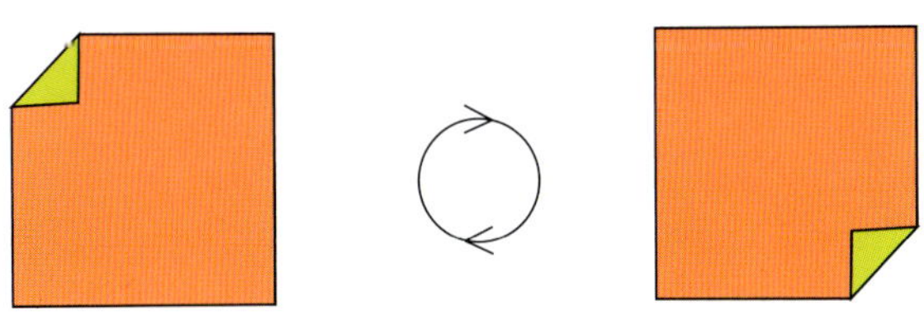

Unsink/Pull out

Techniques

Reverse fold

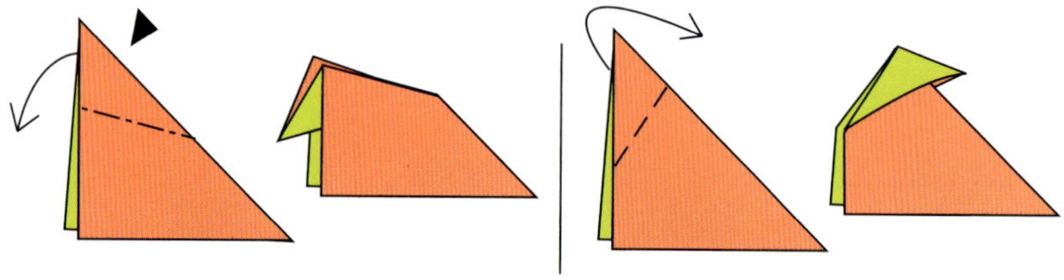

Crimp

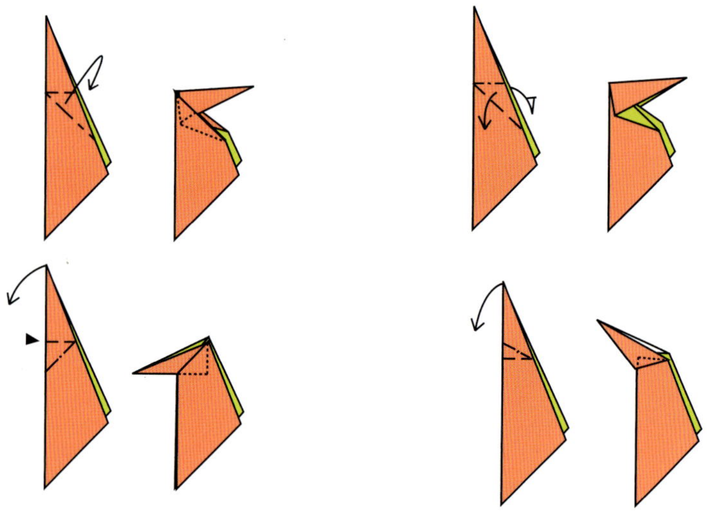

Rabbit ear

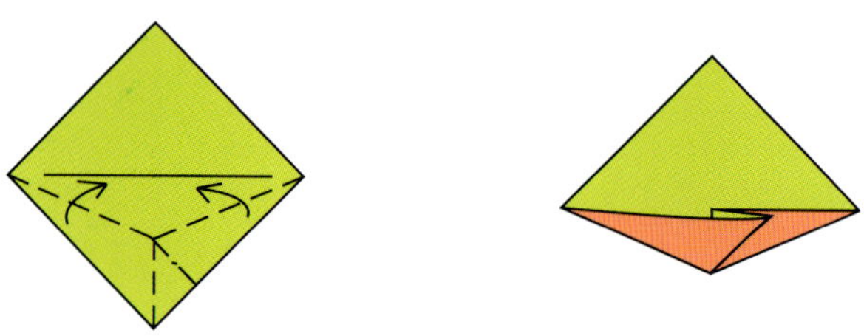

Squash fold

Petal fold

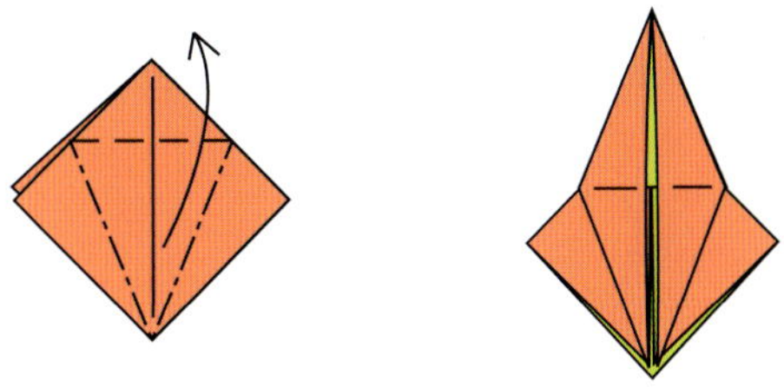

Sink

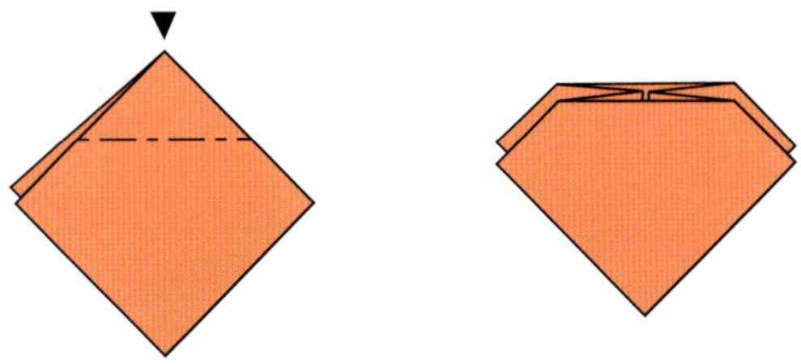

Closed sink

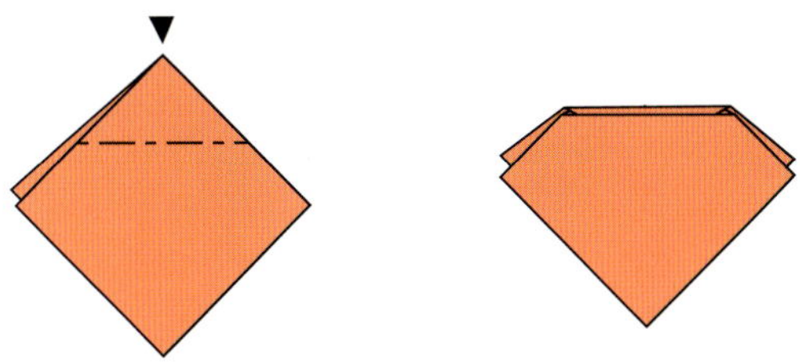

Sink triangularly

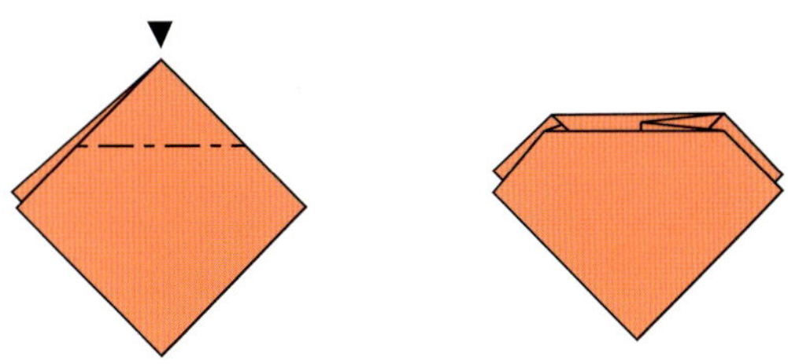

Pleat

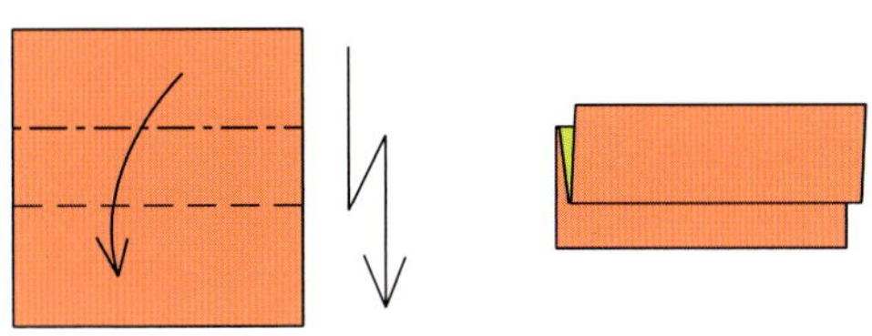

Swivel/pivot

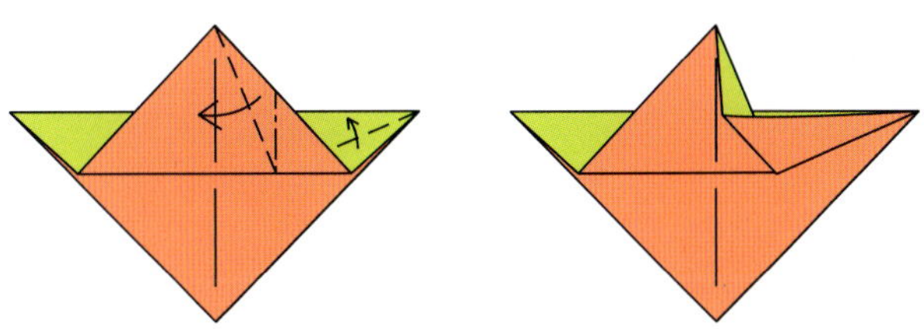

Swan Couple Card

Sy Chen

To learn more about Sy and his journey to origami master, see his bio on page 150.

video: *youtu.be/dItk9XKmbfI*

1

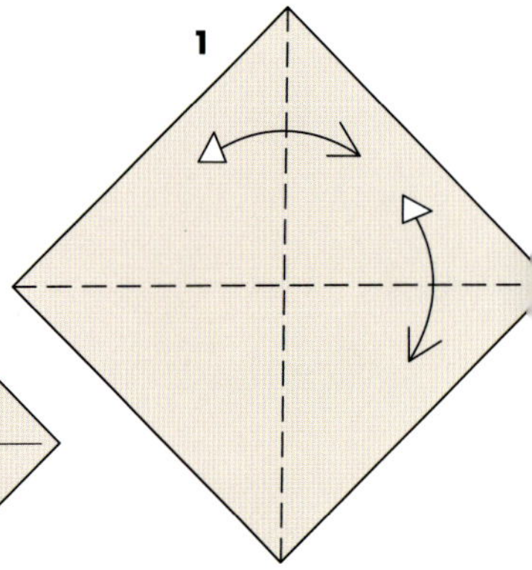

Precrease along the diagonals.

2

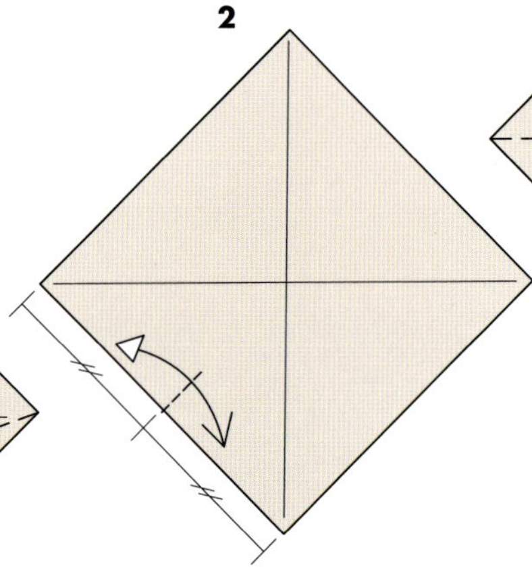

Pinch the lower edge in half.

3

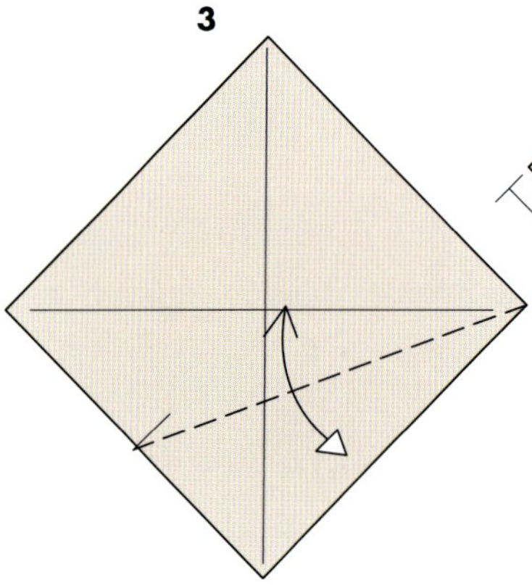

Form a precrease from the corner to the crease.

4

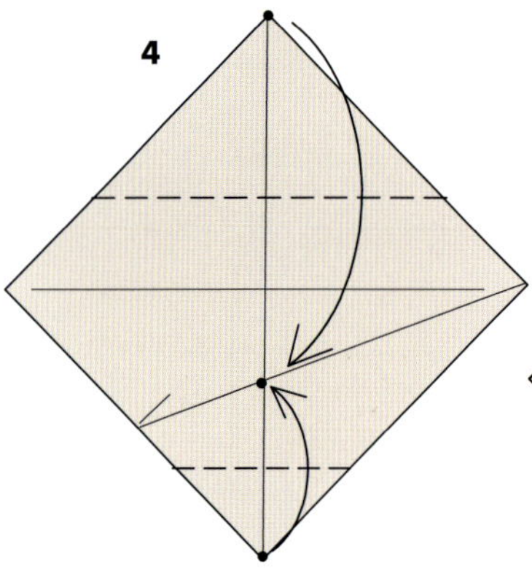

Valley fold toward the dotted intersection.

5

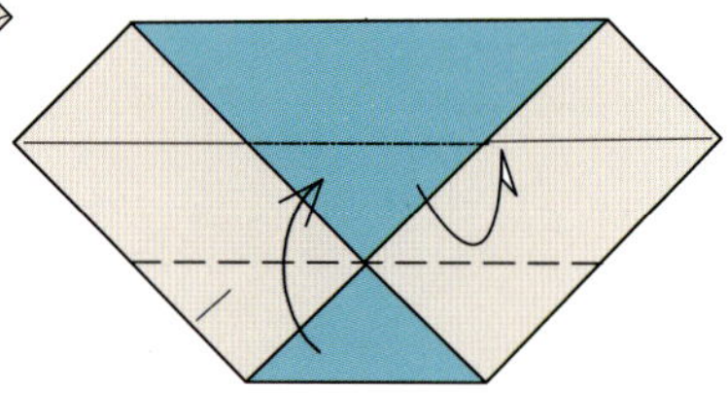

Mountain fold the corner to lie along the center crease. Valley fold the lower section up.

6

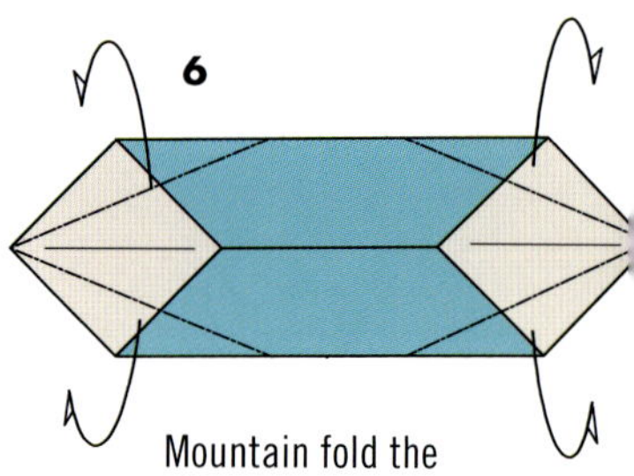

Mountain fold the sides along the angle bisectors.

12

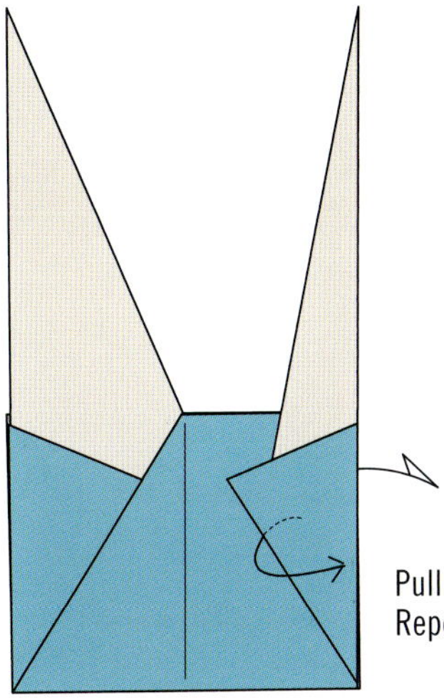

Pull out the trapped layer.
Repeat behind.

13

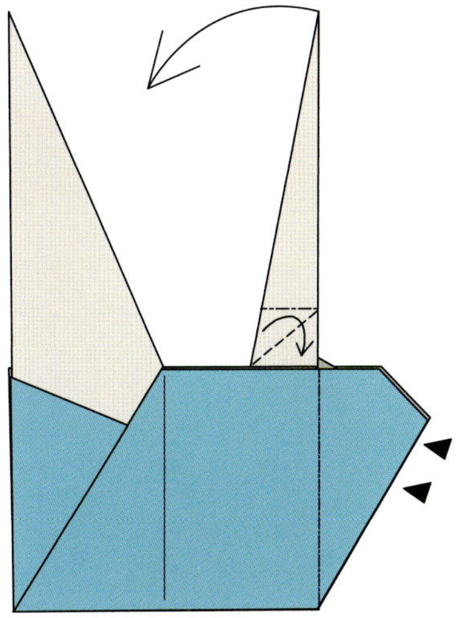

Reverse fold the sides inward.
Crimp the flap down.

11

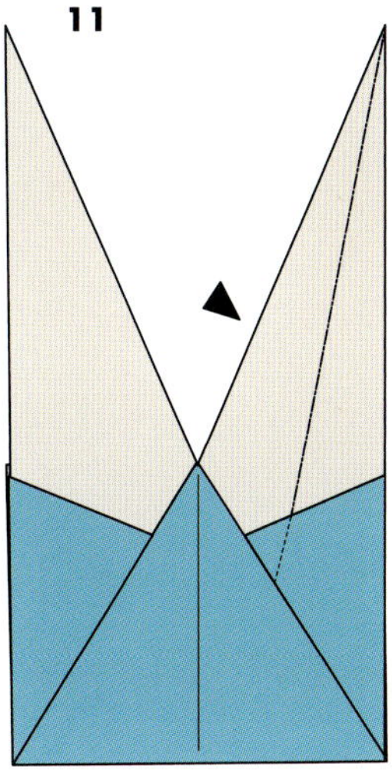

Open sink along the angle bisector.

10

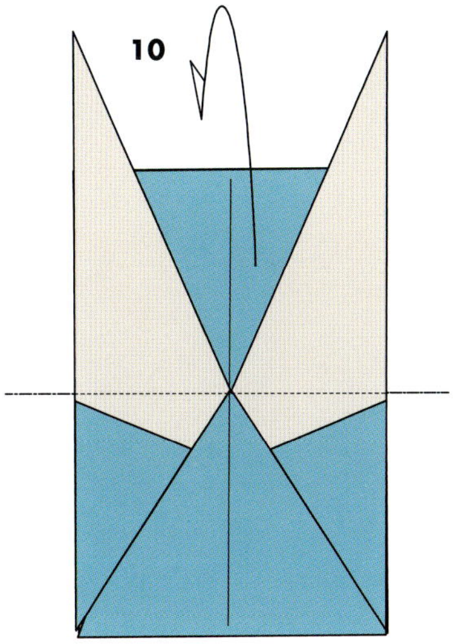

Mountain fold.

9

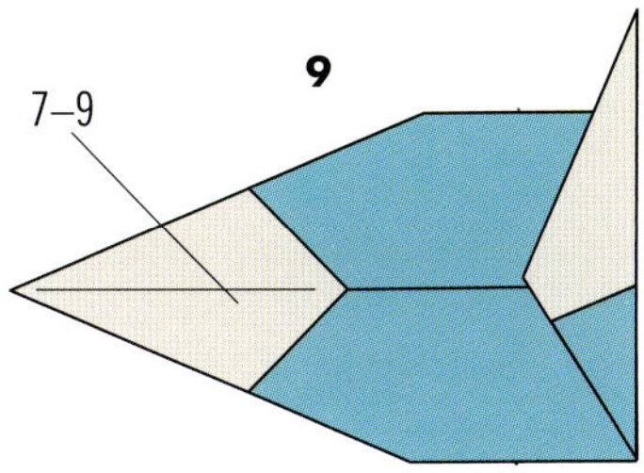

Repeat steps 7–9 in mirror image.

7

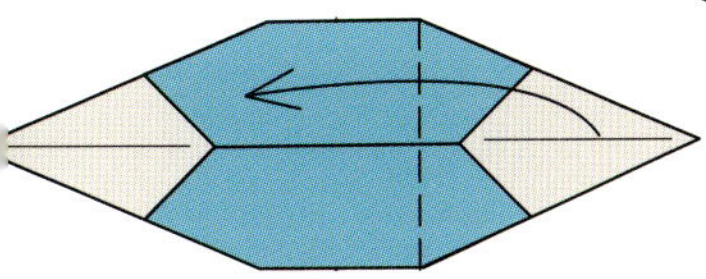

Valley fold along the widest point.

8

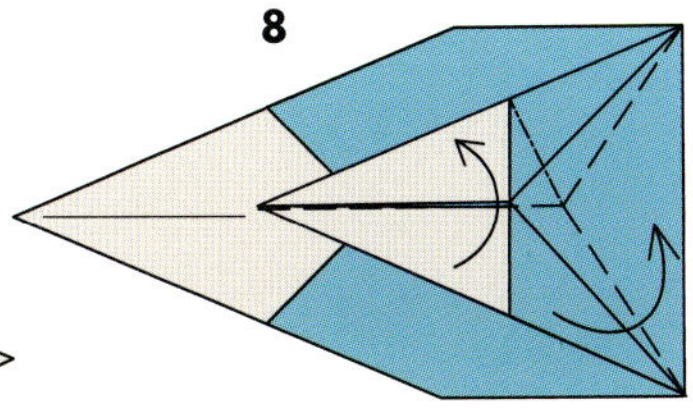

Rabbit ear the flap up.

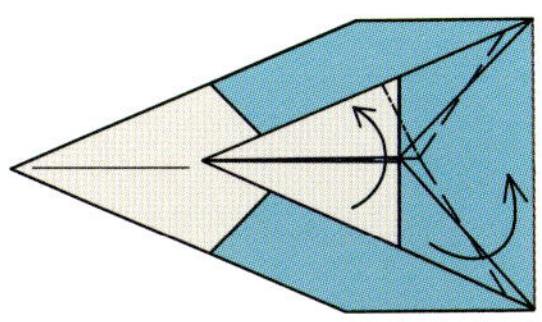

Variation: As a variation, you can shift the rabbit ear location to make the swans closer to each other.

14

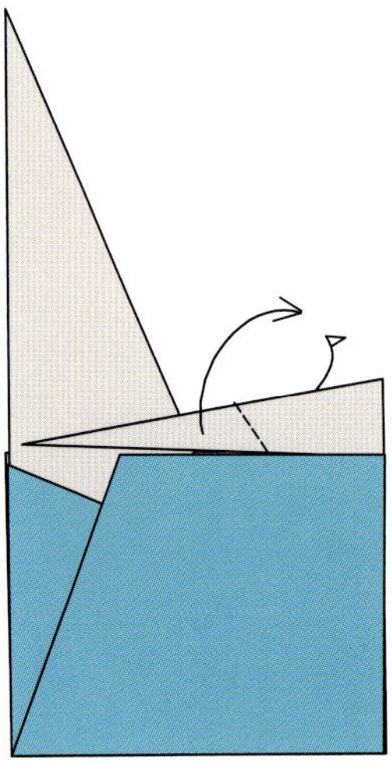

Outside reverse fold.

15

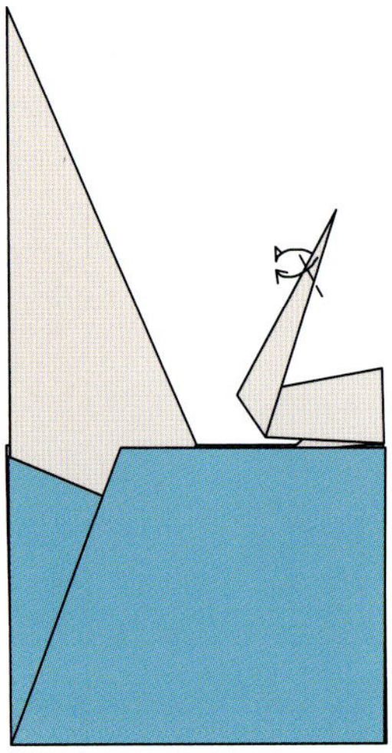

Outside reverse fold.

16

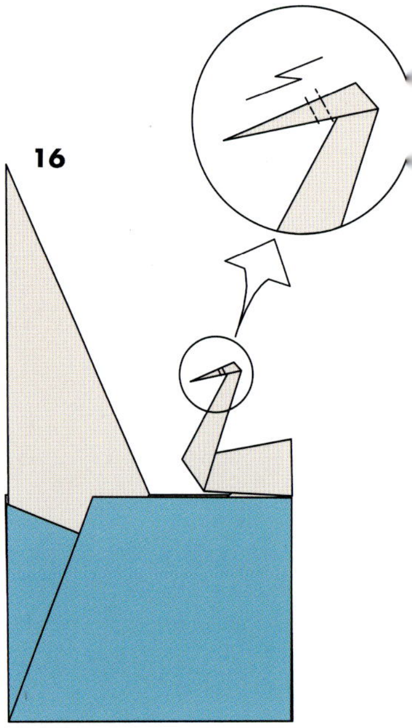

Crimp to form the head.

17

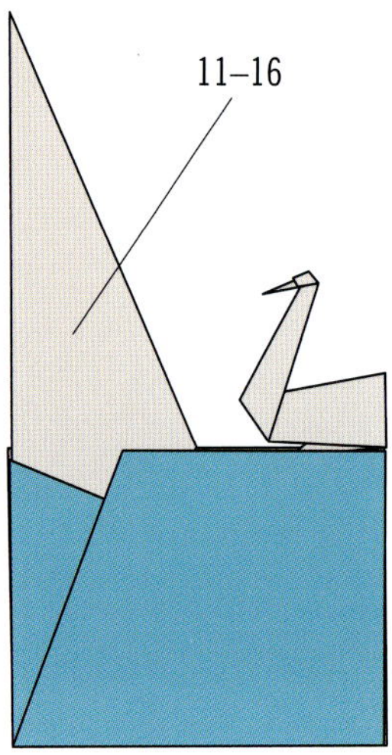

Repeat steps 11–16 in mirror image.

18

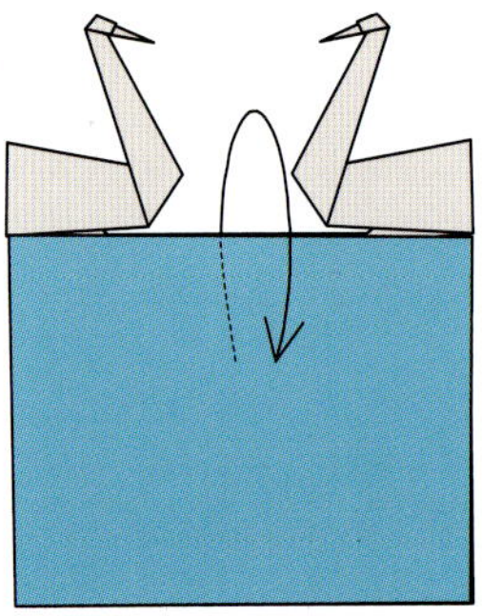

Flip the flap from behind over to close the card.

19

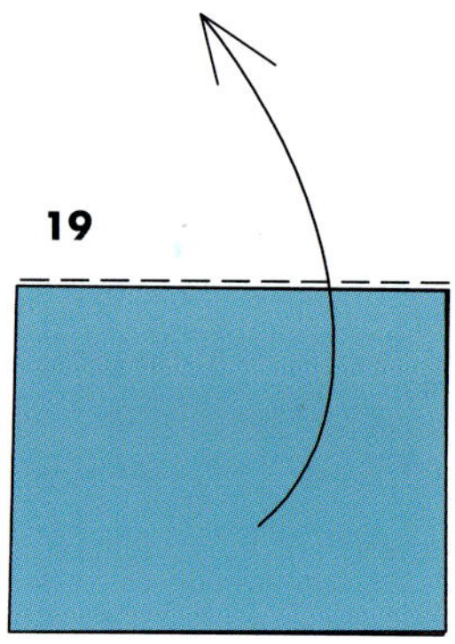

Open out the card to reveal the two swans.

20

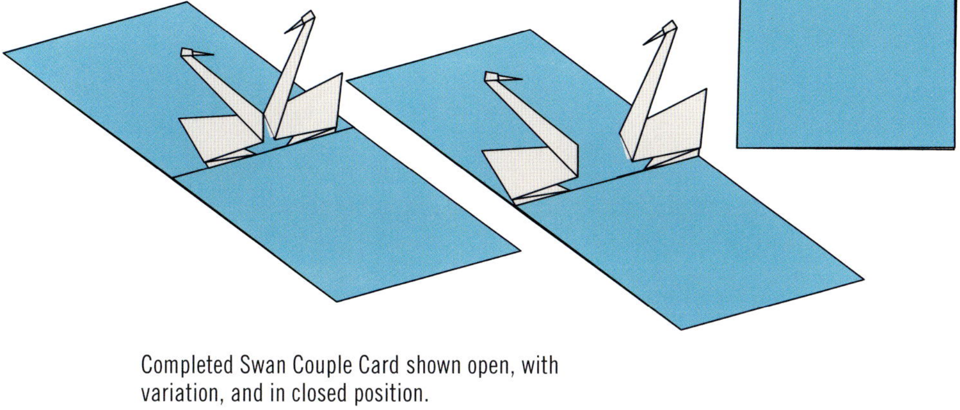

Completed Swan Couple Card shown open, with variation, and in closed position.

Doghouse

Patricia Crawford

To find out what Patricia's favorite origami subject was, see her bio on page 150.

video: *youtu.be/linF8D4ytlA*

1

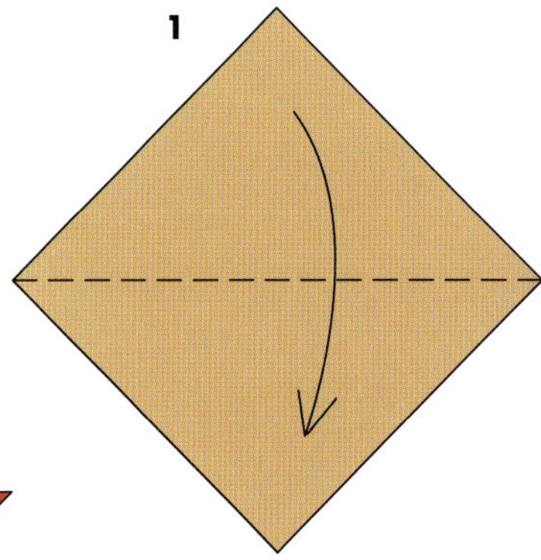

Valley fold in half.

2

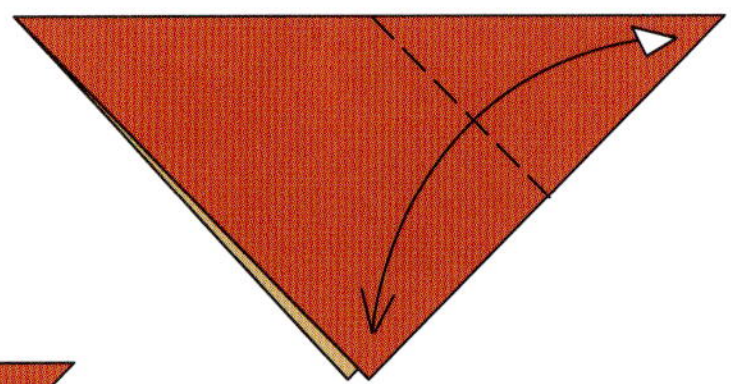

Precrease the right side.

3

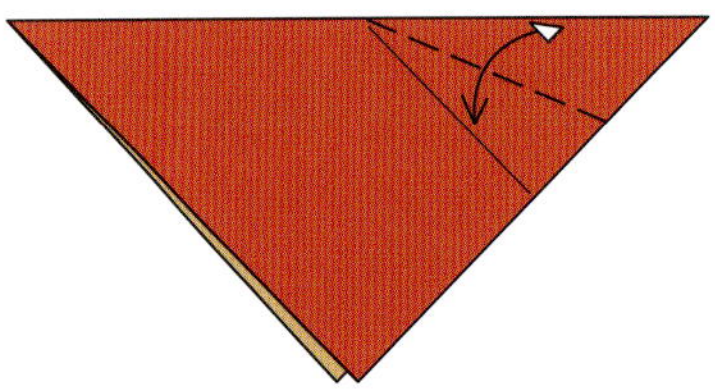

Precrease along the angle bisector.

4

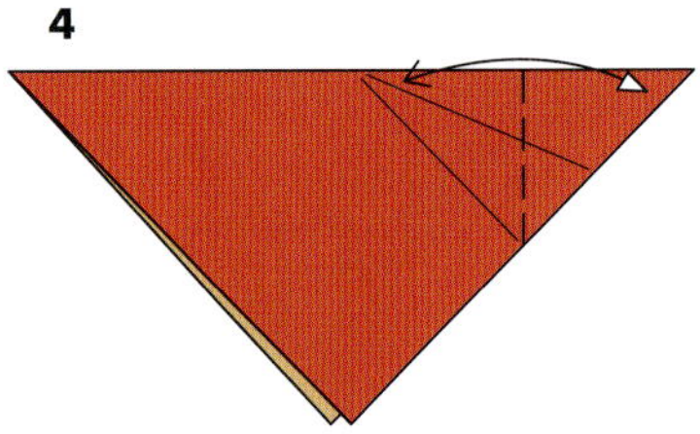

Precrease in half.

5

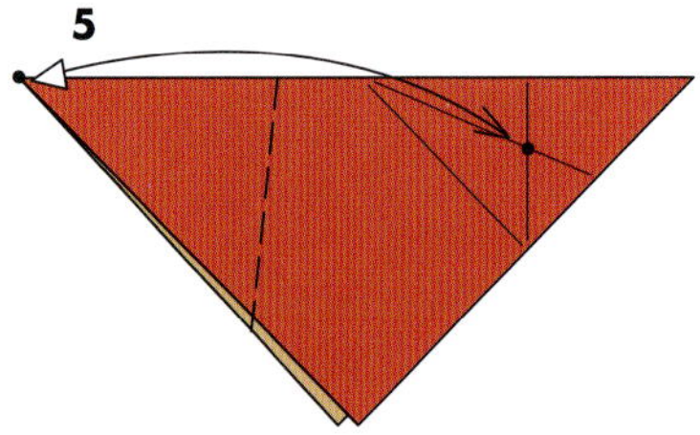

Precrease toward the dotted intersection.

6

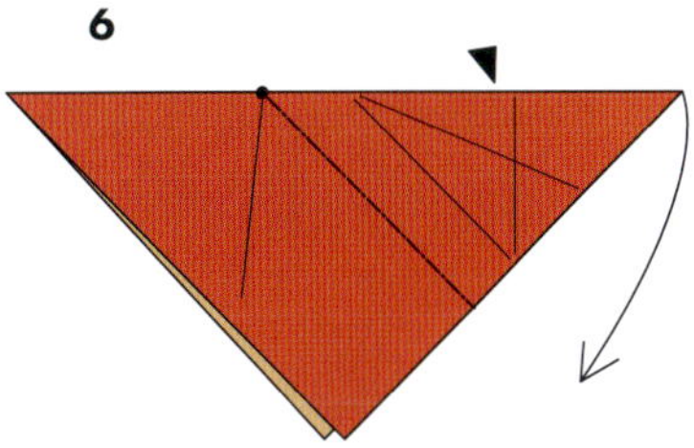

Reverse fold, starting from the indicated point.

7

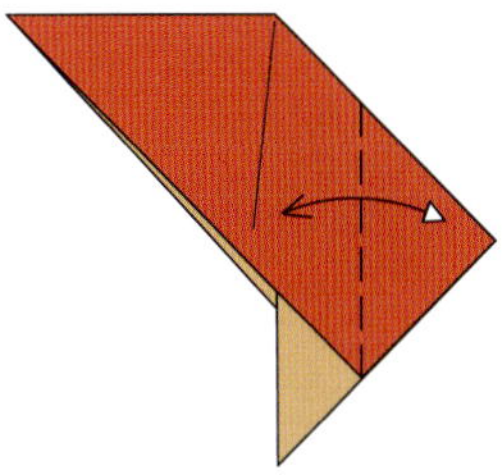

Precrease the flap in half.

8

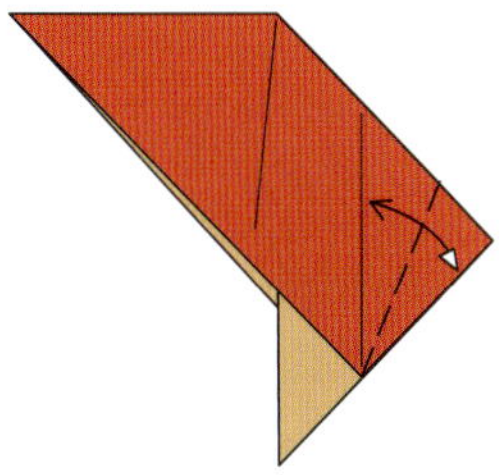

Precrease along the angle bisector.

9

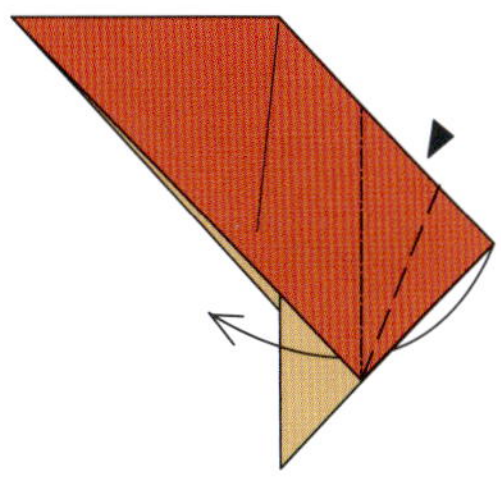

Reverse fold in and then out along the existing creases.

10

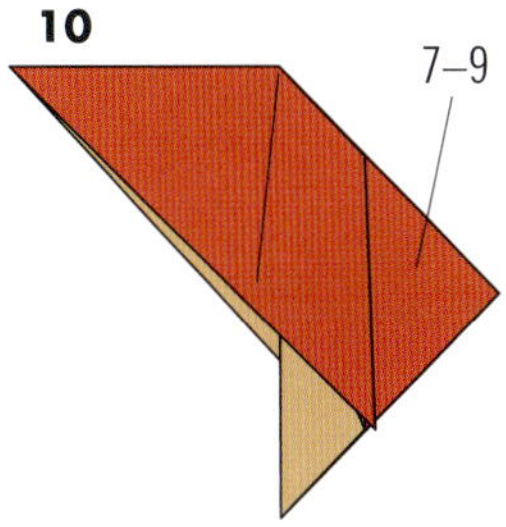

Repeat steps 7–9 behind.

11

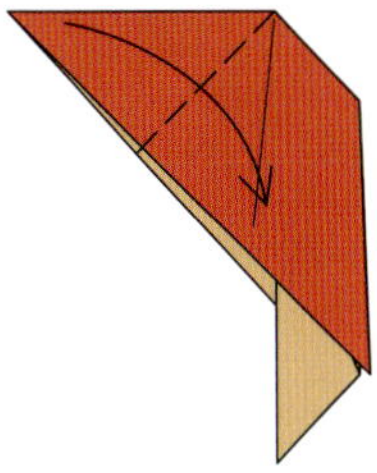

Valley fold down.

12

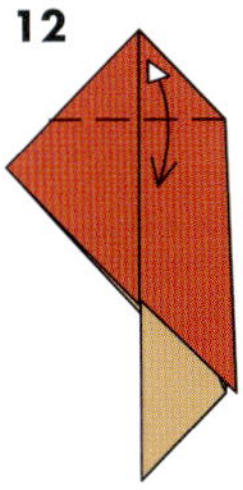

Precrease through all layers.

13

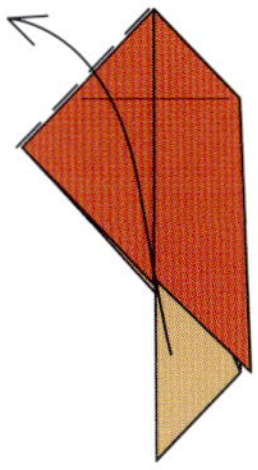

Unfold the flap.

14

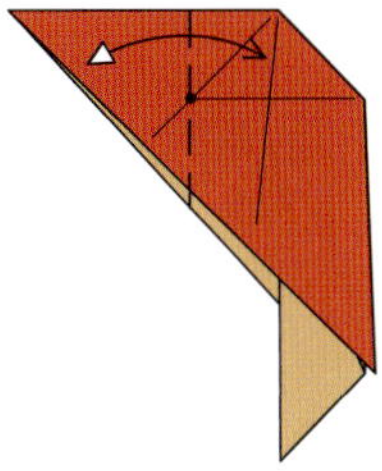

Precrease by continuing along an existing crease.

15

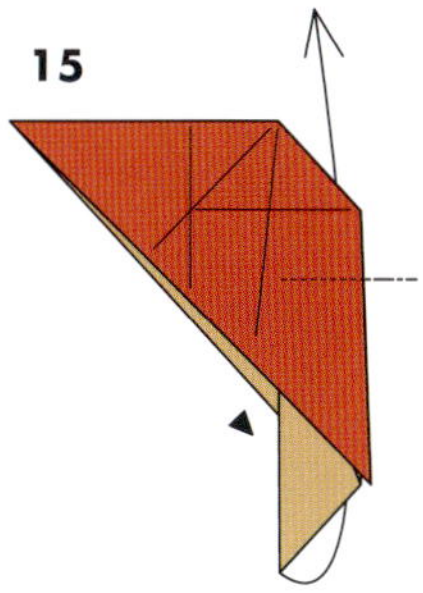

Reverse fold the center flap up as far as possible.

16

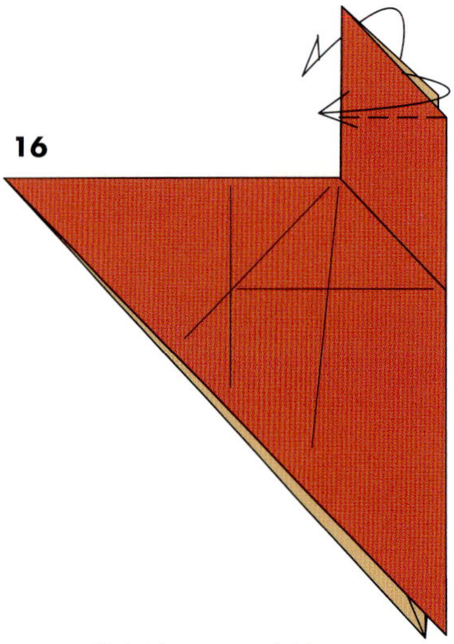

Outside reverse fold.

17

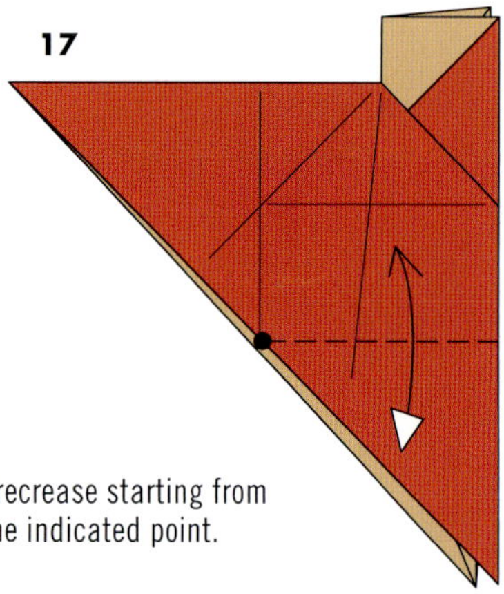

Precrease starting from the indicated point.

18

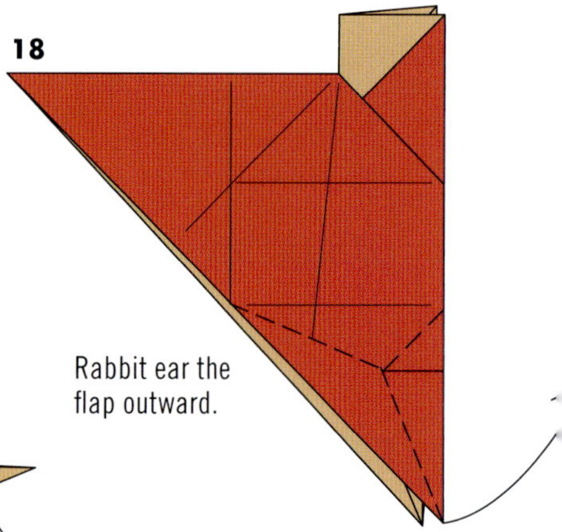

Rabbit ear the flap outward.

19

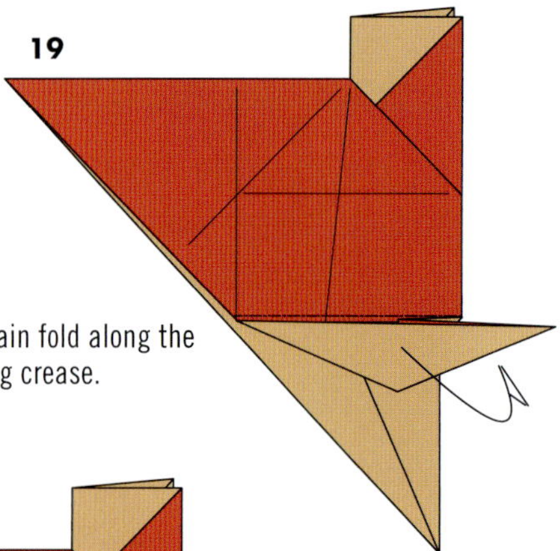

Mountain fold along the existing crease.

20

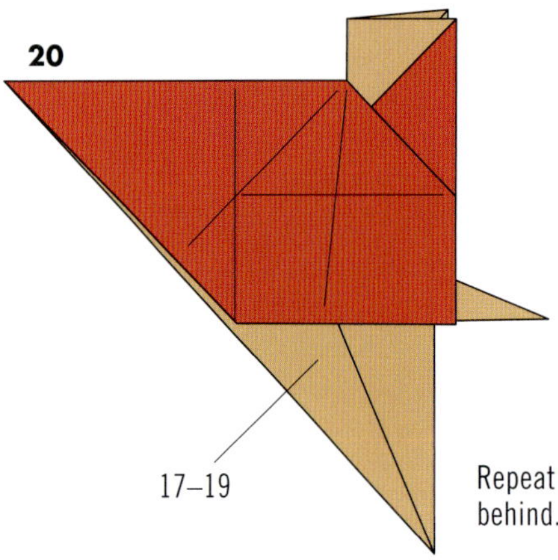

Repeat steps 17–19 behind.

21

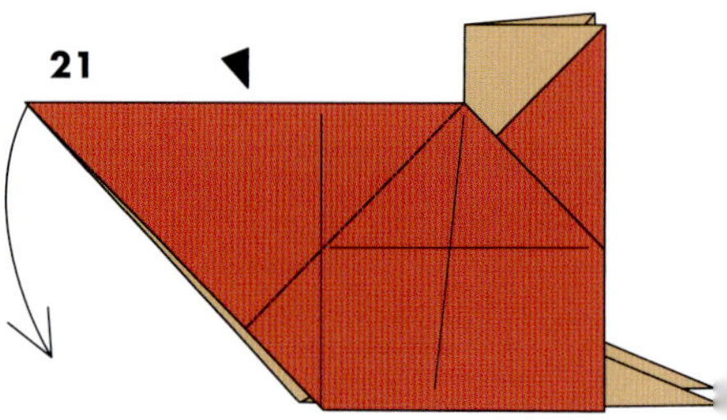

Reverse fold along the existing crease.

22

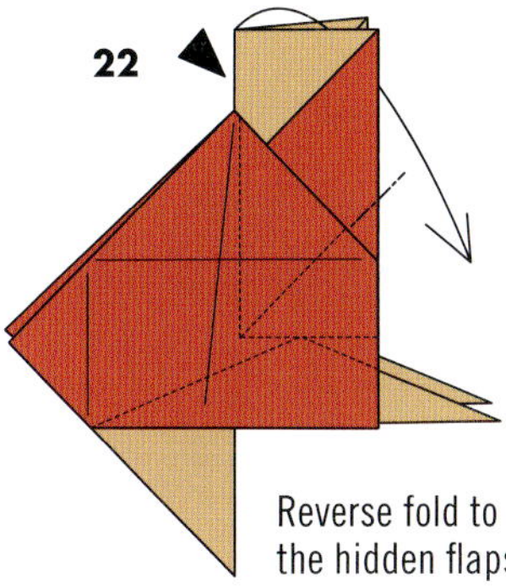

Reverse fold to lie above the hidden flaps.

23

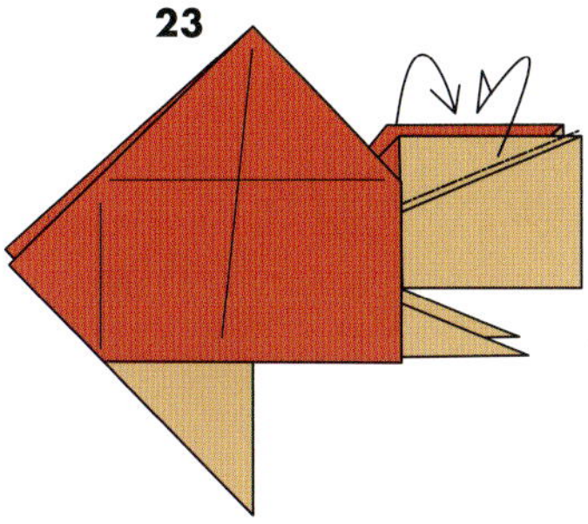

Tuck the edges inside.

24

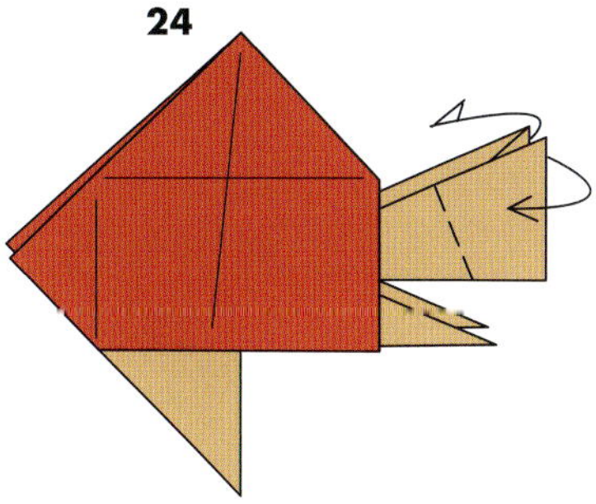

Outside reverse fold.

25

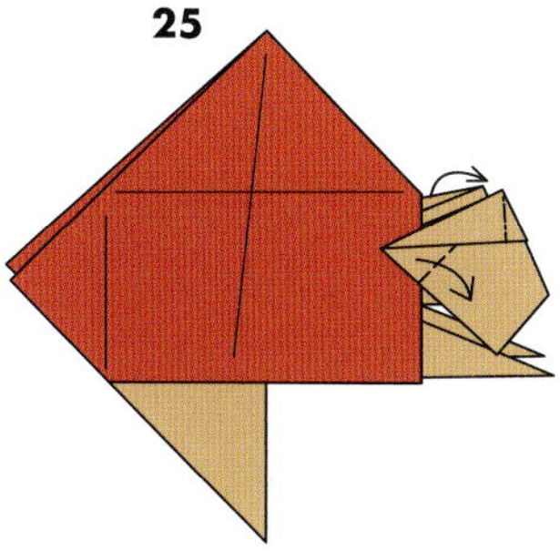

Squash fold. Repeat behind.

26

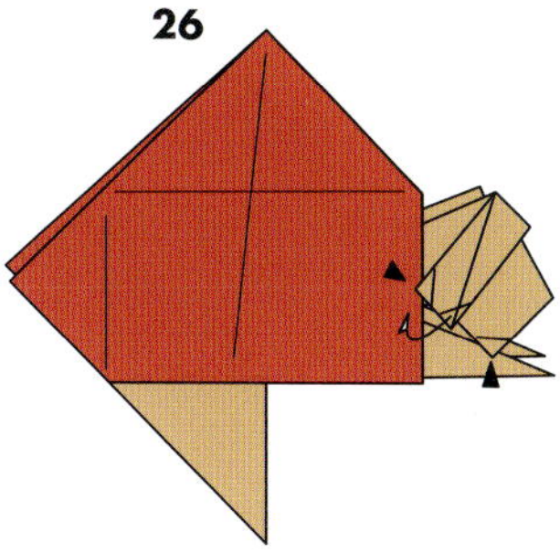

Shape with reverse folds and mountain folds.

27

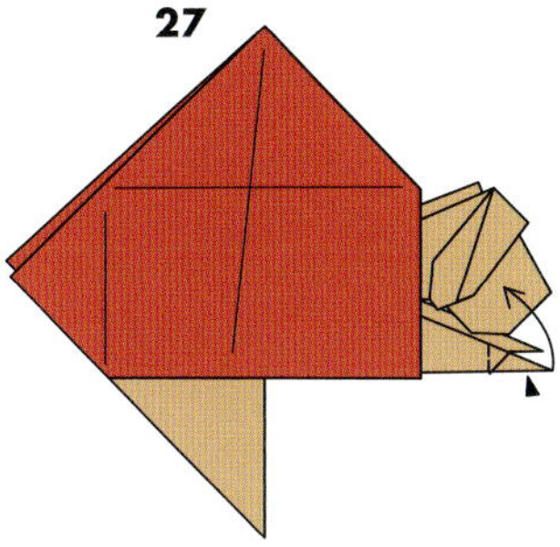

Spread squash the flap up.

28

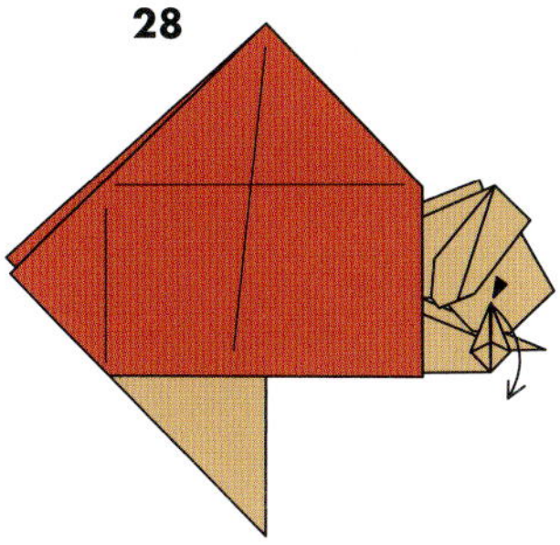

Spread squash the flap down.

29

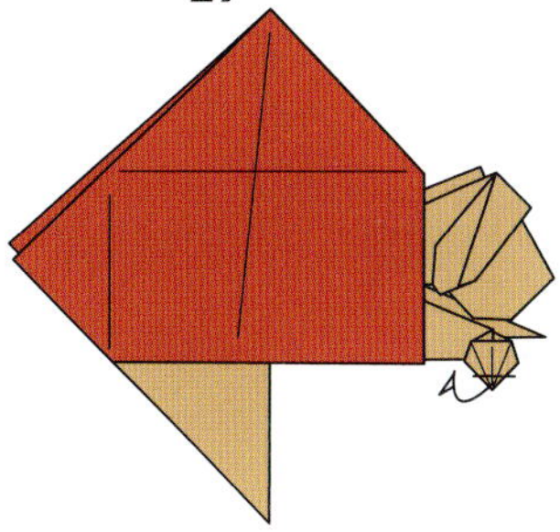

Mountain fold the tip.

30

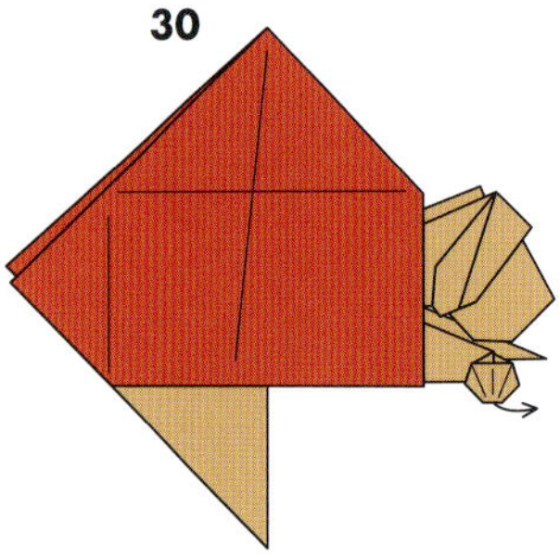

Open out the flap.

31

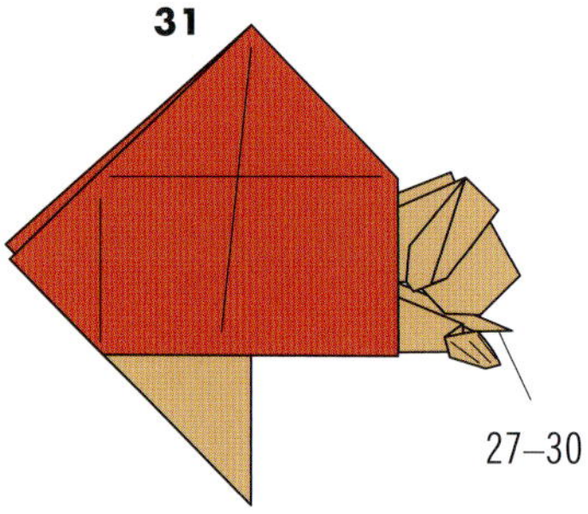

Repeat steps 27–30 behind.

32

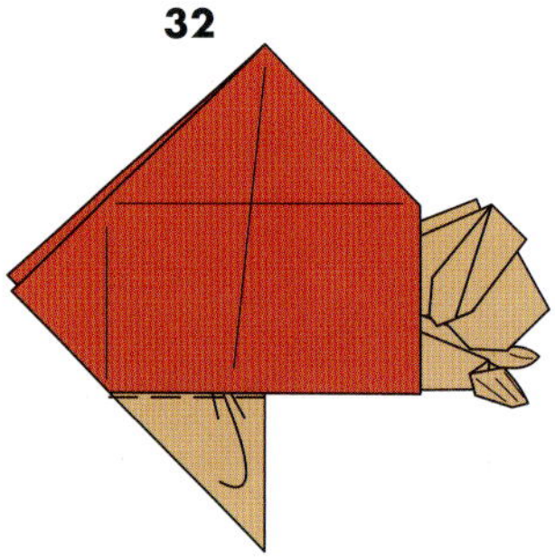

Tuck the center flap in.

33

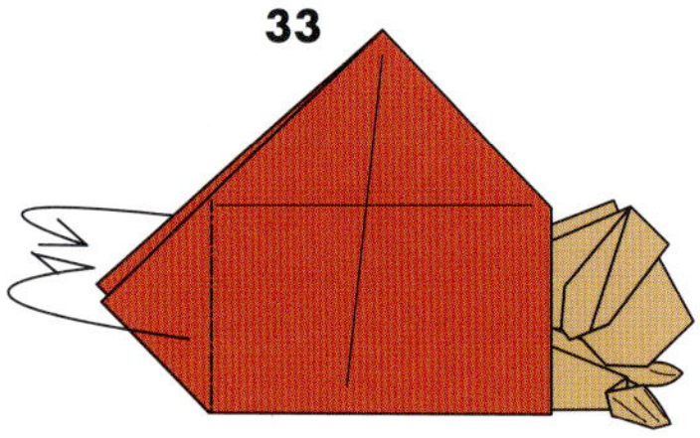

Tuck the side flaps in along the existing creases.

34

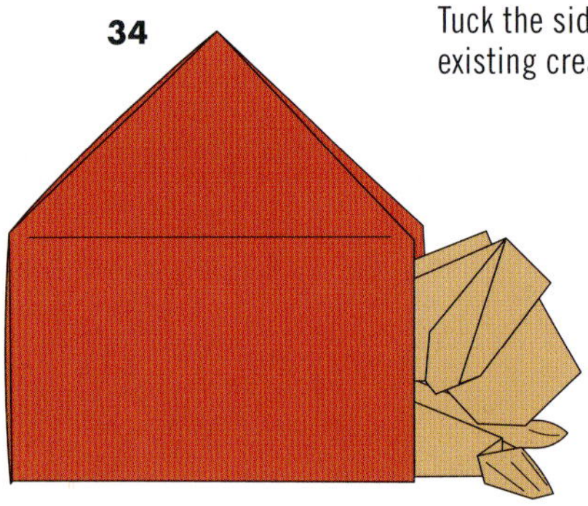

Completed Doghouse.

Harlequin

Neal Elias

One of the few origami masters to have a folding technique named after him. Check out Neal's story on page 155.

video: *youtu.be/BXbmBIRhuW0*

1

Precrease the top edge in half with a mountain fold.

2

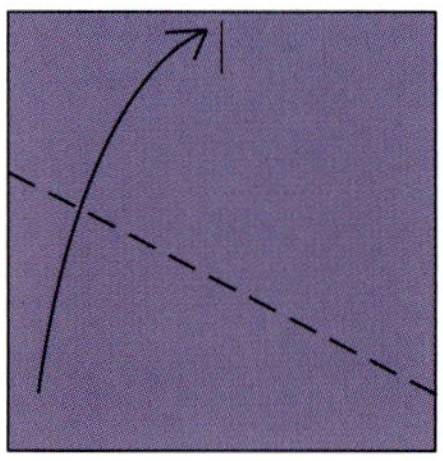

Valley fold the corner to meet the crease.

3

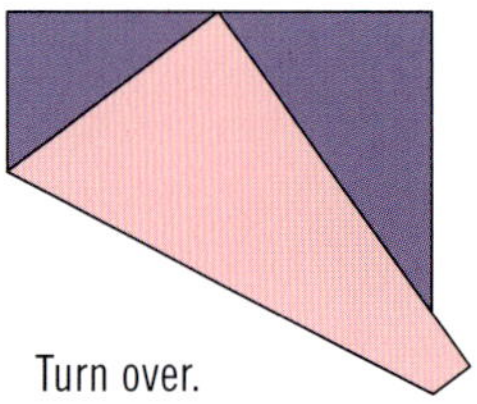

Turn over.

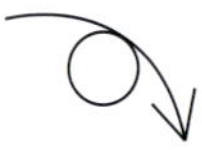

4

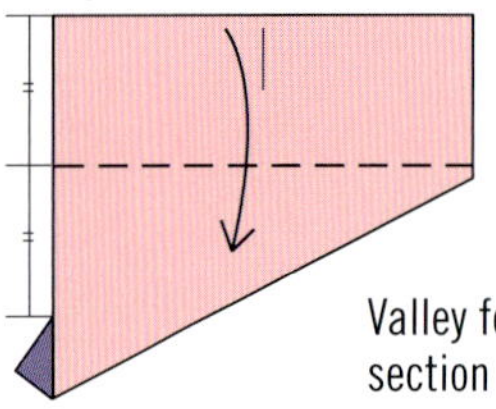

Valley fold the indicated section in half.

5

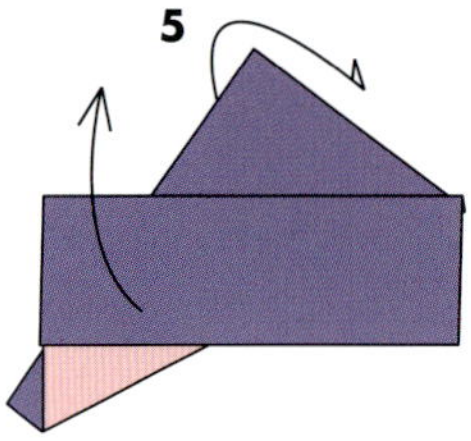

Unfold completely to the colored side.

6

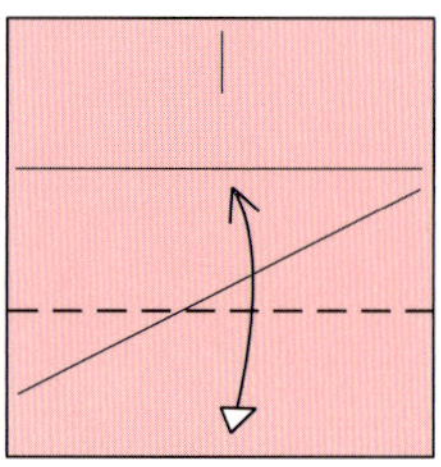

Precrease the lower section in half.

7

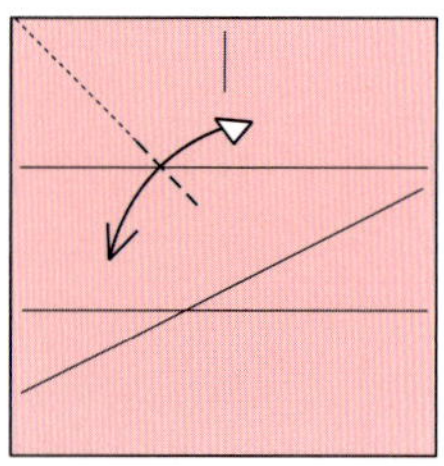

Form a pinch through the crease along the angle bisector.

8

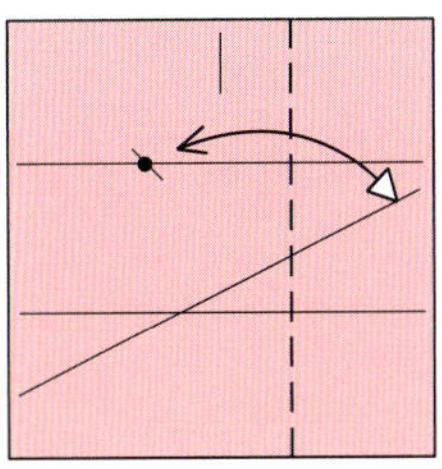

Precrease to the indicated intersection.

9

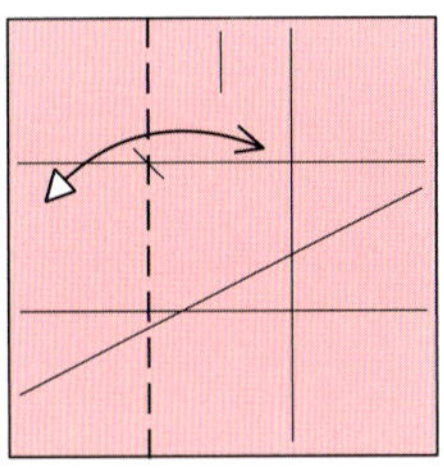

Precrease the left section in half.

10

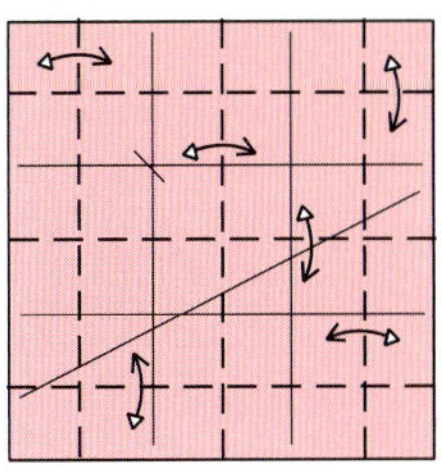

Precrease each section in half, both horizontally and vertically.

11

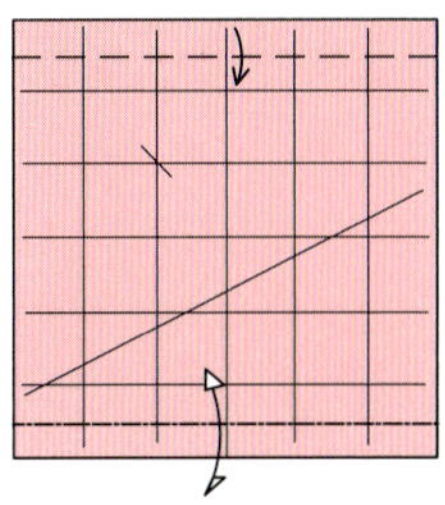

Valley fold at the top and precrease at the bottom with a mountain fold.

12

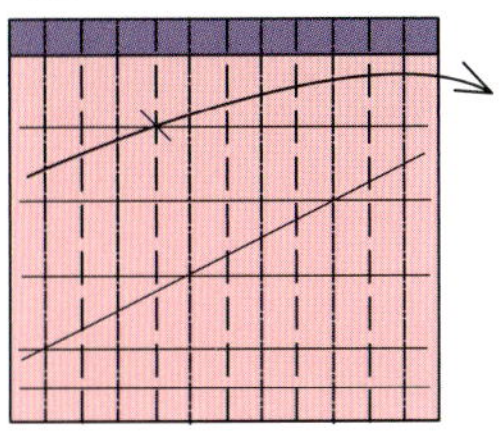

Pleat the model like a fan, by inserting mountain folds.

13

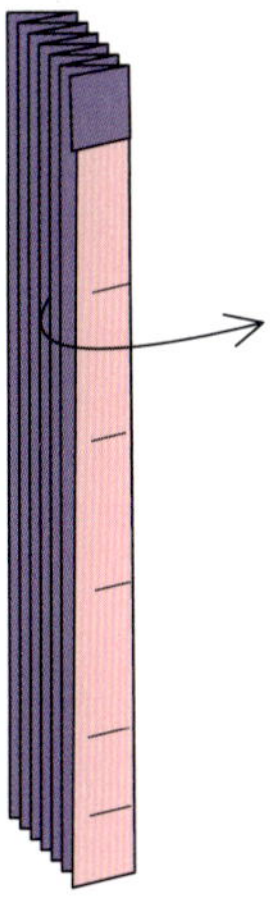

Open out three sets of pleats.

14

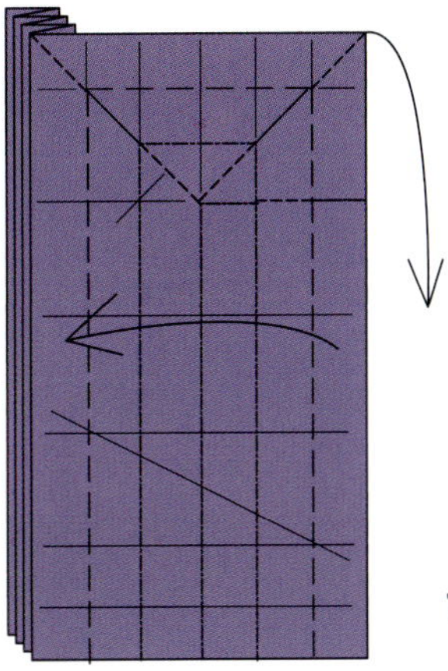

Pull the corner down while pleating inward (Elias Stretch).

15

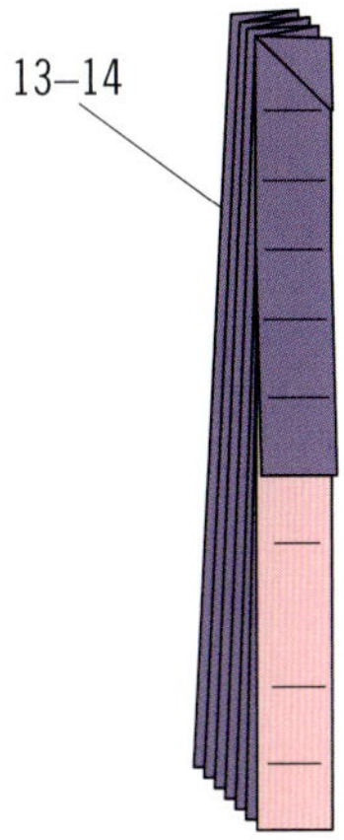

Repeat steps 13–14 behind.

16

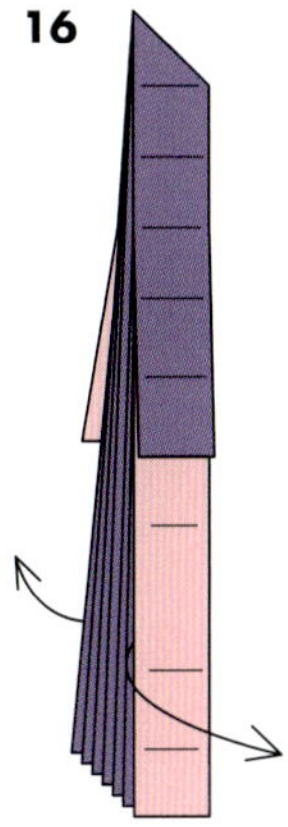

Spread apart the pleats at the bottom.

17

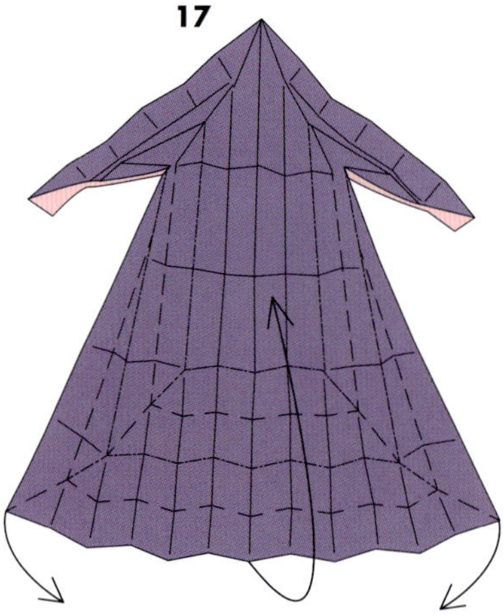

Pull the corners down while pleating inward (Elias Stretch).

18

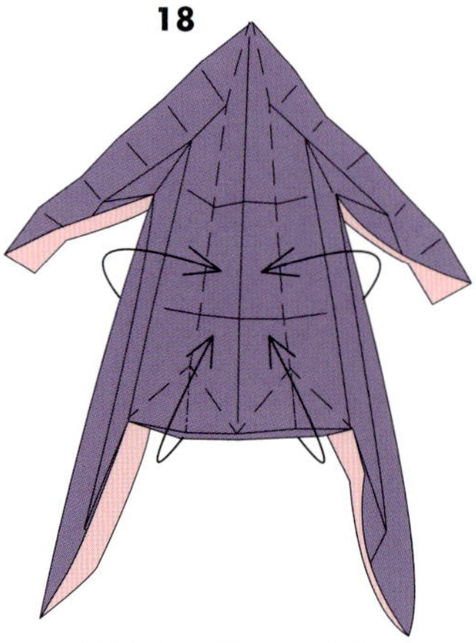

Fold the sides in while inserting reverse folds.

19

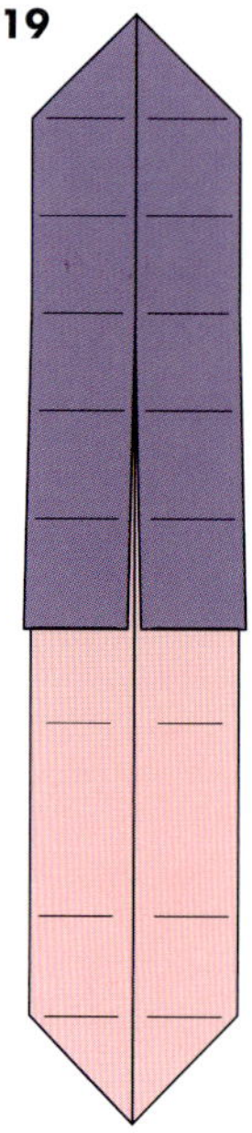

Turn over.

20

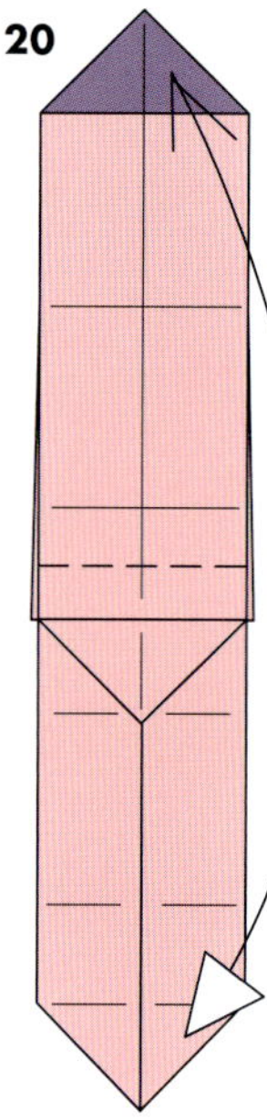

Precrease in half.

21

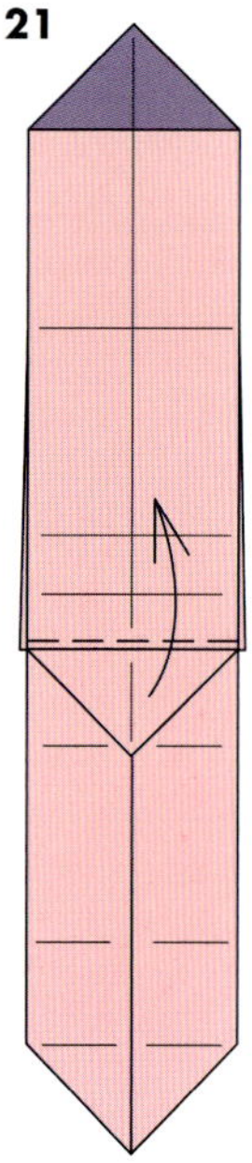

Valley fold the center flap up.

22

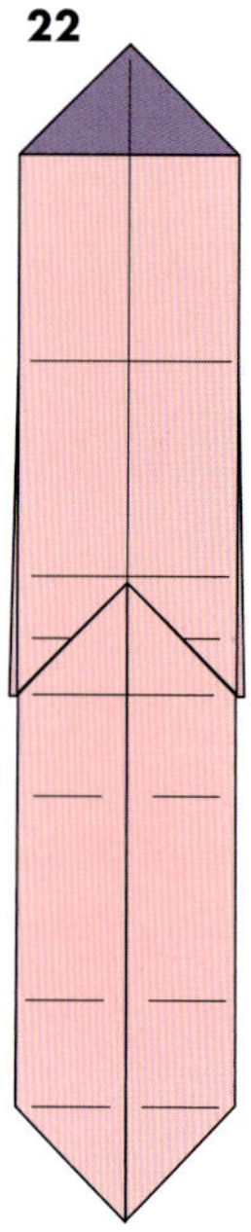

Turn over.

23

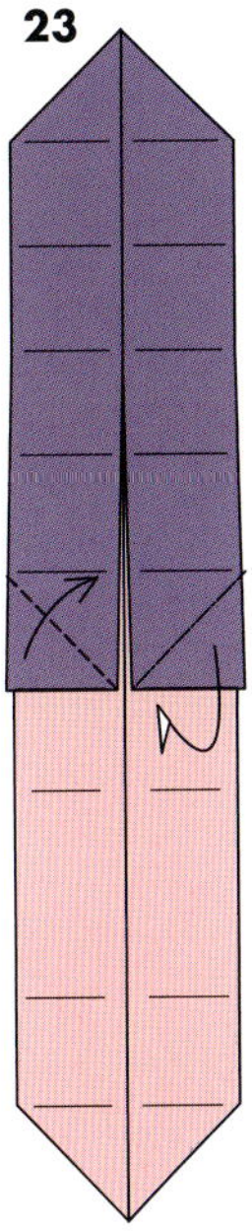

Valley fold at the left and mountain fold at the right.

24

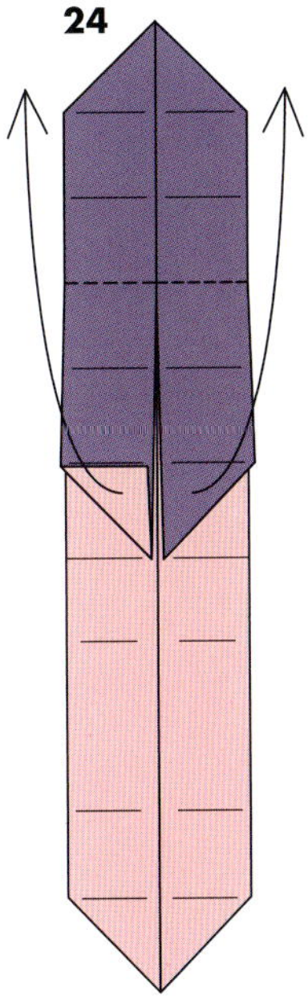

Swing both flaps up.

25

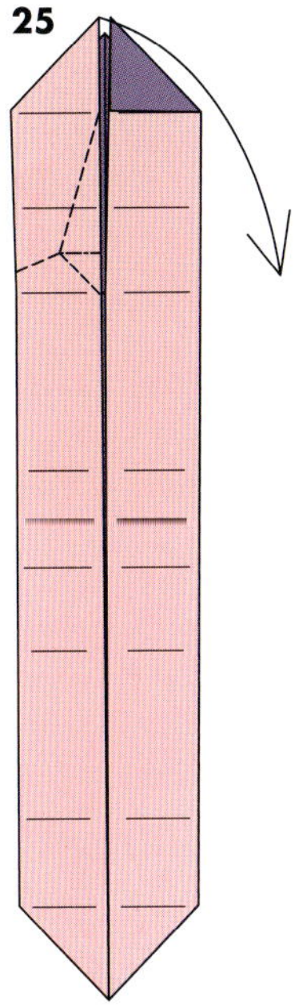

Rabbit ear the flap over. The folds should meet at the center of the flap.

26

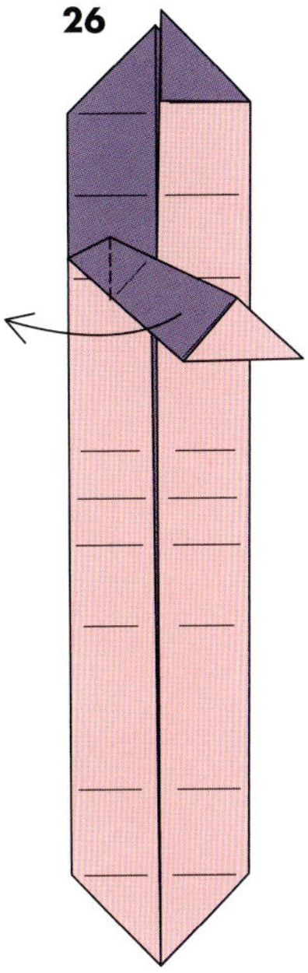

Lightly swing the flap over.

27

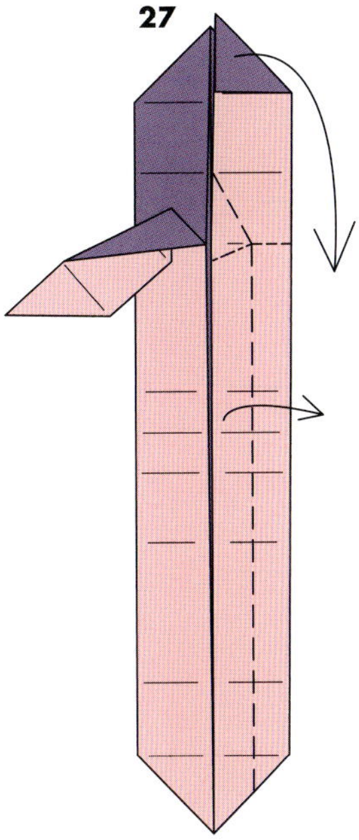

Valley fold over a single layer while bringing the flap back down. Allow a swivel to form.

28

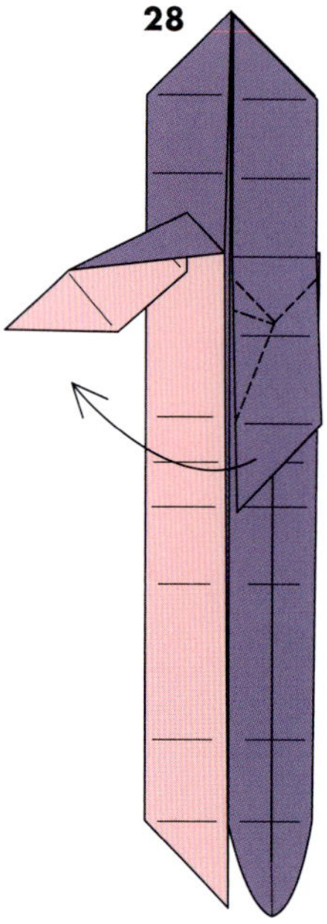

Rabbit ear the flap over.

29

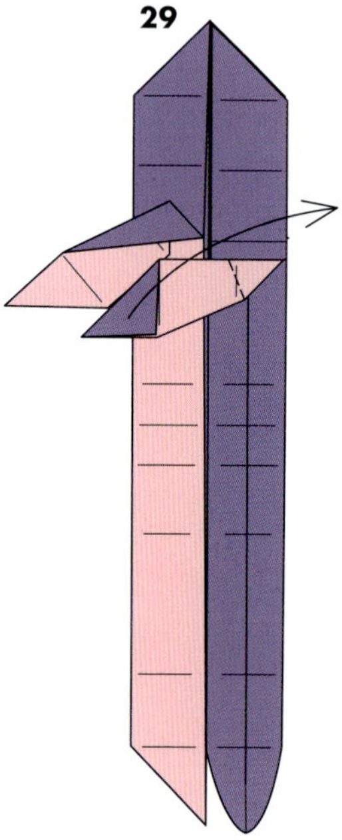

Lightly swing the flap over.

30

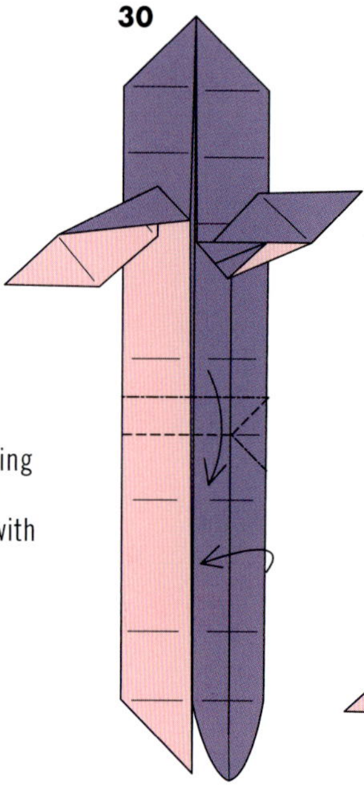

Pleat along the existing creases, pulling the single layer inward with a swivel fold.

31

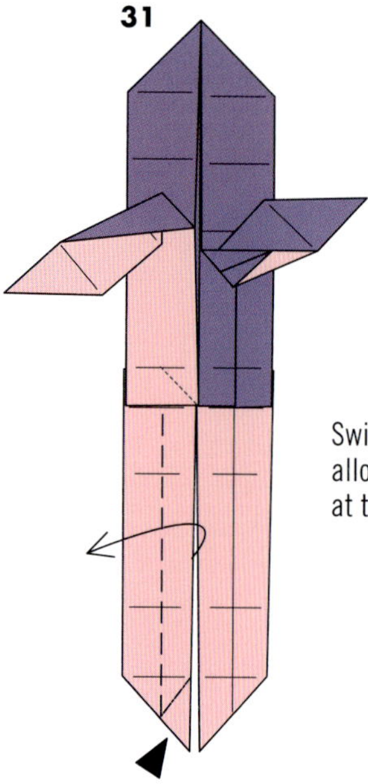

Swivel a single layer over, allowing a squash to form at the bottom.

32

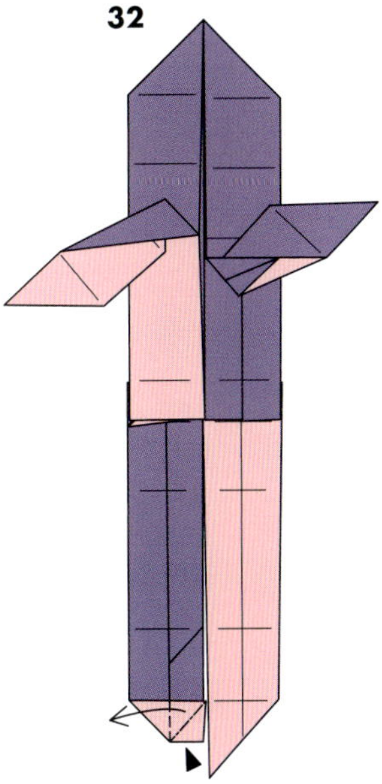

Squash the flap over.

33

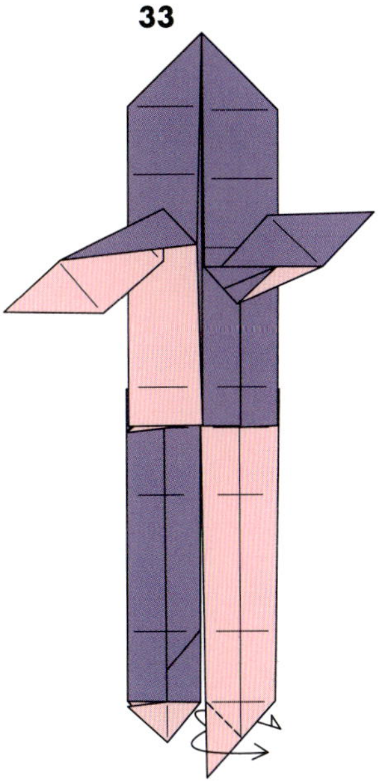

Outside reverse fold.

34

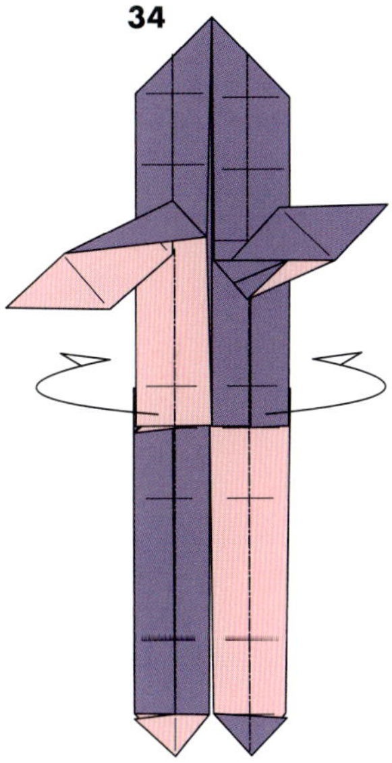

Mountain fold the sides in half.

35

Turn over.

36

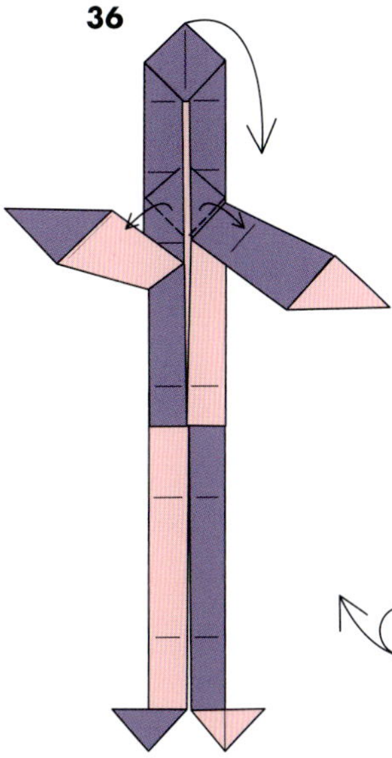

Squash the flap down.

37

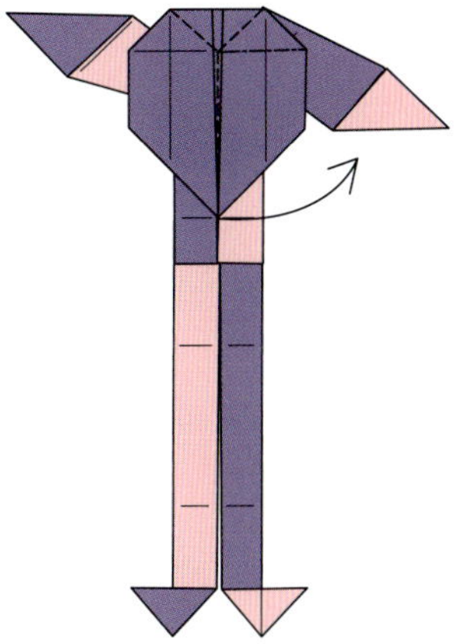

Rabbit ear the flap.

38

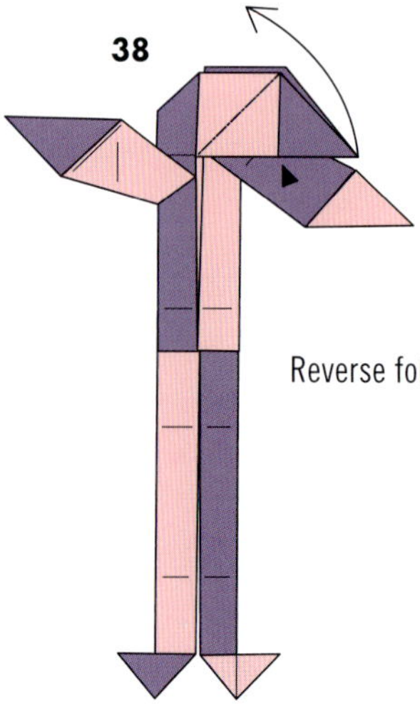

Reverse fold up.

39

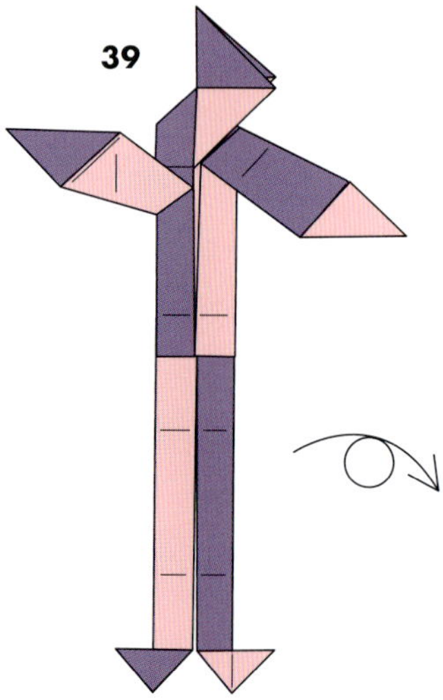

Turn over.

40

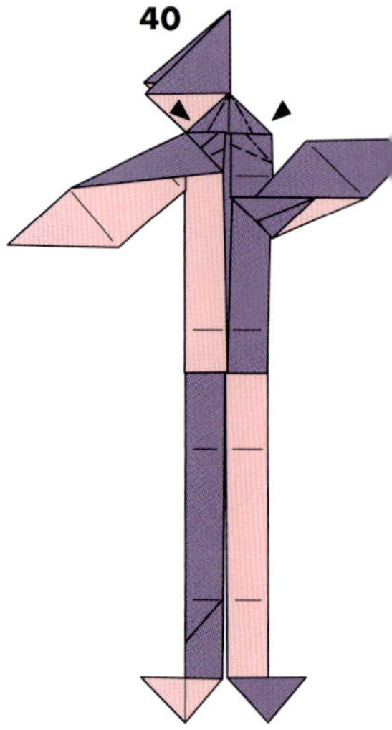

Spread squash the corners.

41

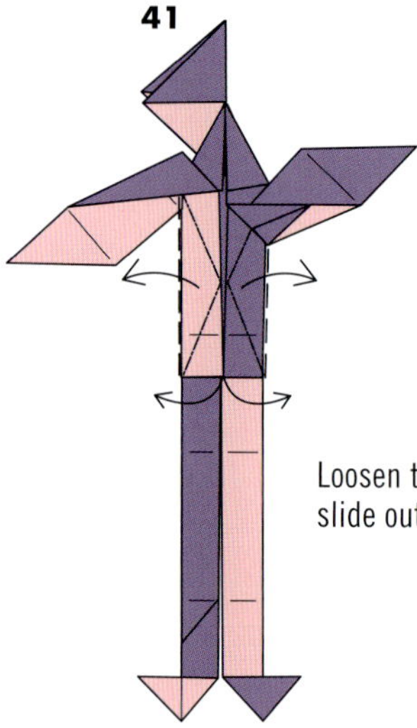

Loosen the pleats at the midsection and slide out a layer at each side.

42

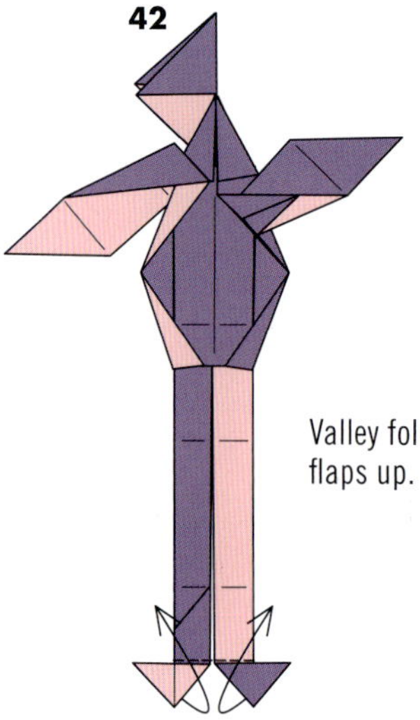

Valley fold the bottom flaps up.

43

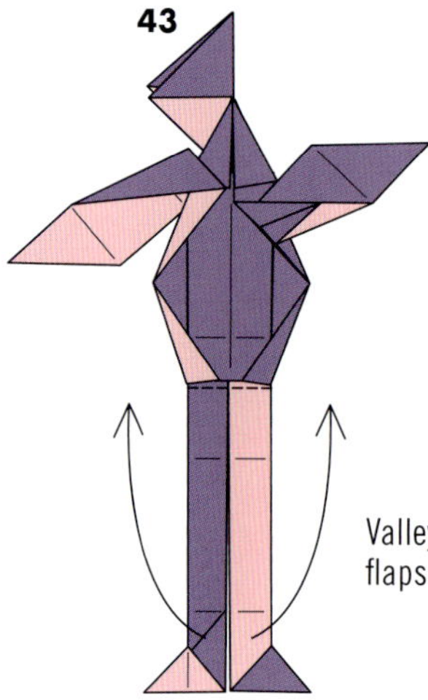

Valley fold the flaps up.

44

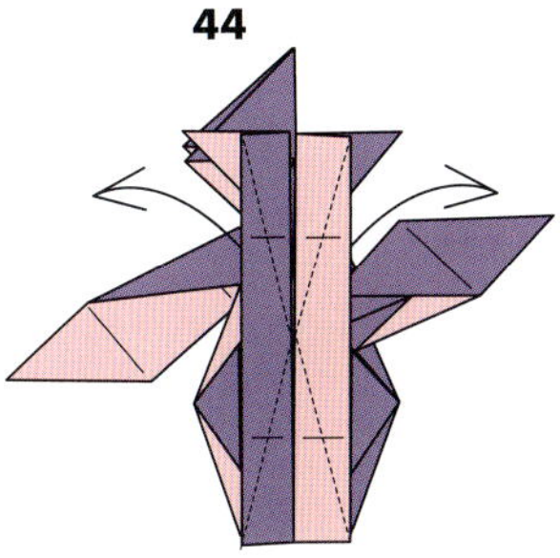

Slide the side layers outward.

45

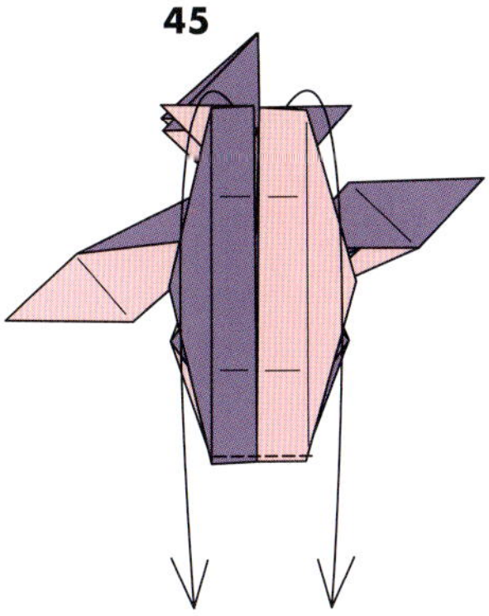

Valley folds the flaps down as far as possible.

46

Valley fold the bottom flaps down.

47

Turn over.

48

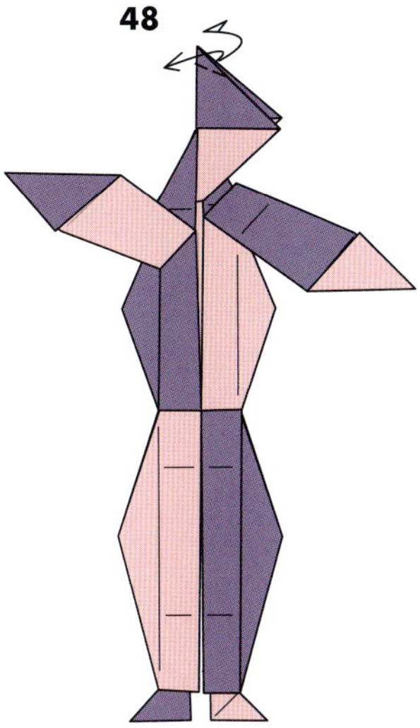

Outside reverse fold.

49

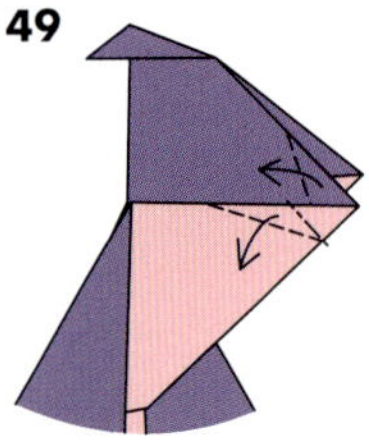

Swivel fold.

50

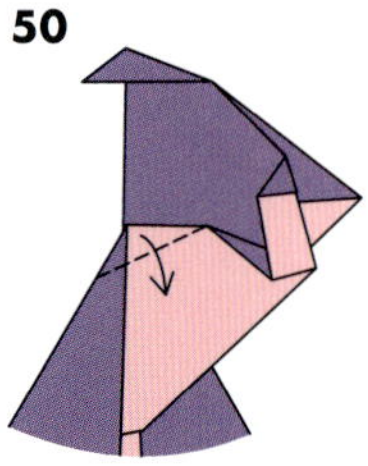

Valley fold down.

51

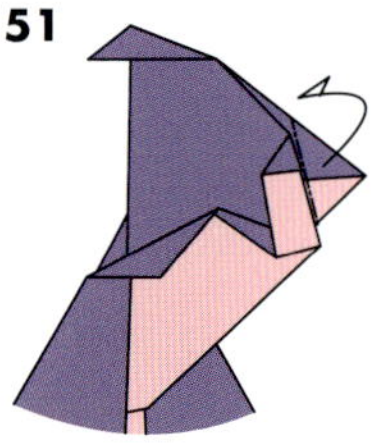

Mountain fold.

52

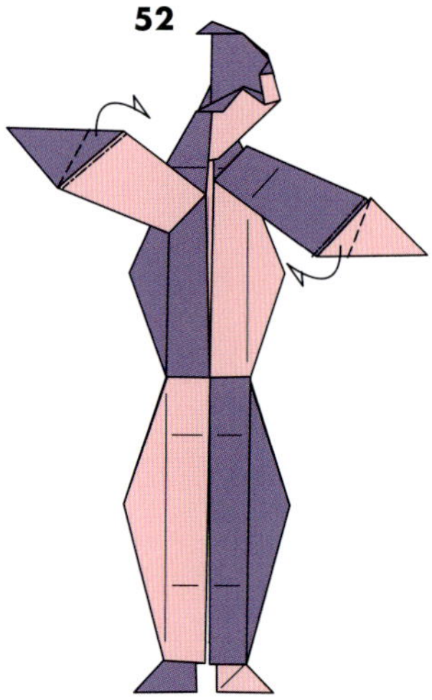

Pleat the triangular sections.

53

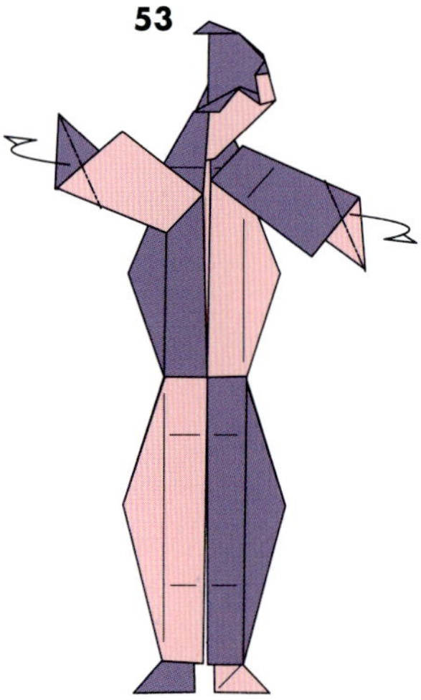

Mountain fold the flaps.

54

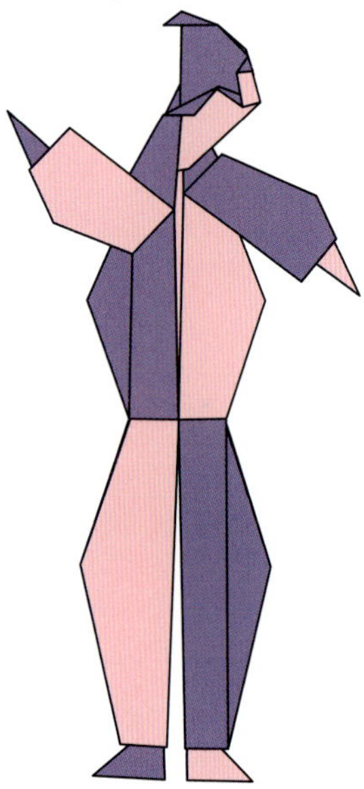

Completed Harlequin.

Christmas Tree

Peter Engel

After graduating from Harvard and Columbia, Peter spent a decade abroad—turn to his bio on page 151 to find out where and how it impacted his origami craft.

video: *youtu.be/iy6lH8koNVg*

Begin with a square the same size as the one used for Santa and the Toy Bag. A 10" (25 cm) square produces a tree 10 ¼" (26 cm) tall.

1

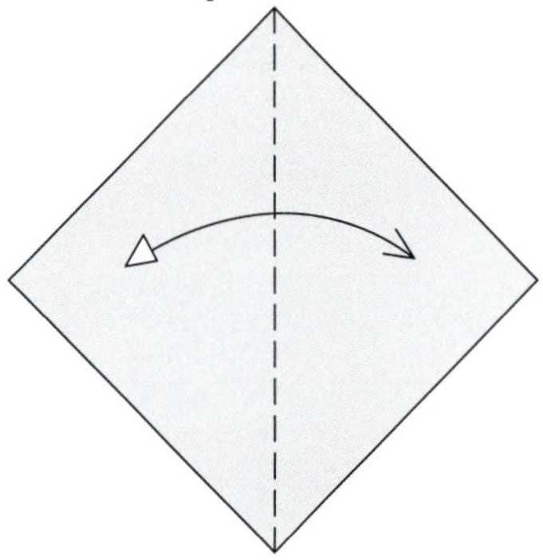

Fold and unfold along the diagonal.

2

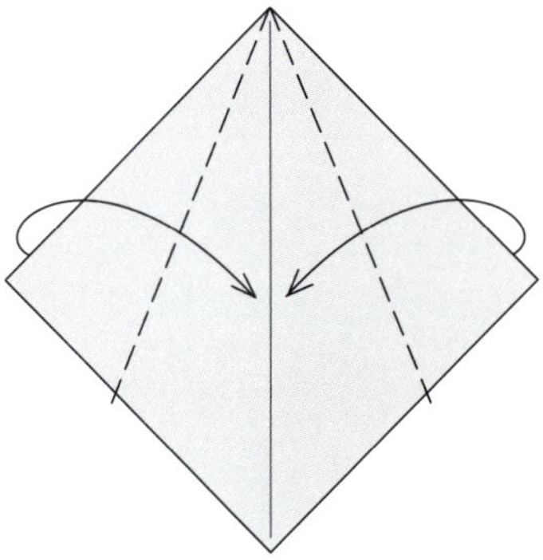

Fold the edges to the centerline.

3

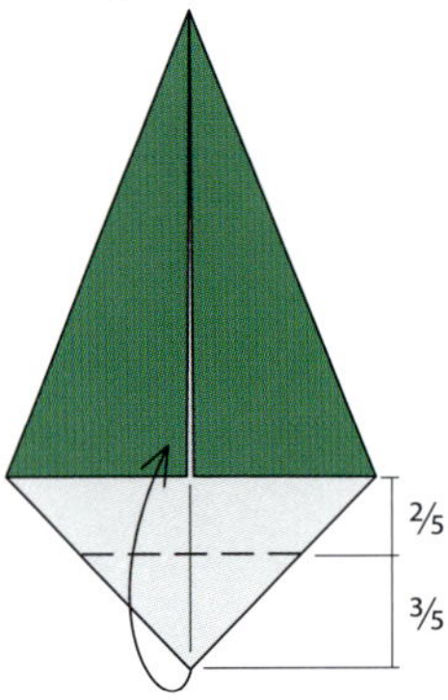

Fold the corner to the centerline. The proportions do not need to be exact.

4

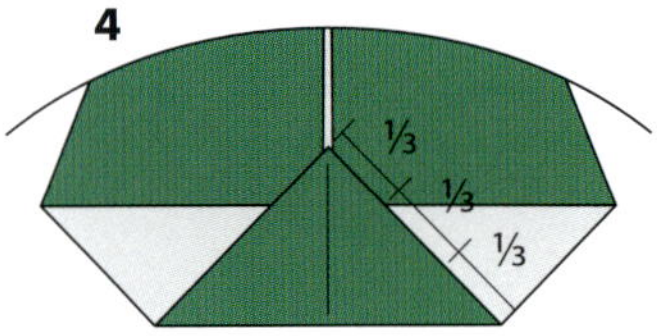

After folding step 3, the proportions will be as shown.

5

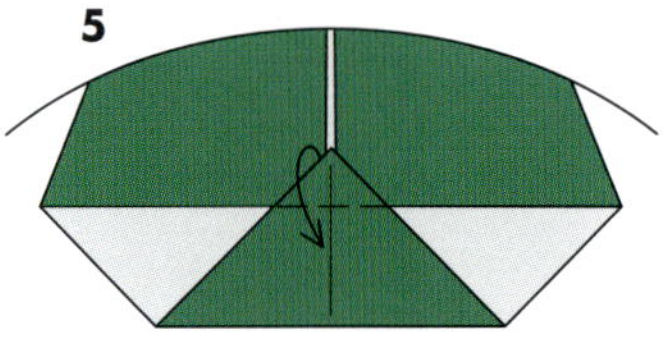

Fold along the edge behind.

6

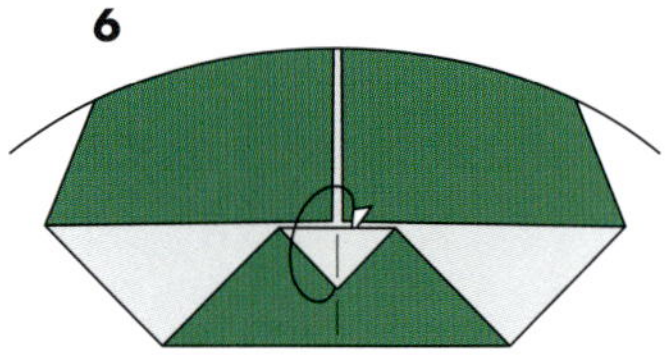

Swing the corner behind.

7

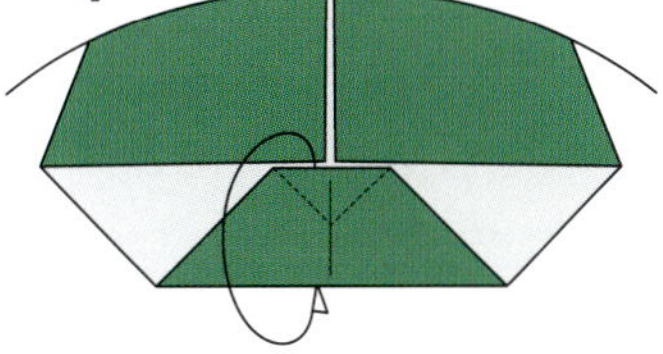

Swing the layer and corner behind and up.

8

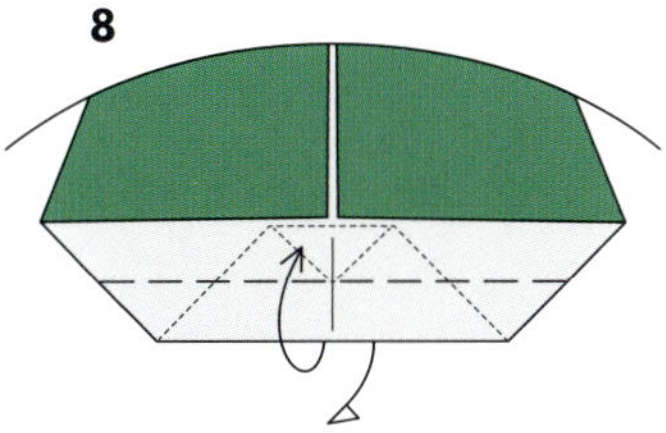

Fold the top layer only edge to edge. The bottom layer swings forward.

9

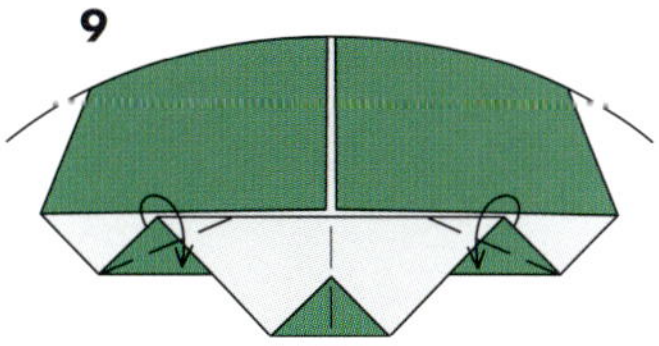

Fold edge to edge.

10

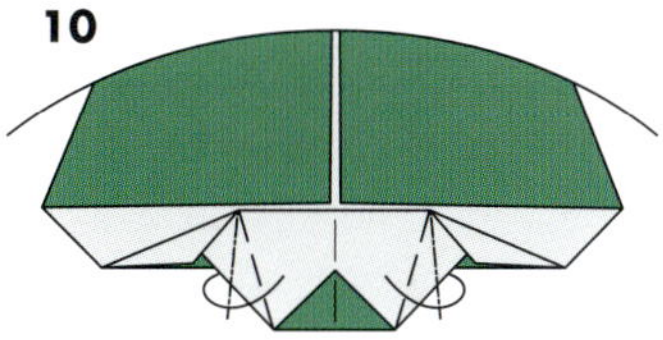

Swivel fold toward the center.

11

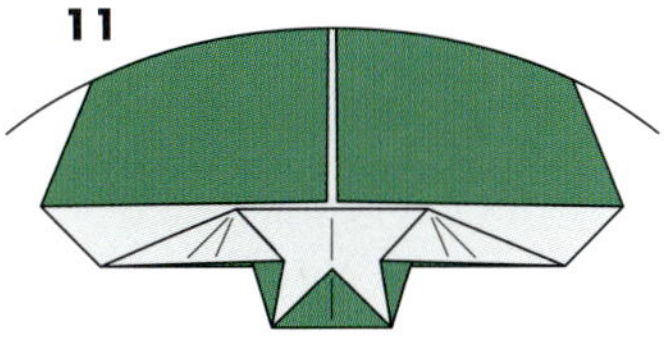

The trunk is completed. Turn over.

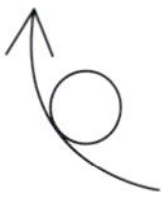

12

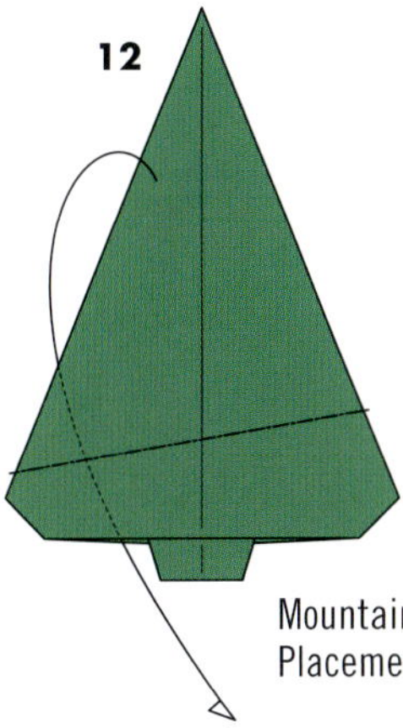

Mountain fold at an angle. Placement is approximate.

13

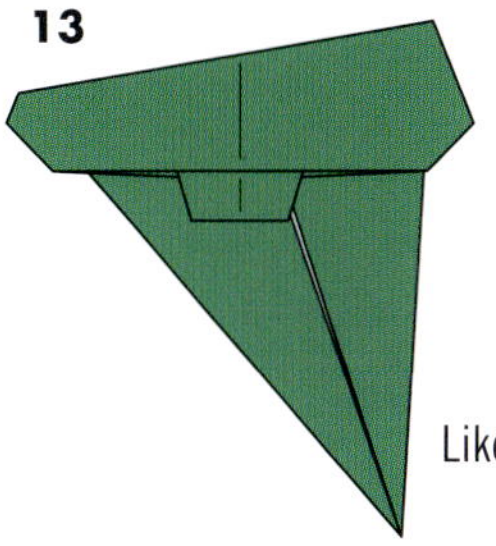

Like this. Turn over.

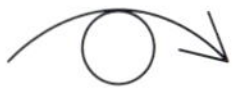

14

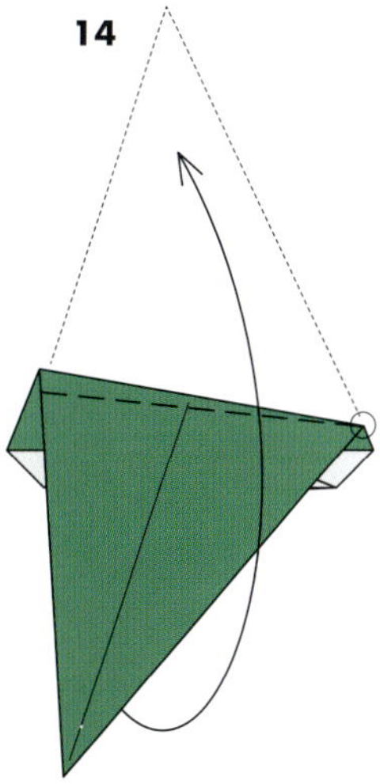

Fold through the circled point at a slightly different angle.

15

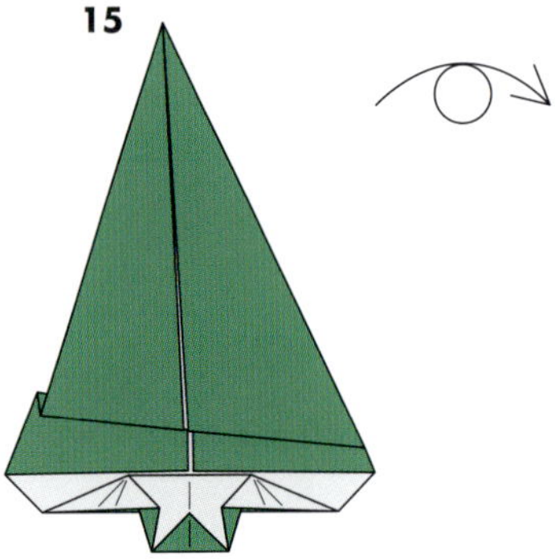

The result is a narrow pleat. Turn over.

16

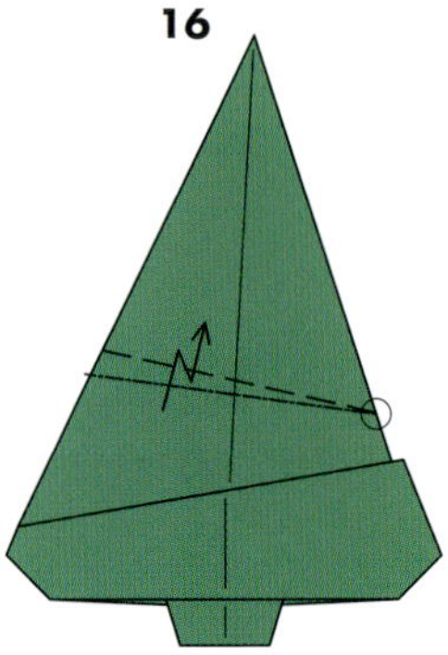

Form a second pleat, as in 12–14, but sloping in the opposite direction.

17

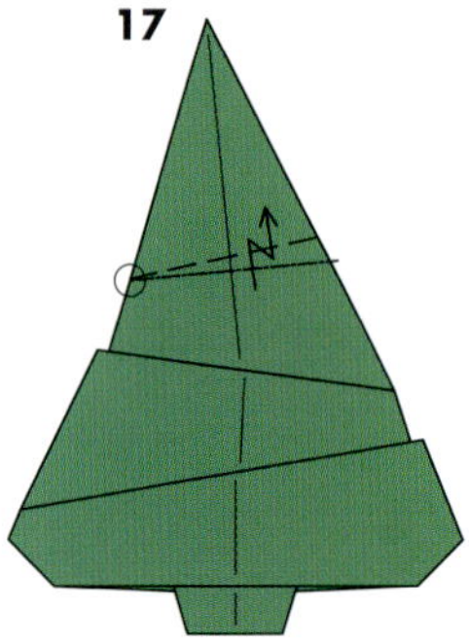

The third pleat.

18

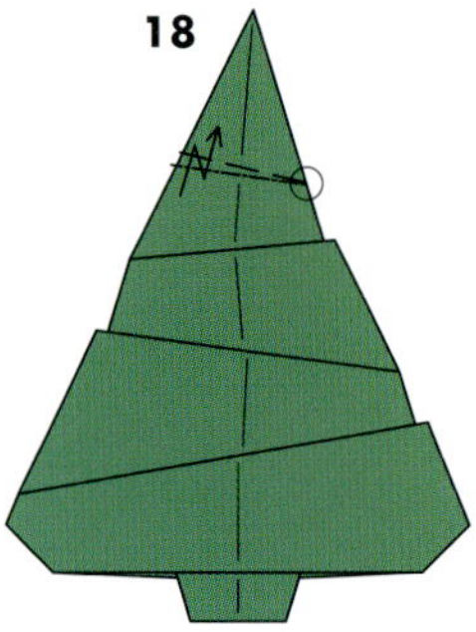

The fourth pleat. Add further pleats as desired.

19

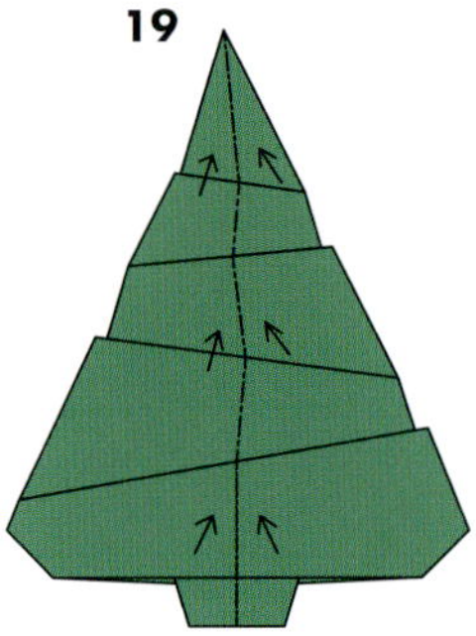

Mountain-fold the irregular centerline to make the tree slightly three-dimensional.

20

Fold three waterbombs to make a stack of Christmas gifts.

21

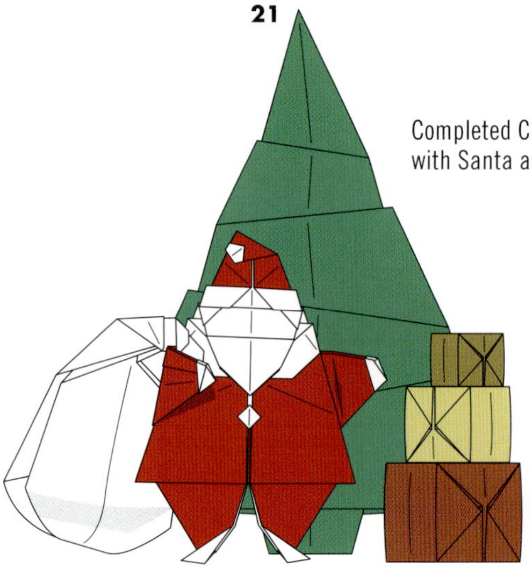

Completed Christmas Tree, with Santa and his Toy Bag.

Santa Claus

Peter Engel

video: *youtu.be/pguwZ6bdk7c*

1

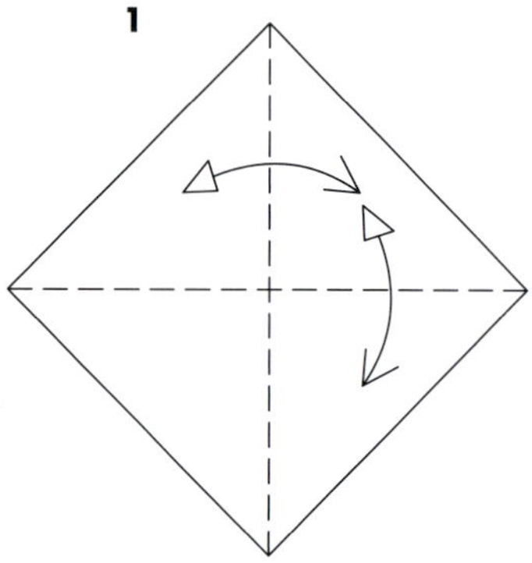

Fold and unfold along the diagonals.

2

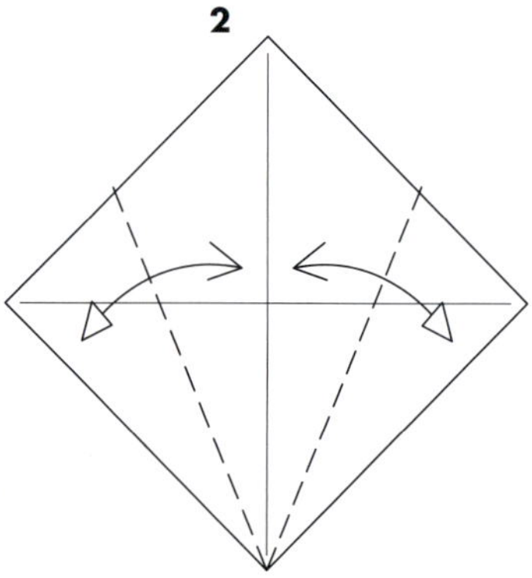

Fold the edges to the centerline and unfold.

3

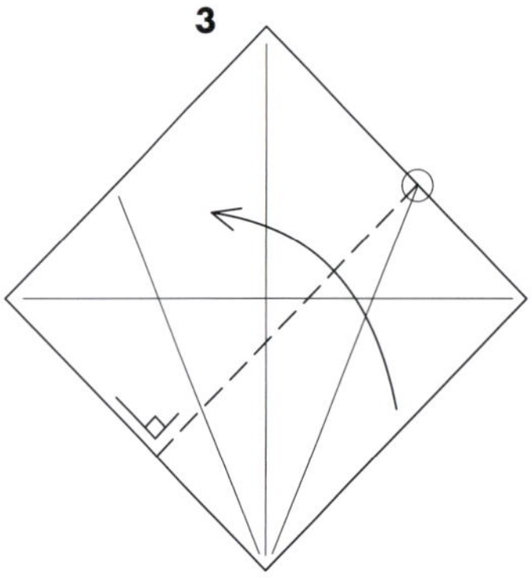

Fold parallel to the edge through the circled point.

4

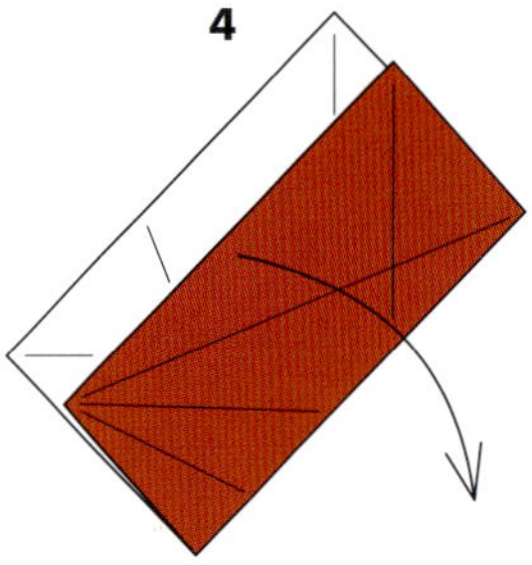

Unfold.

5

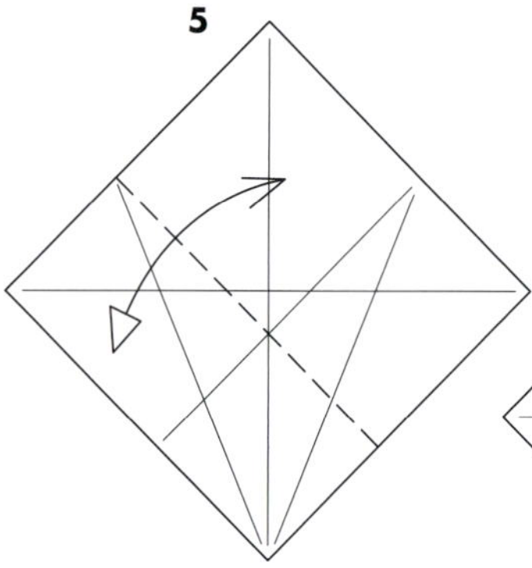

Fold and unfold as in steps 3–4.

6

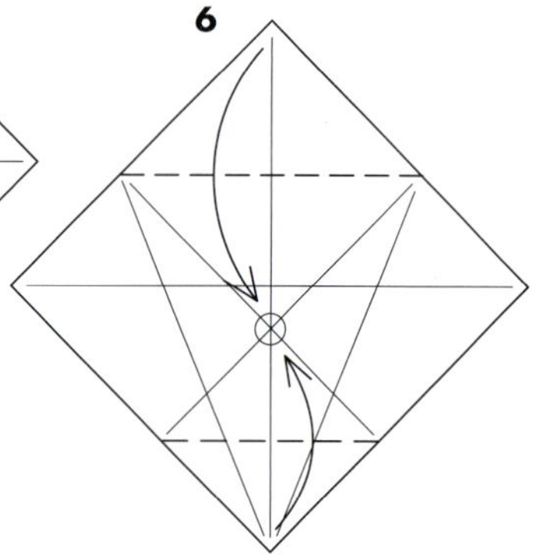

Fold the corners to the circled point.

7

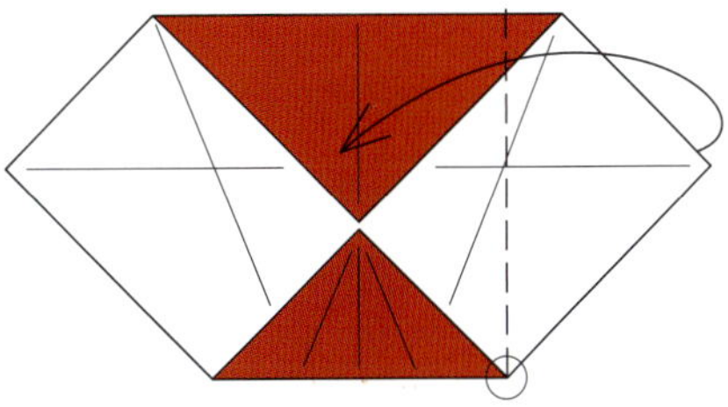

Valley fold vertically through the circled point.

8

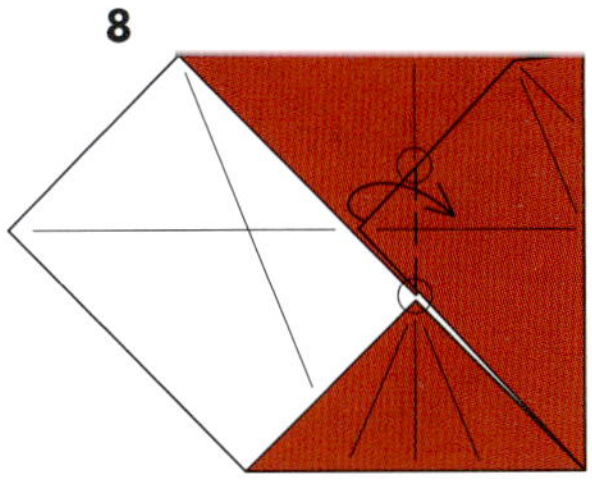

Fold the corner along the hidden centerline.

9

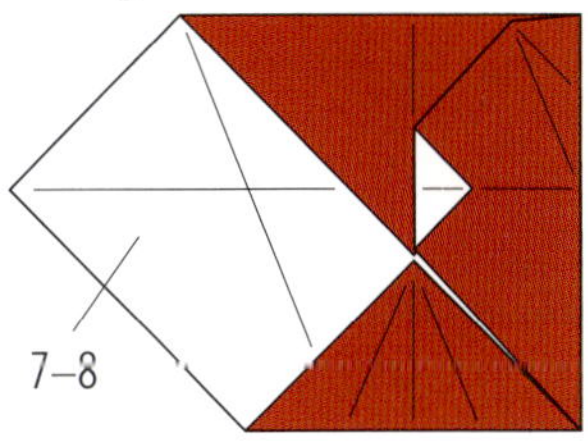

Repeat steps 7–8 on the left side.

10

Next diagram shows the circled area enlarged.

11

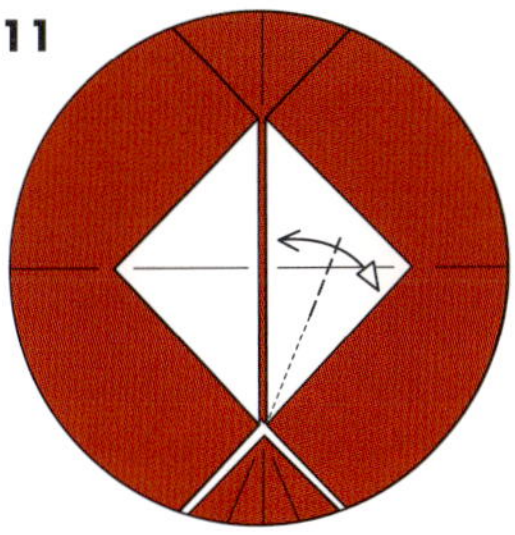

Fold edge to edge, marking only where the fold crosses the horizontal crease.

12

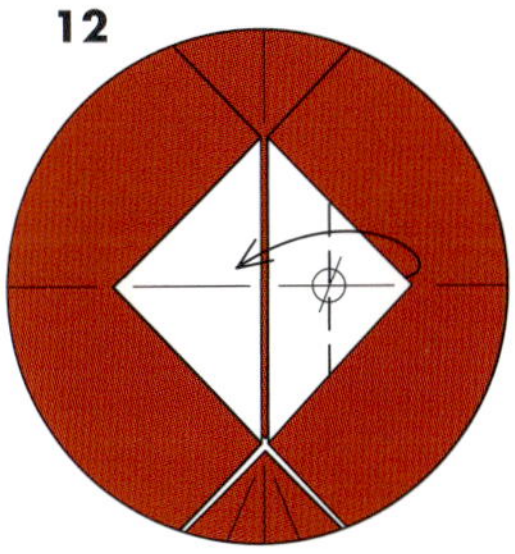

Fold the corner at the marked intersection.

13

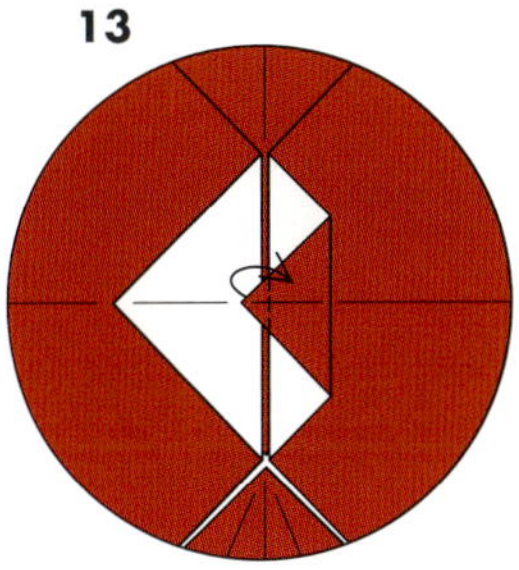

Fold the corner along the centerline.

14

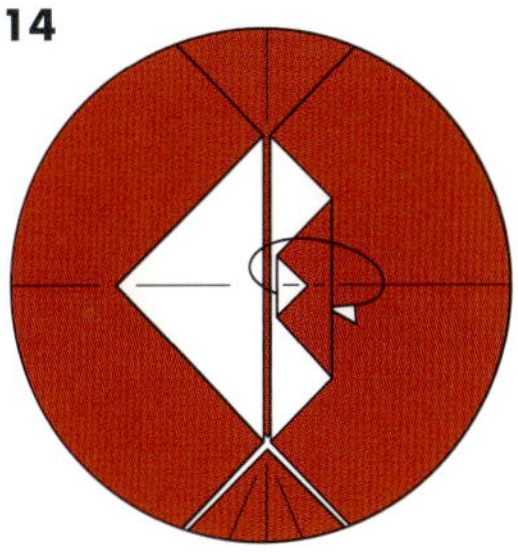

Swing the layers to the right and behind.

15

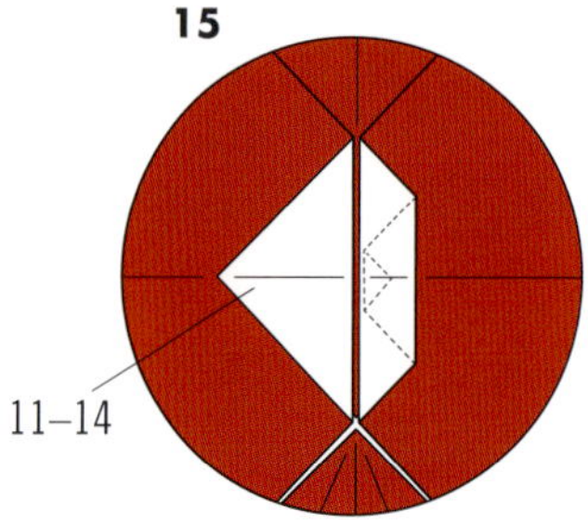

Repeat steps 11–14 on the left.

16

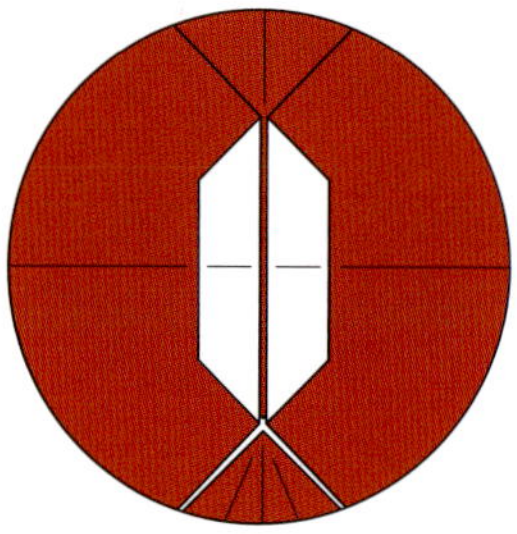

Both sides completed. The white flaps will become Santa's collar.

17

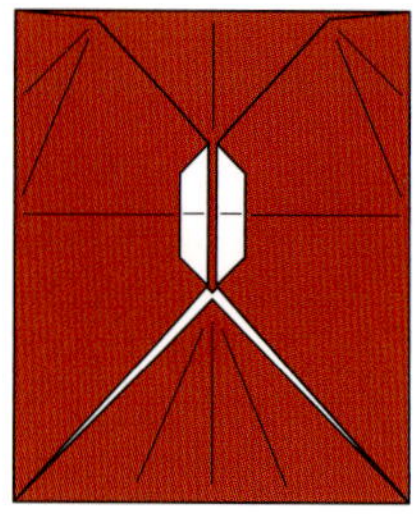

Turn over.

18

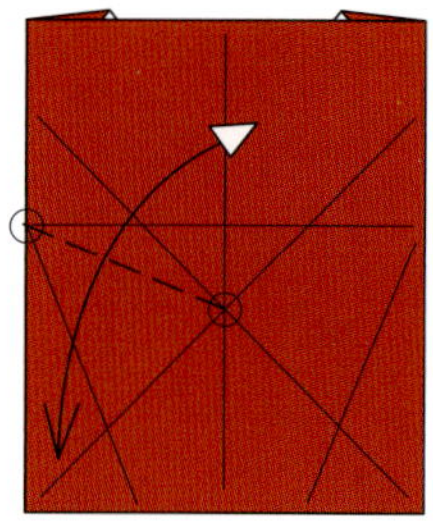

Fold and unfold, creasing only between the circled points.

19

Repeat 18 on the right.

20

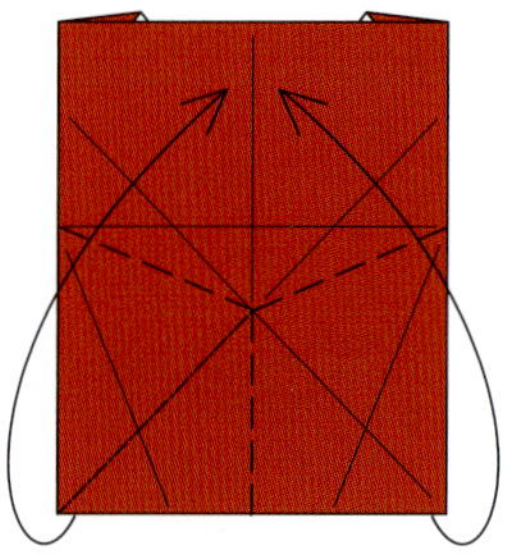

Rabbit's ear along the existing creases.

21

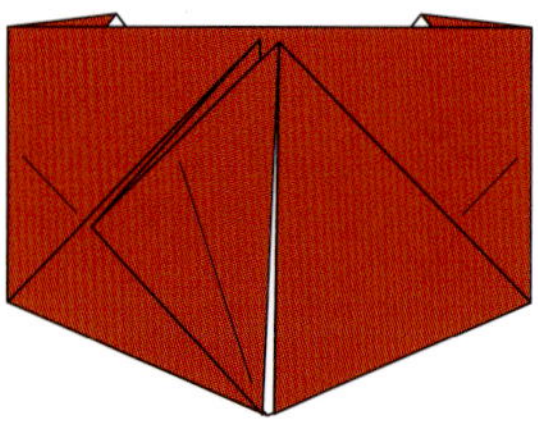

Rotate 180 degrees.

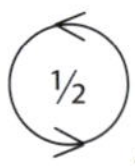

22

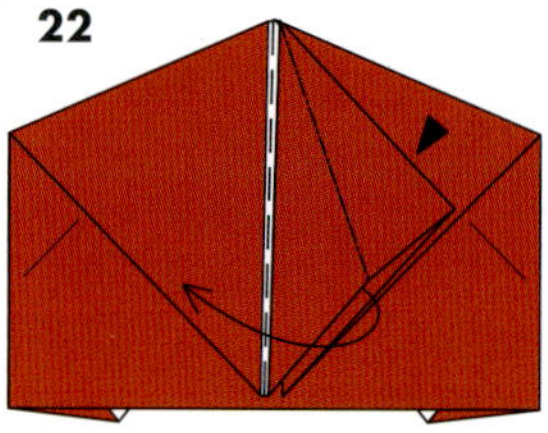

Squash fold.

23

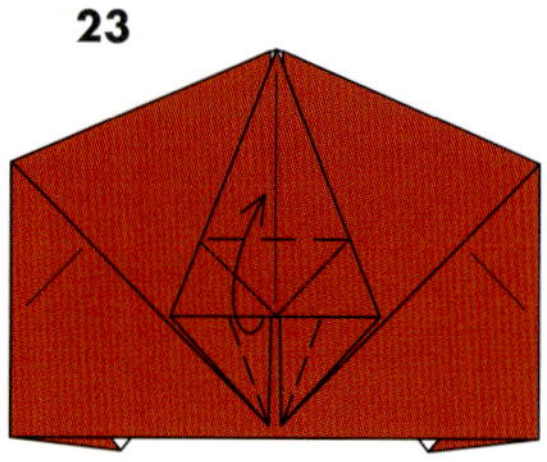

Petal fold.

24

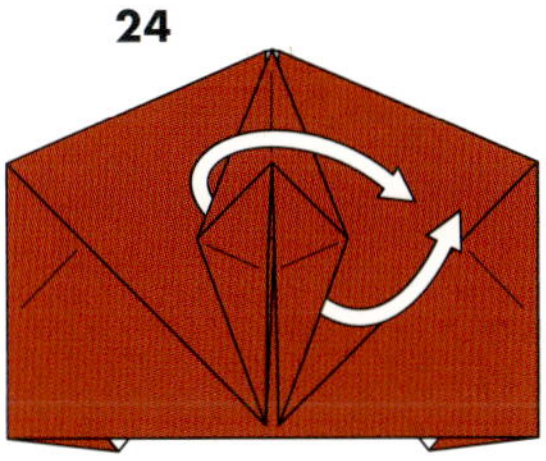

Unwrap carefully and pull out loose paper.

25

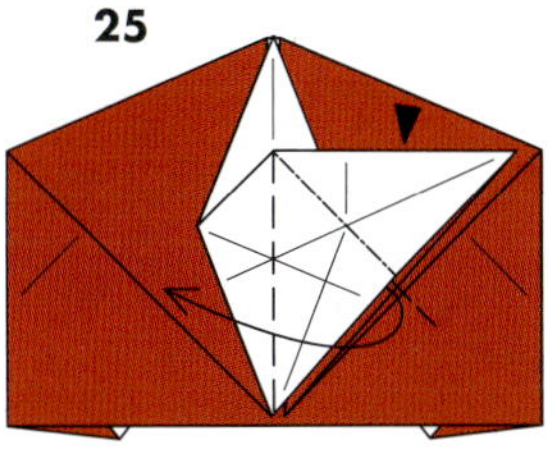

Squash fold.

26

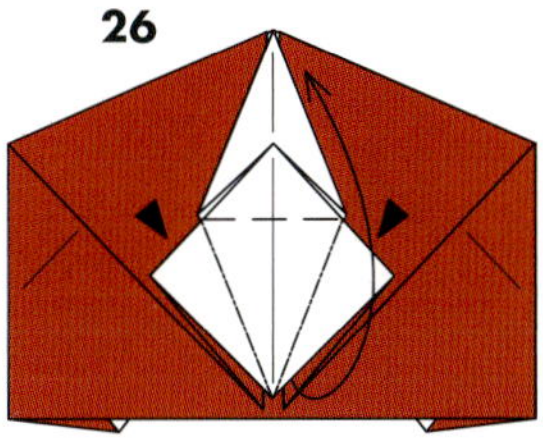

Petal fold.

27

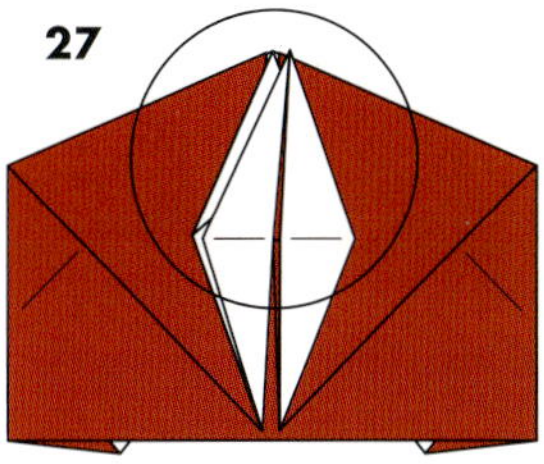

Next diagram shows the circled area enlarged.

28

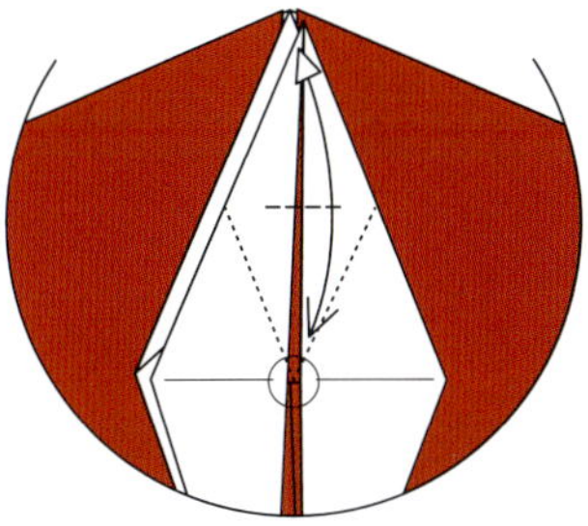

Mark by folding the top corner to the circled point.

29

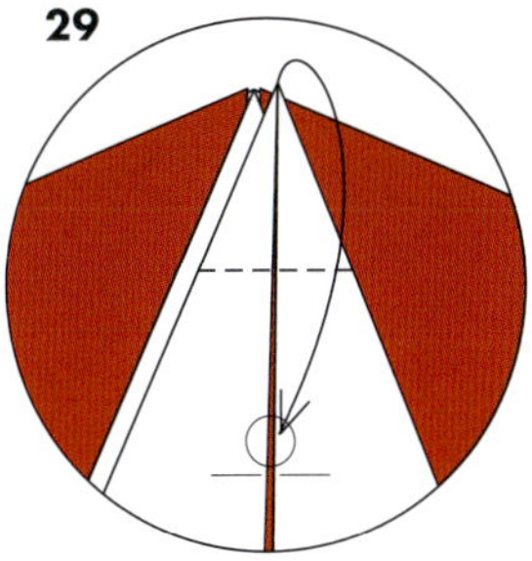

Fold the corner to just above the mark and crease firmly.

30

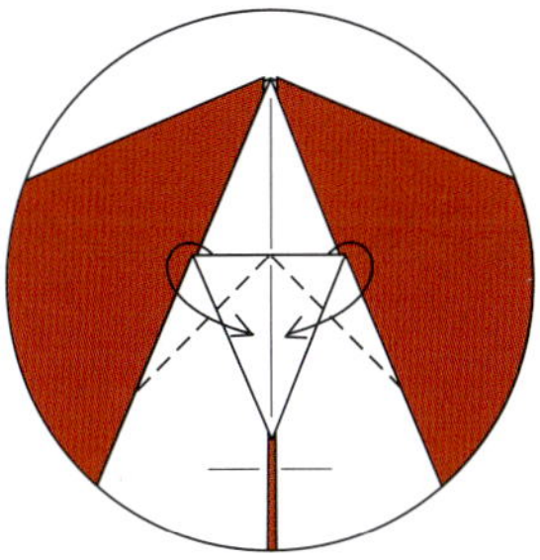

Fold the top edges to the centerline.

31

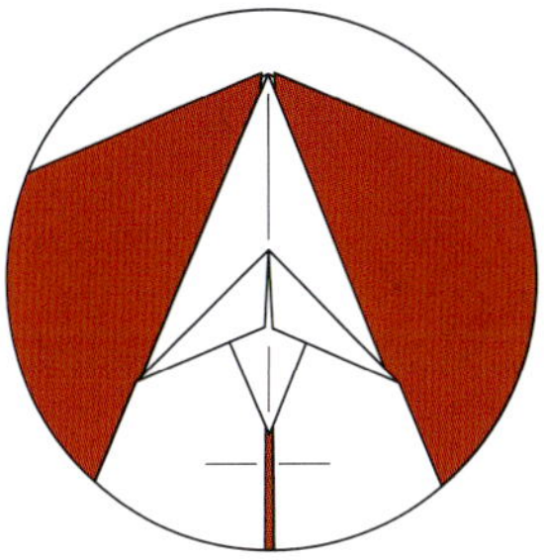

Crease firmly and unfold to 29.

32

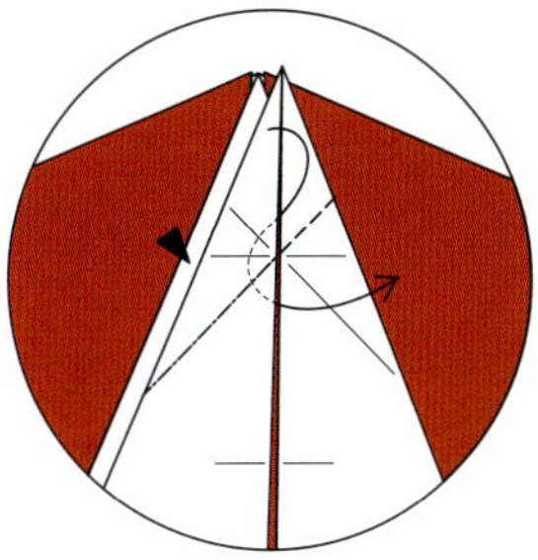

Inside reverse fold along the existing creases.

33

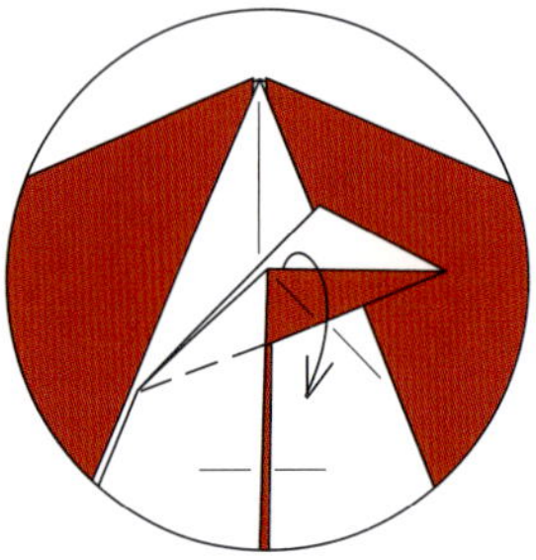

Swing the top layer down.

34

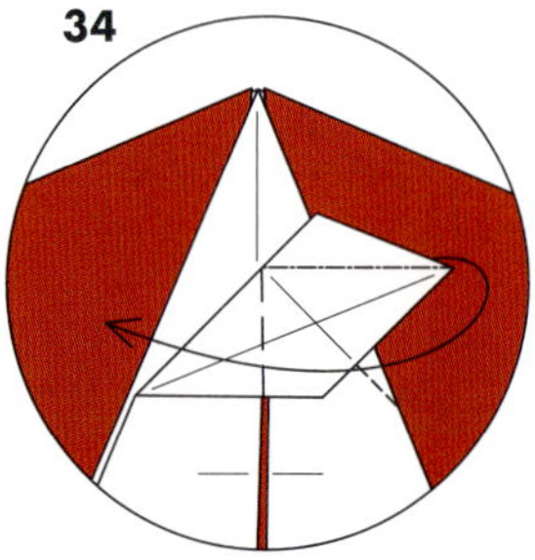

Swing to the left. The flap at the top right folds down automatically.

35

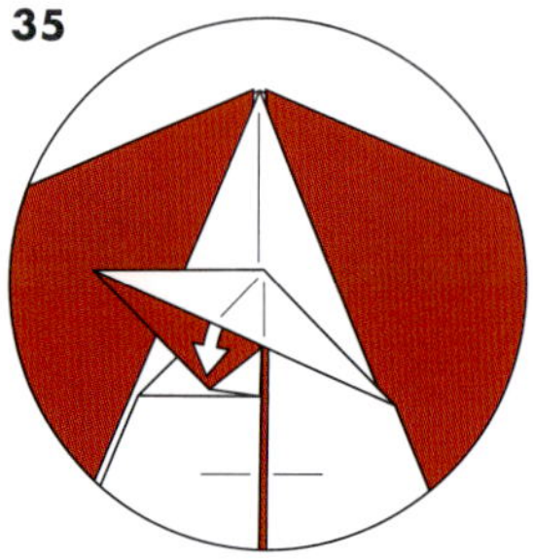

Pull out the loose paper.

36

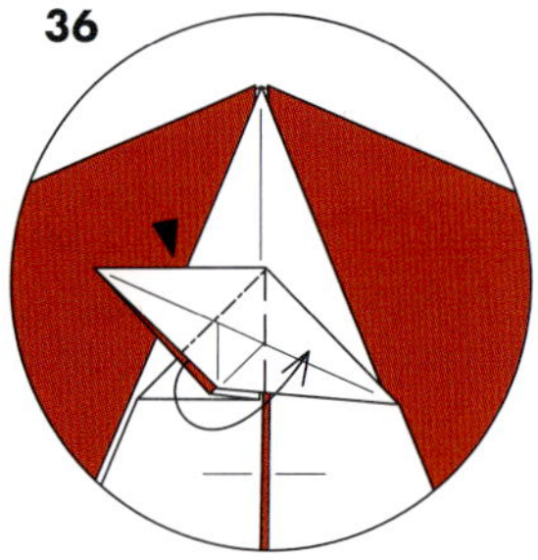

Squash-fold.

37

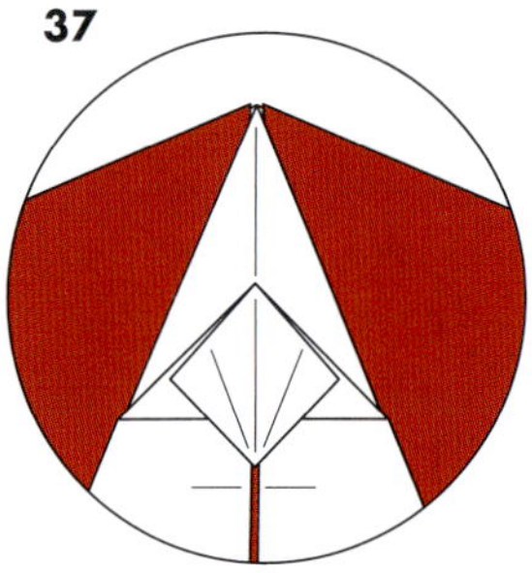

The square will be Santa's button.

38

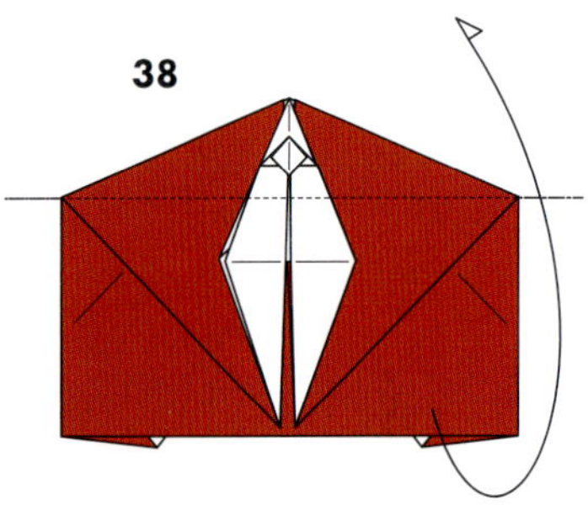

Swing the bottom portion behind and up.

39

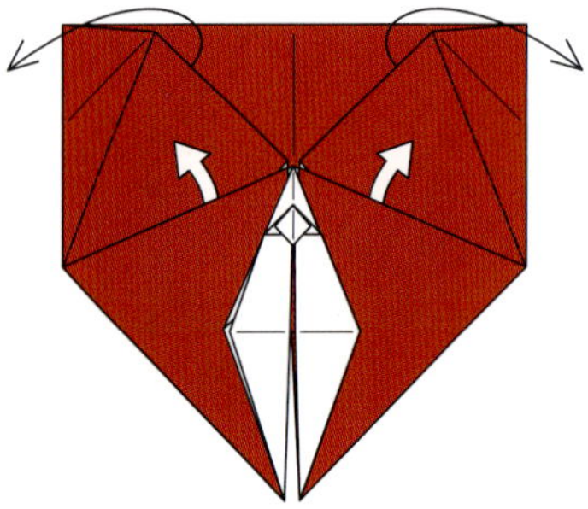

Pull out loose paper.

40

Tuck white flaps, including button, beneath adjacent colored flaps.

41

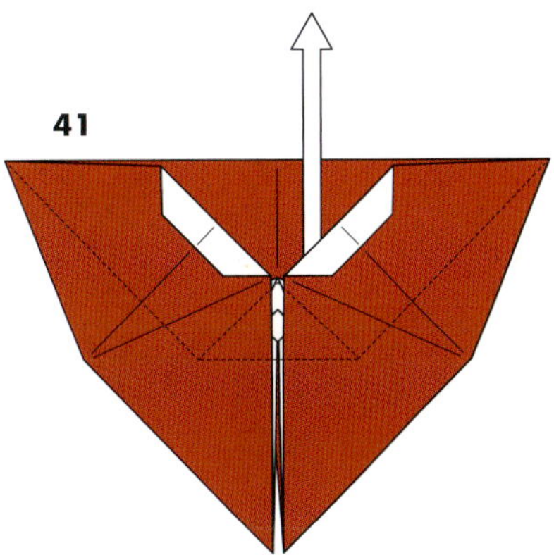

Pull out the hidden flap.

42

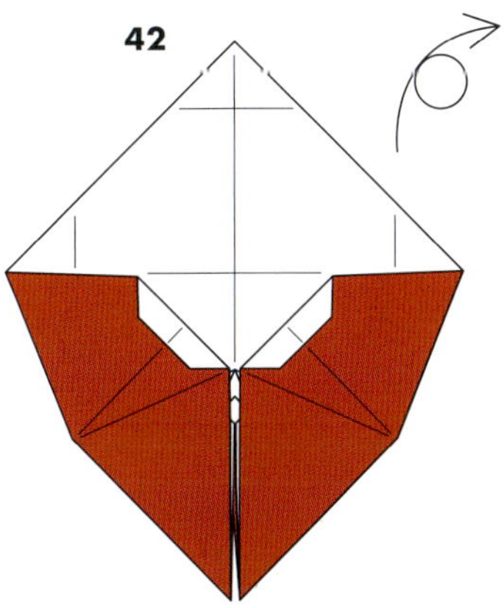

Turn over.

43

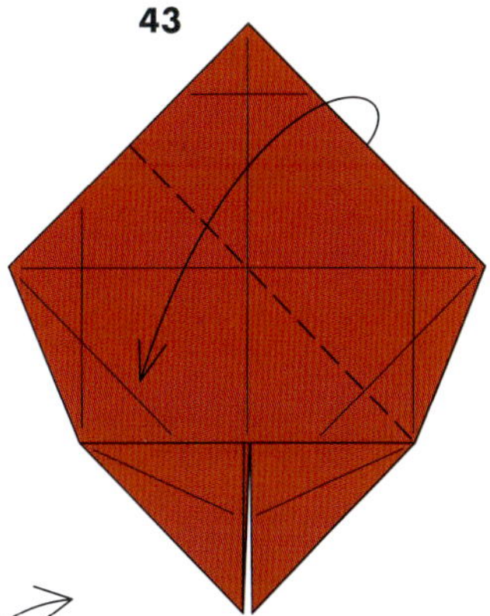

Fold the edge to met the existing crease.

44

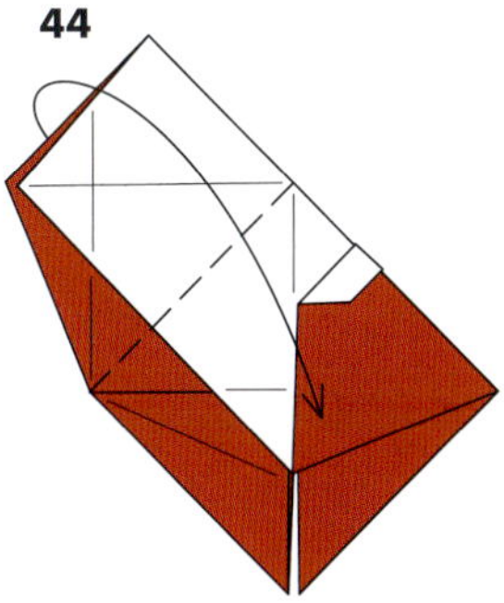

Fold the left-hand flap down and to the right.

45

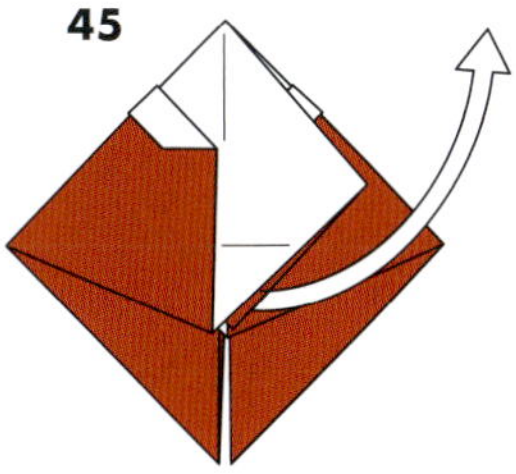

Pull out loose paper and flatten.

46

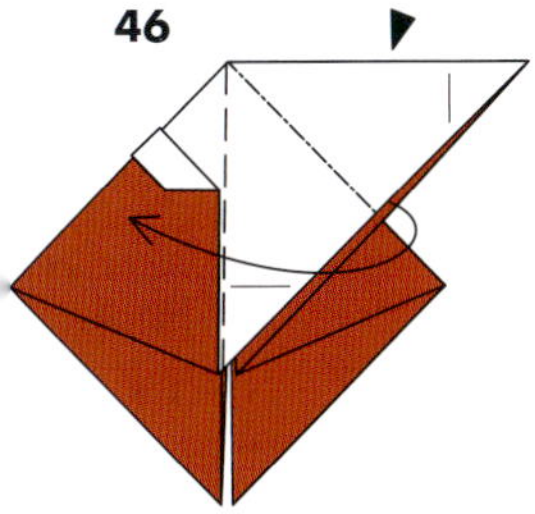

Squash-fold.

47

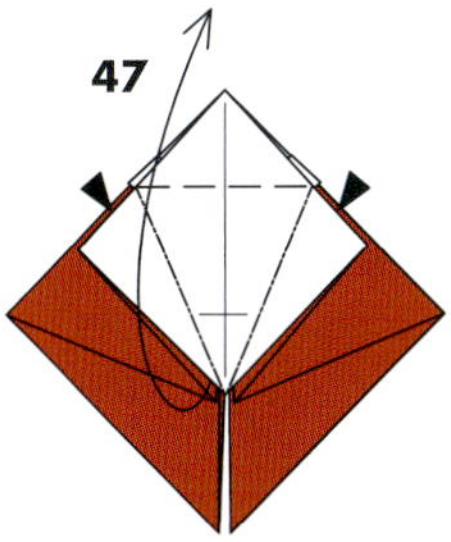

Petal-fold.

48

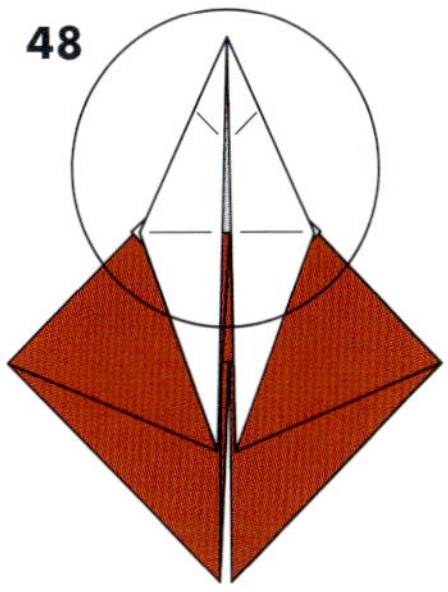

The next diagram shows the circled area enlarged.

49

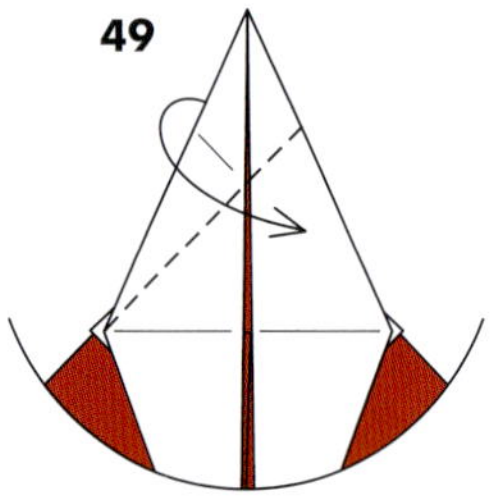

Fold along the hidden edge directly behind.

50

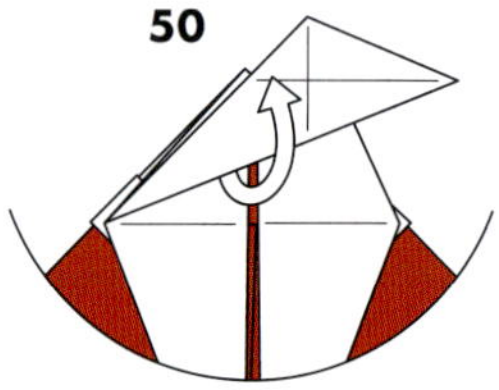

Pull out the inner layer.

51

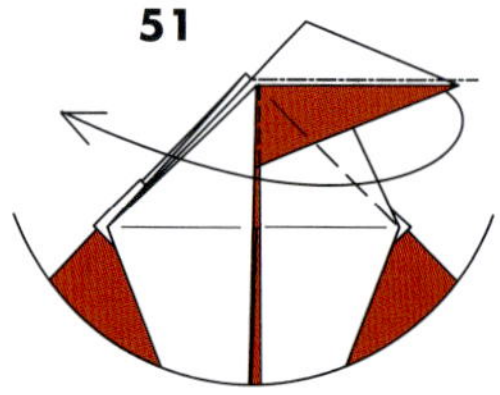

Swing flap to the left.

52

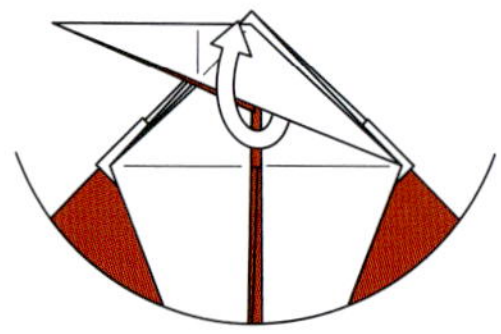

Pull out the inner layer.

53

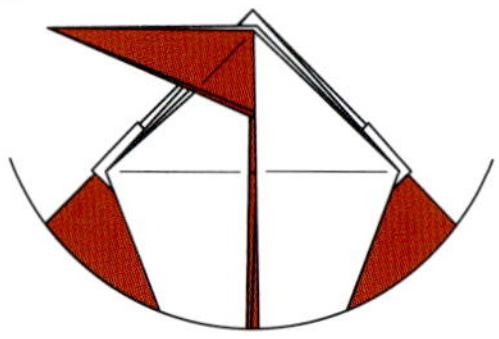

The colored triangular flap will become Santa's head and hat.

54

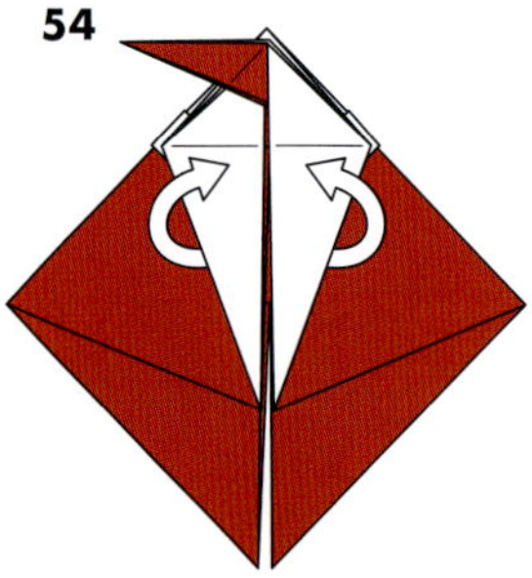

Tuck white flaps into colored flaps beneath.

55

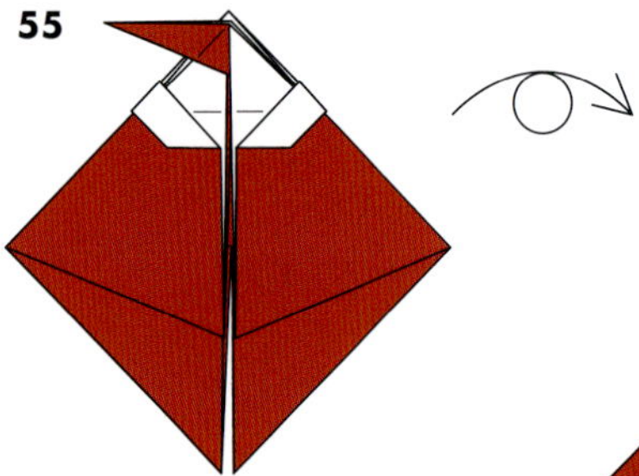

Turn over.

56

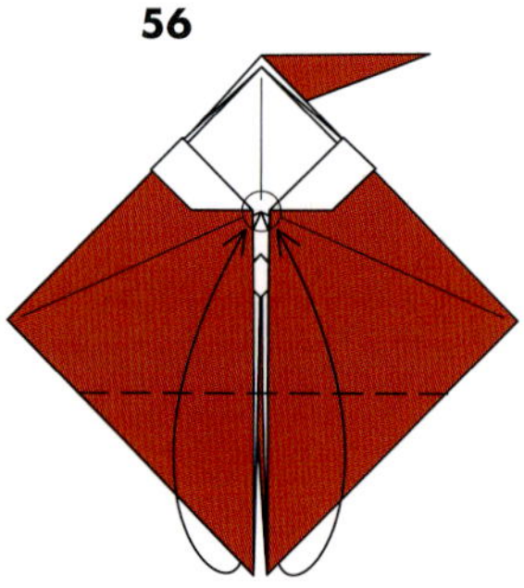

Fold the bottom flaps to the circled point.

57

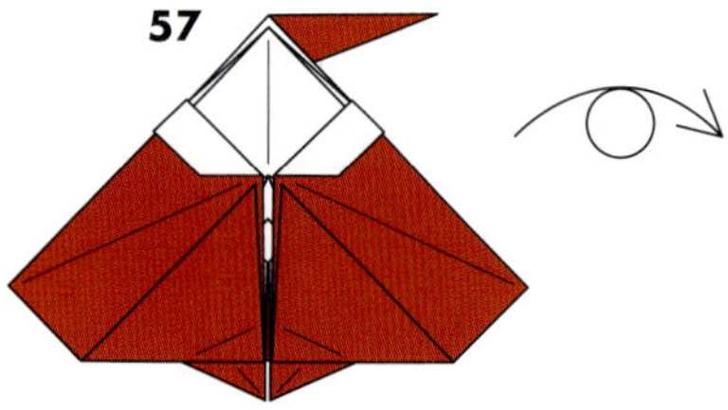

Turn over.

63

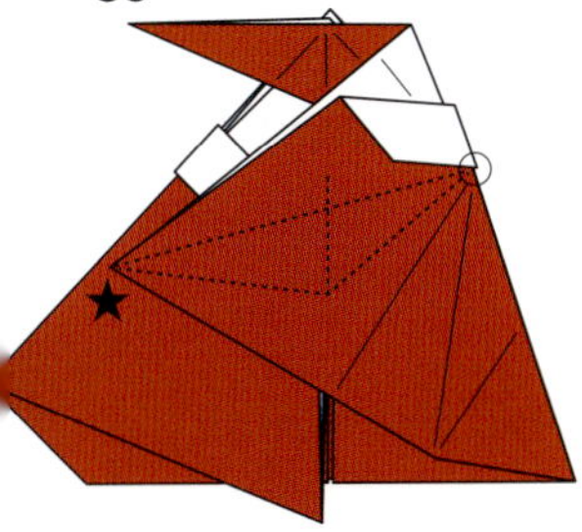

Sequence completed. The dotted lines show the location of the loose paper folded in step 61.

64

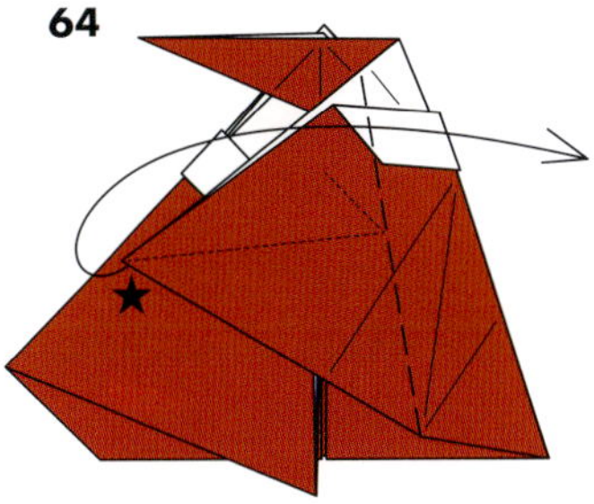

Swing the starred flap to the right while simultaneously stretching the loose paper folded in 61. Look ahead to the next diagram.

65

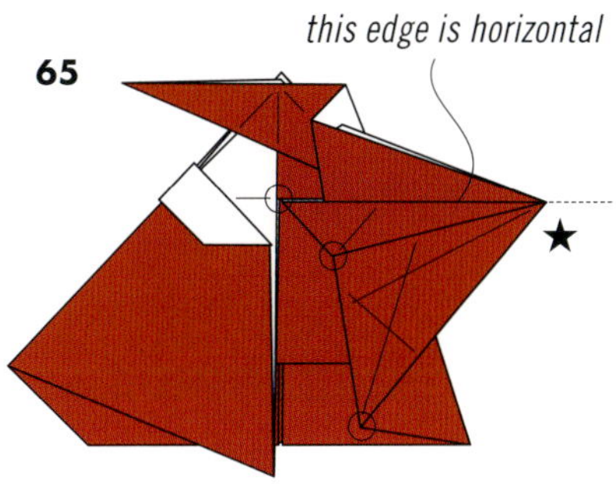

Like this. Note location of the newly circled points.

62

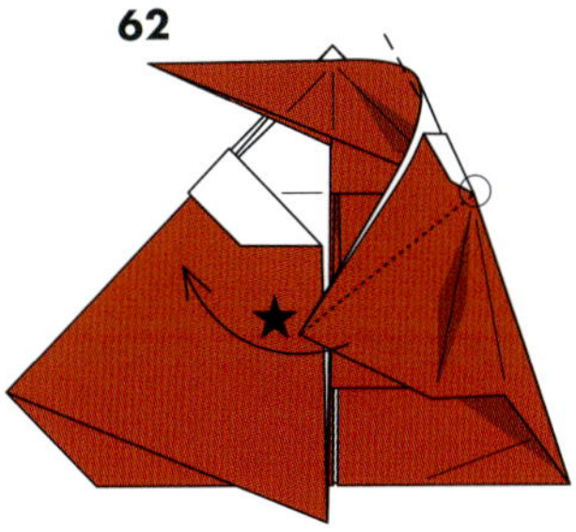

Continue swinging the starred flap to the left and flatten.

61

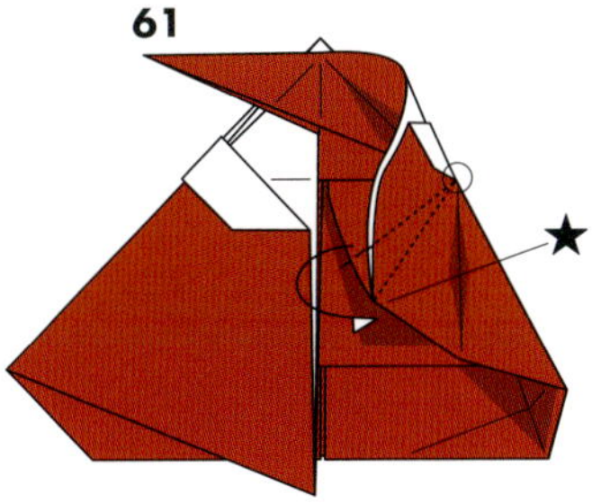

This step occurs while the starred corner is being swung to the left. Following the arrow, swing down the loose paper to where it lands naturally.

60

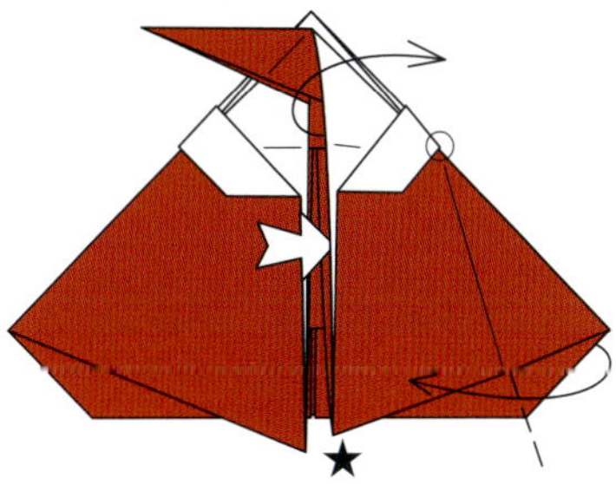

Swing the starred corner up and to the left, pivoting at the circled point. The next two diagrams show this step in motion.

59

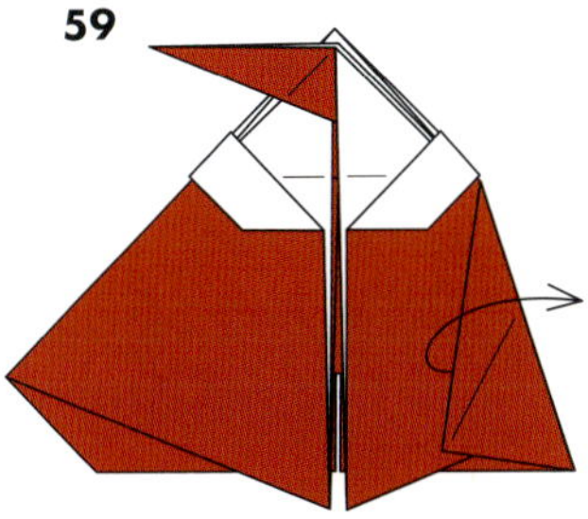

Unfold.

58

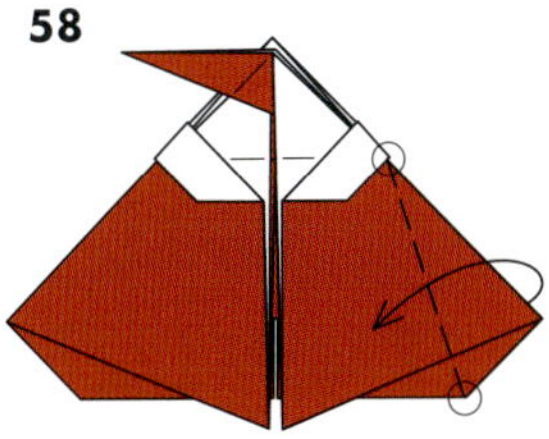

Fold the corner along the line connecting the circles.

66

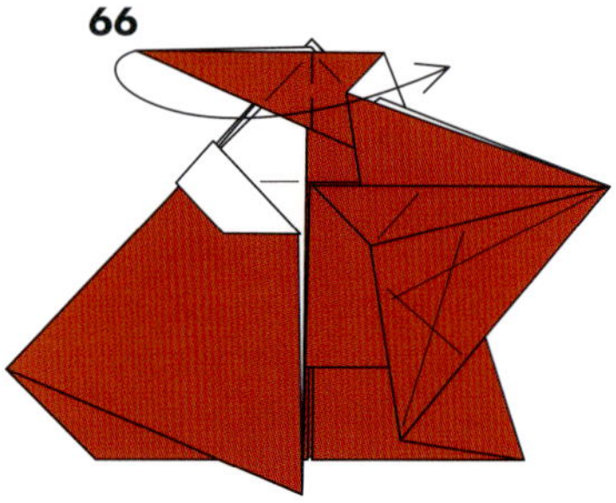

Swing the top flap to the right.

67

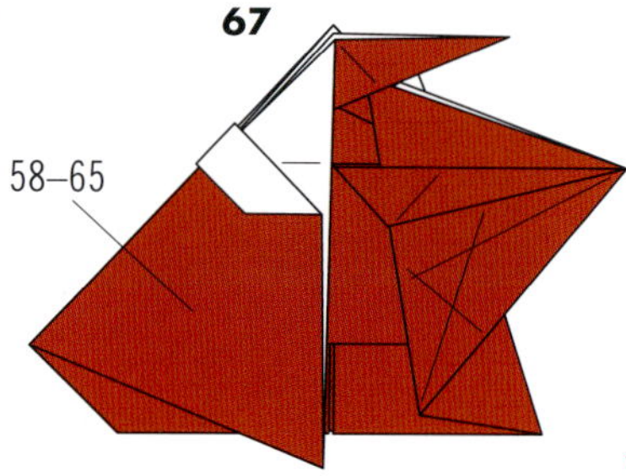

Repeat steps 58–65 on the left side.

68

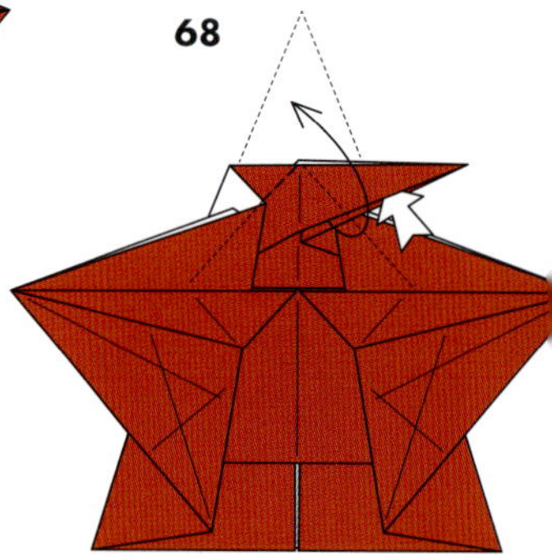

Open and flatten the triangular flap.

69

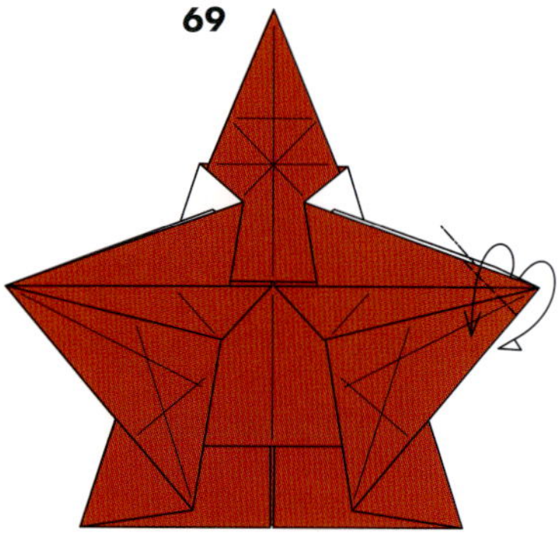

Outside reverse-fold the tip to form a cuff. See 70–72 for detailed instructions.

70

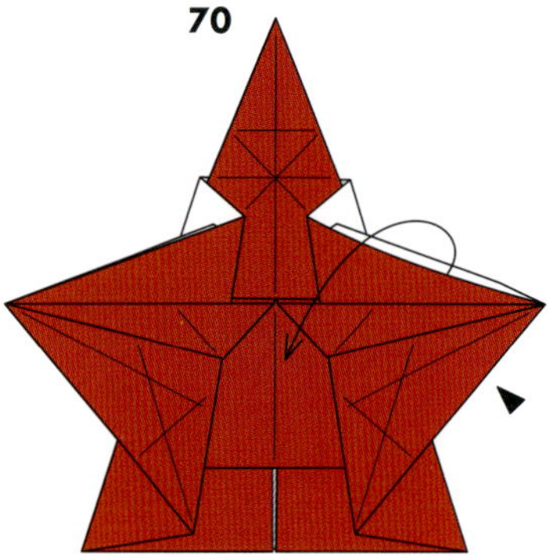

Open the pocket, but do not crease.

71

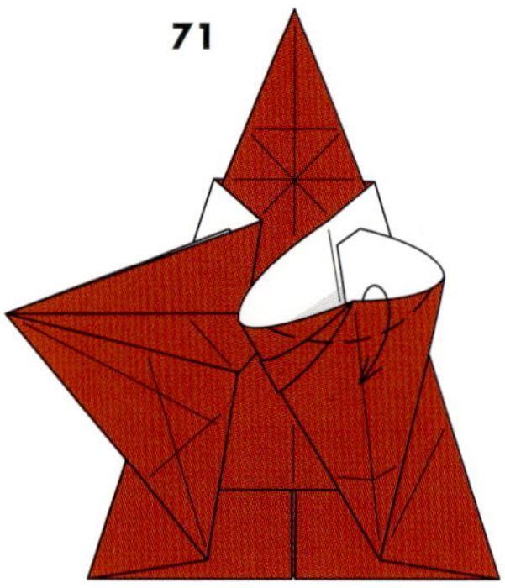

Fold down only the tip.

72

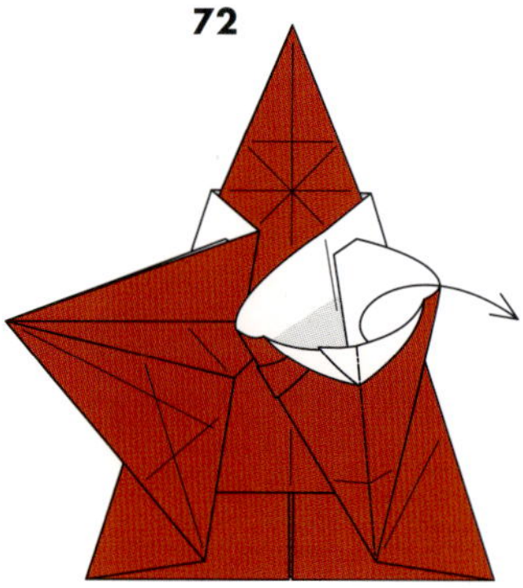

Return the flap to its position in 69.

73

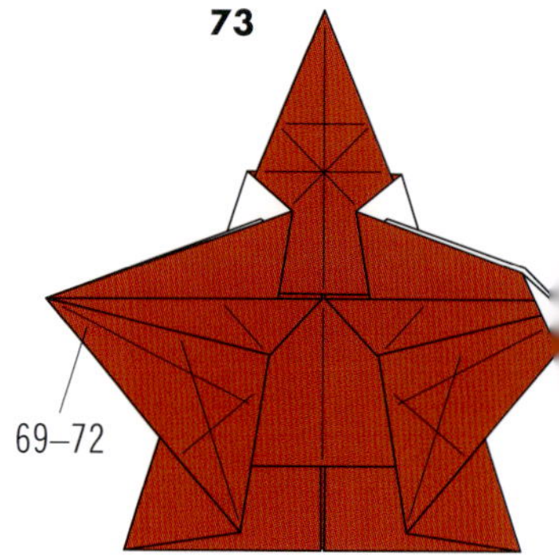

Repeat steps 69–72 on the left side.

74

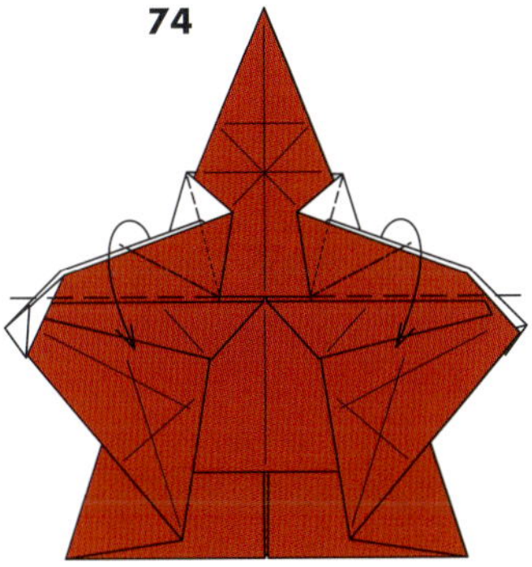

Swivel-fold along the horizontal edges.

75

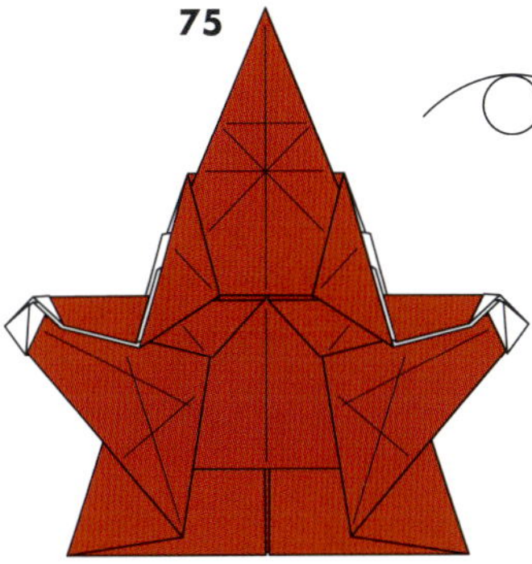

Turn over.

76

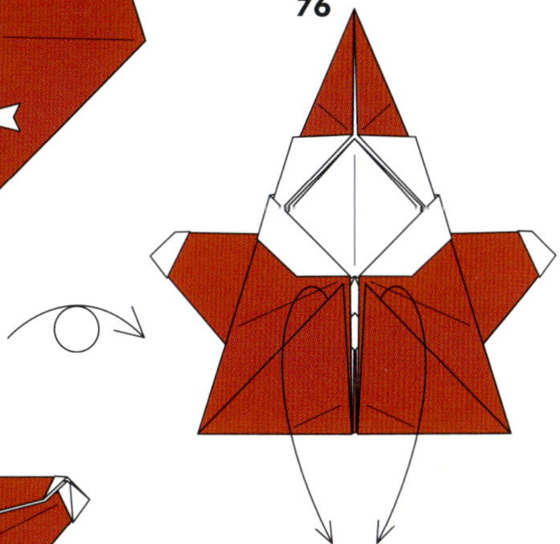

Swing down the two triangular flaps.

77

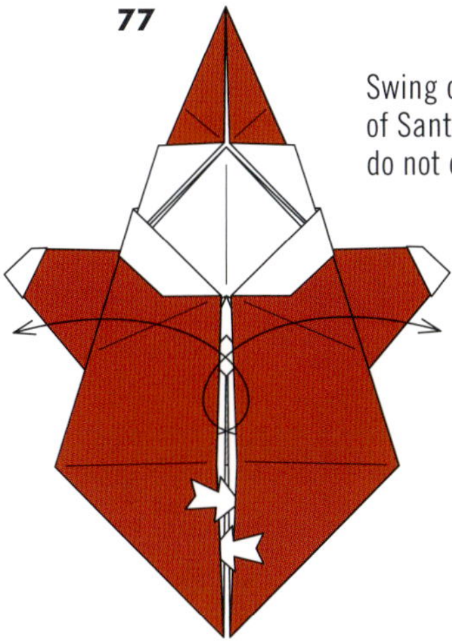

Swing open the sides of Santa's coat but do not crease.

78

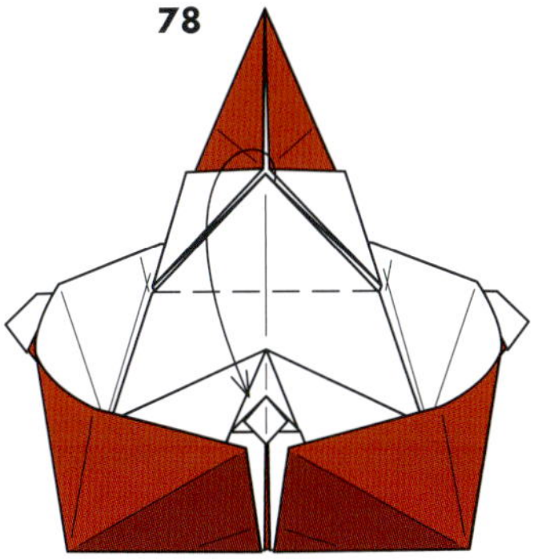

Swing down the white triangular flap. This will be Santa's beard.

79

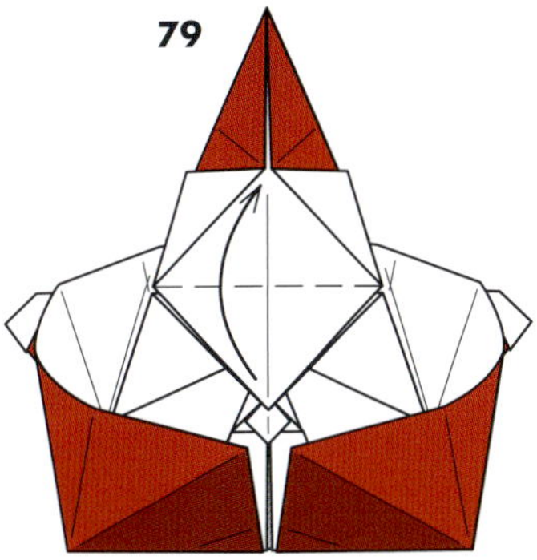

Crease firmly and unfold.

80

Enlarged view.

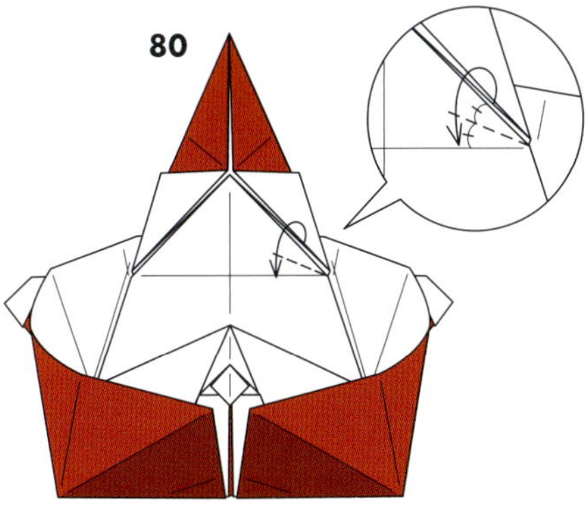

Fold the edge to the horizontal line. Crease only where shown.

81

Enlarged view.

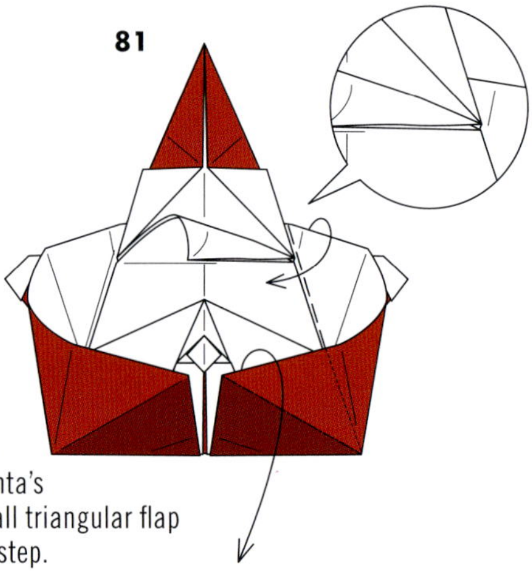

Swing the corner back down. The collar of Santa's coat will cover the small triangular flap folded in the previous step.

82

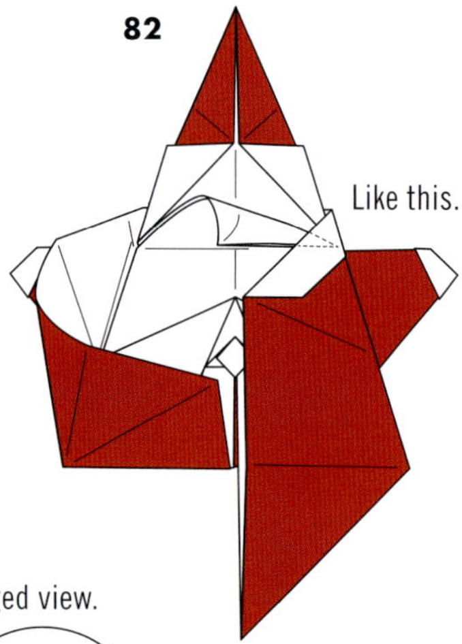

Like this.

83

Enlarged view.

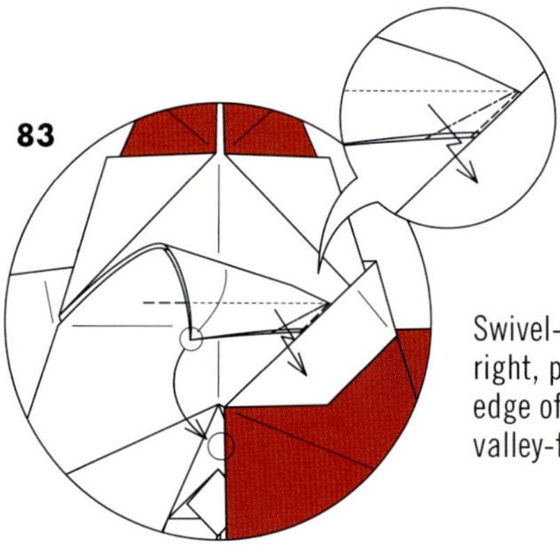

Swivel-fold the white flap to the right, pressing it against the edge of the collar to form the valley-fold.

84

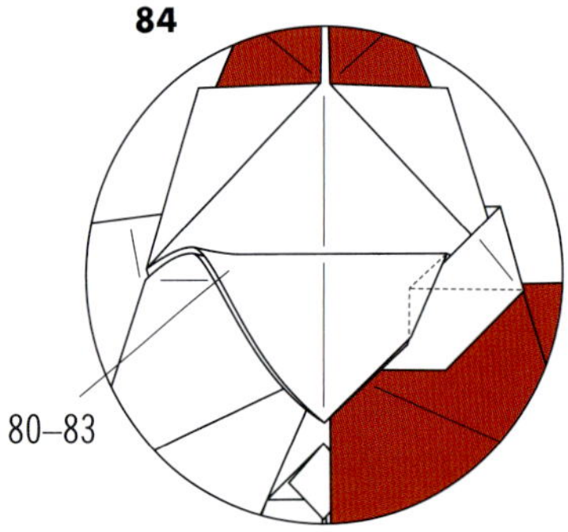

Like this. Repeat steps 80–83 on the left side.

85

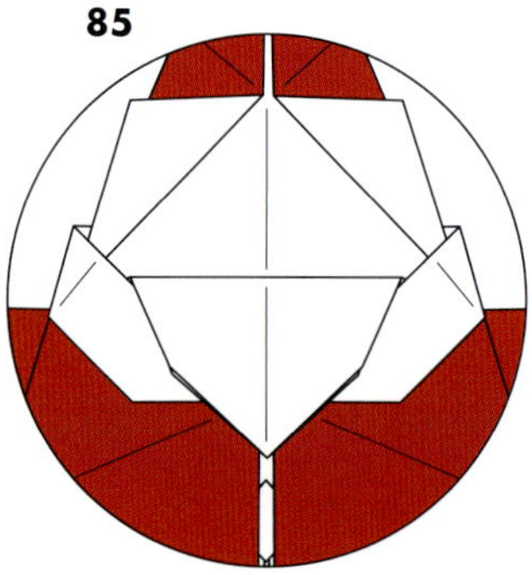

Press the beard down firmly. Reopen Santa's coat to its position in step 80.

86

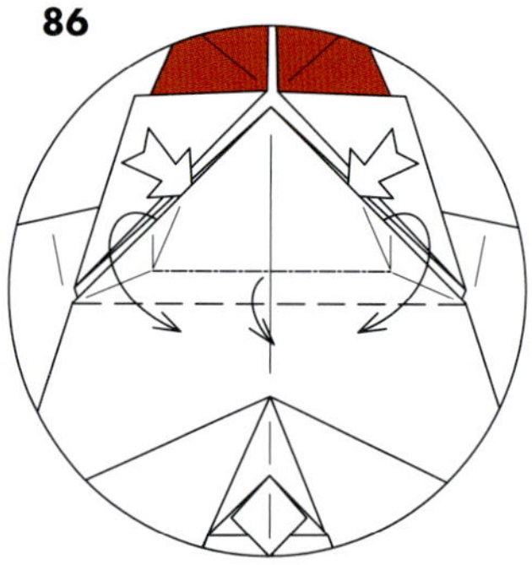

Spread-squash the bottom of the flap along the existing creases. The beard will become three-dimensional and stick out from the rest of the model. Look ahead to the next diagram.

92

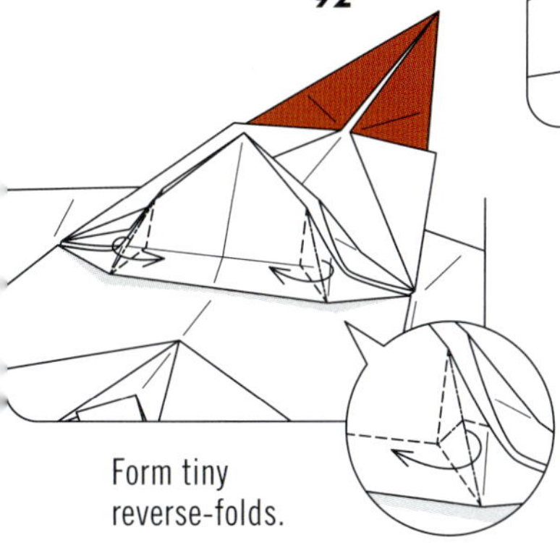

Form tiny reverse-folds.

93

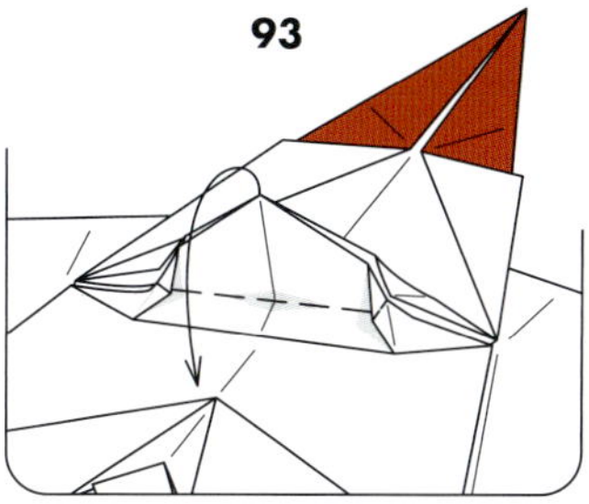

Flatten completely.

94

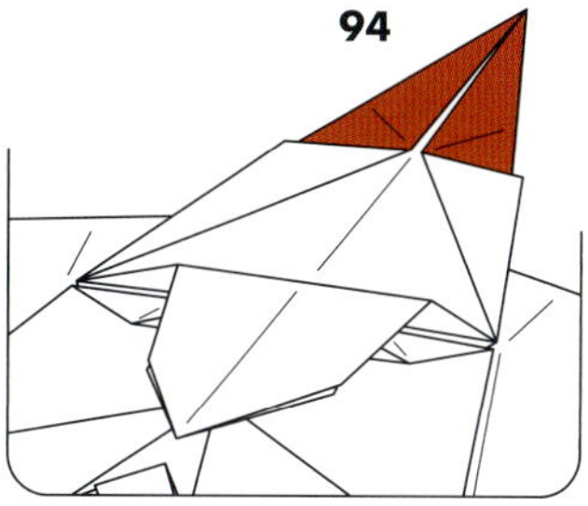

Like this. Turn over.

91

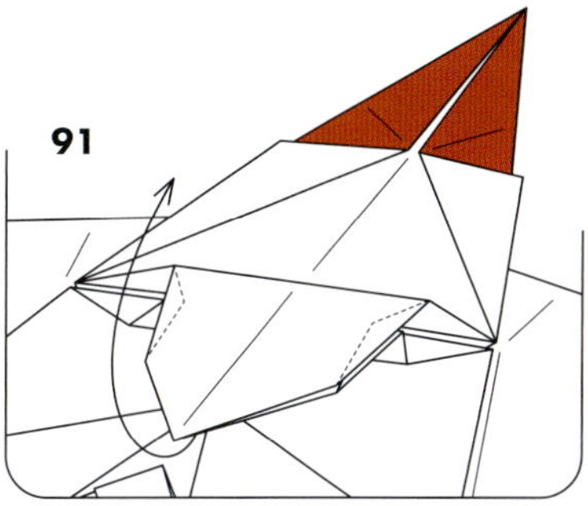

Like this. Raise the beard again.

90

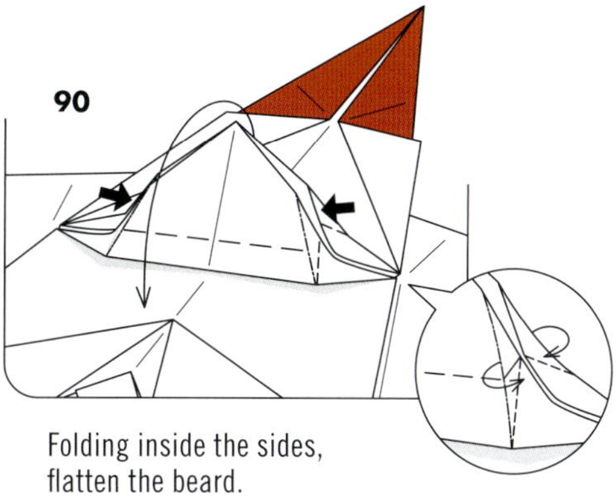

Folding inside the sides, flatten the beard.

87

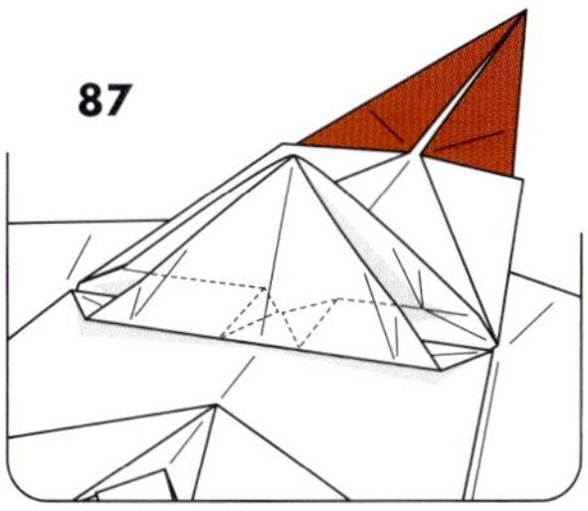

The central part of the flap will be squashed inside.

88

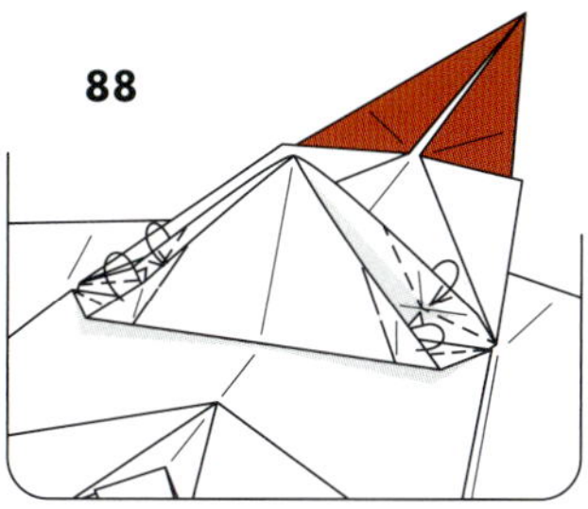

Fold the edges inside using the existing creases.

89

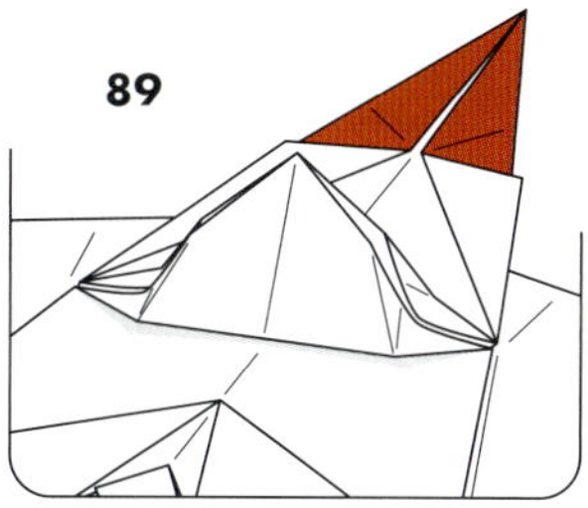

Like this.

95

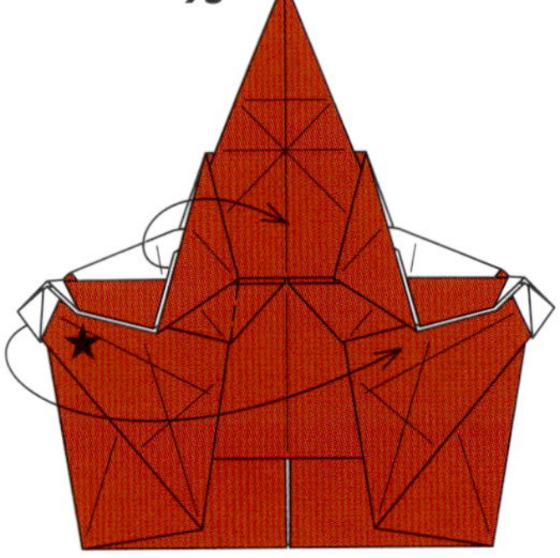

Swing the starred left-hand flap over to the right. It is necessary to open out some of the paper as shown.

96

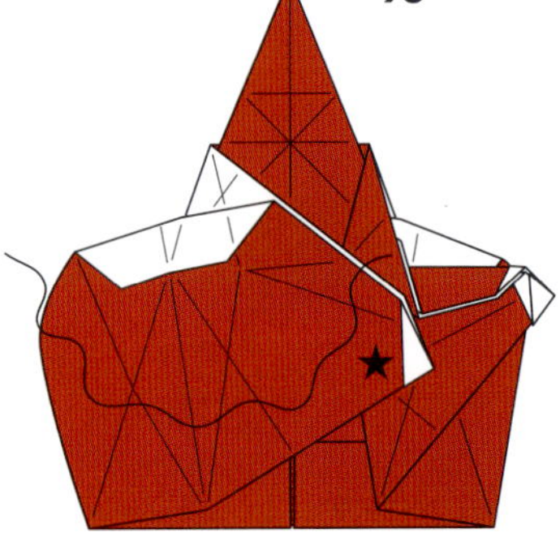

The next diagram is a transparent view.

97

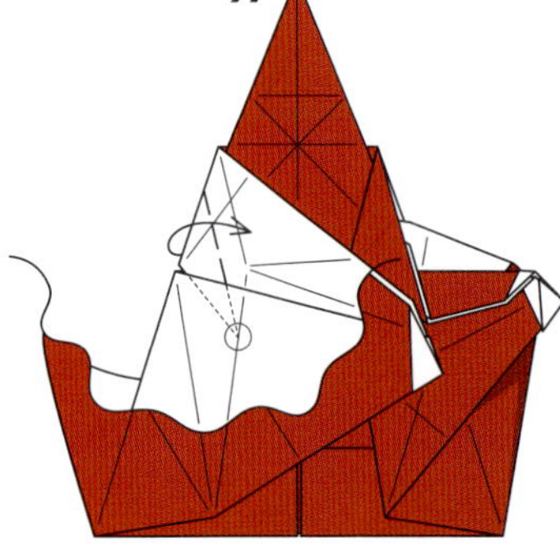

This sequence narrows Santa's head. through the hidden circled point. Loo ahead to the next diagram for anothe reference point. Tweezers are extreme helpful here.

98

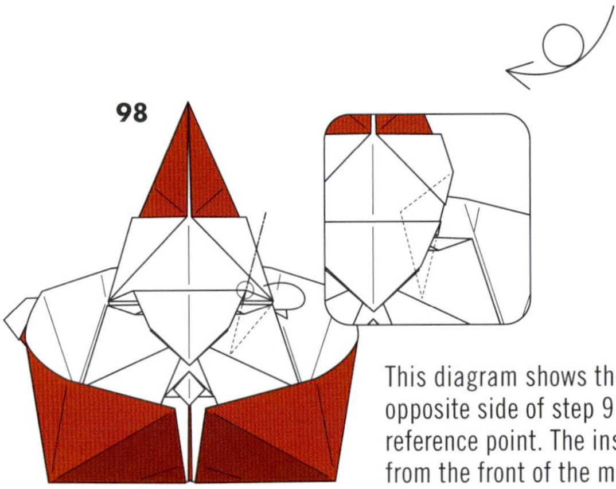

This diagram shows the front of the model and the opposite side of step 97. The circle shows the second reference point. The inset shows the completed fold seen from the front of the model. Turn over.

99

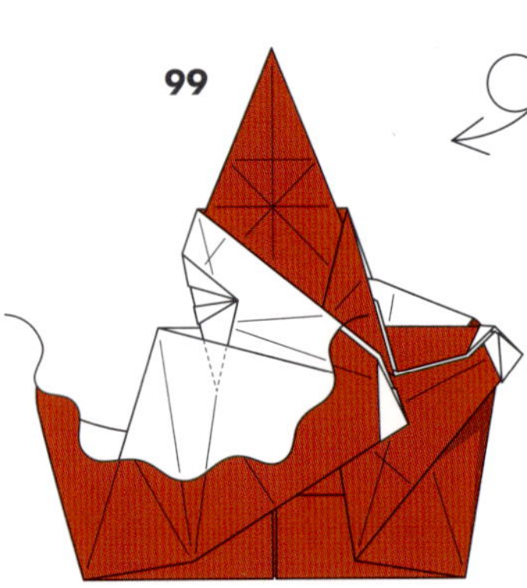

This view shows the completed fold seen from the rear of the model.

100

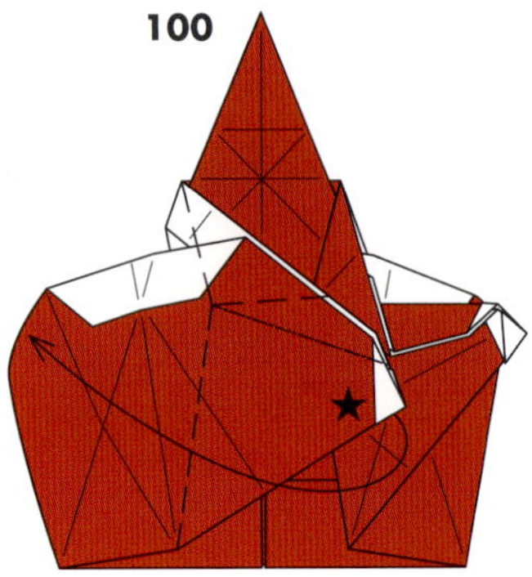

Swing the starred flap back to the left and reassemble the existing creases. Note that a portion the little flap folded in 97 and 98 gets folded again in the process.

101

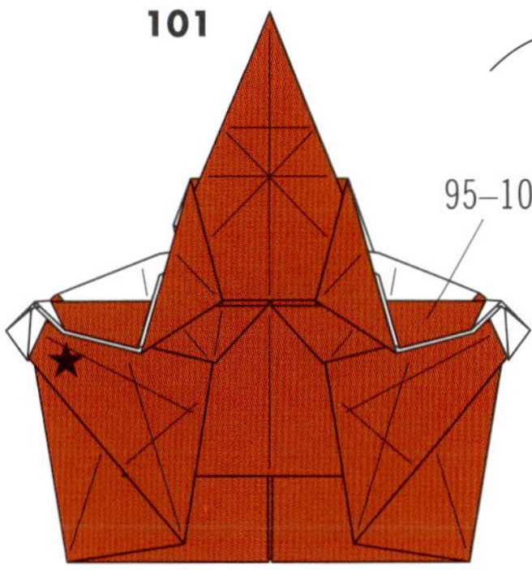

Repeat steps 95–100 on the right side.

102

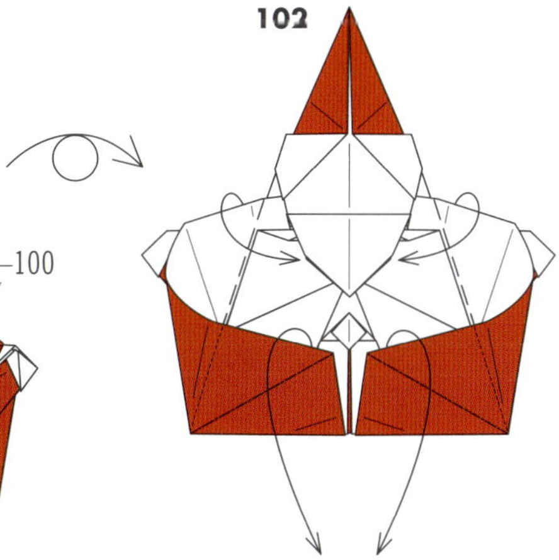

Swing down the corners to their original position.

103

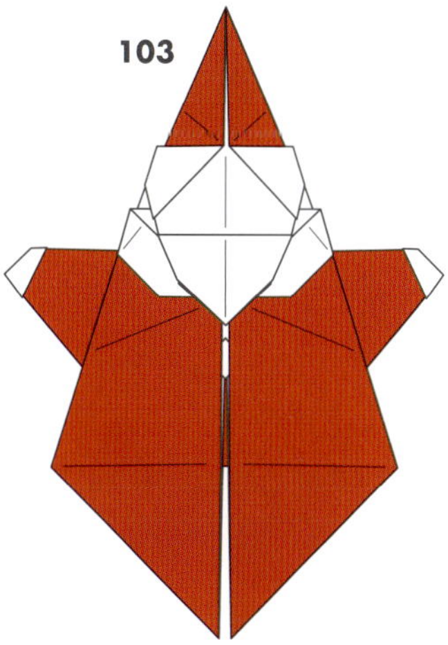

The next diagram shows the head enlarged.

104

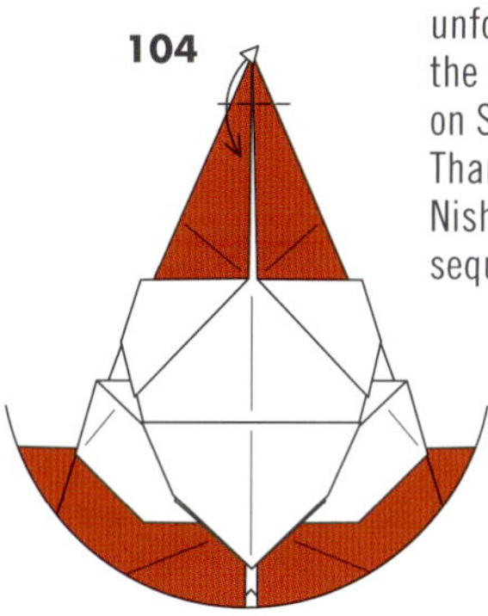

Fold the tip and unfold to precrease the pompom on Santa's hat. Thanks to Seiji Nishikawa for this sequence.

105

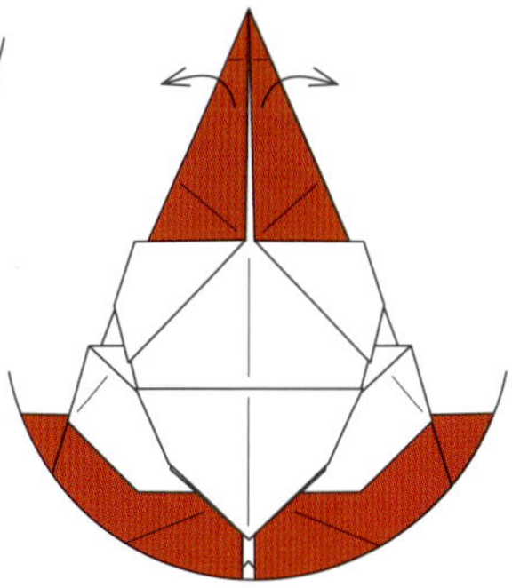

Swing open the sides of the tip.

106

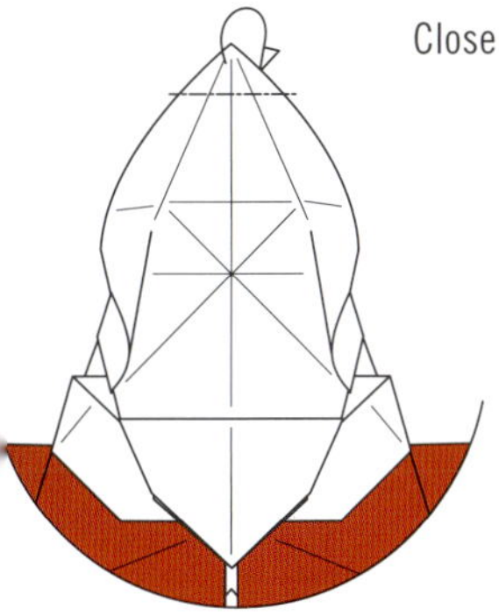

Fold behind along the crease made in 104.

107

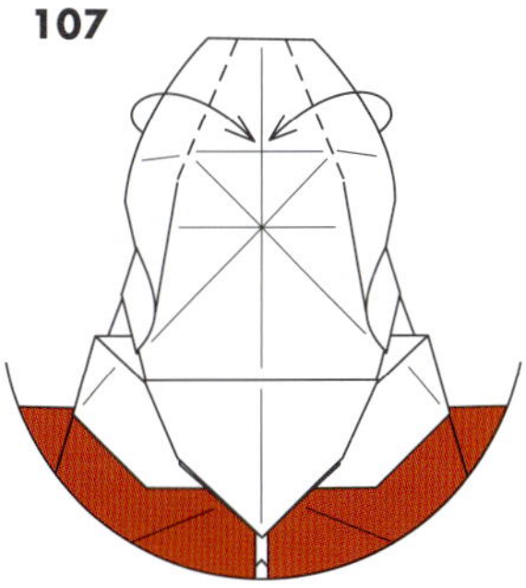

Close the flap.

108

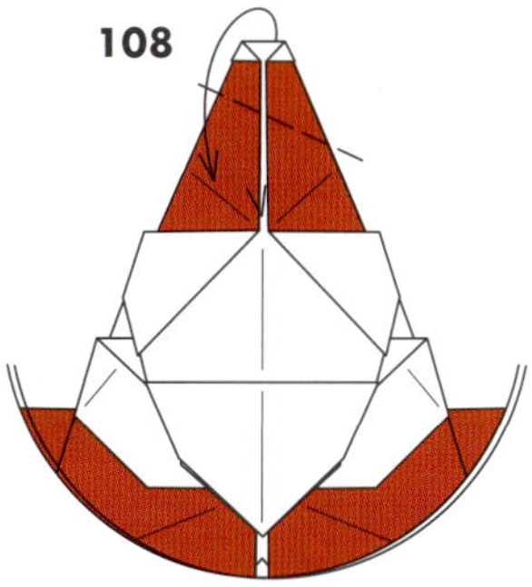

Fold down the tip.

109

Reference point.

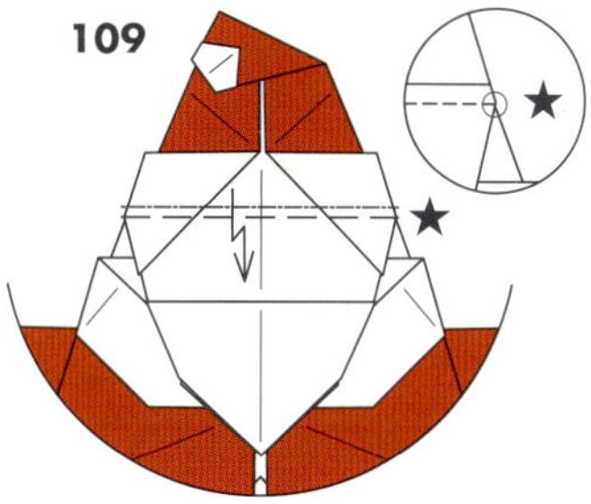

Pleat slightly.

110

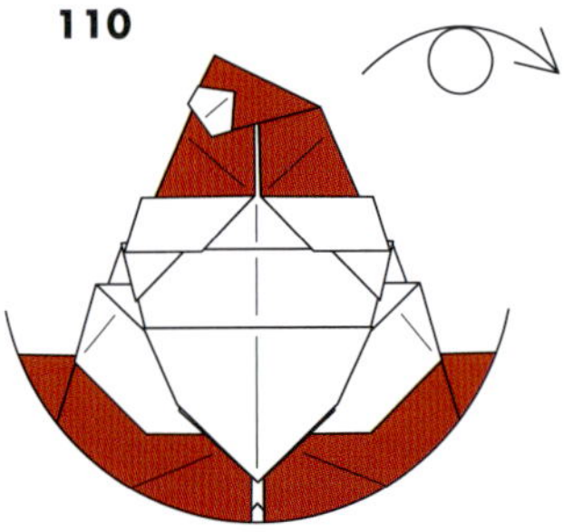

Santa's head and hat are complete. Turn over.

111

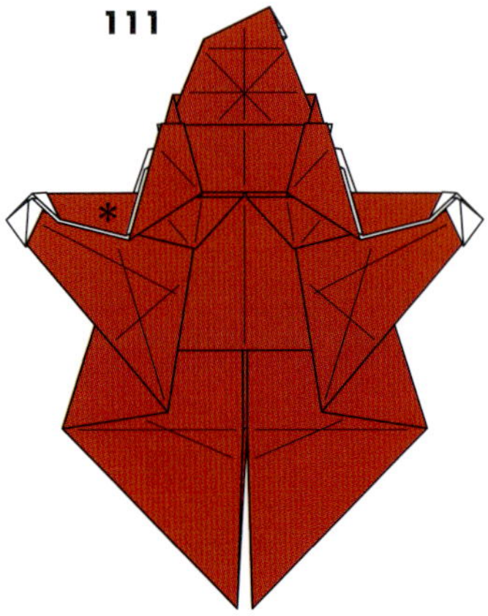

Separate two layers and bring the top one, marked with a star, inside.

112

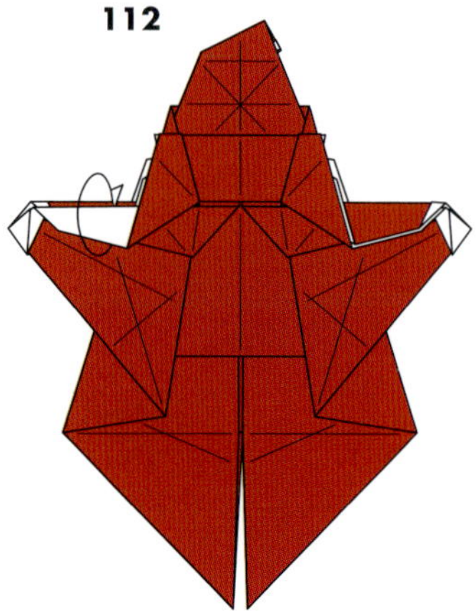

Fold the upper layer inside.

113

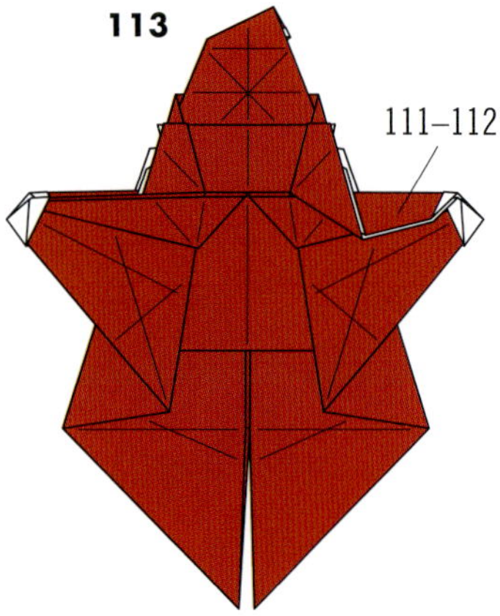

Repeat steps 111–112 on the right side.

114

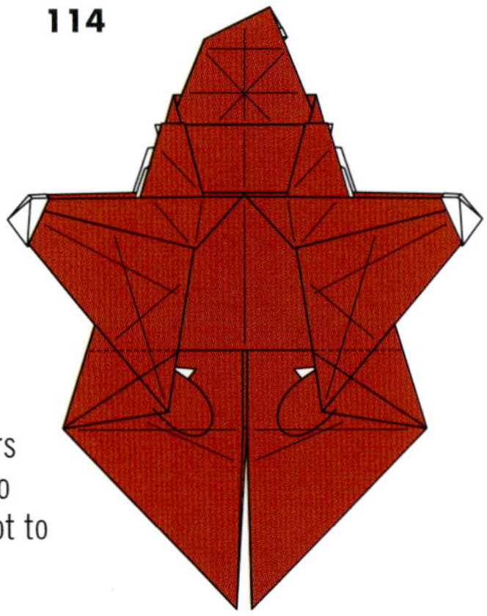

Tuck the corners behind and into the furthest slot to lock the back.

115

Turn over.

116

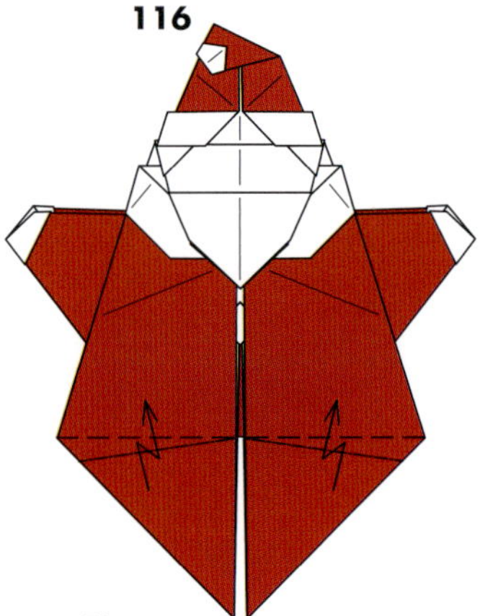

Pleat.

117

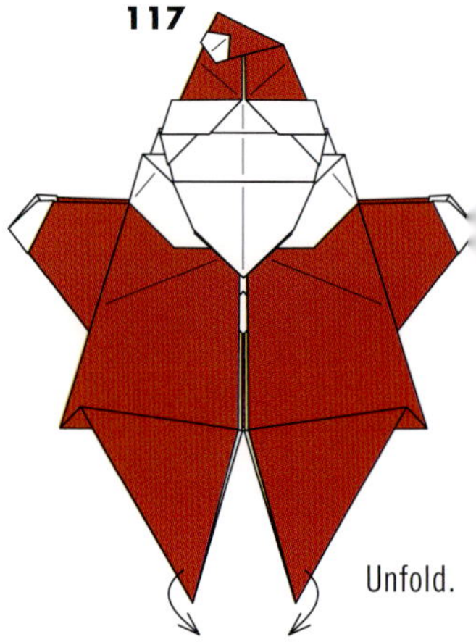

Unfold.

123

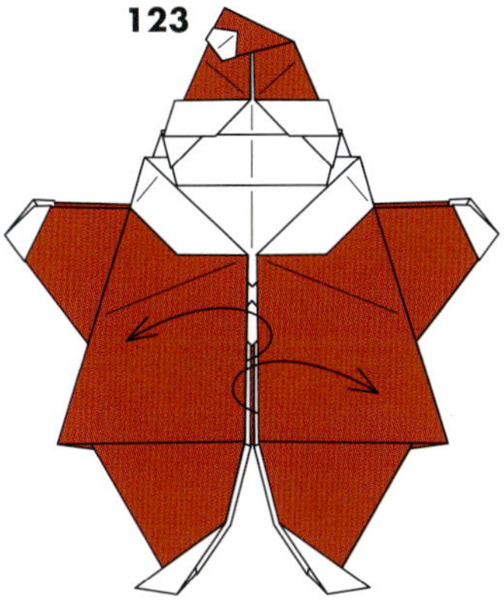

Swing open the sides of Santa's coat enough to see inside

124

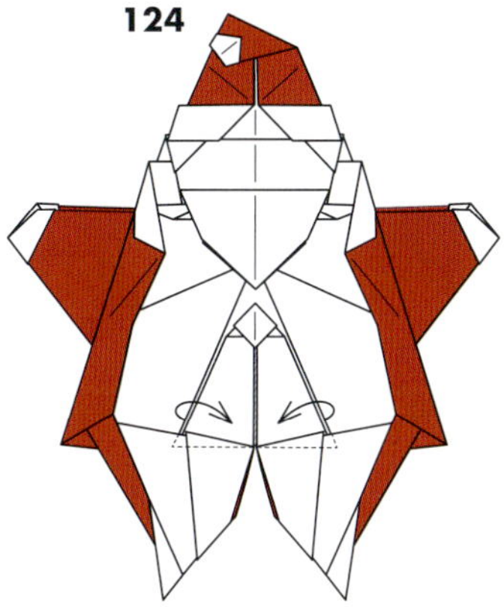

Pull out the tiny pleated flaps.

122

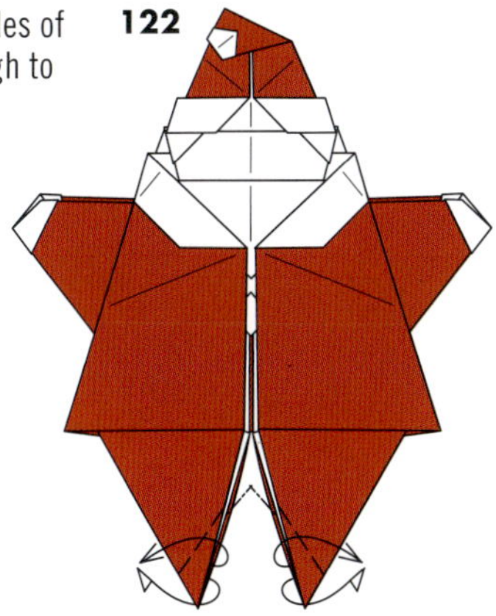

Outside reverse-fold along the creases just made.

121

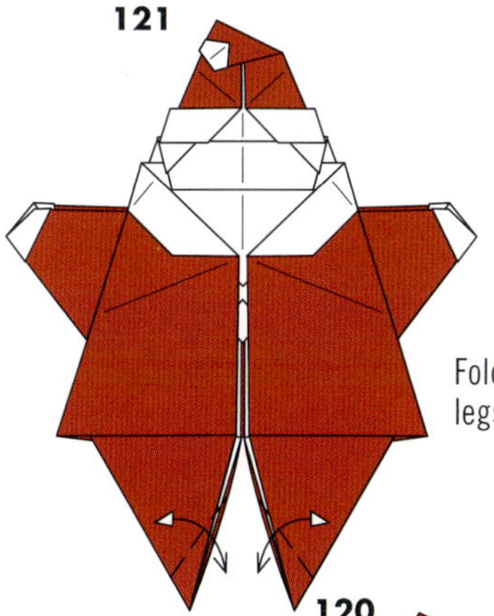

Fold and unfold the legs to form feet.

120

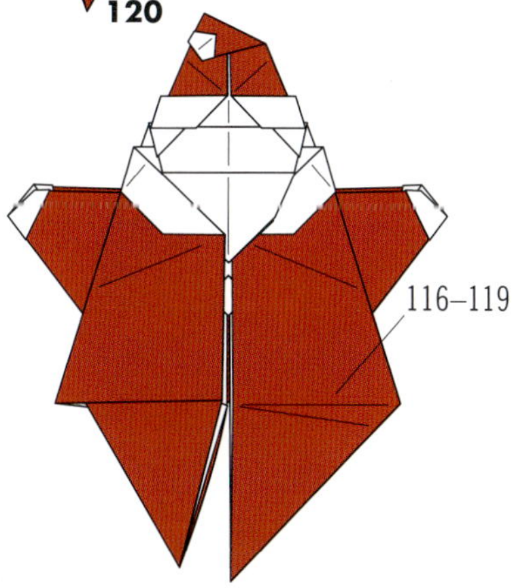

Repeat steps 116–119 on the right side.

118

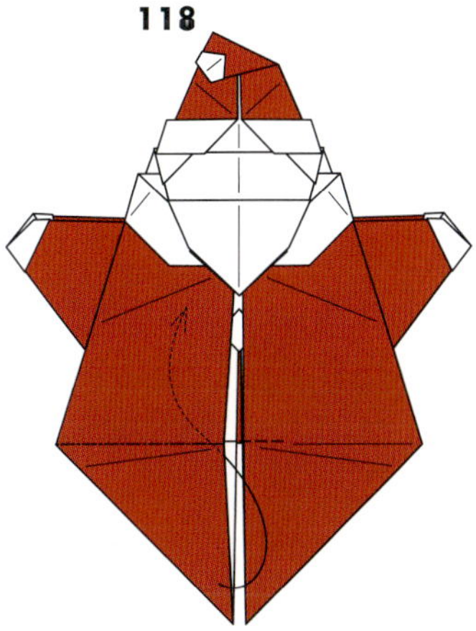

Inside reverse fold along the horizontal creases.

119

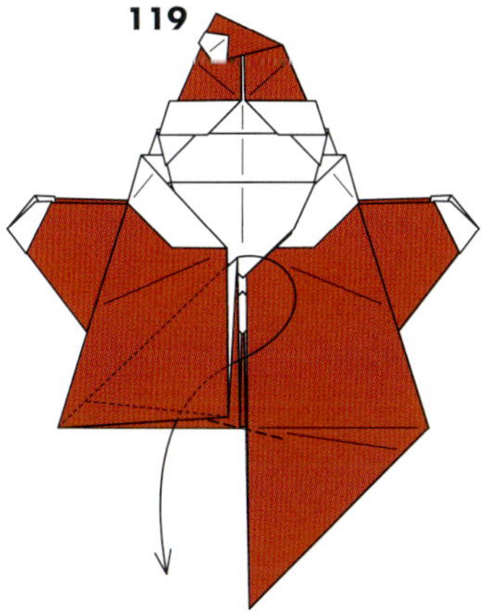

Inside reverse fold along the angled creases.

125

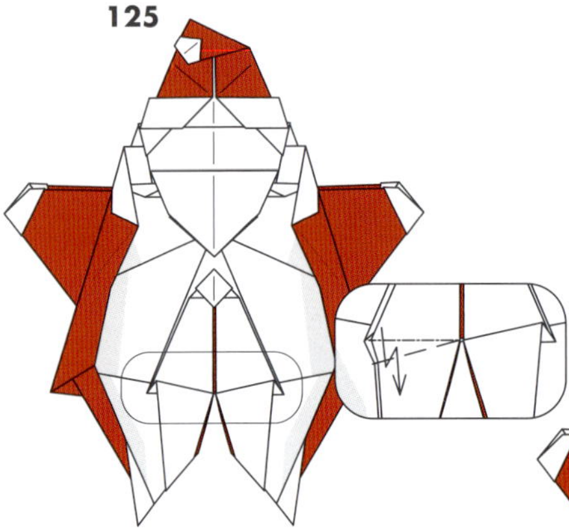

Reverse the mountain and valley folds of the pleated flaps.

126

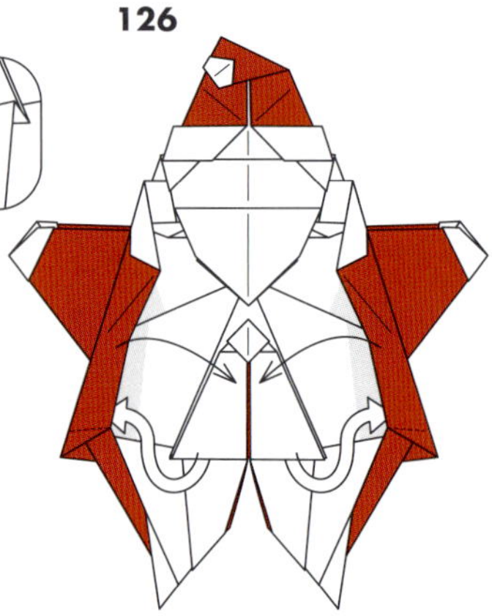

Close the coat while tucking the pleated flaps into the corresponding slots in the sides of the coat.

127

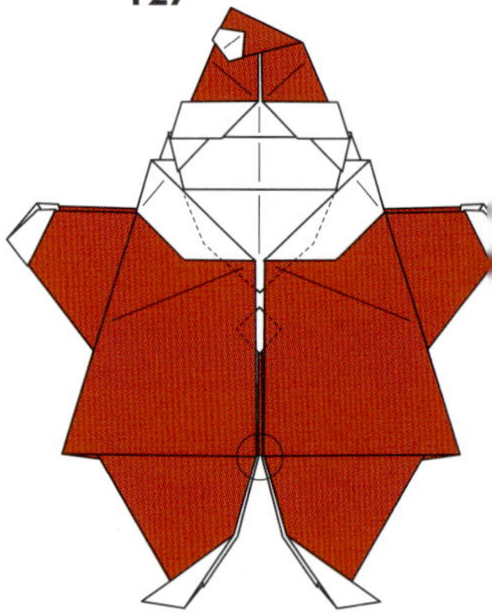

Santa's coat is locked at the circl point. Bring the beard and button the front of the coat. Turn over.

128

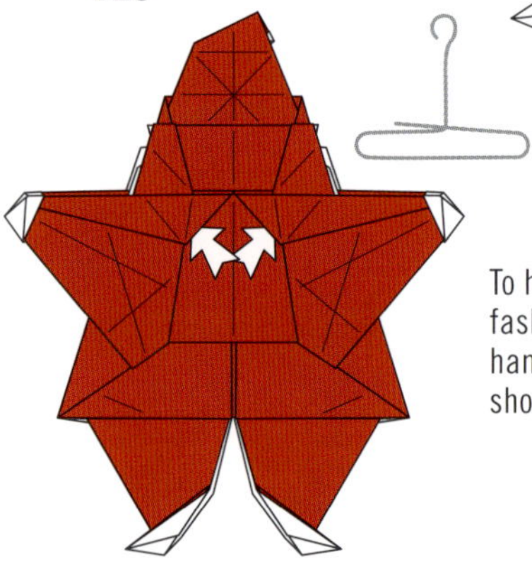

To hang the model as an ornament, fashion a paper clip into a tiny hanger and insert into pockets at shoulders.

129

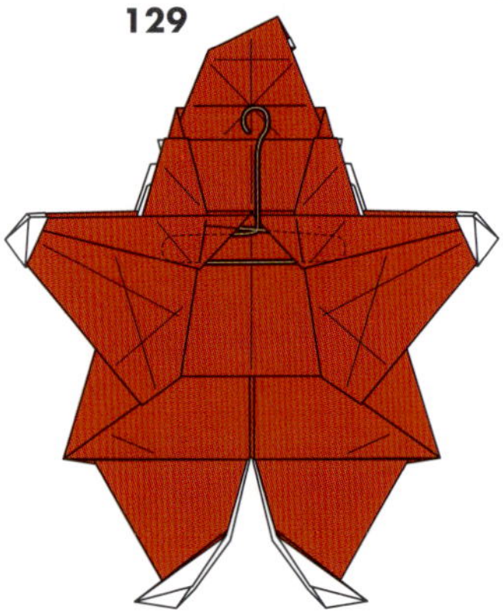

Paper clip inserted. Turn over.

130

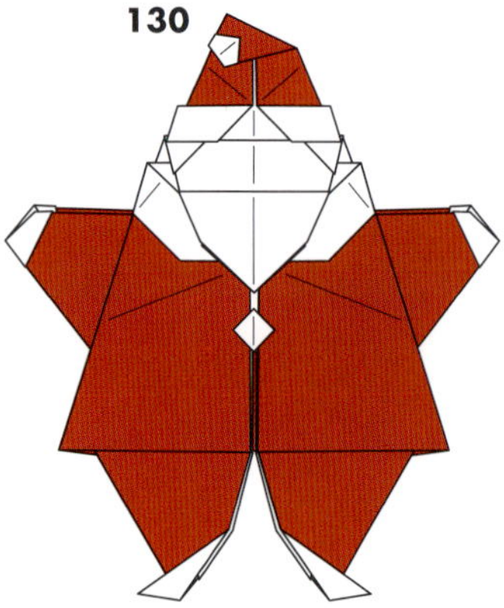

Completed Santa Claus.

Santa's Toy Bag

Begin with a square the same size as the one used for Santa.

1

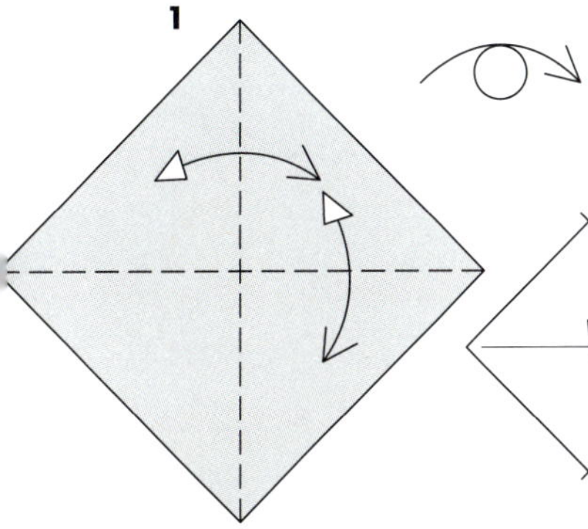

Fold and unfold along the diagonals. Turn over.

2

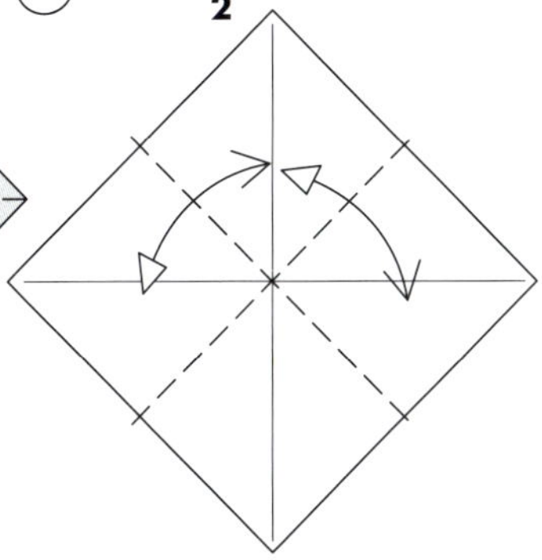

Fold edge to edge and unfold.

3

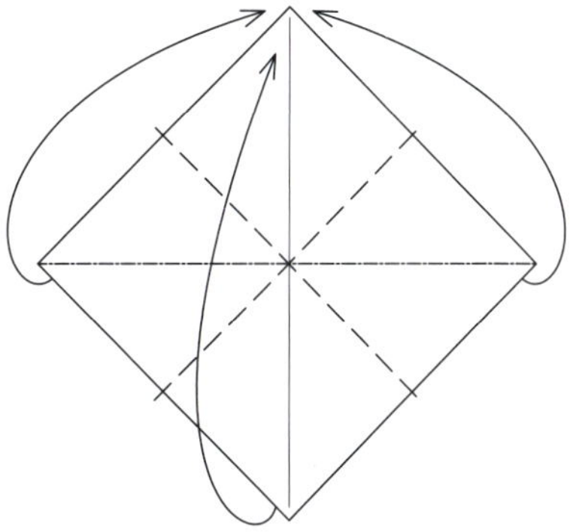

Collapse along the existing creases.

4

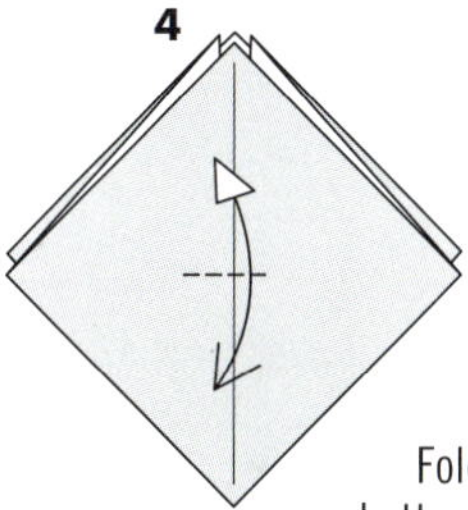

Fold the top corner to the bottom corner and unfold. Press lightly only where shown.

5

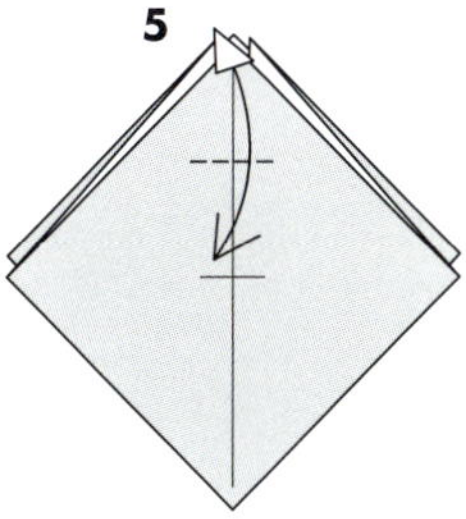

Fold the top corner to the mark made in the previous step and unfold. Press lightly only where shown.

6

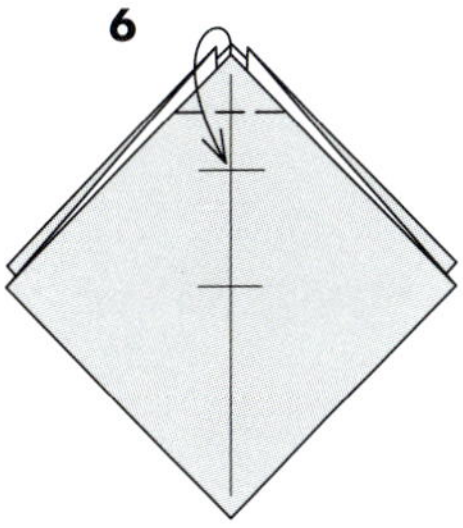

Fold the top corner to the mark. Press lightly across the full width.

7

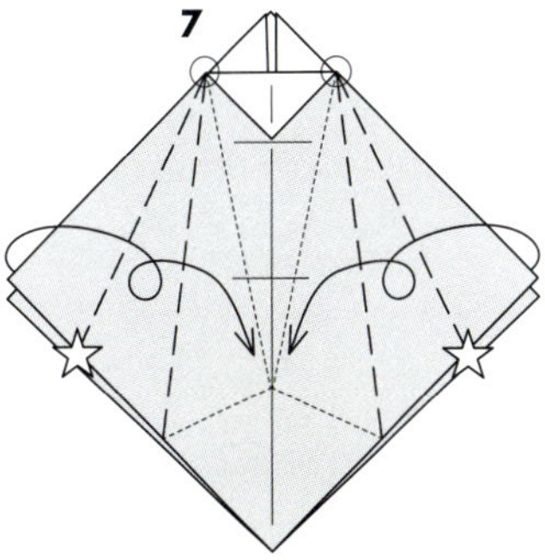

Fold over and over so that the starred points meet on the centerline.

8

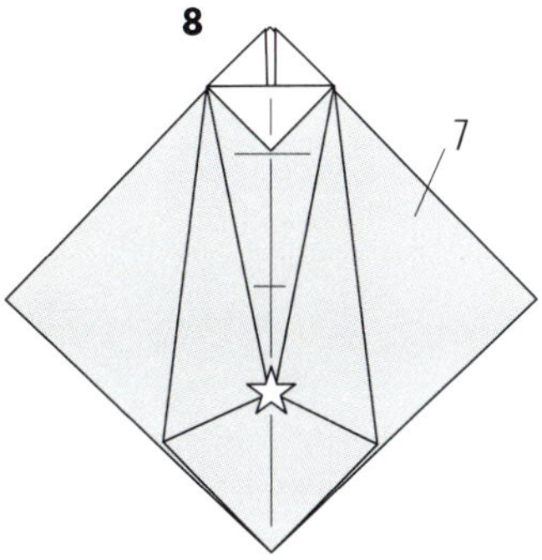

Repeat step 7 behind.

9

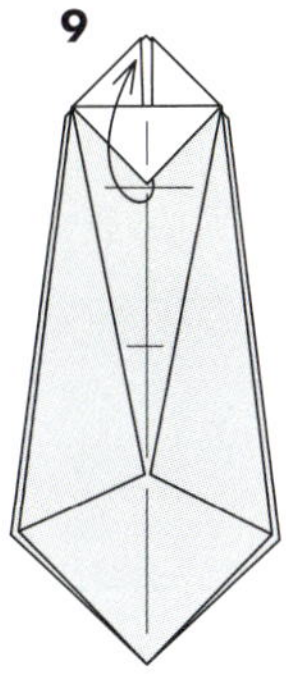

Unfold the white flap.

10

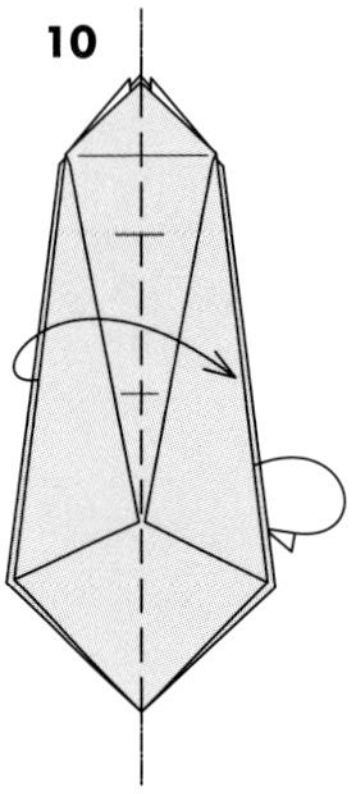

Swing the left flap to the right and the rear right flap to the left.

11

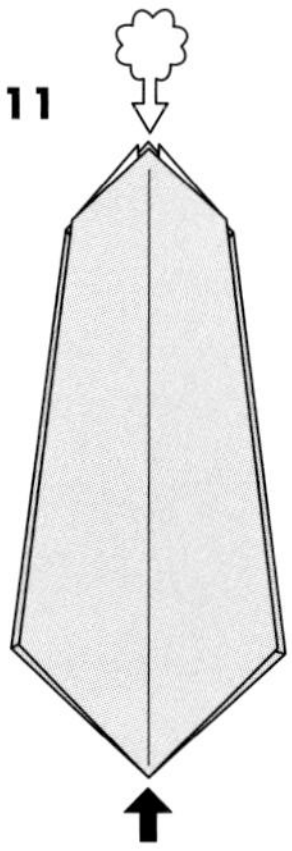

Blow into the top while rounding the bottom. The bag will become three-dimensional.

12

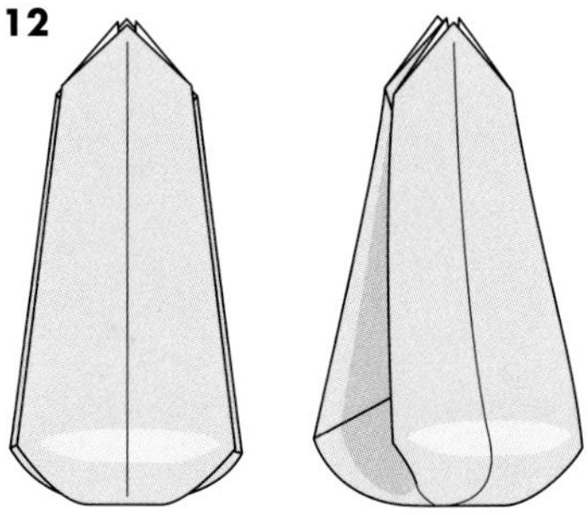

Like this. Side view.

13

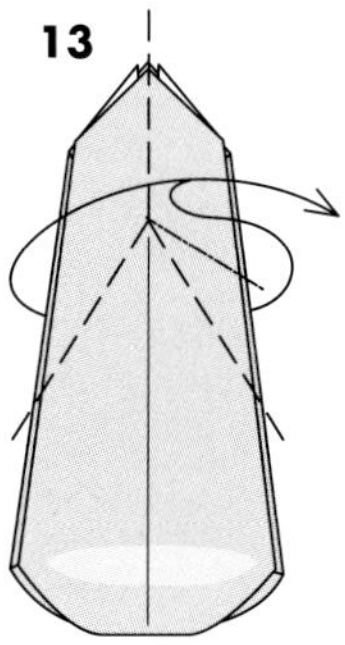

Fold all the layers together, making a thick rabbit's ear.

14

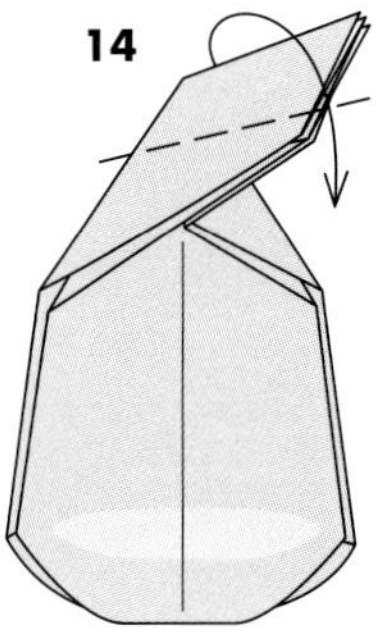

Fold all the layers down.

15

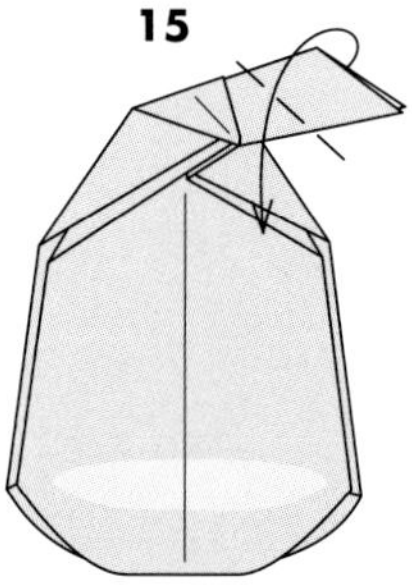

Fold all the layers again to hook the tip of the bag.

16

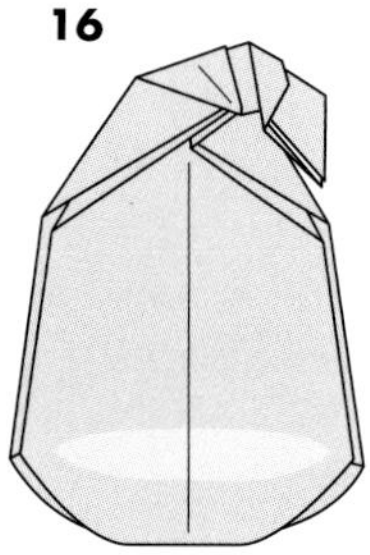

Completed Santa's Toy Bag.

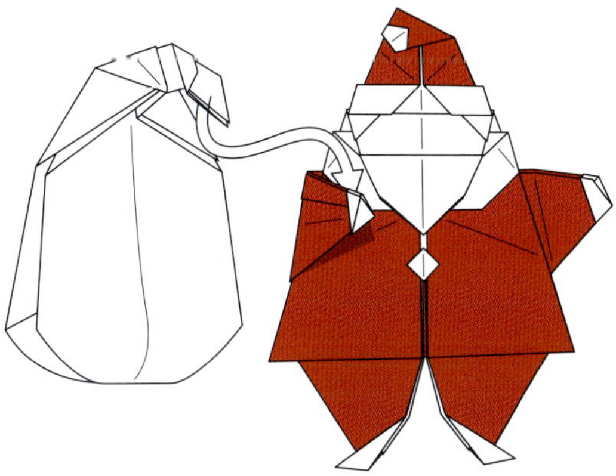

Bend Santa's arm and tuck the hook of the bag into the crook of Santa's arm.

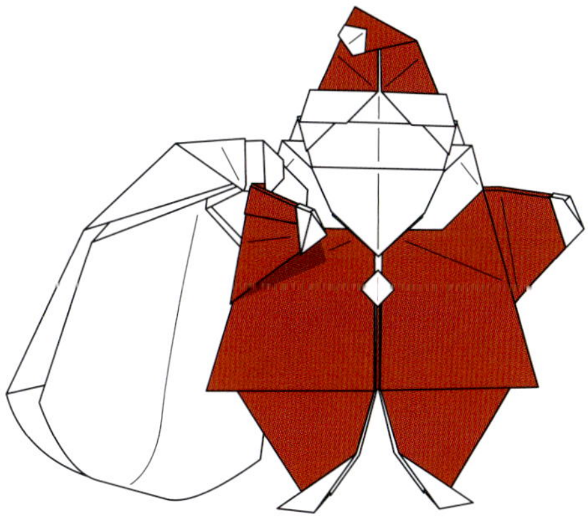

Completed Santa Claus with his Toy Bag.

Dragon Slayer

Paul Frasco

Paper isn't the only medium Paul works with. To find out what his other, unexpected, specialty is, see his bio on page 151.

video: *youtu.be/lTQmdKRFjA4*

1

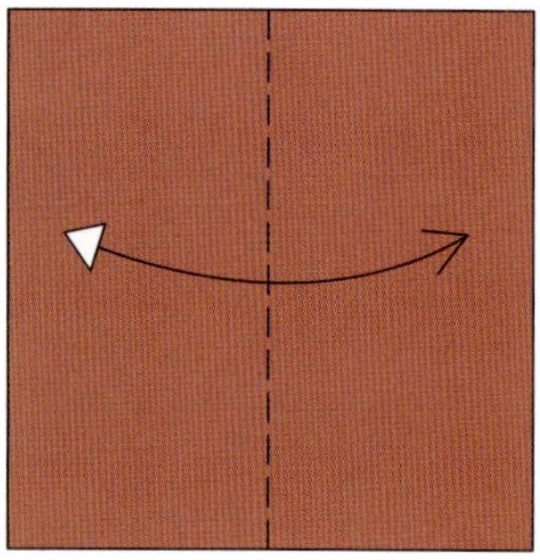

Precrease in half.

2

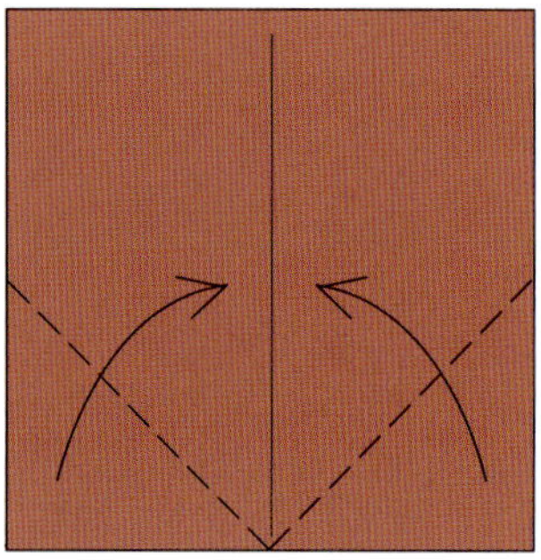

Valley fold to the center.

3

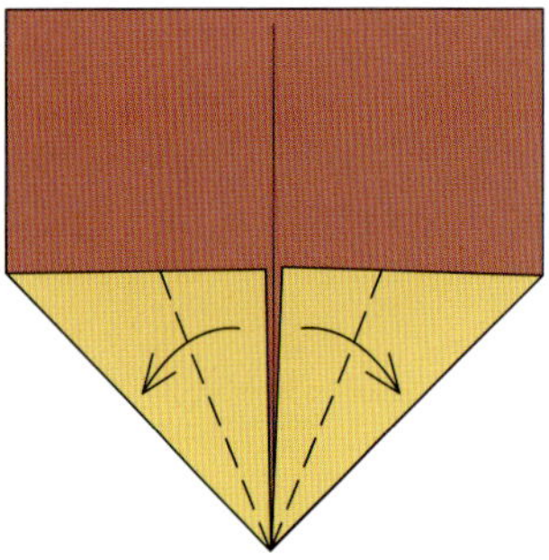

Valley fold outward.

4

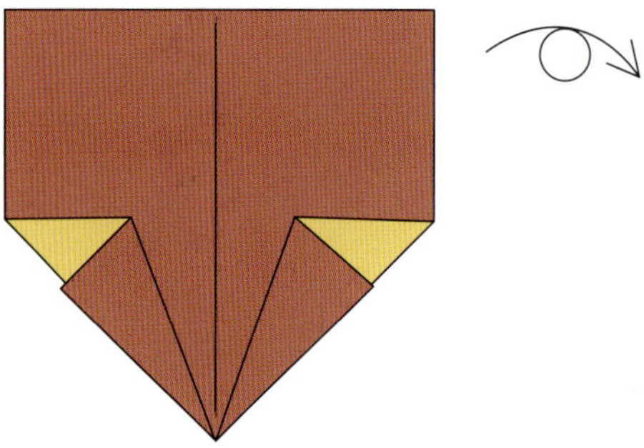

Turn over.

5

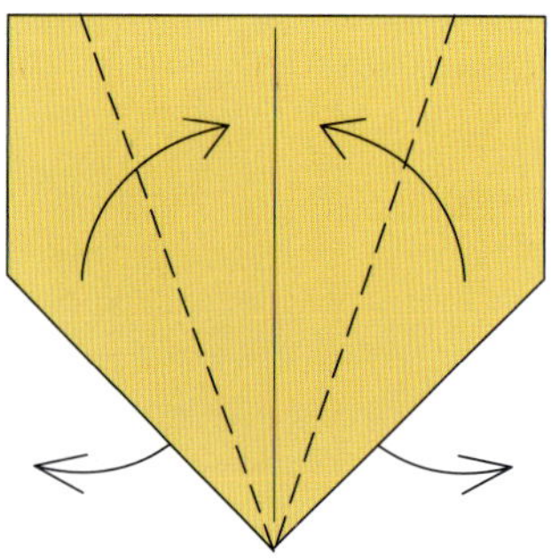

Valley fold to the center, allowing the flaps from behind to swing outward.

6

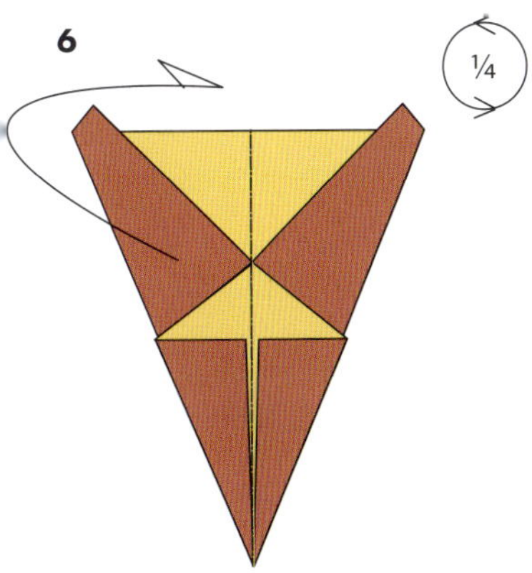

Mountain fold in half and rotate.

7

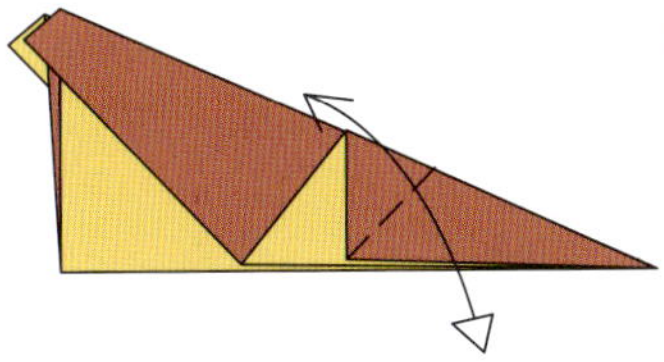

Precrease through all layers.

8

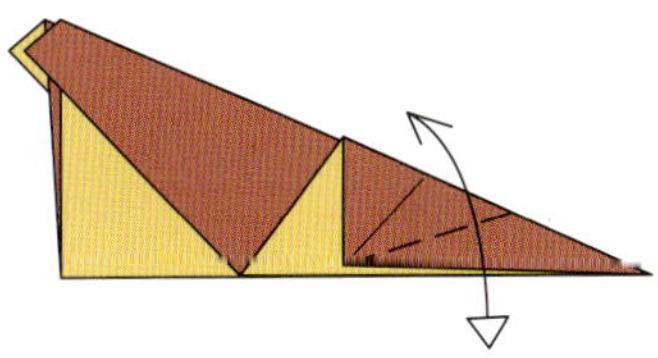

Precrease through all layers.

9

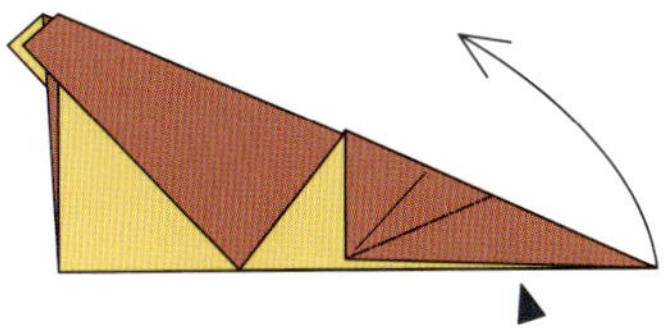

Reverse fold up.

10

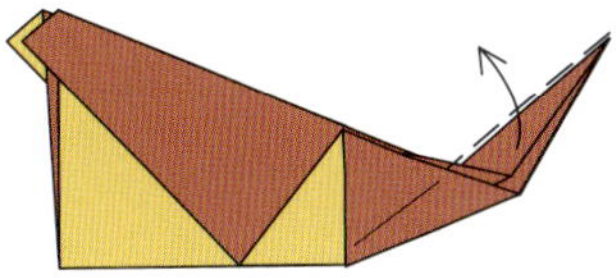

Valley fold the trapped layer up.

11

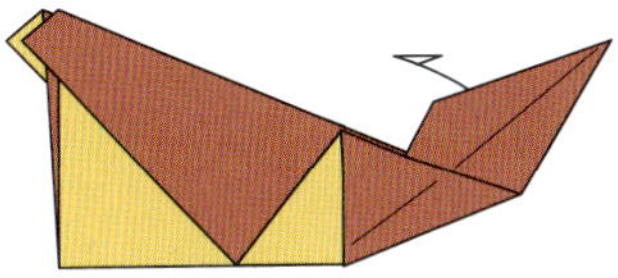

Valley fold the trapped layer behind up.

12

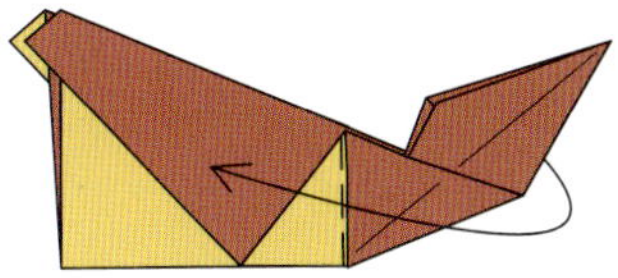

Valley fold.

13

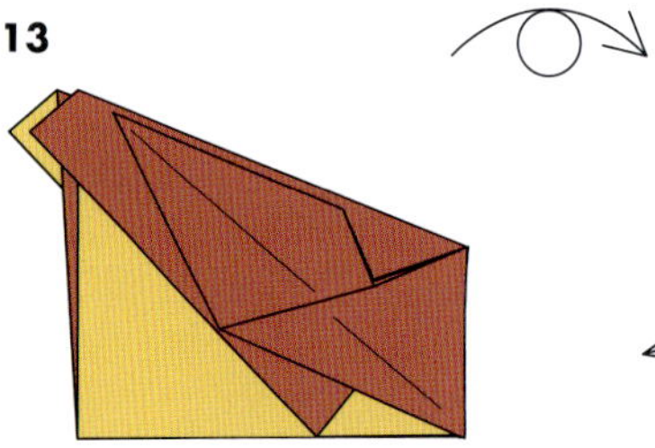

Turn over.

14

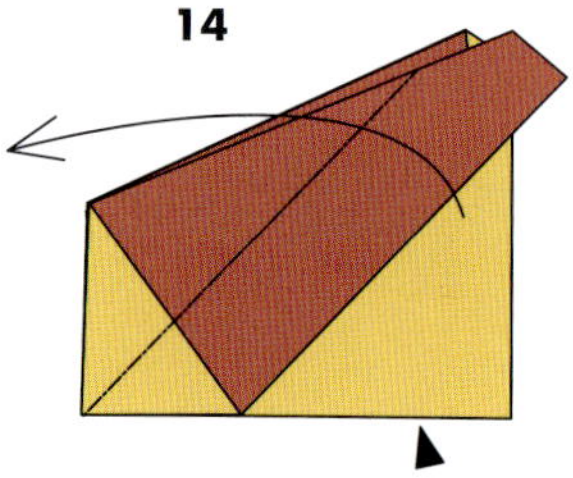

Squash fold.

15

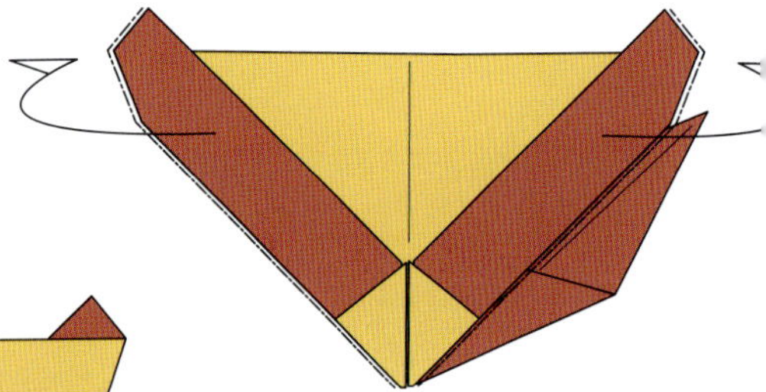

Wrap around a single layer at each side.

16

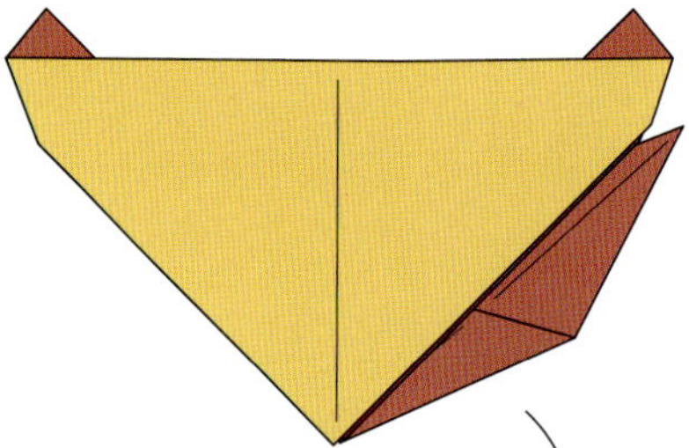

Turn over.

17

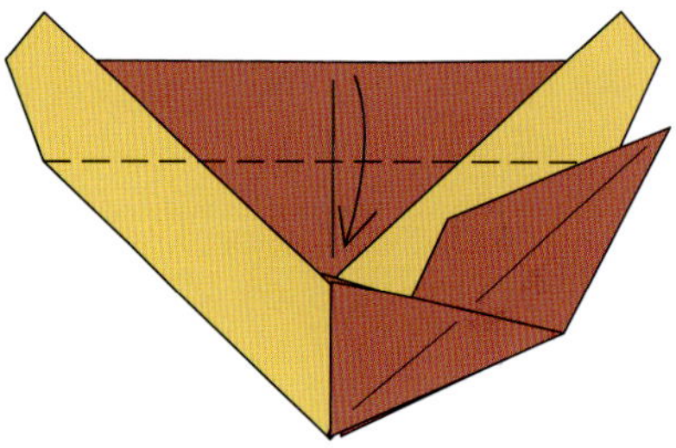

Valley fold down.

18

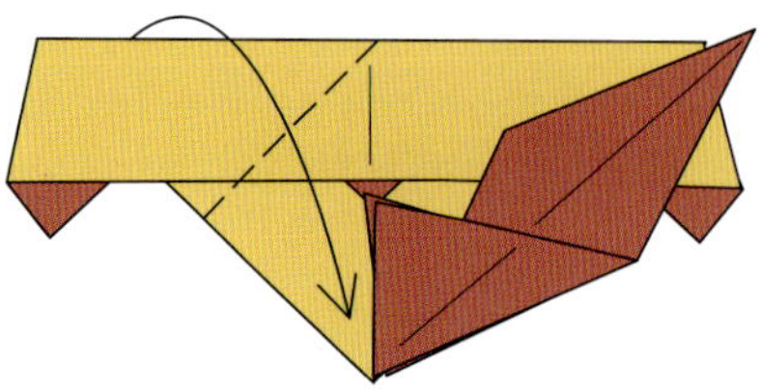

Valley fold down.

19

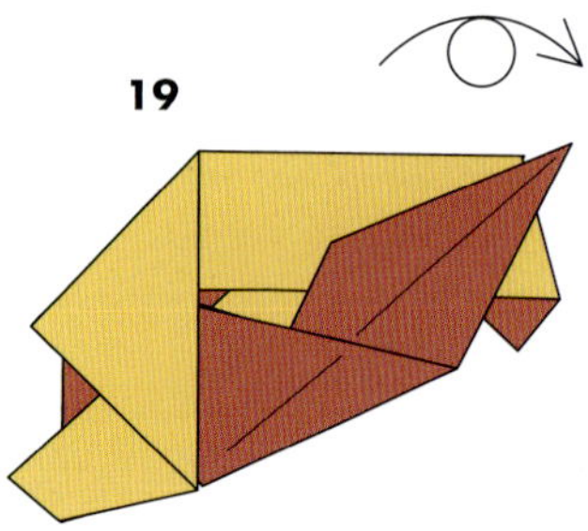

Turn over.

20

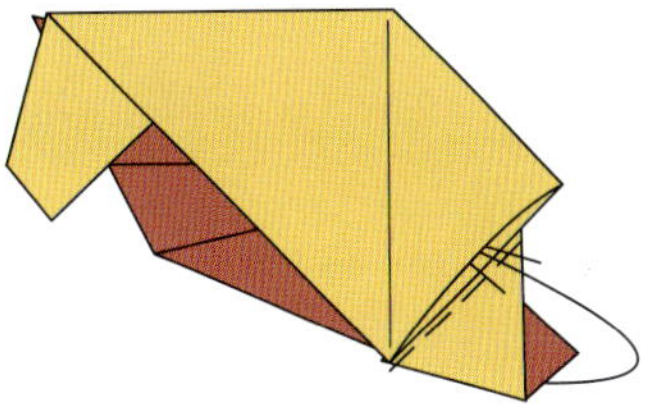

Valley fold the flap into the pocket.

21

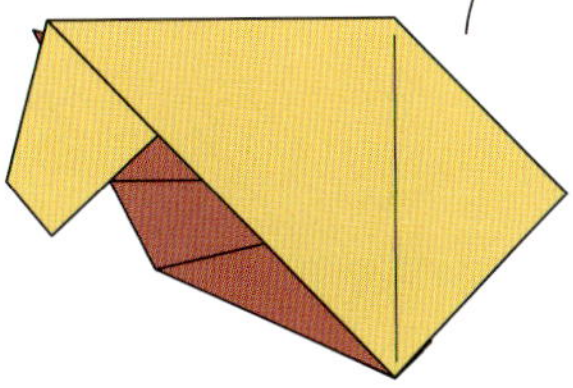

Turn over.

22

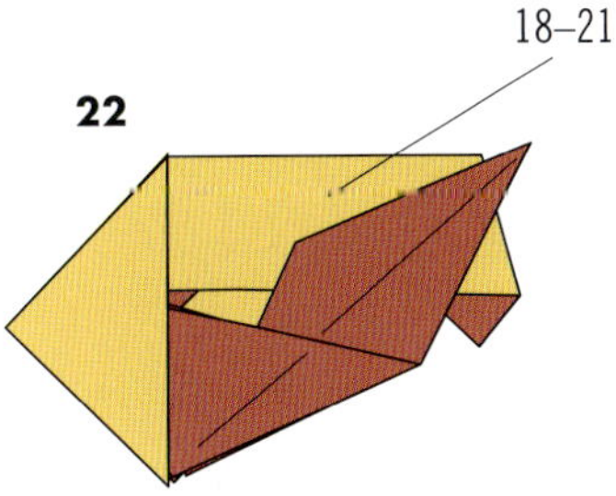

Repeat steps 18–21 in mirror image.

23

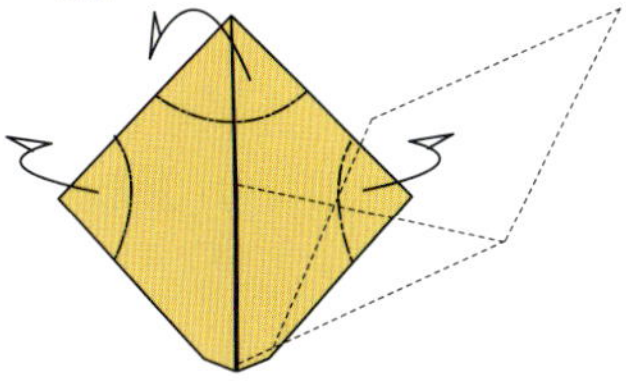

Shape the corners with rounded mountain folds.

24

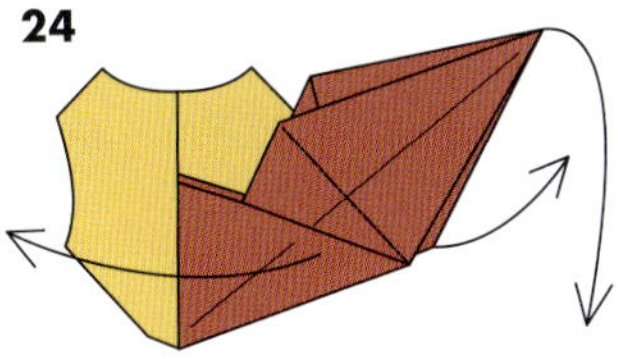

Spread apart the flap. The model will not lie flat.

25

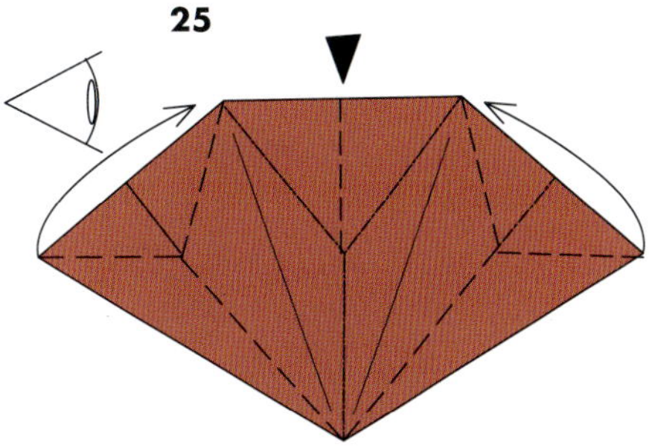

Close the flap back up by squashing the center upward and rabbit earring the sides.

26

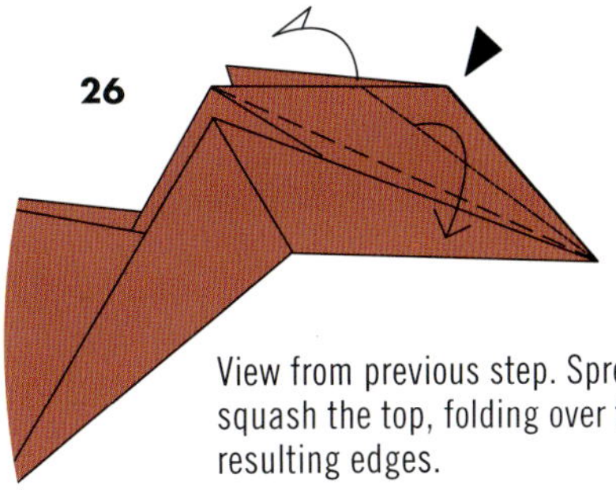

View from previous step. Spread squash the top, folding over the resulting edges.

27

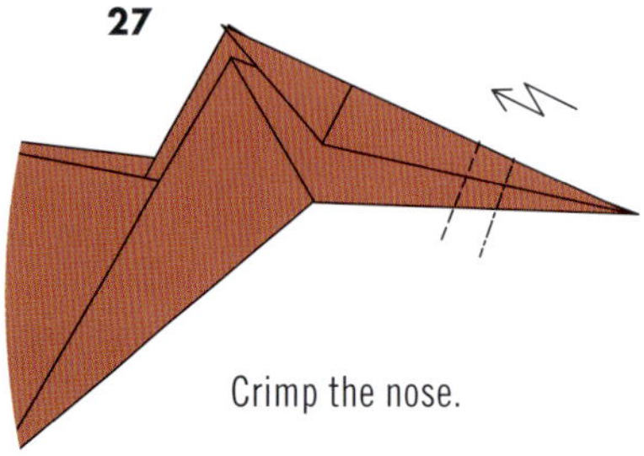

Crimp the nose.

28

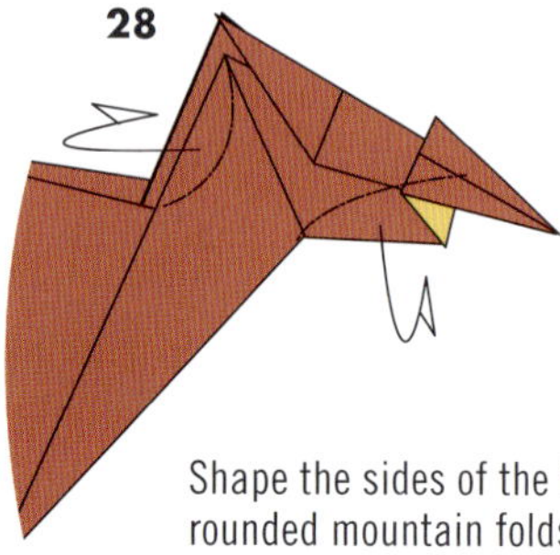

Shape the sides of the head with rounded mountain folds.

29

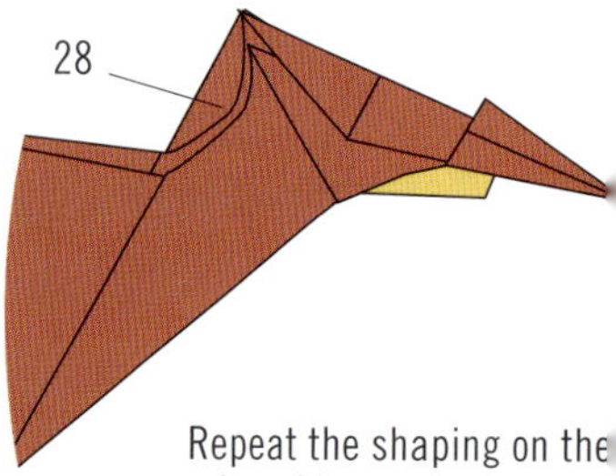

Repeat the shaping on the other side.

30

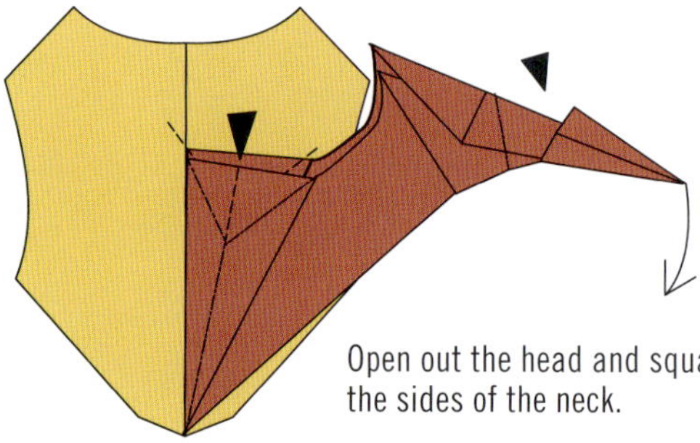

Open out the head and squash the sides of the neck.

31

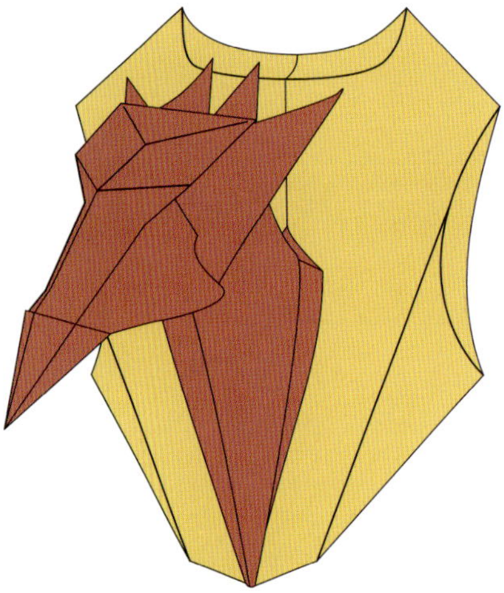

Completed Dragon Slayer.

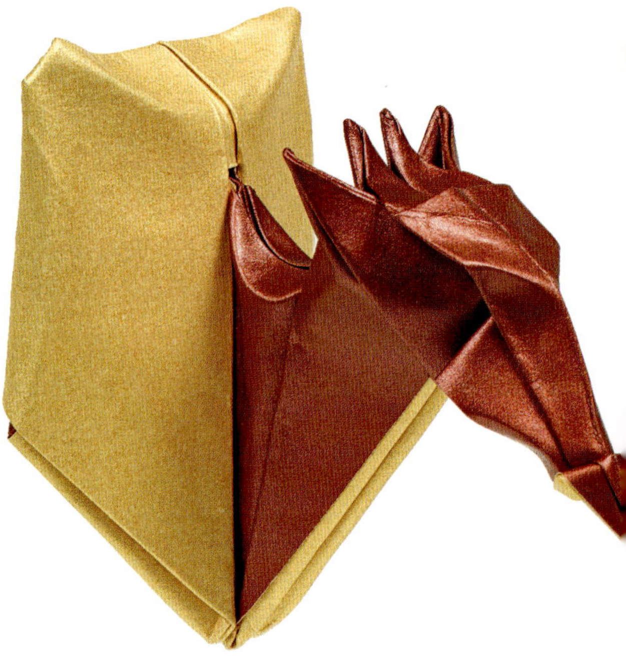

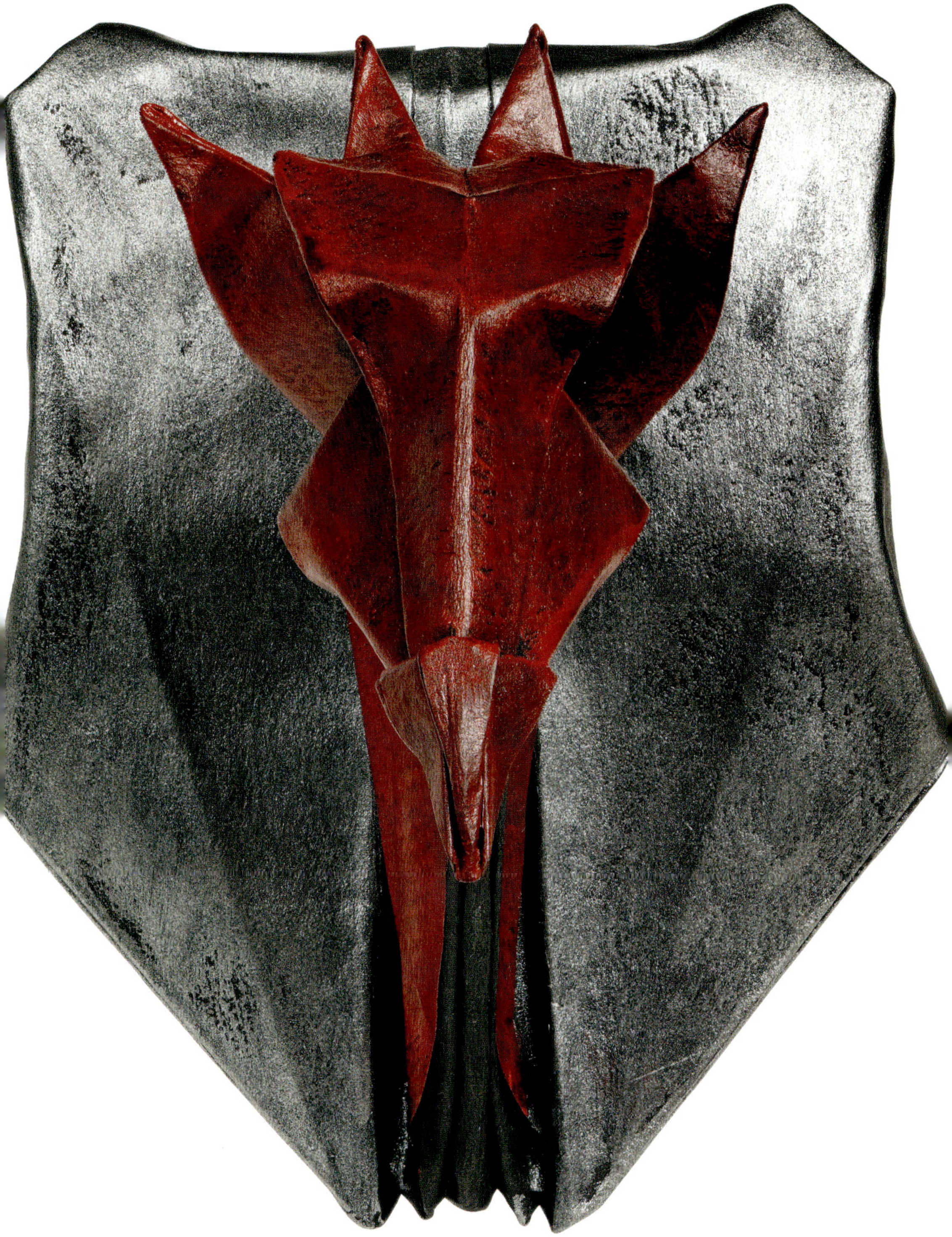

Convertible Bag

Gay Merrill Gross

Gay feels strongly that origami instructions should be easy to follow. Turn to her bio on page 156 to learn why.

video: *youtu.be/a5pvlUcDBQM*

1

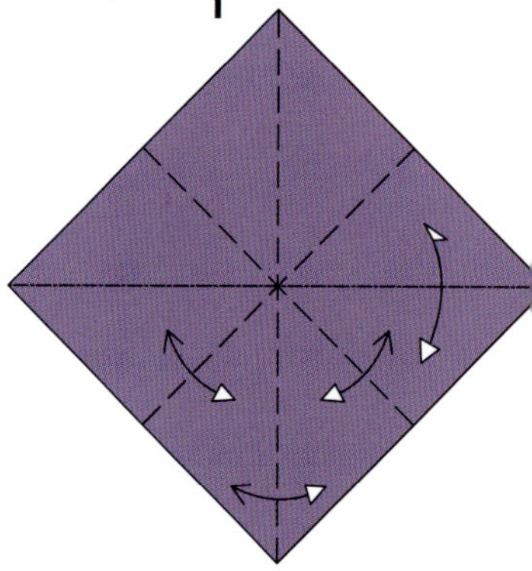

Begin with the colored side up. Precrease in half in the indicated directions.

2

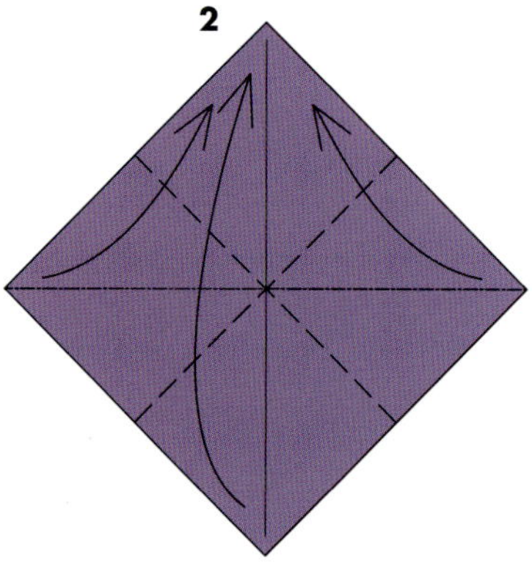

Collapse the points upward.

3

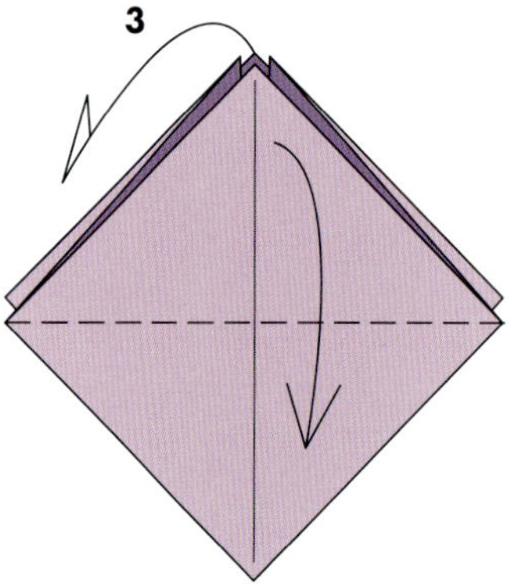

Valley fold a single layer both front and back.

4

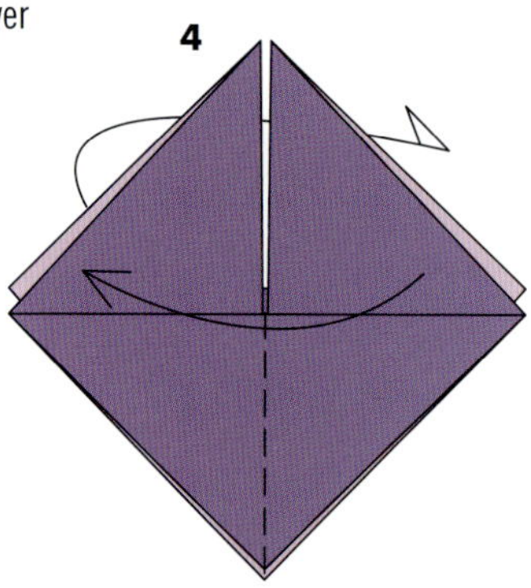

Swing over a flap at each side.

5

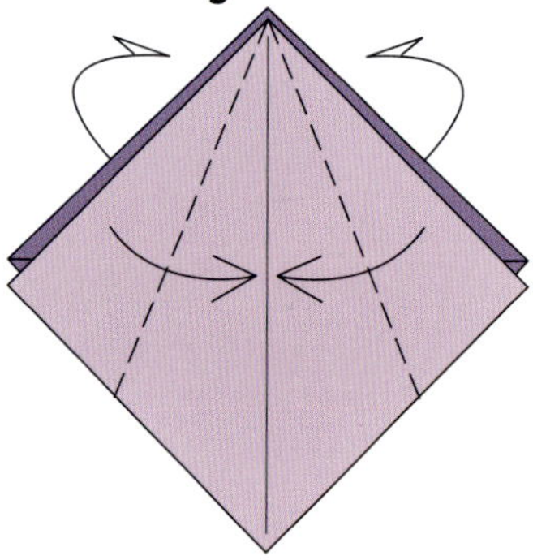

Valley fold the sides inward, both front and back.

6

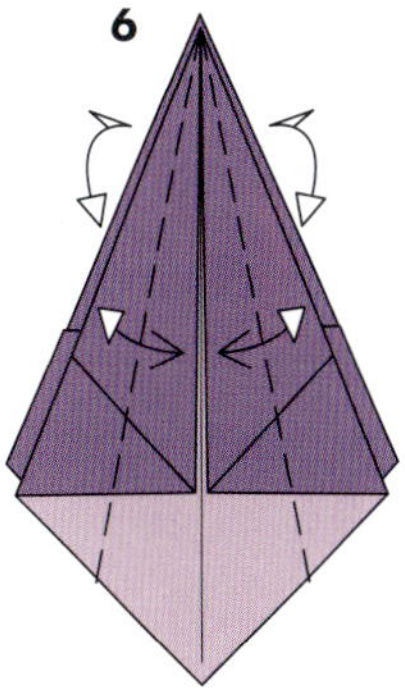

Precrease the front and back along the angle bisectors.

7

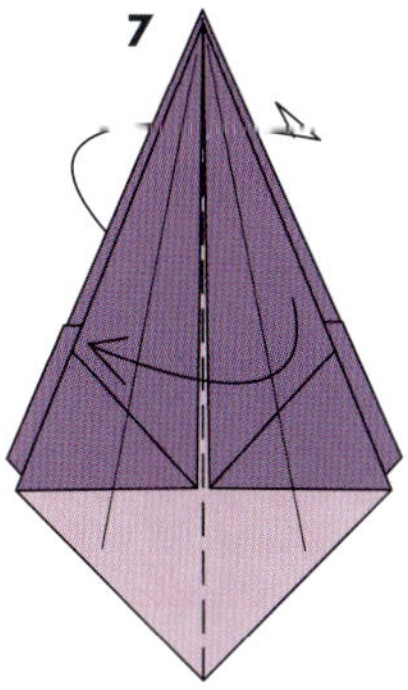

Swing over a flap at each side.

8

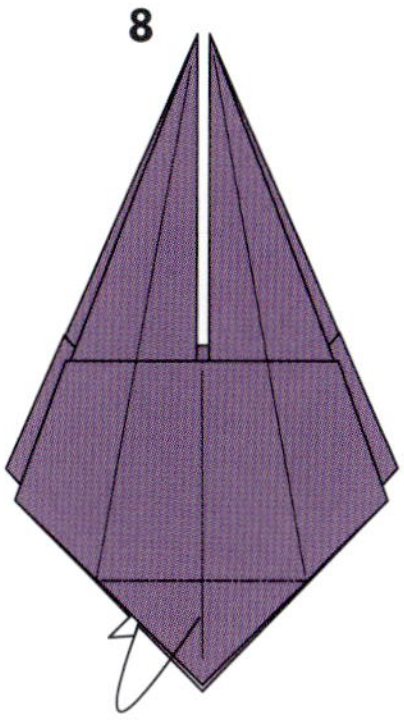

Mountain fold the single layer, noting where the fold hits the creases.

9

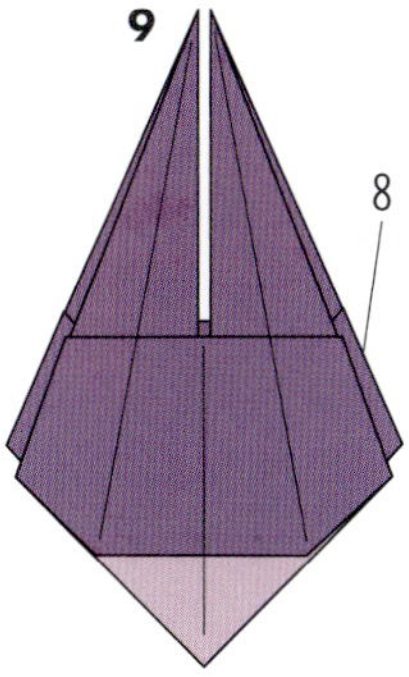

Repeat step 8 behind.

10

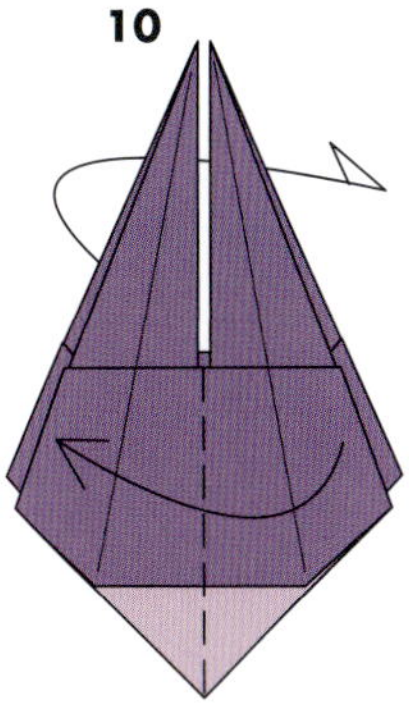

Swing over a flap at each side.

11

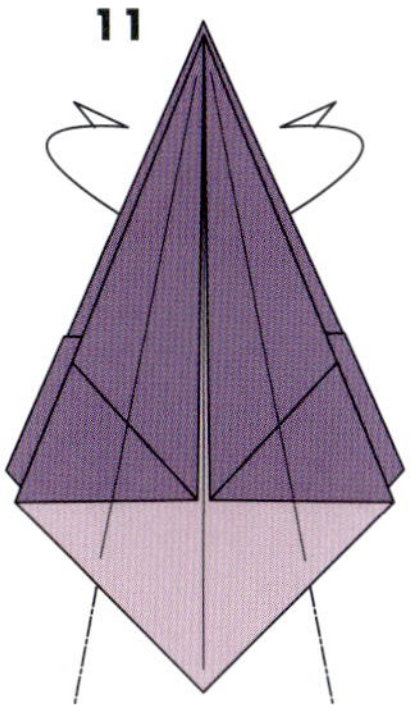

Mountain fold the rear flaps along the existing creases.

12

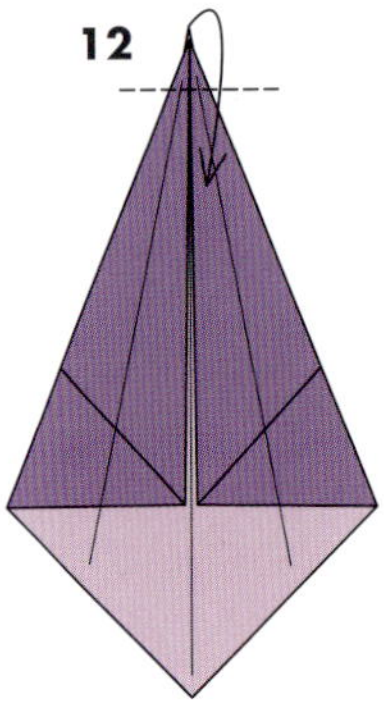

Valley fold the two flaps together.

13

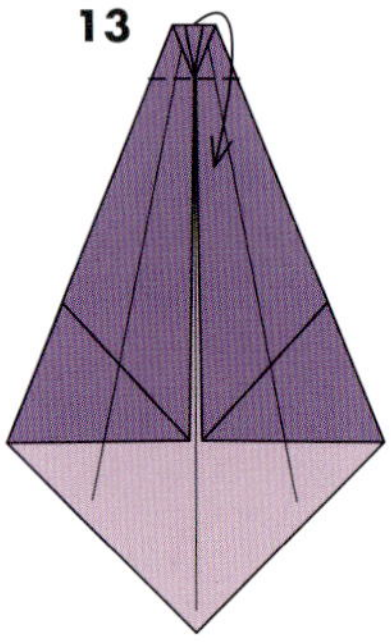

Valley fold the cluster of flaps down again.

14

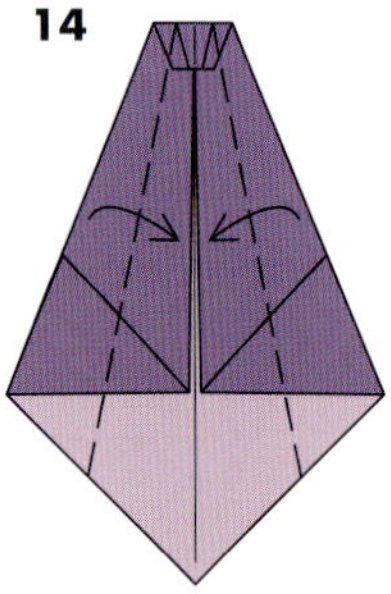

Valley fold the sides in along the existing creases.

15

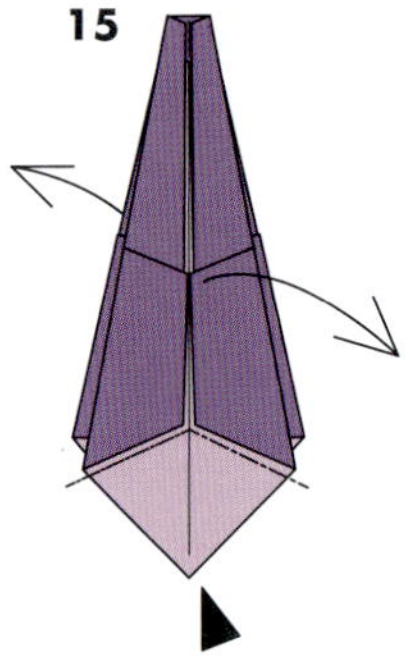

Open the bag and then push up on the base, forming mountain folds on the white section along the colored edges and creating a long folded groove that projects up into the bag.

16

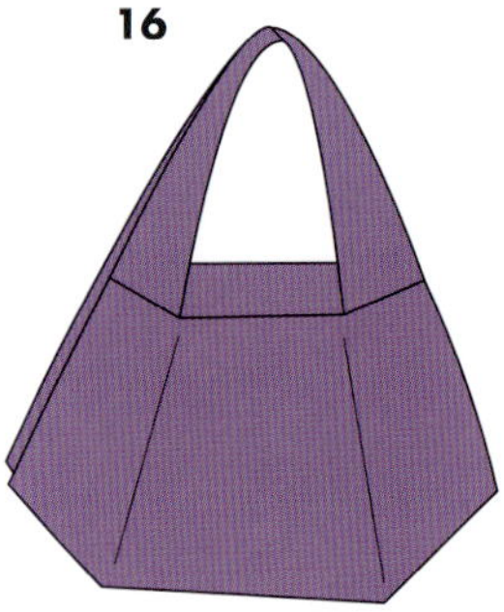

Completed Convertible Bag in first position.

17

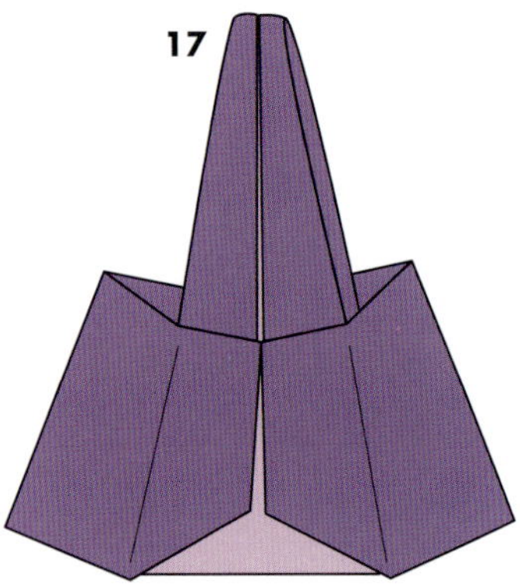

Completed Convertible Bag, after opening it and re-collapsing it in the opposite direction.

Frog

Beth Johnson

See Beth's bio on page 152 to find out what her signature style element is.

video: *youtu.be/3XS7eB0H2BA*

1

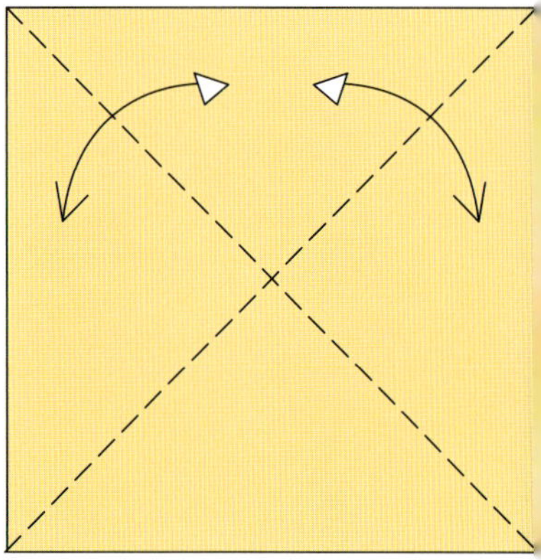

Precrease along the diagonals.

2

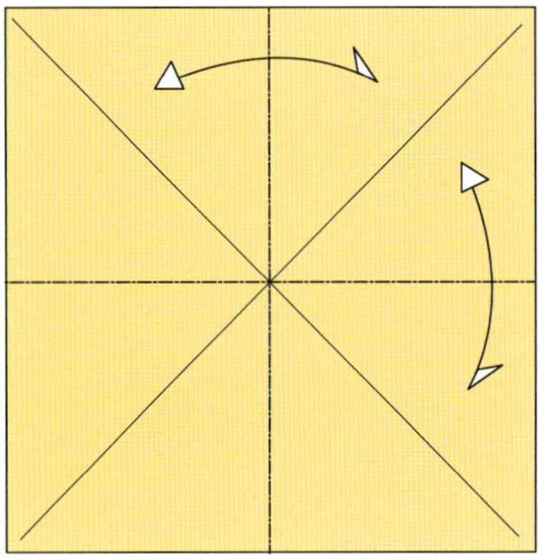

Precrease with mountain folds.

3

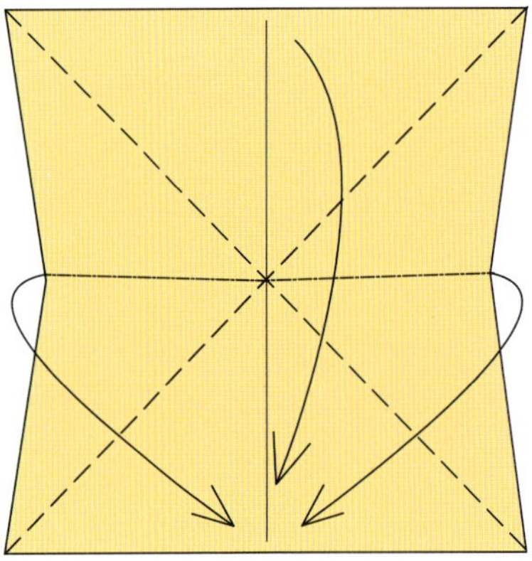

Collapse downward (Waterbomb Base).

4

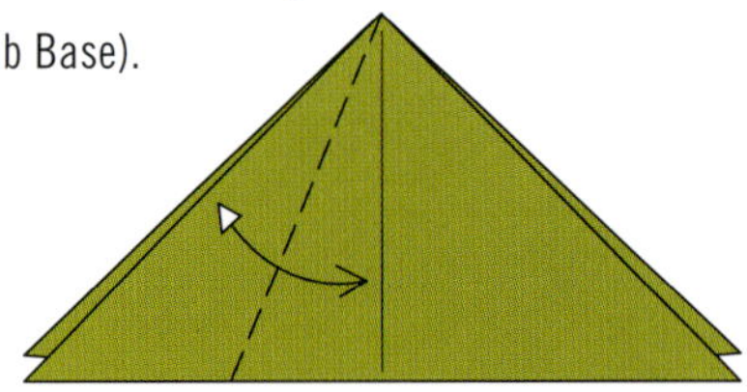

Precrease along the angle bisector.

5

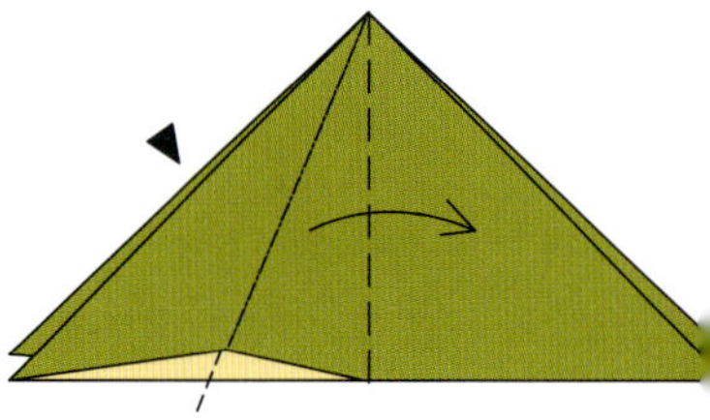

Squash fold the top flap.

6

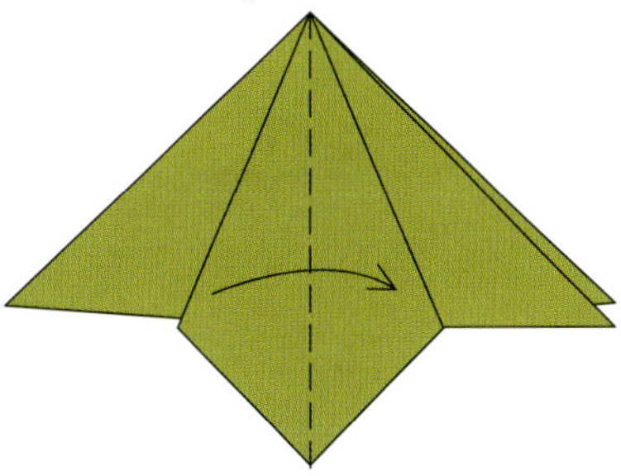

Swing over one layer.

7

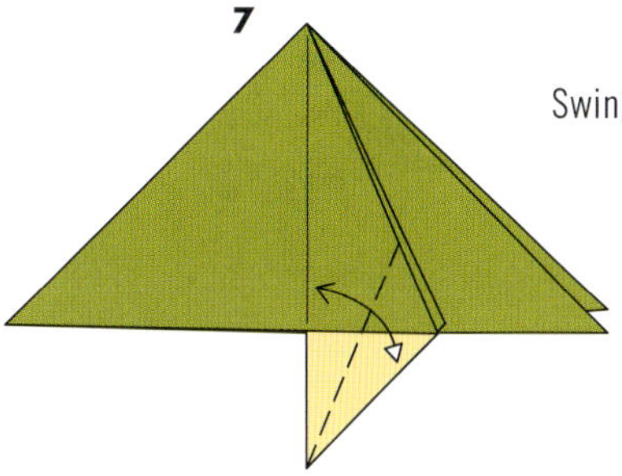

Precrease along the angle bisector, through the top flap only.

8

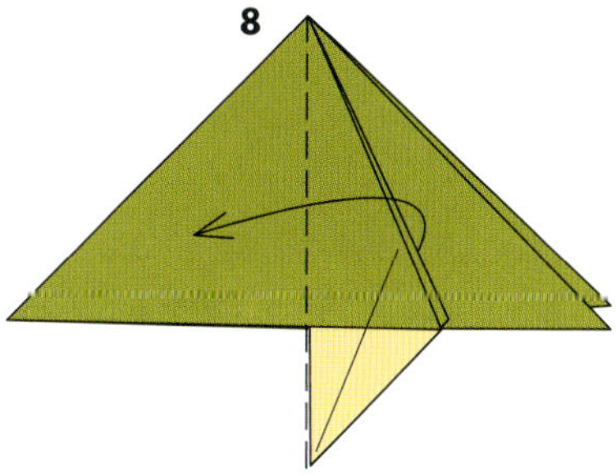

Swing over two flaps.

9

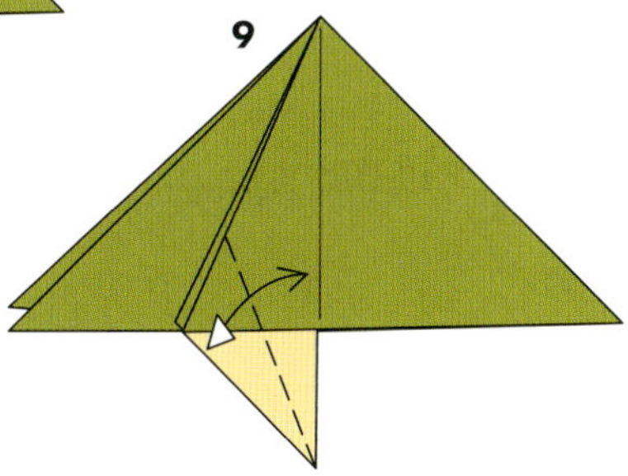

Precrease along the angle bisector, through the top flap only.

10

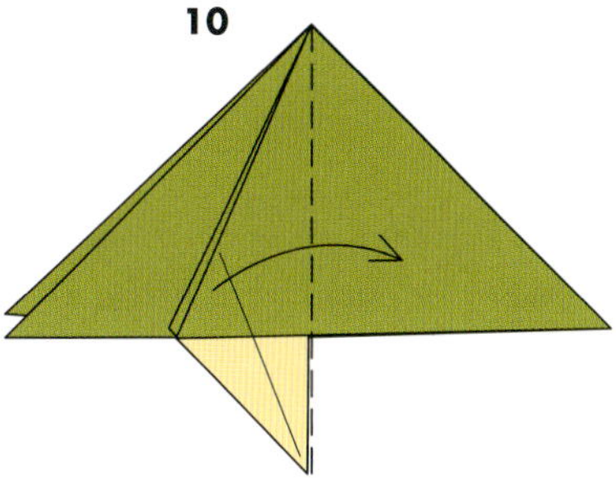

Swing over the top layer.

11

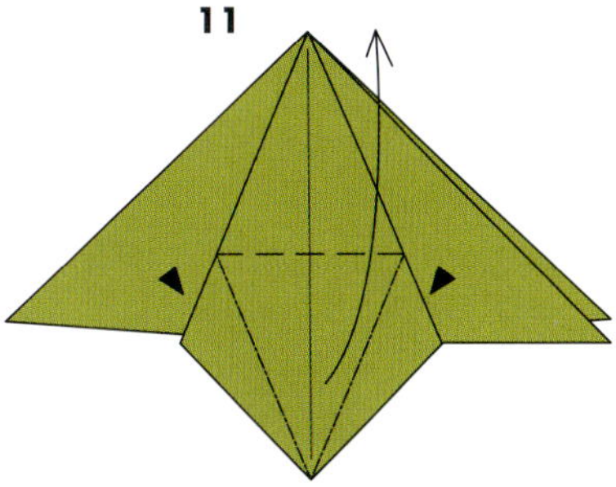

Petal fold.

12

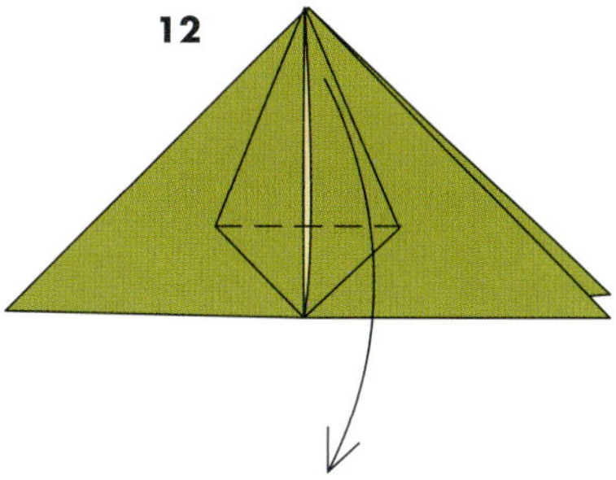

Swing down the top flap.

13

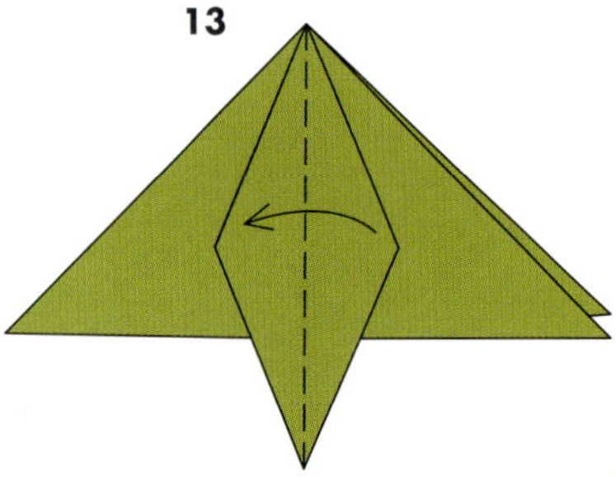

Swing over one flap.

14

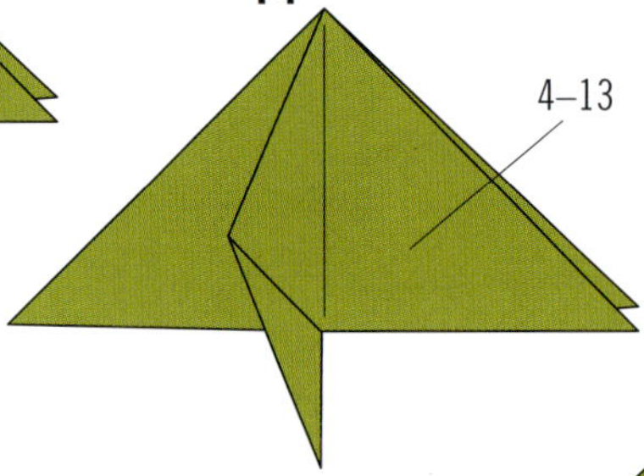

Repeat steps 4–13 in mirror image.

15

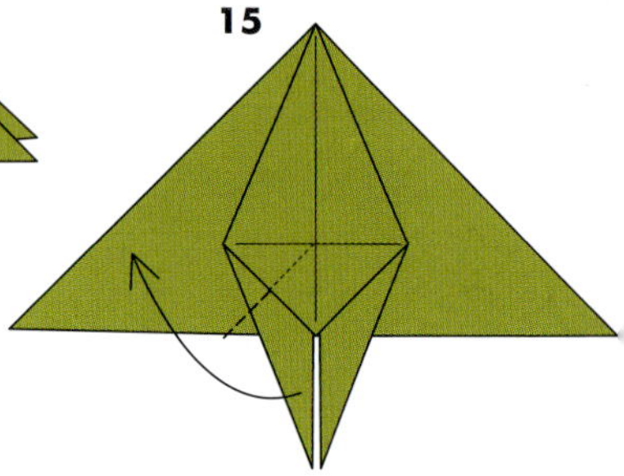

Valley fold over.

16

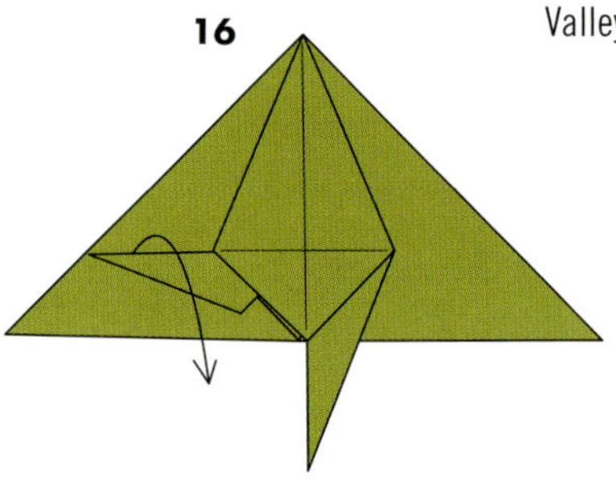

Swing the flap back down.

17

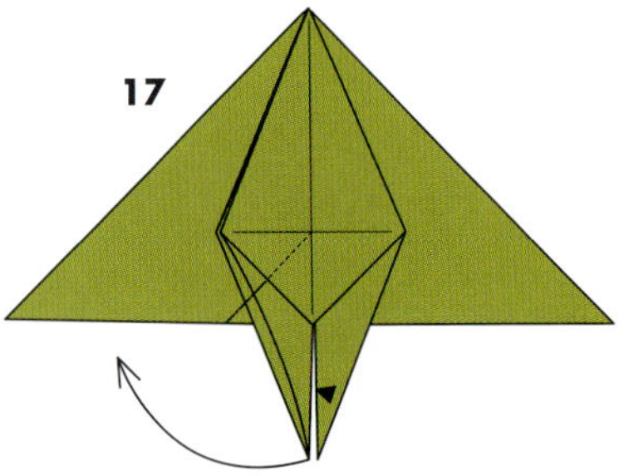

Reverse fold along the existing crease.

18

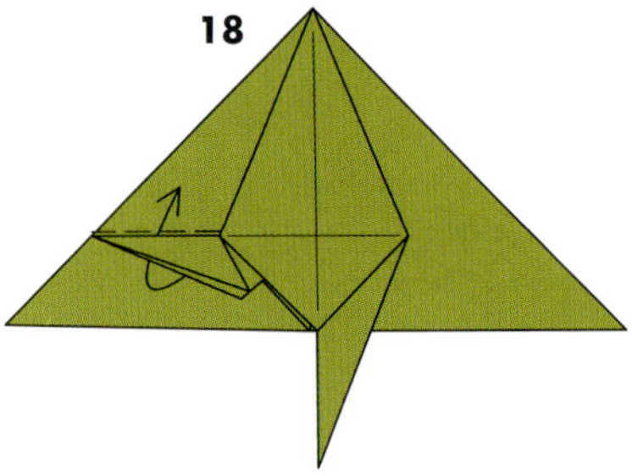

Swivel fold the bottom layer of the flap by pulling it up, and reversing the folds from the previous step.

19

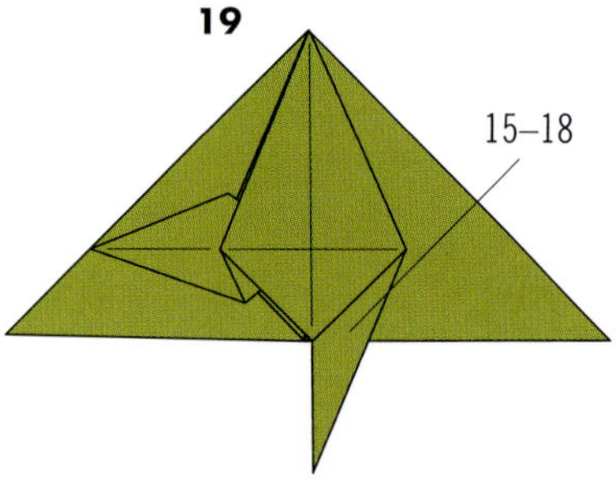

Note that the flap is seamless on the top, and the raw edges are on its backside. Repeat steps 15–18 in mirror image.

26

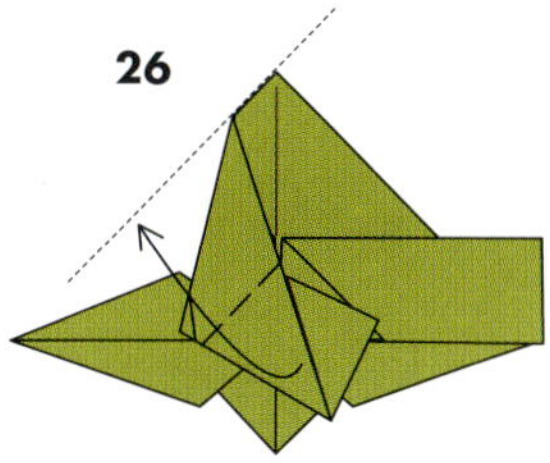

Valley fold to the imaginary line (an extension of the top edge).

25

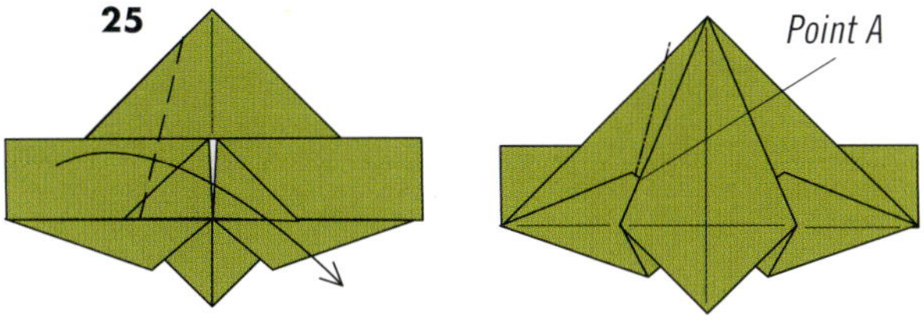

Valley fold over at an angle. The fold should pass though point A, as shown in the next drawing (the view from the opposite side).

24

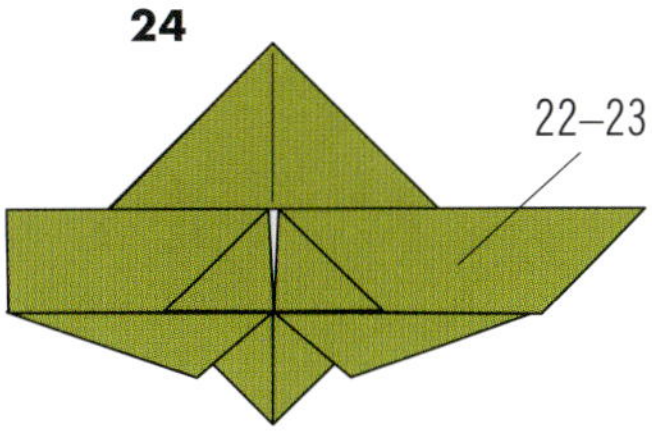

Repeat steps 22–23 in mirror image.

23

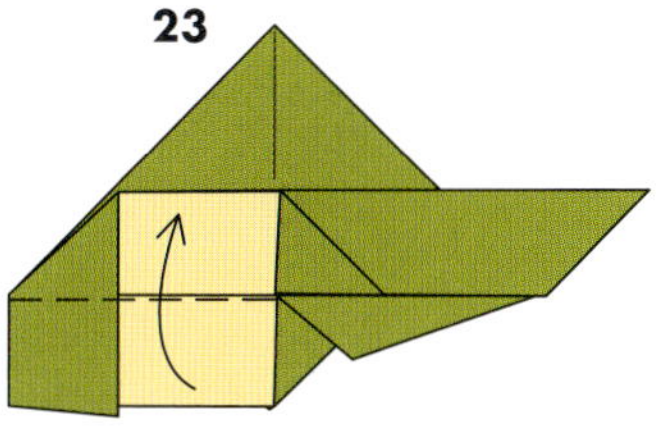

Valley fold the single layer back up.

22

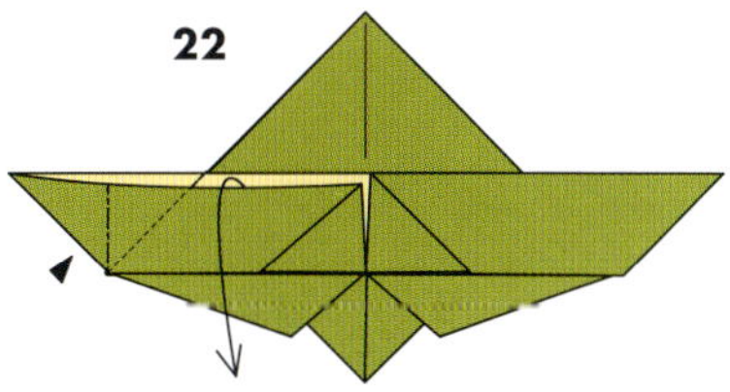

Swing down the top single layer, allowing a squash to form.

20

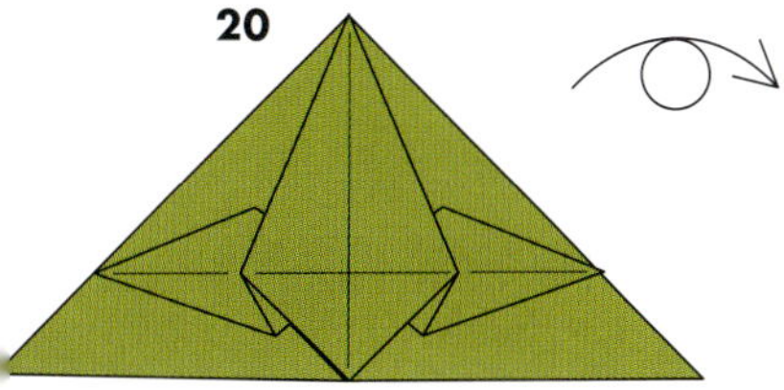

Turn over.

21

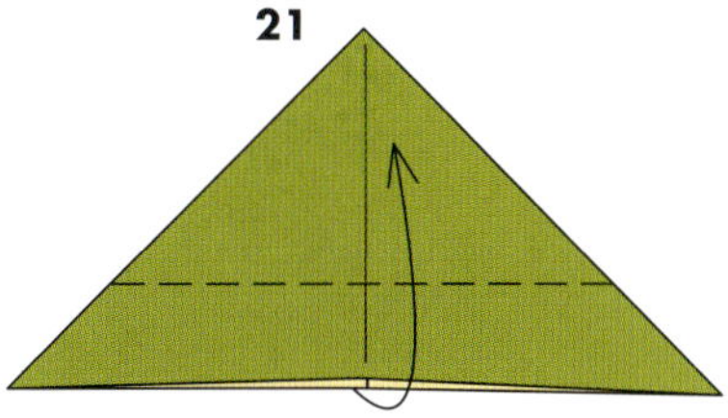

Valley fold the bottom edge up as far as possible.

27

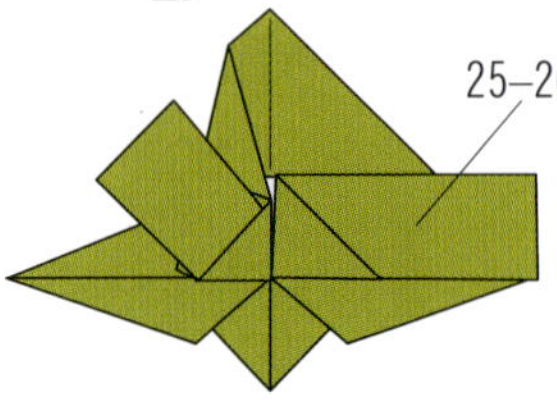

Repeat steps 25–26 in mirror image.

28

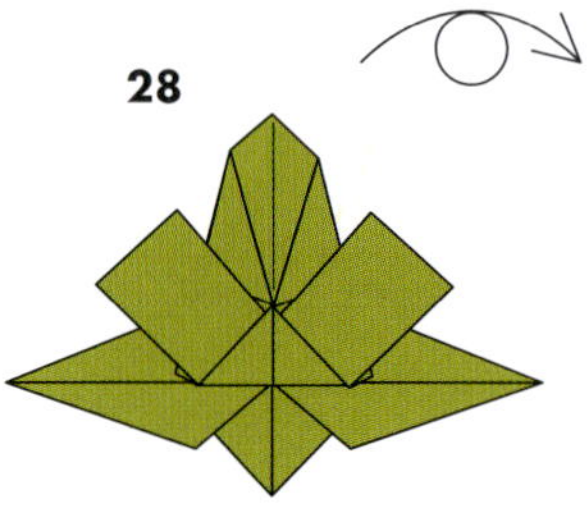

Turn over.

29

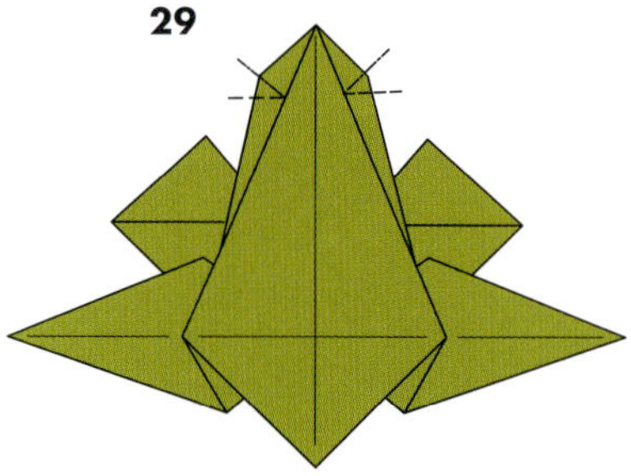

Crimp the lower layer to form eyes.

30

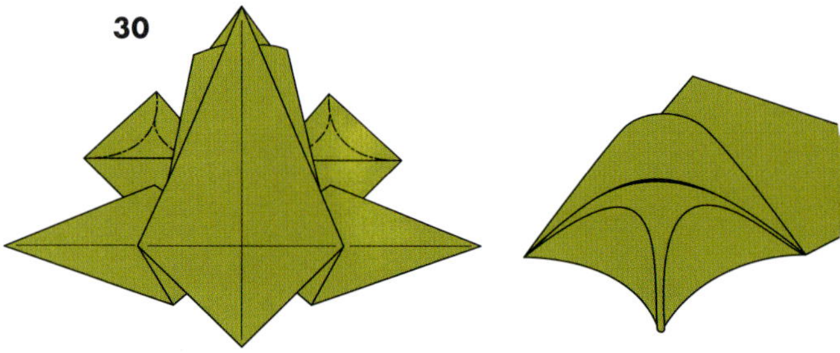

Shape the front toes with curved mountain folds. Round the feet into a dome-like shape. See the side image of a completed front view for reference.

31

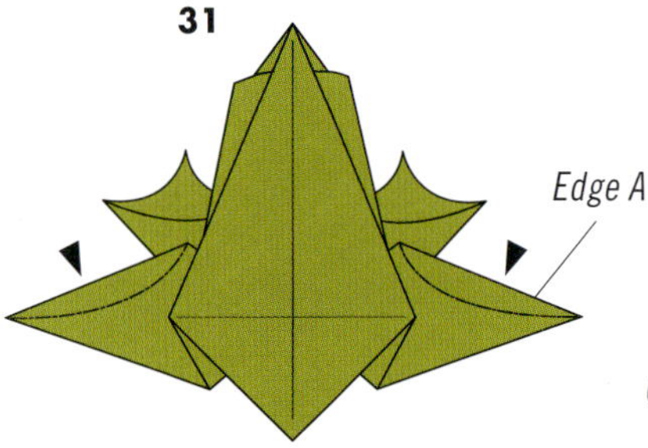

Spread apart the edge of the legs using curved mountain folds. See the side image of the completed front view to see where the edges shift to.

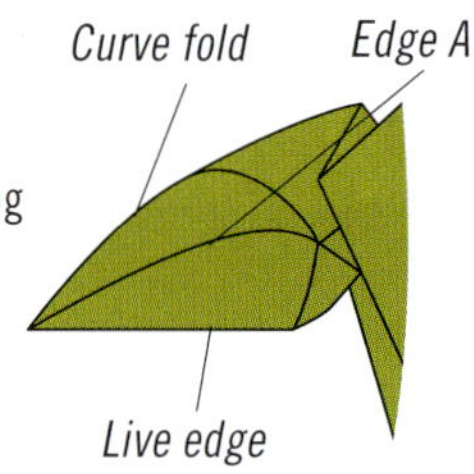

32

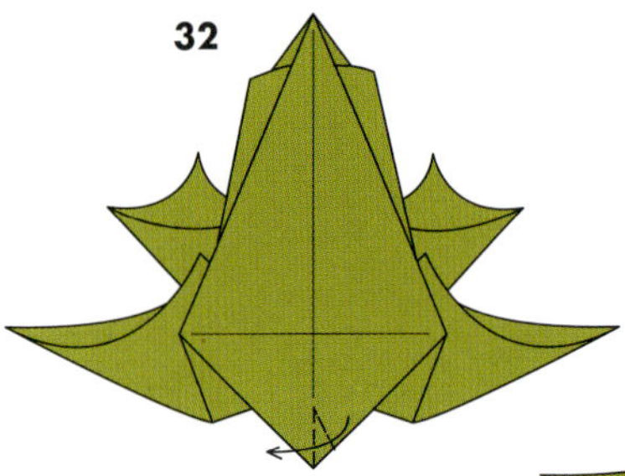

Form a small pleat to give the body a 3D shape.

33

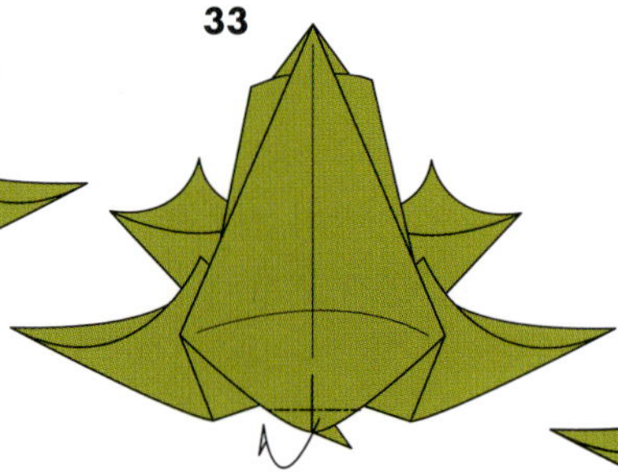

Lock the pleat with a mountain fold through all the layers.

34

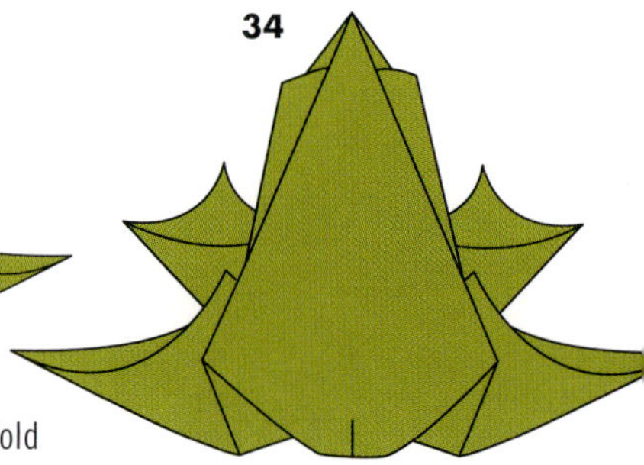

Completed Frog.

Bee

Marc Kirschenbaum

Read more about Marc, the editor of this book, on page 153.

video: *youtu.be/0BAyYm_e2M4*

1

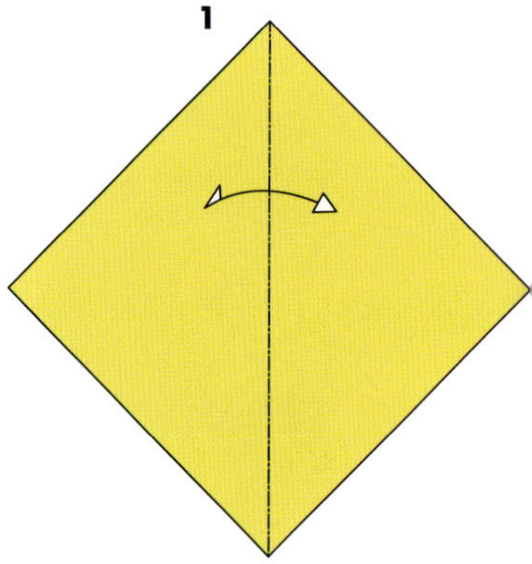

Precrease with a mountain fold.

2

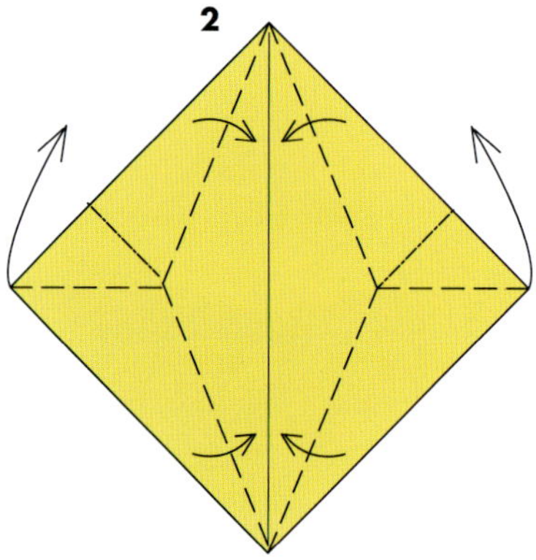

Rabbit ear the sides.

3

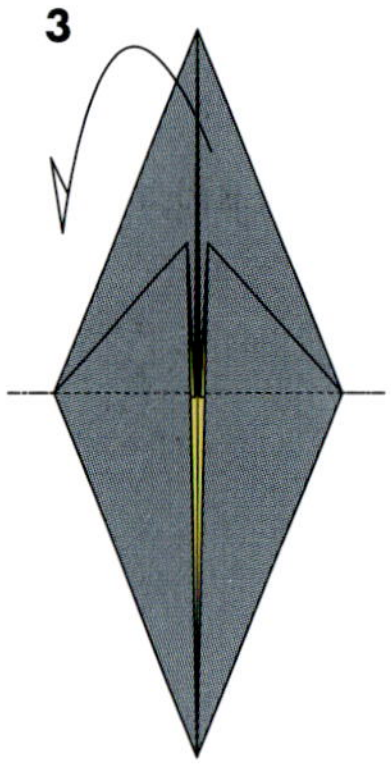

Mountain fold the top flap down.

4

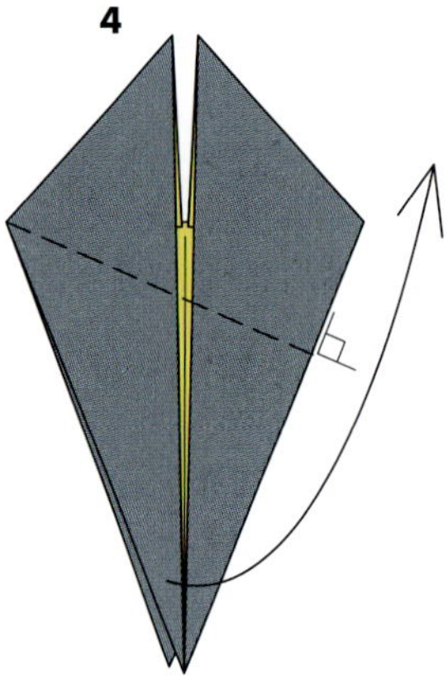

Valley fold up.

5

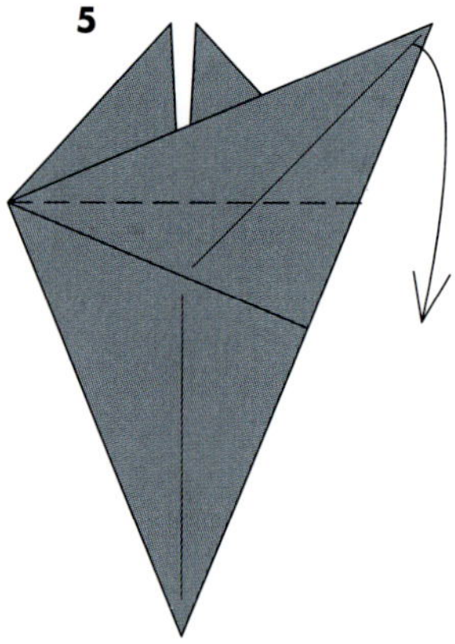

Valley fold down.

6

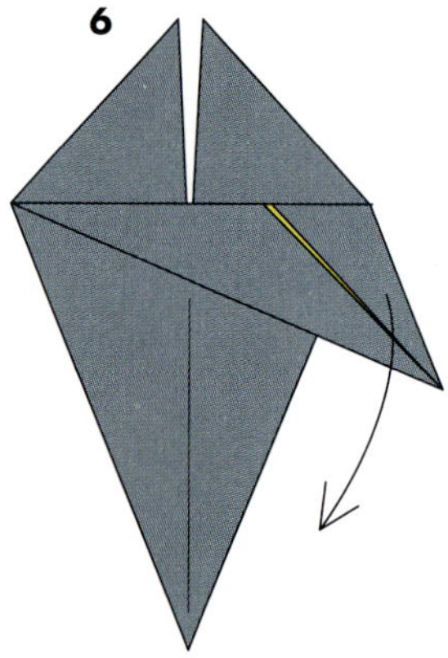

Unfold the pleat.

7

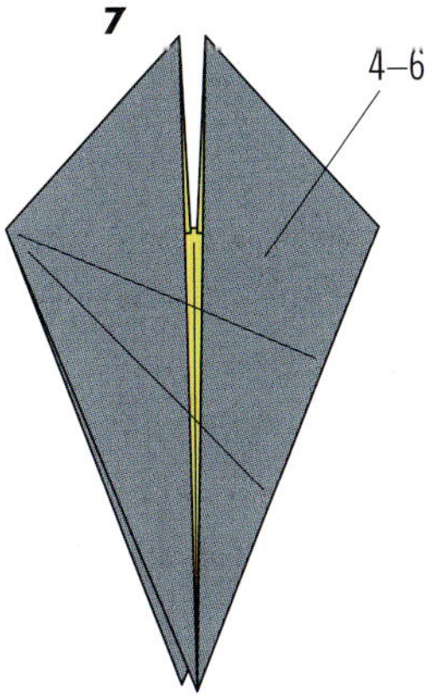

Repeat steps 4–6 in mirror image.

8

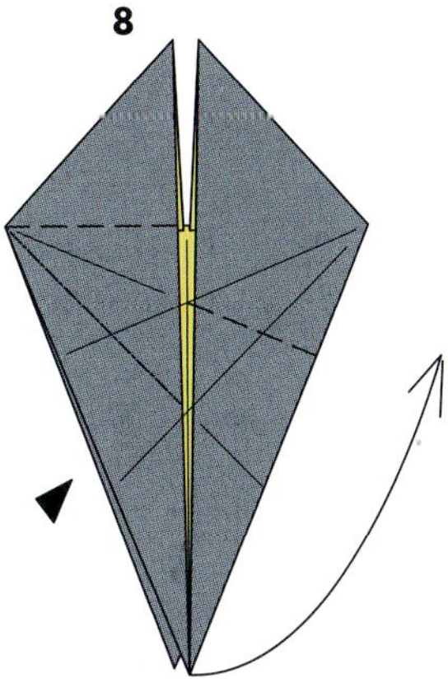

Squash fold.

9

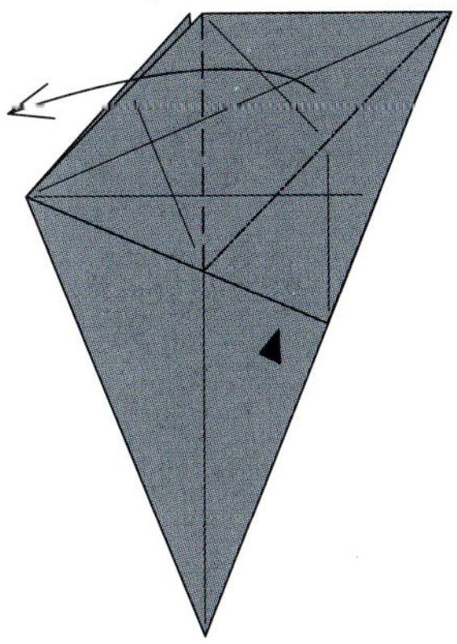

Squash fold.

10

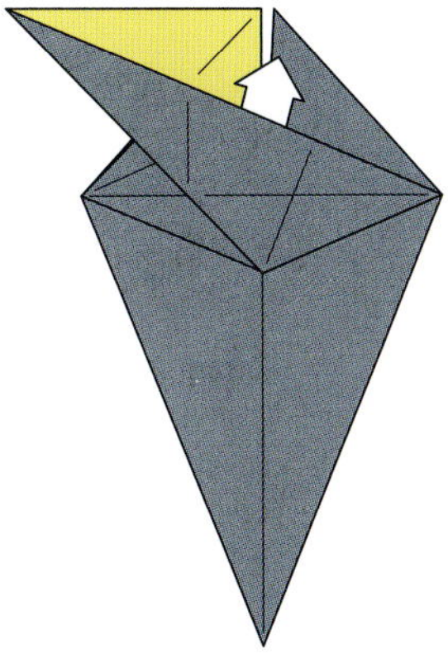

Pull out the trapped single layer.

11

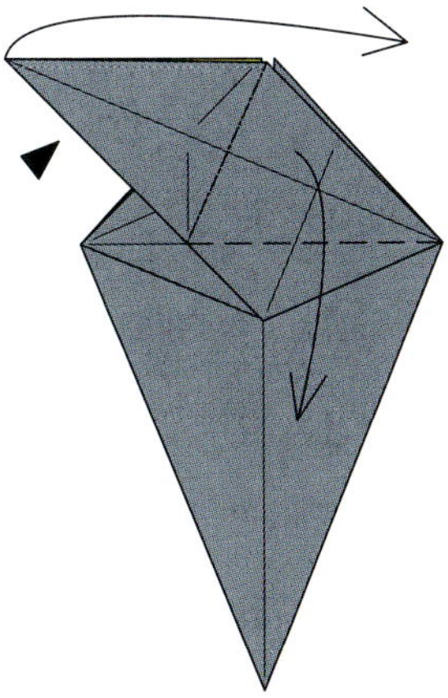

Squash fold.

12

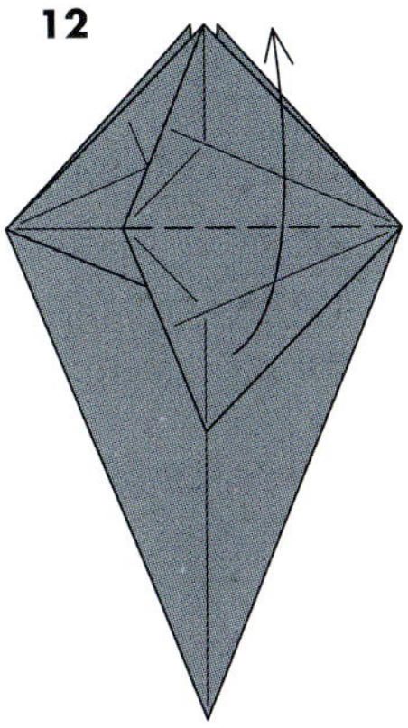

Valley fold up.

13

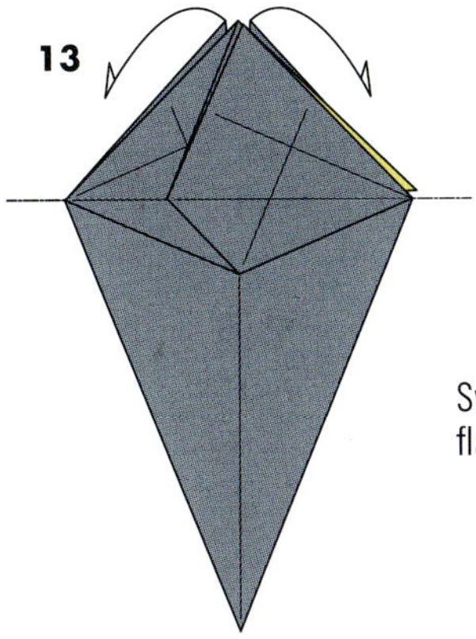

Swing the rear flaps down.

14

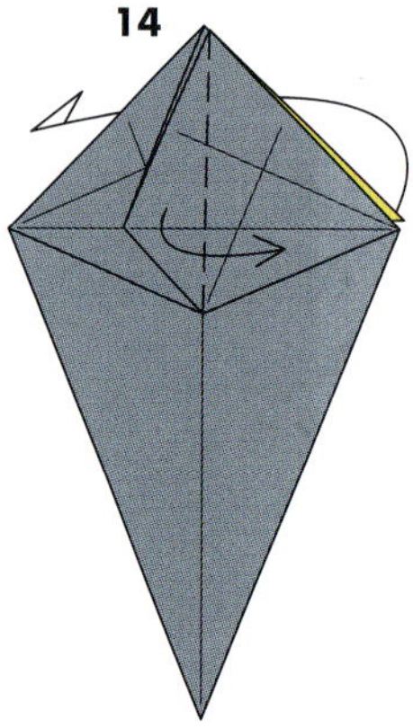

Swing over a layer at each side.

15

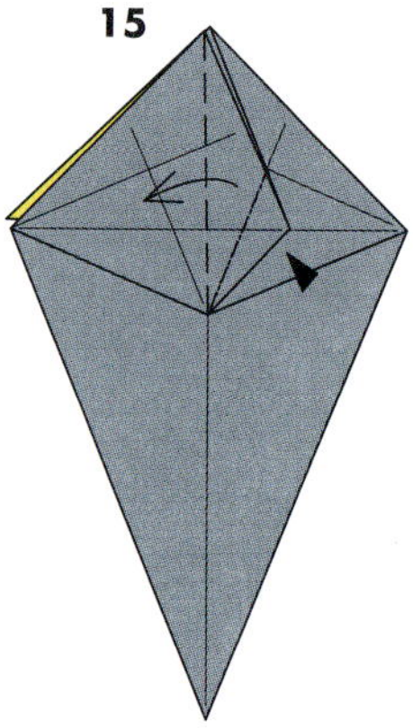

Spread squash
the center flap.

16

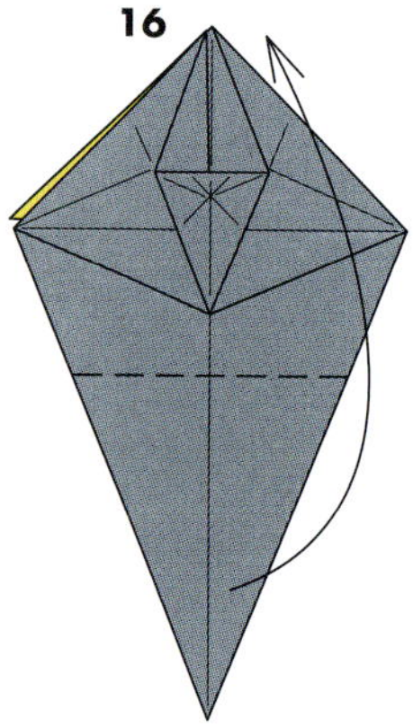

Valley fold up.

17

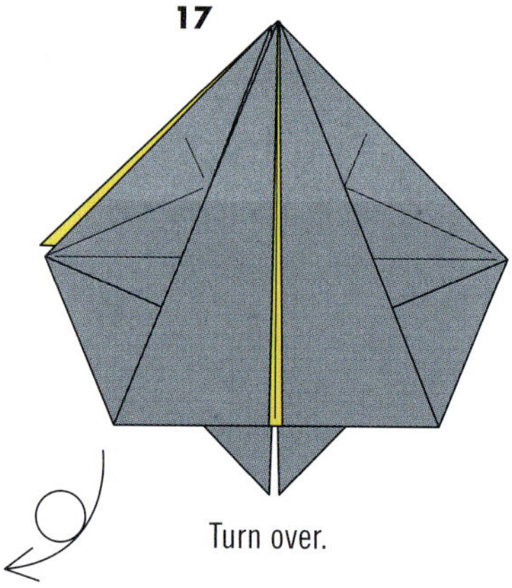

Turn over.

18

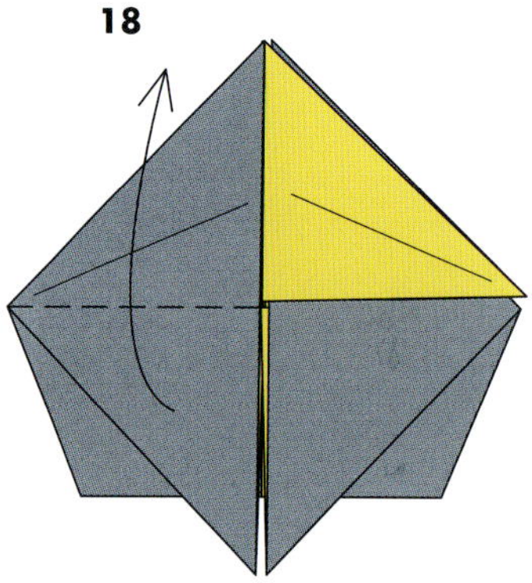

Swing one flap up.

19

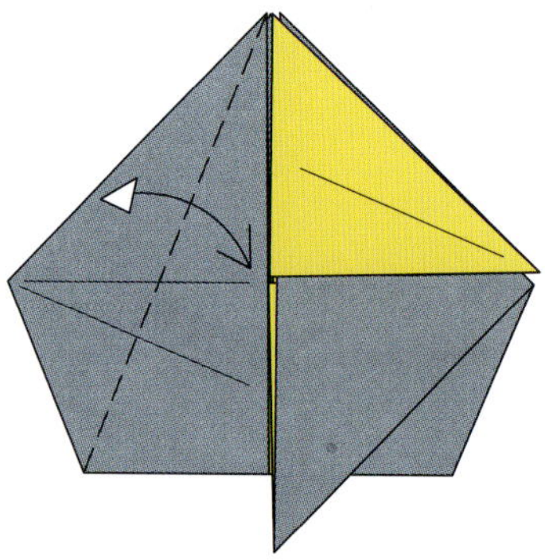

Precrease through all layers.

20

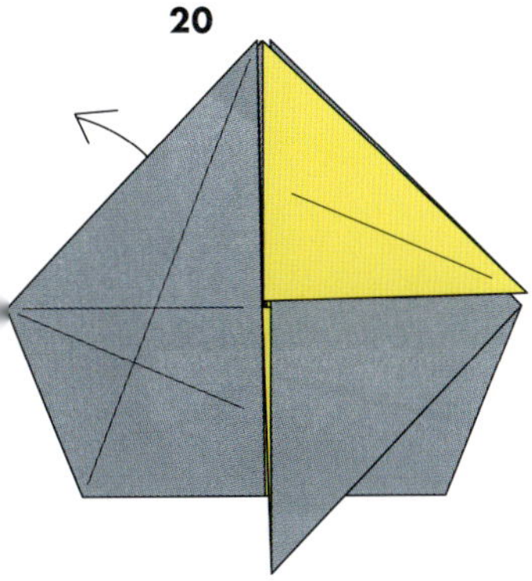

Pull out one layer.

21

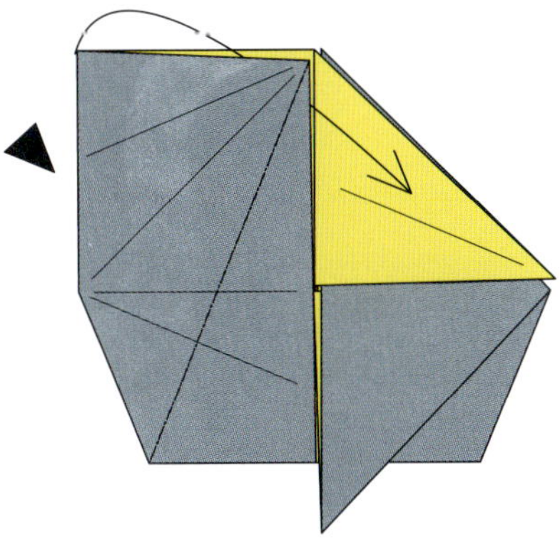

Closed reverse fold.

22

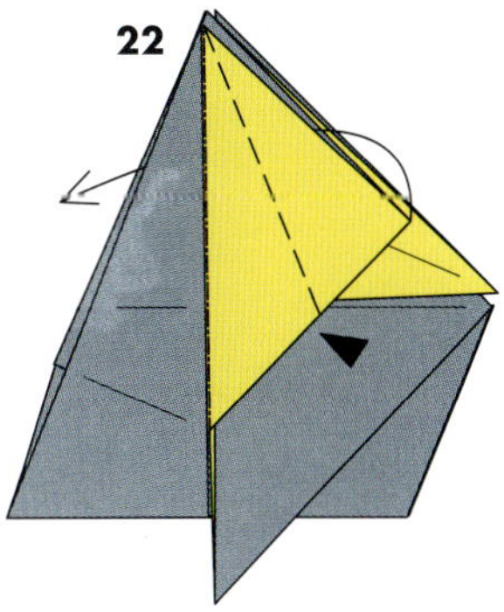

Reverse fold in and out along the existing creases,

23

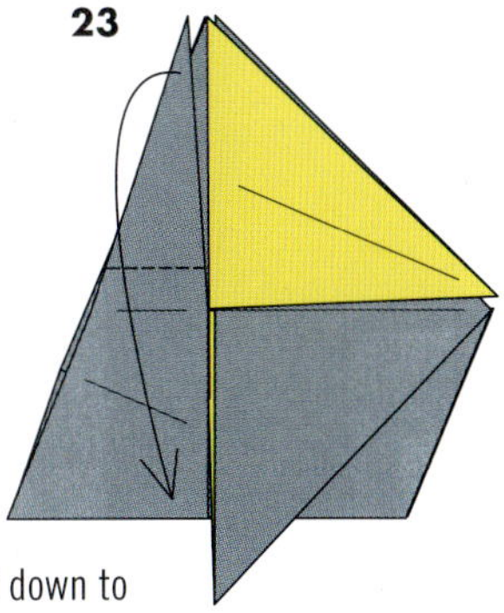

Valley fold down to the edge.

24

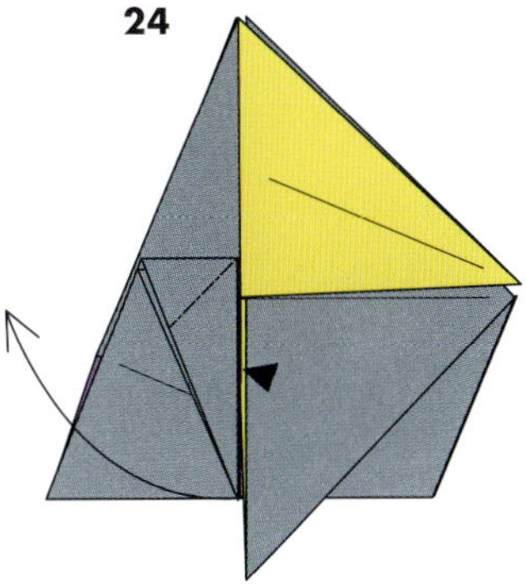

Spread squash.

25

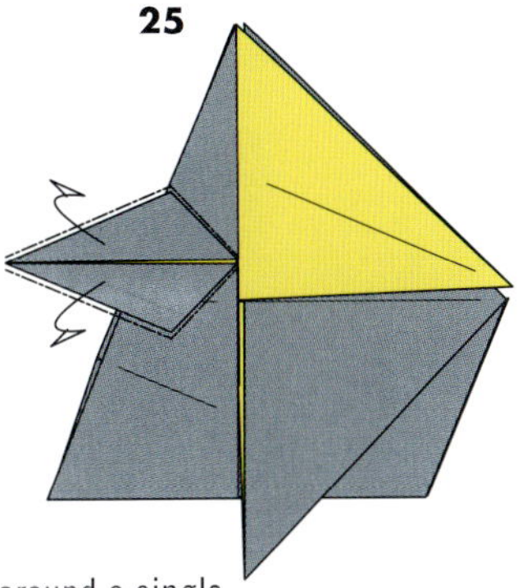

Wrap around a single layer at each side.

26

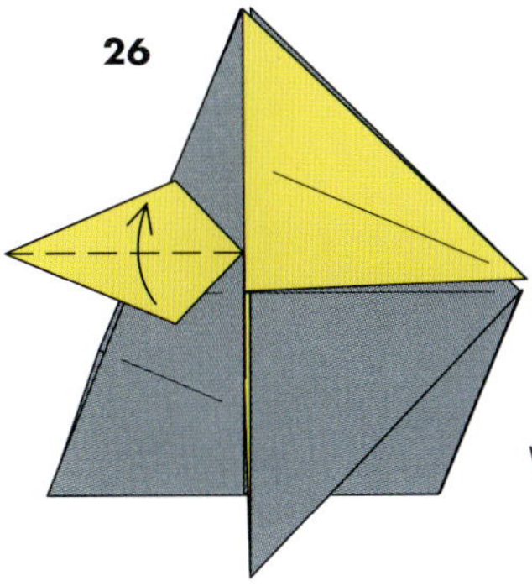

Valley fold in half.

27

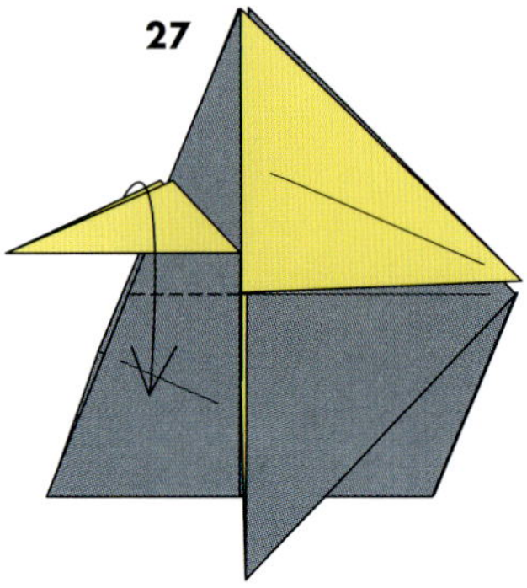

Swing down.

28

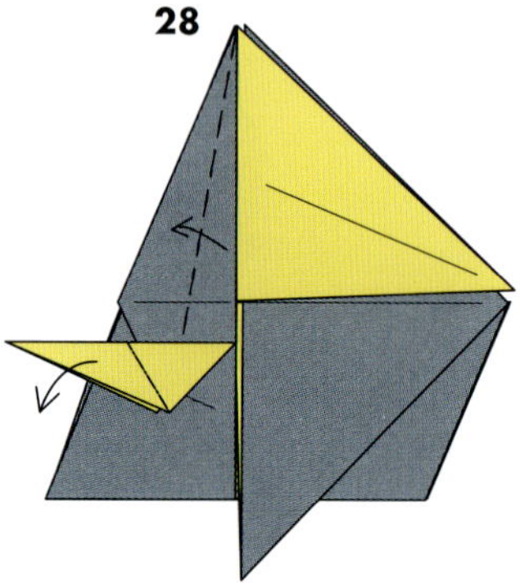

Swivel the top single layer.

29

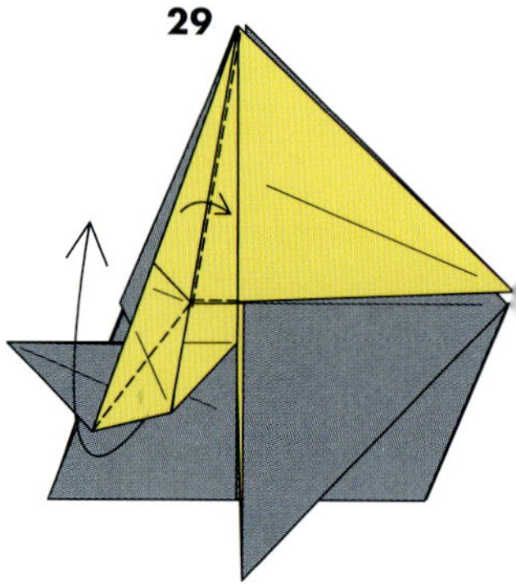

Valley fold up while swiveling the layer back over.

30

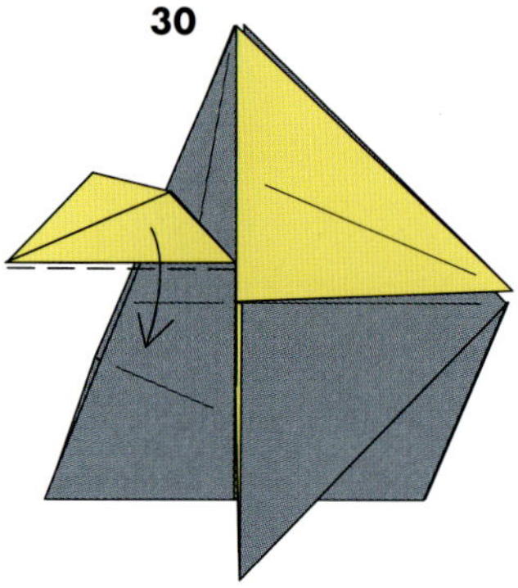

Open out the flap.

31

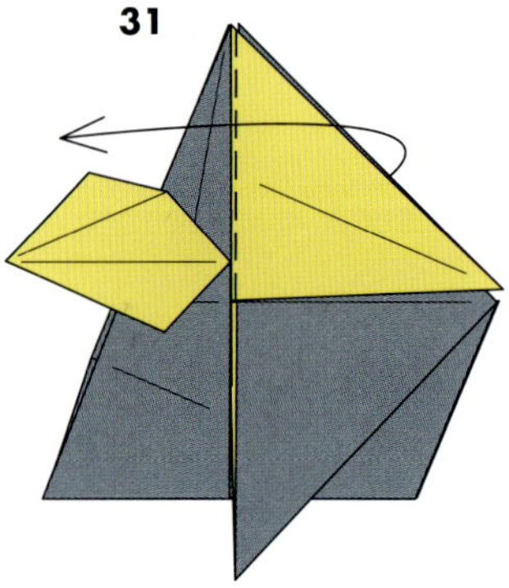

Swing over the center flap.

32

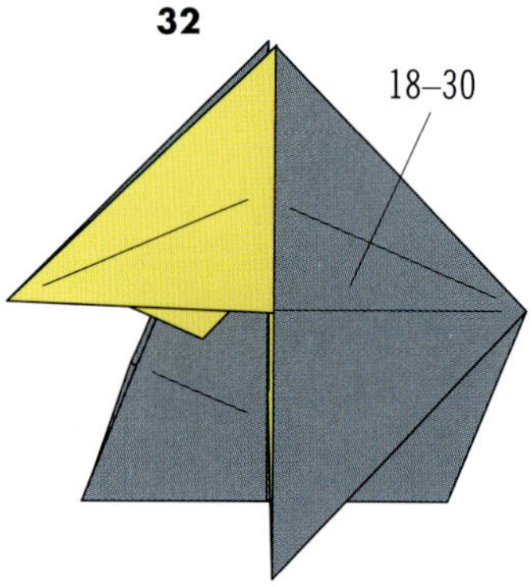

Repeat steps 18–30 in mirror image.

33

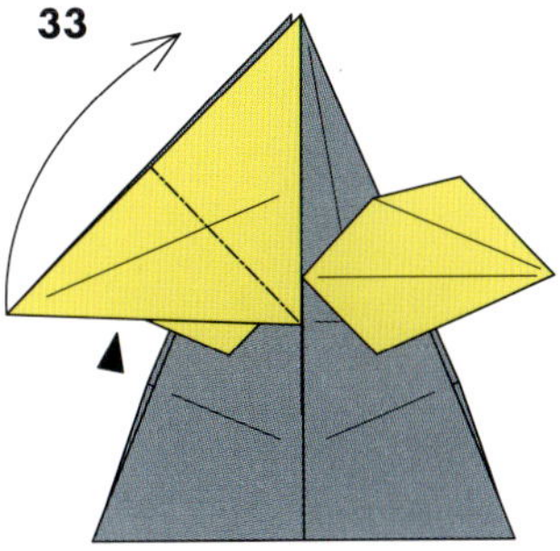

Squash fold.

34

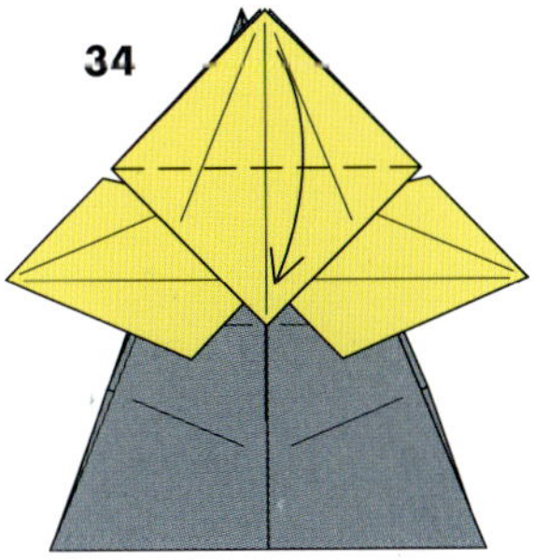

Valley fold down.

35

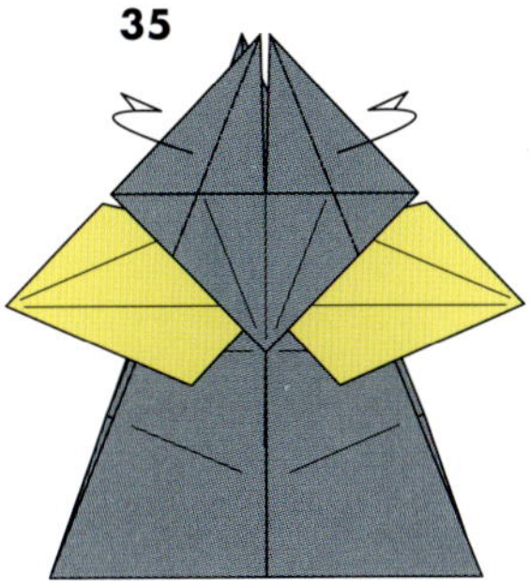

Mountain fold the sides.

36

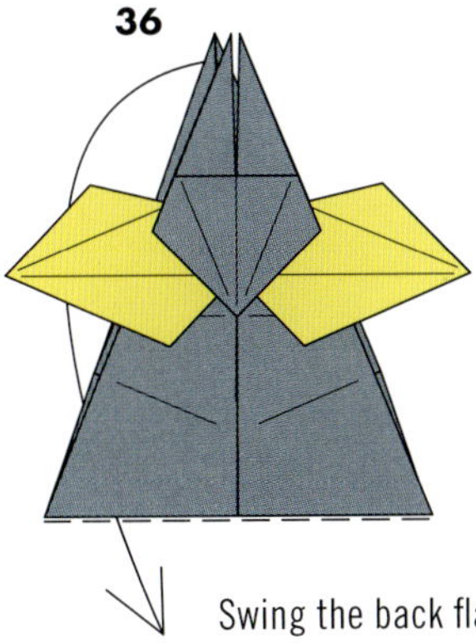

Swing the back flap down.

37

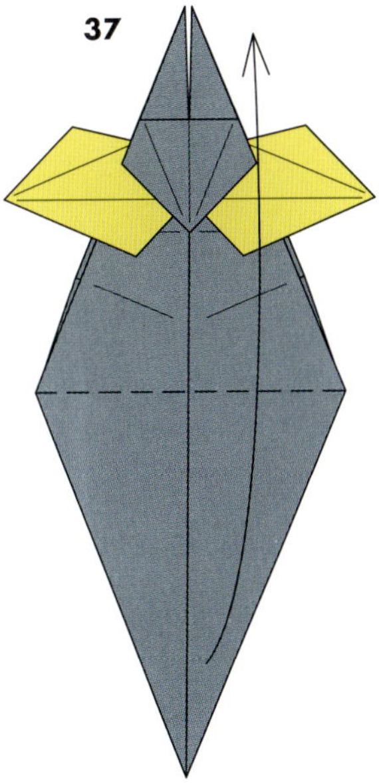

Valley fold the flap up.

38

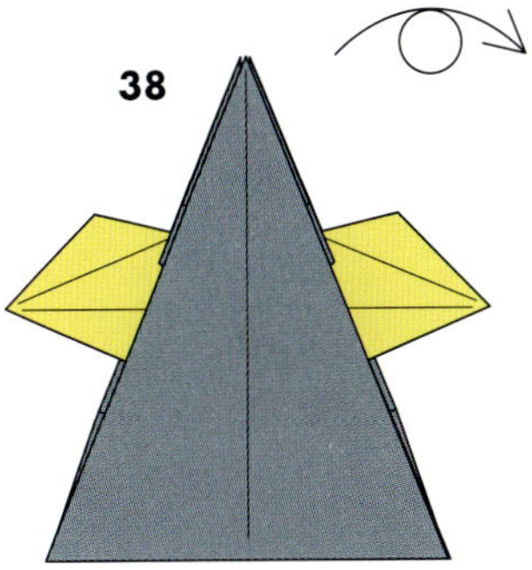

Turn over.

39

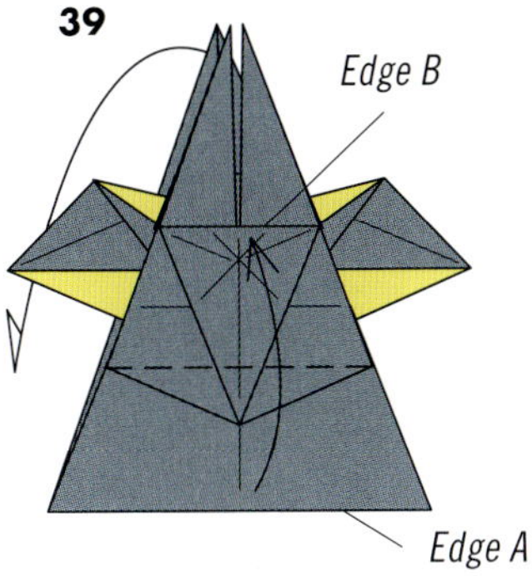

Valley fold edge A toward edge B, allowing the back flap to flip out.

40

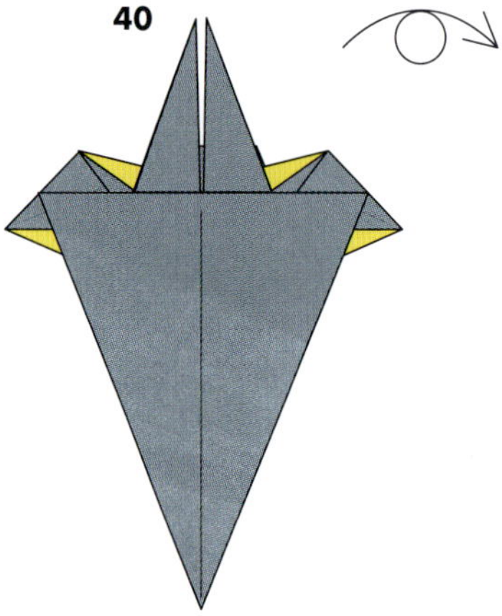

Turn over.

41

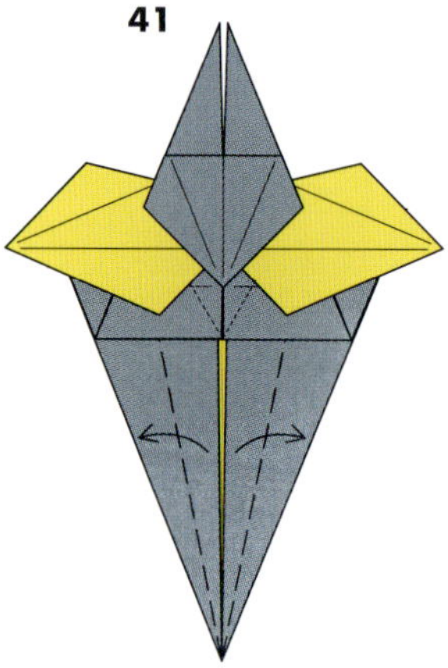

Valley fold the edges outward, allowing hidden swivels to form.

42

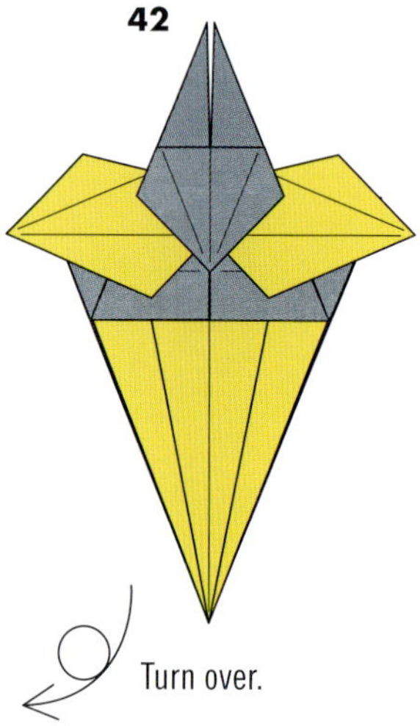

Turn over.

43

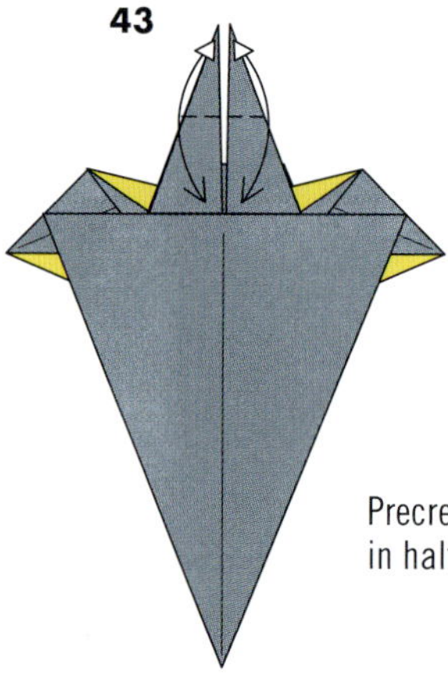

Precrease the top flaps in half.

44

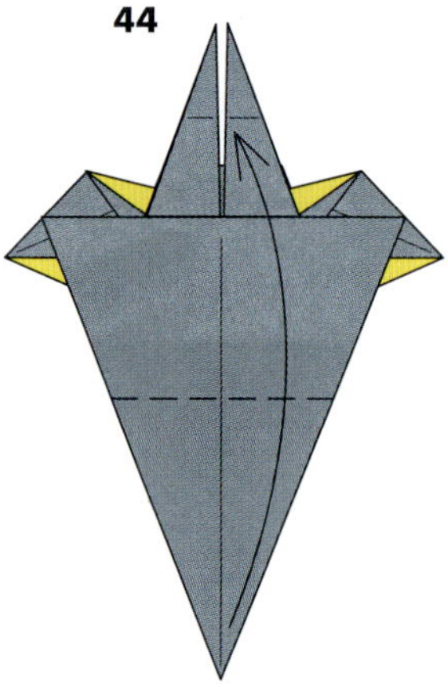

Valley fold toward the last creases.

45

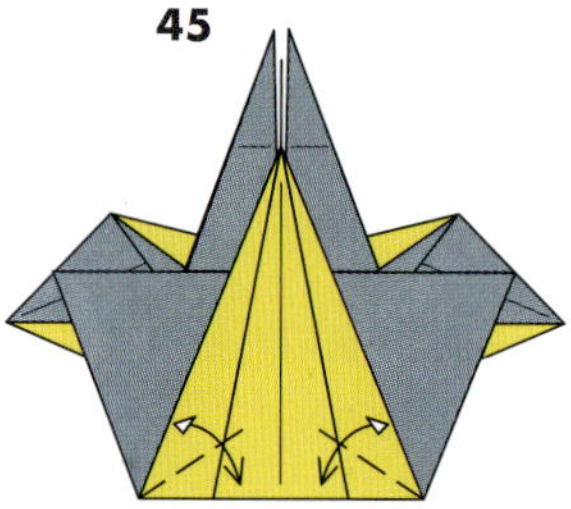

Precrease along the angle bisectors.

46

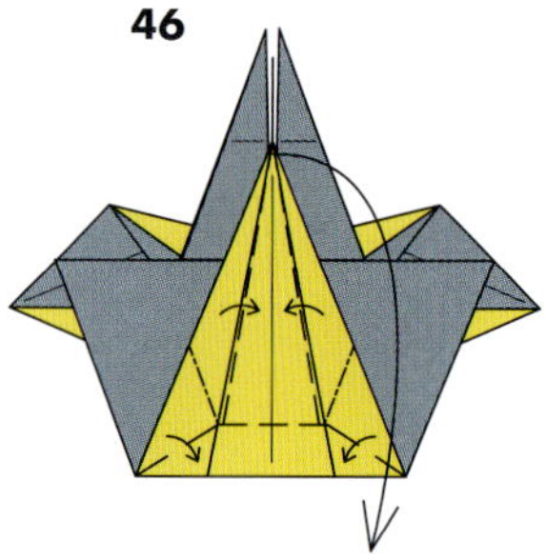

Valley fold down while swiveling in the sides.

47

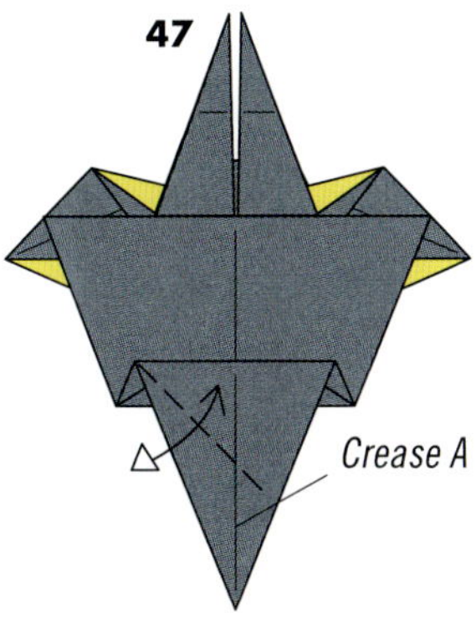

Precrease, such that crease A lies horizontal.

48

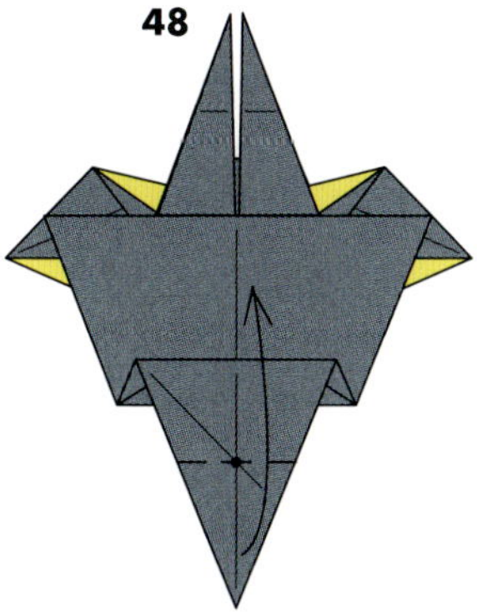

Valley fold through the dotted intersection.

49

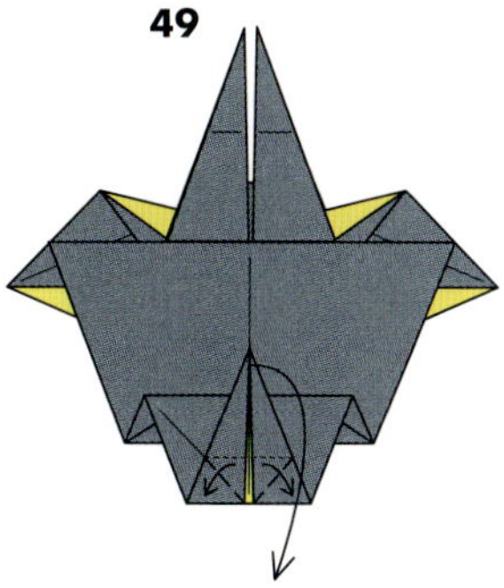

Squash fold the flap down.

50

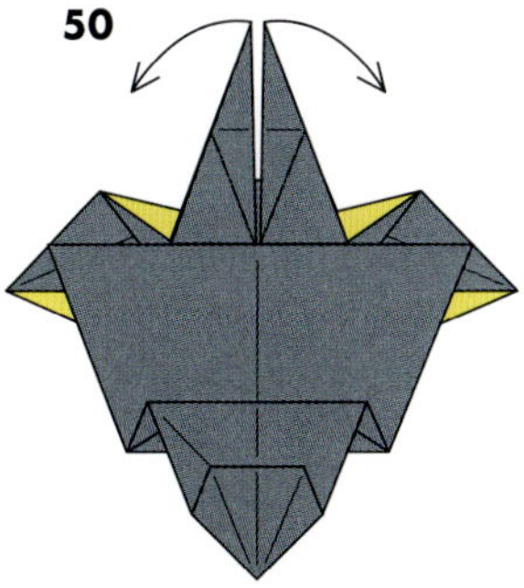

Reverse fold outward, being sure to distribute the layers evenly.

51

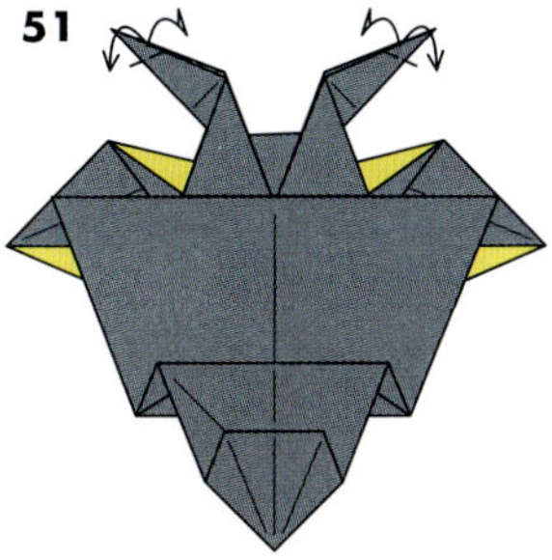

Outside reverse fold each flap.

52

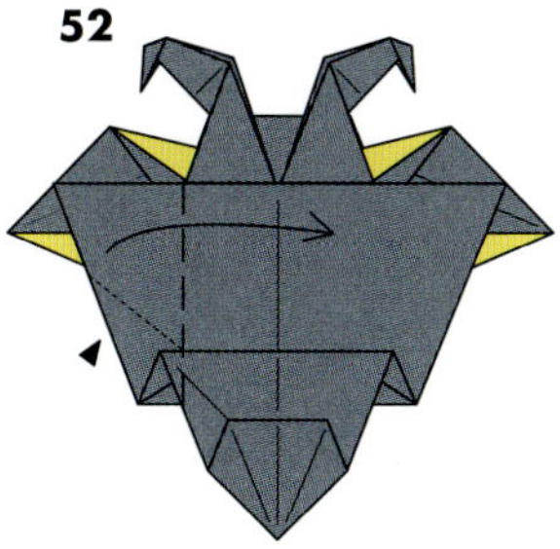

Valley fold the side over, allowing a squash fold to form.

53

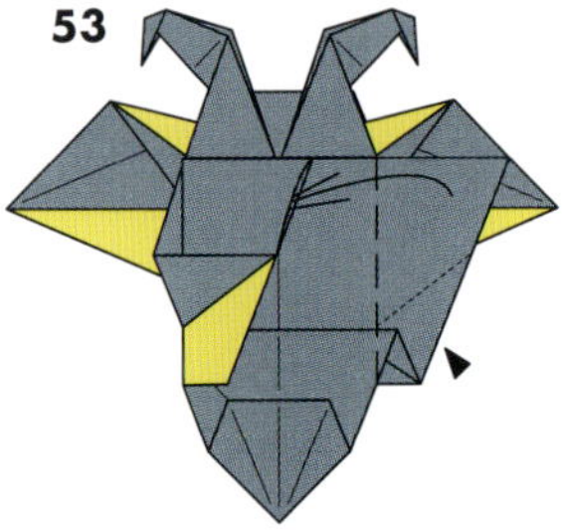

Valley fold the other side over, tucking it into the pocket.

54

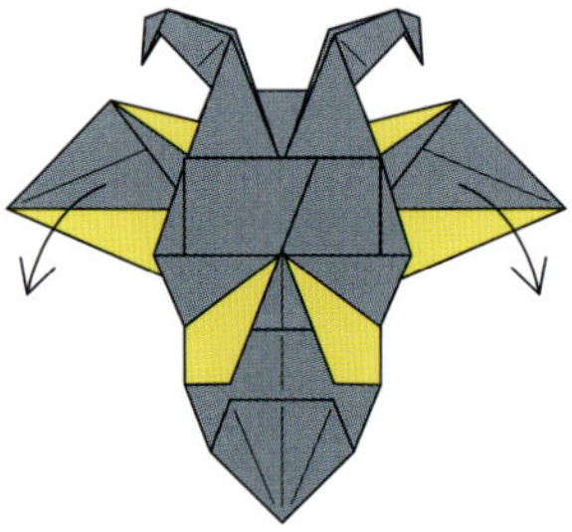

Turn over and adjust the wings as desired.

55

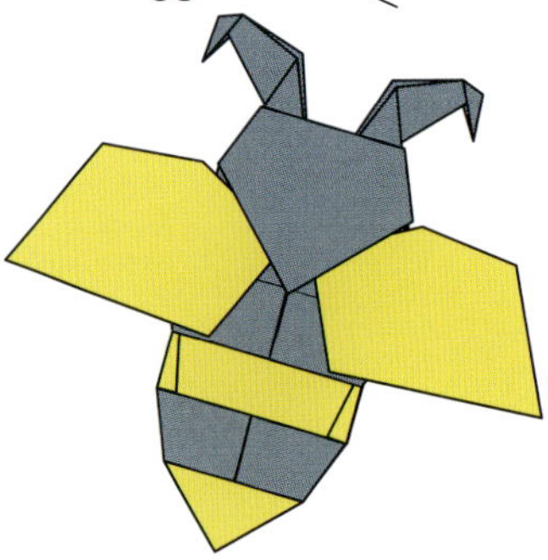

Completed Bee.

Tiger

Jason Ku

A precociously talented origami master, Jason brought origami to MIT in the 2000s. See his bio on page 157 for more.

video: *youtu.be/x6mscholP34*

1

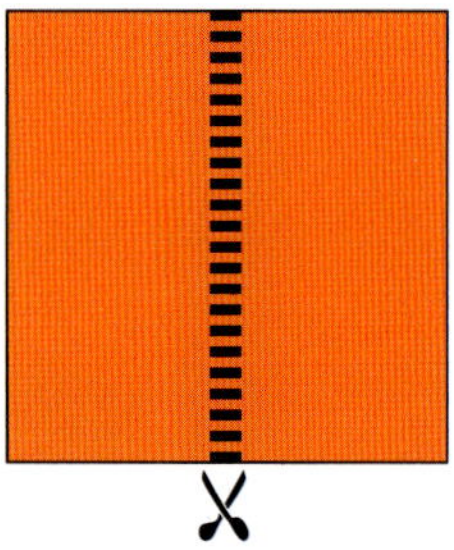

Cut a square in half. Both pieces will be used.

2

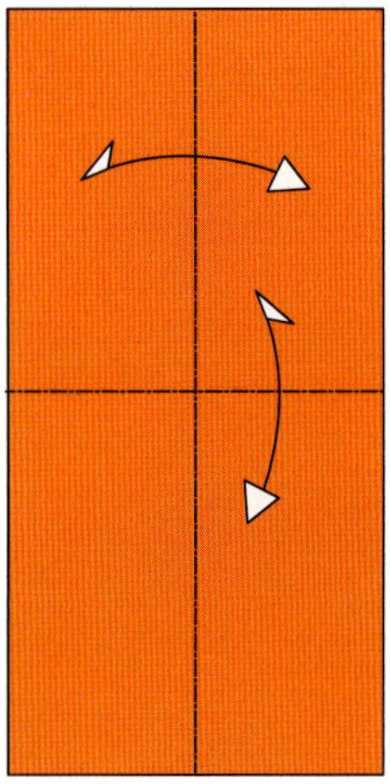

Precrease the first piece in half with mountain folds.

3

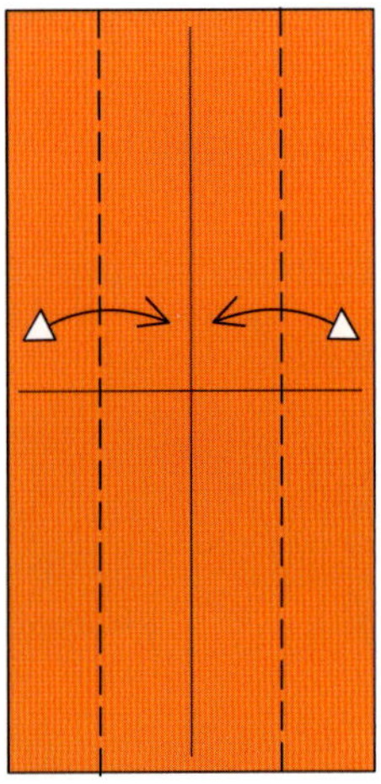

Precrease the sides in half.

4

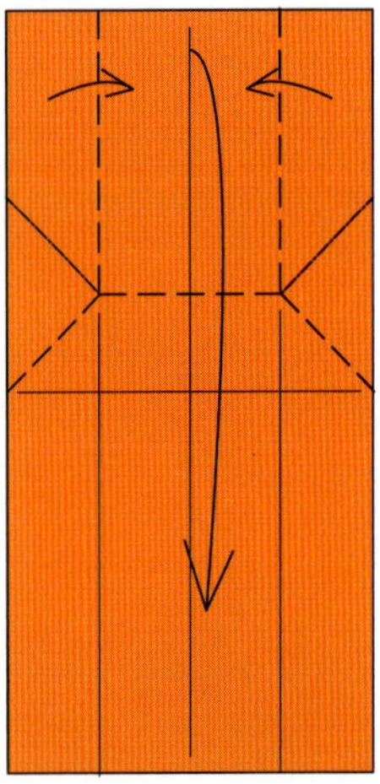

Valley fold down while swiveling the sides in.

5

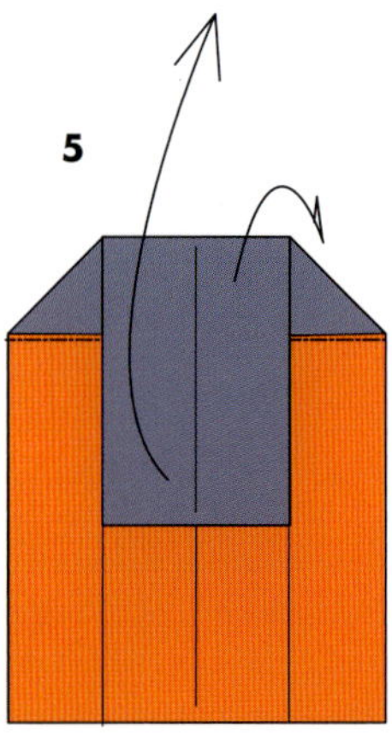

Flip the top section up.

6

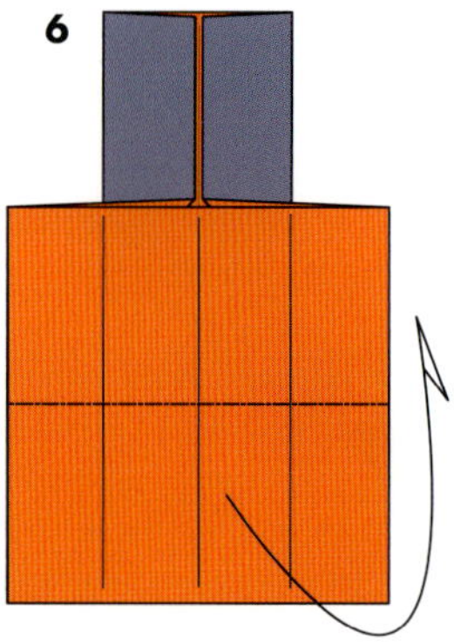

Mountain fold the bottom section in half.

13

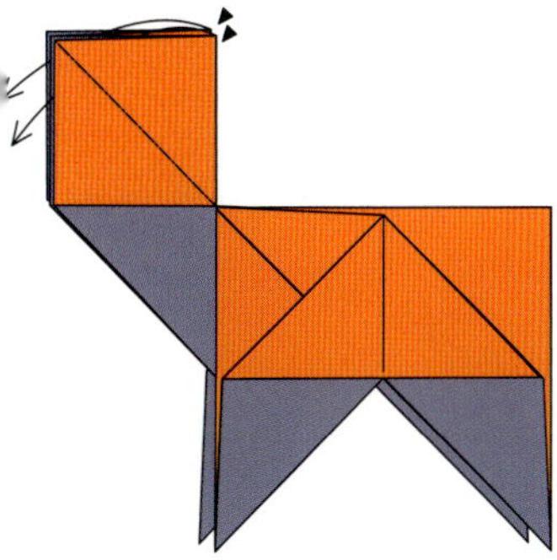

Reverse fold the two corners.

14

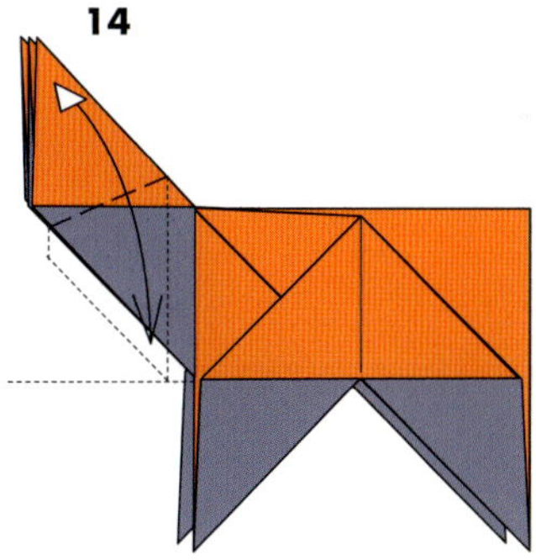

Precrease the cluster of flaps, noting the imaginary line.

15

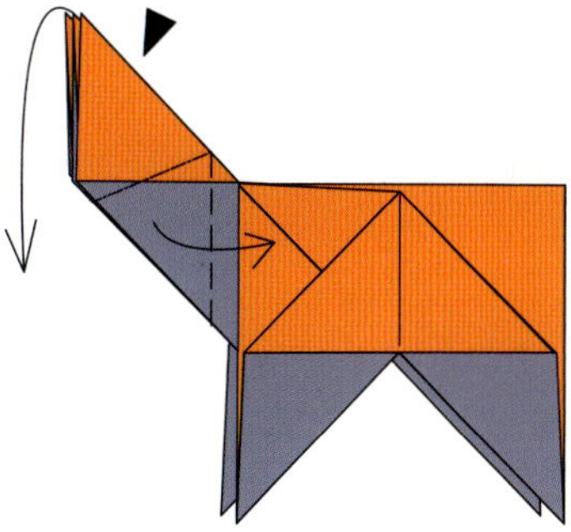

Squash fold down, allowing the left side to be thicker.

12

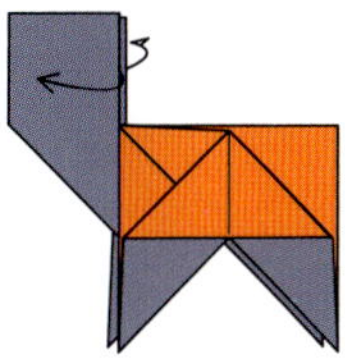

Wrap around a single layer at each side.

11

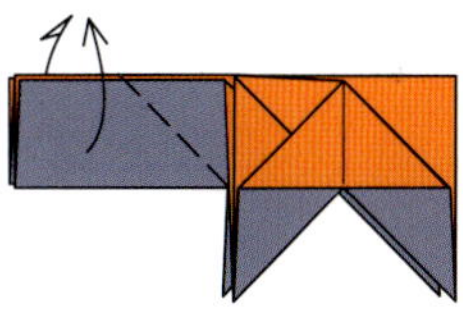

Outside reverse fold.

10

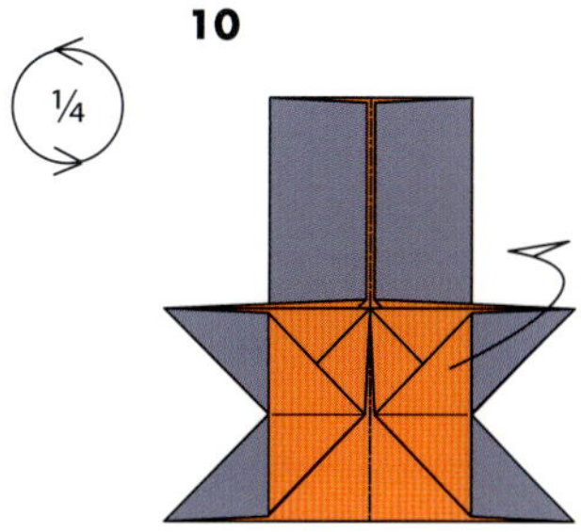

Mountain fold in half and rotate.

7

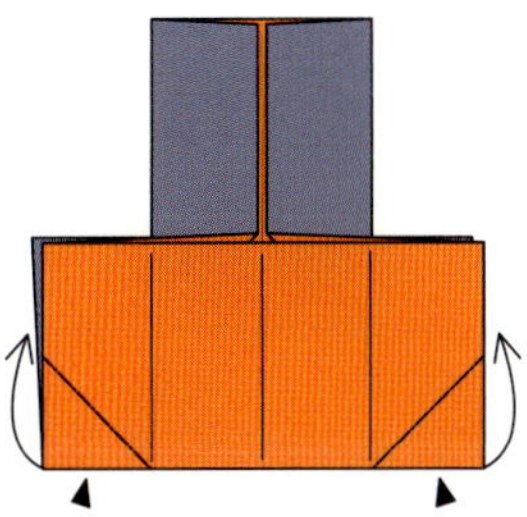

Reverse fold the bottom corners.

8

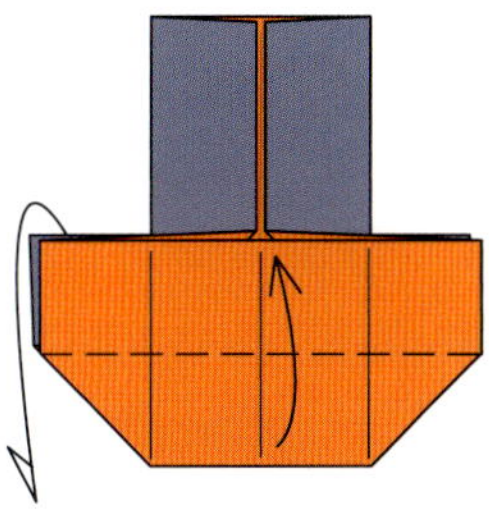

Valley fold, allowing the back flap to flip down.

9

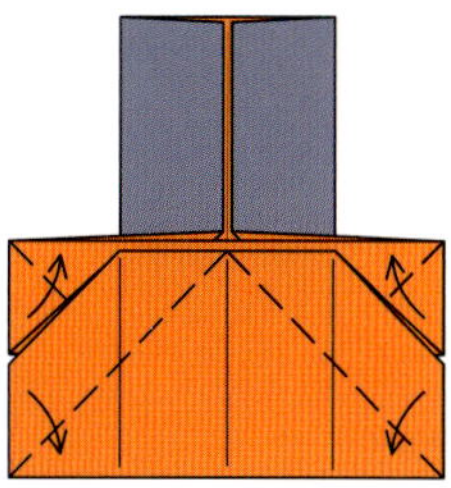

Valley fold, allowing the center to spread apart.

16

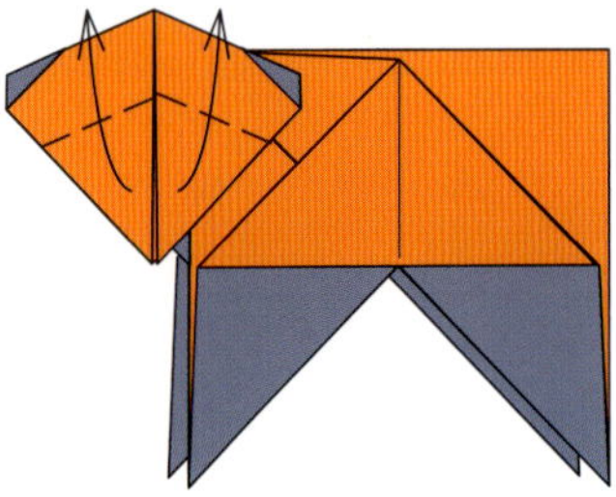

Valley fold the flaps up, such that the outer edges are straight.

17

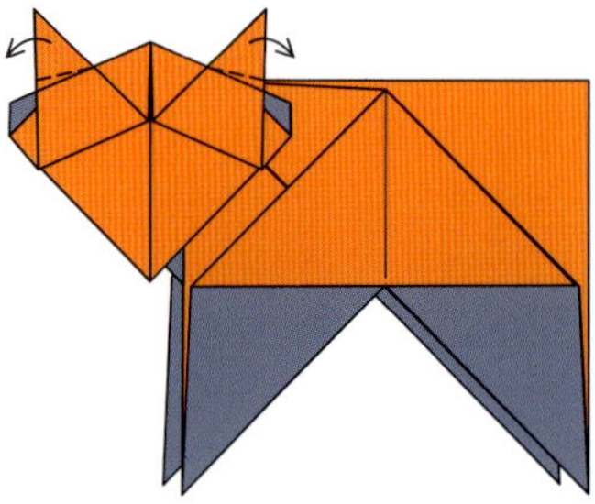

Pleat the ears around the edge.

18

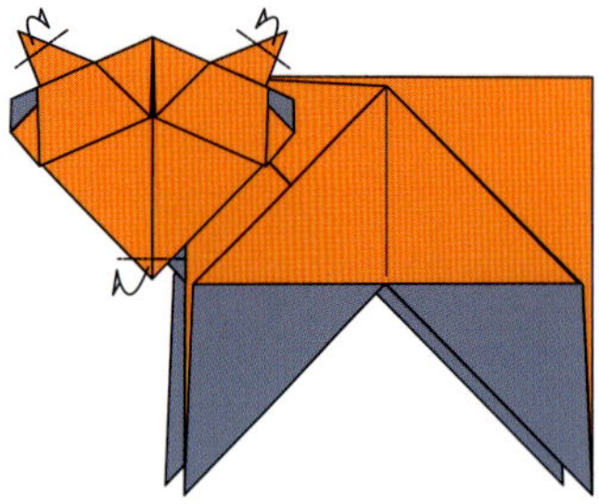

Mountain fold the three corners.

19

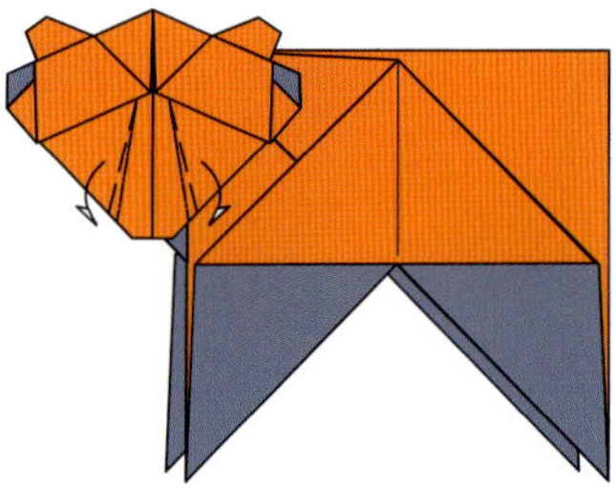

Add pleats to form the nose.

20

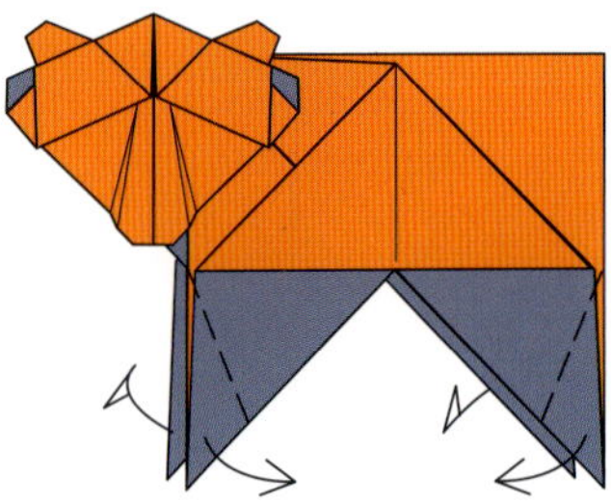

Valley fold the four legs.

21

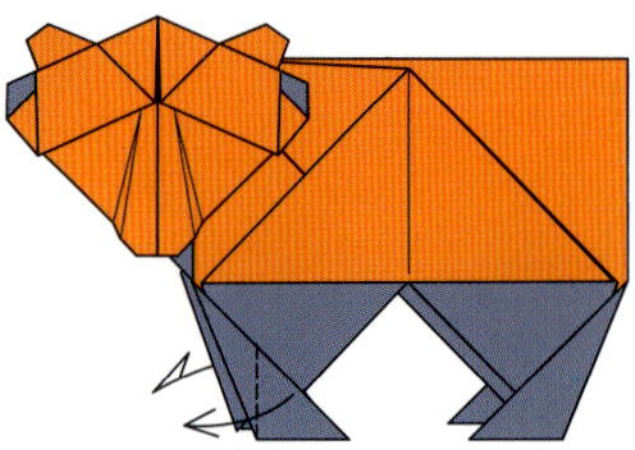

Valley fold the front legs.

22

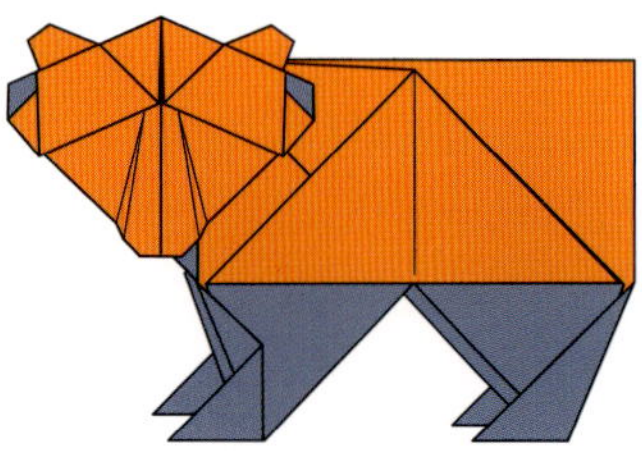

Completed body section.

23

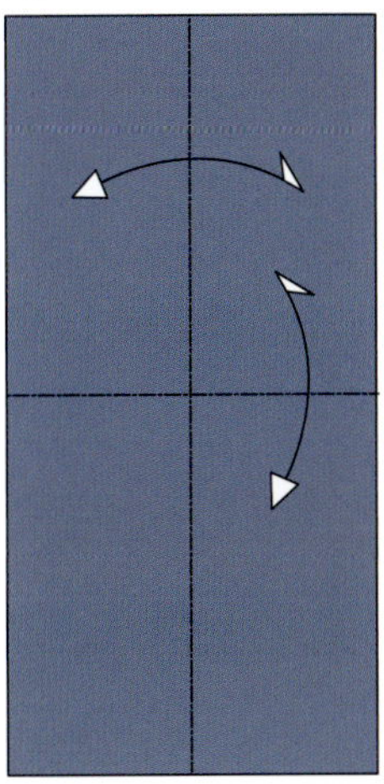

Precrease the second piece with mountain folds.

24

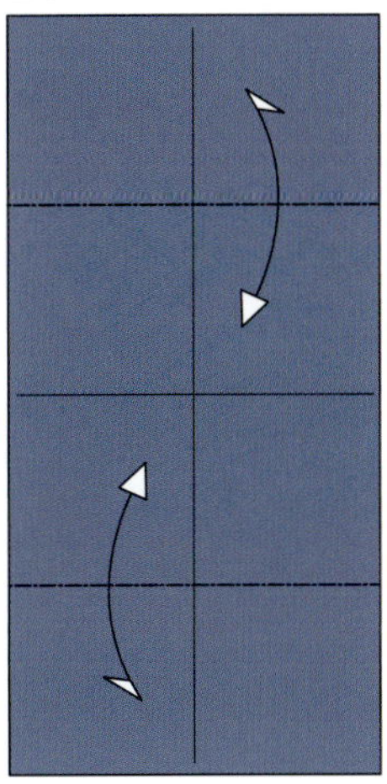

Precrease again with mountain folds.

25

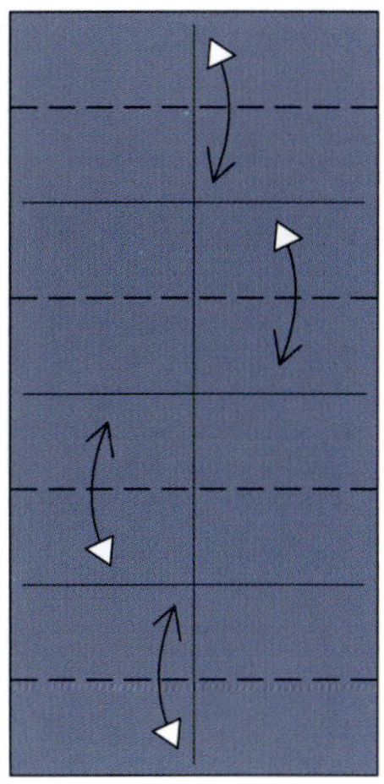

Precrease the sections in half with valley folds.

26

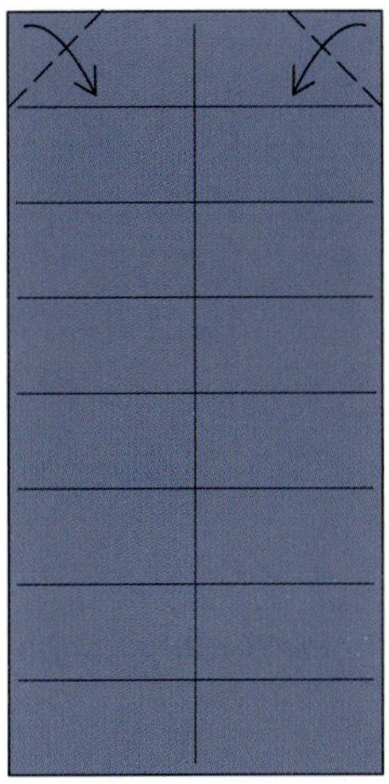

Valley fold the top corners.

27

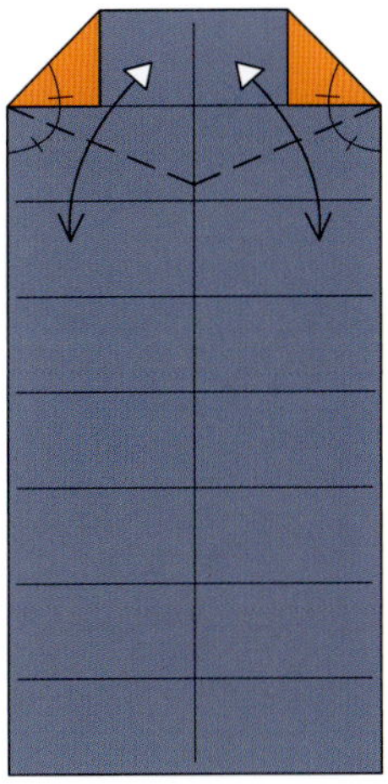

Precrease along the angle bisectors.

28

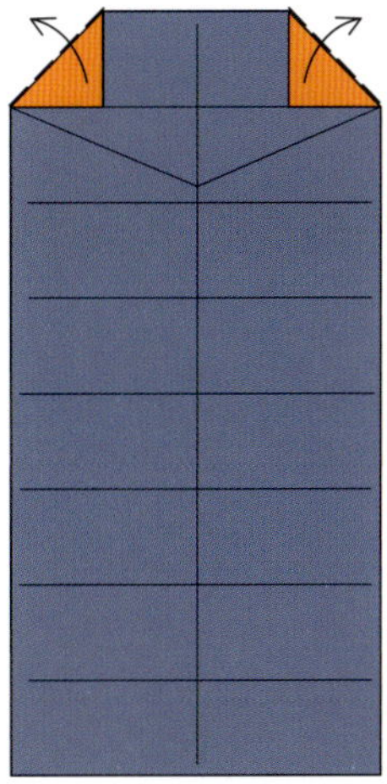

Unfold the top corners.

29

Valley fold the corners down.

30

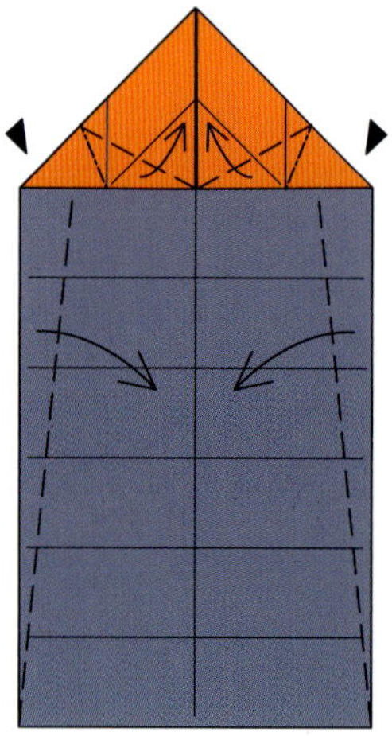

Swivel the sides in. The mountain folds lie on existing creases.

31

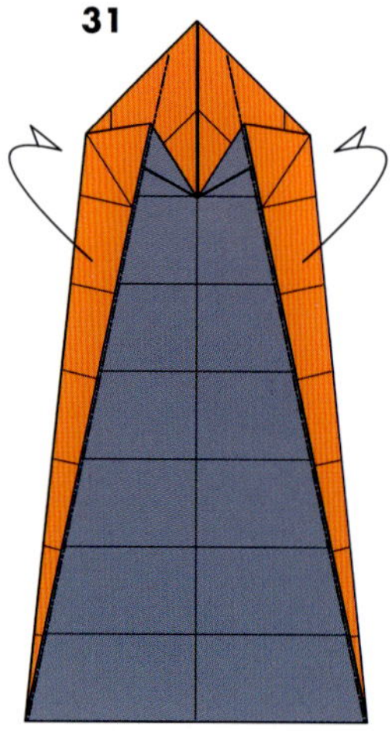

Mountain fold the sides.

32

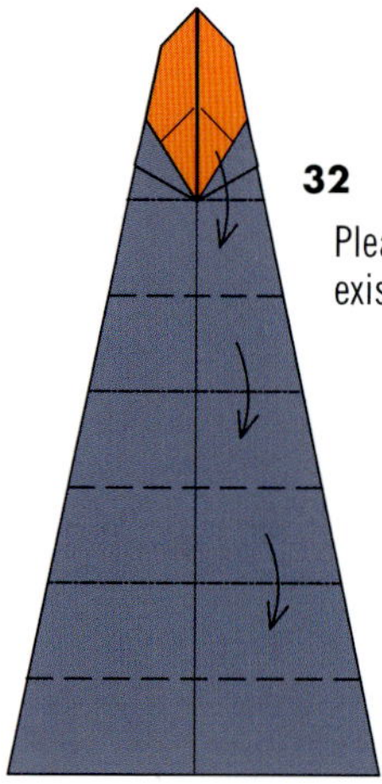

Pleat along the existing creases.

33

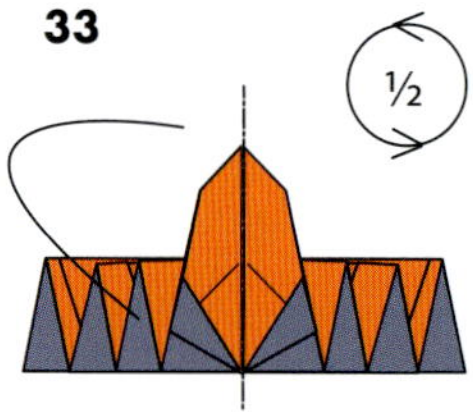

Mountain fold in half and rotate.

34

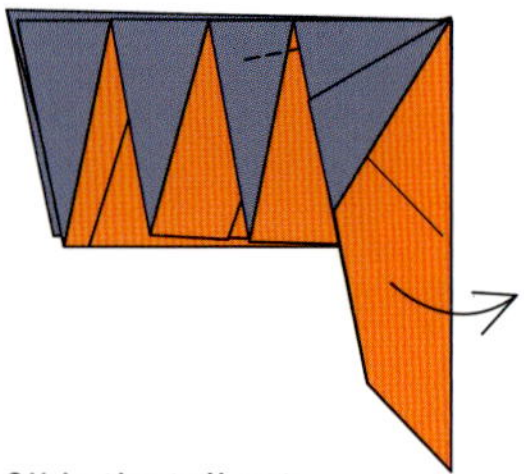

Slide the tail out.

35

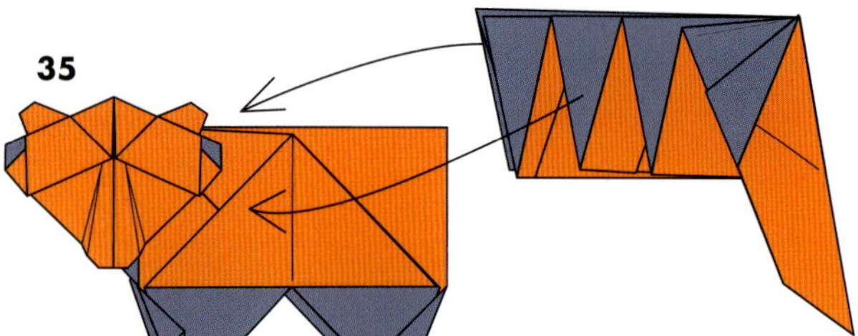

Tuck the striped section around the body section. You can tuck the tips of the stripes into the pockets on the body, or simply glue the sections together.

36

Completed Tiger.

A Butterfly for Reiko Tuttle

Michael LaFosse

See Michael's bio on page 154 to learn what enables him to make his origami creatures super realistic.

video: *youtu.be/vMnvFVjnYbI*

1

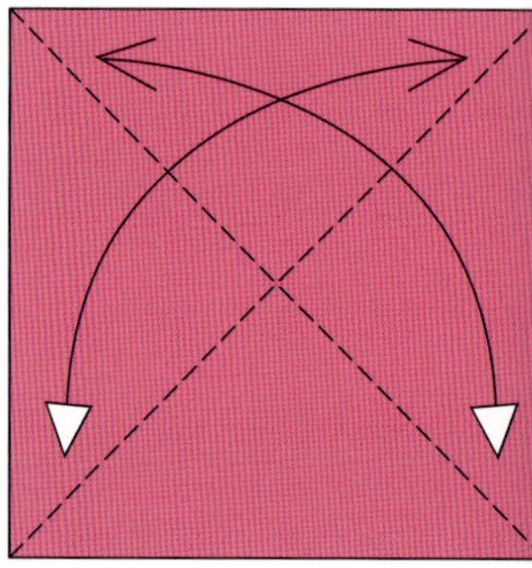

Begin with the colored side up. Precrease along the diagonals.

2

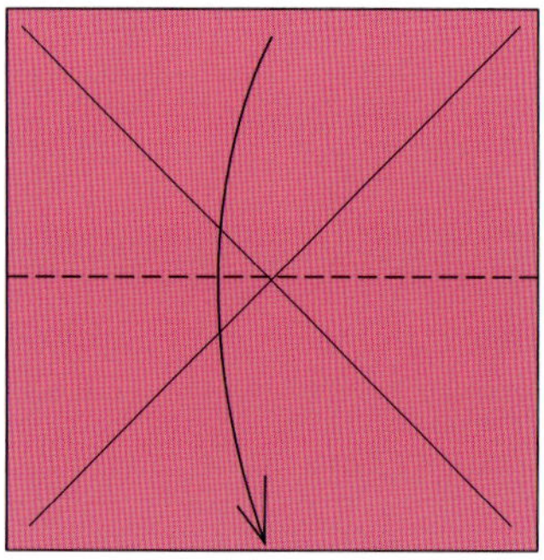

Valley fold in half.

3

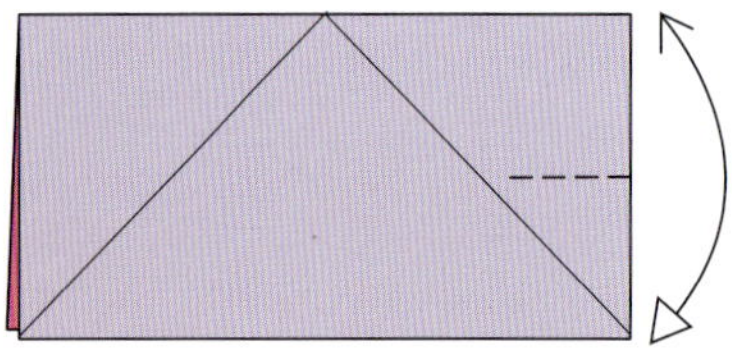

Precrease the top layer in half.

4

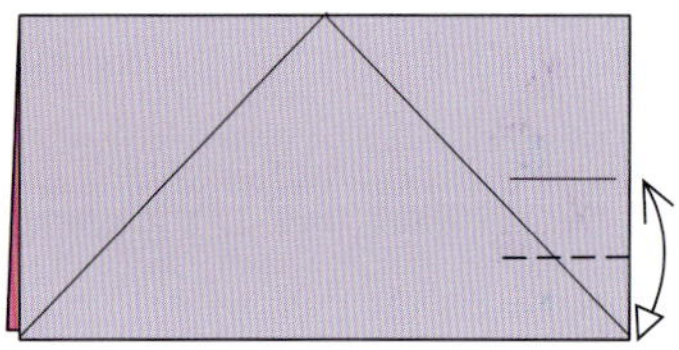

Precrease the lower section in half.

5

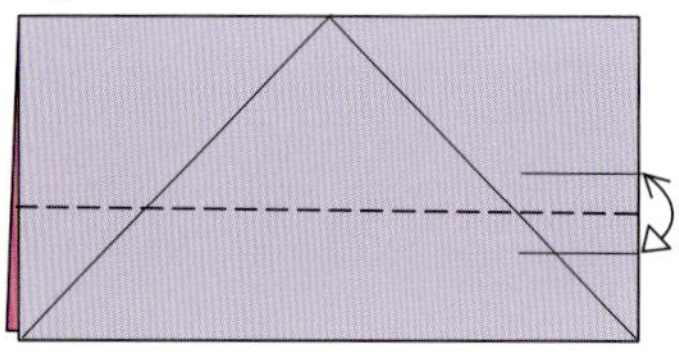

Precrease by bringing the two creases together.

6

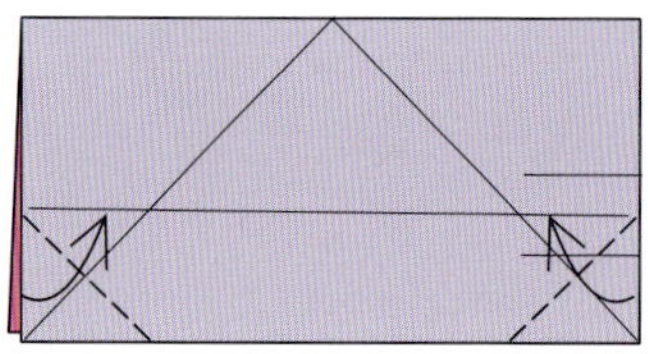

Valley fold the corners to the last crease.

7

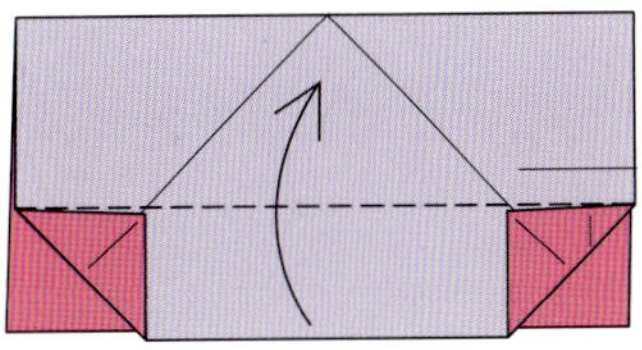

Valley fold along the existing crease.

8

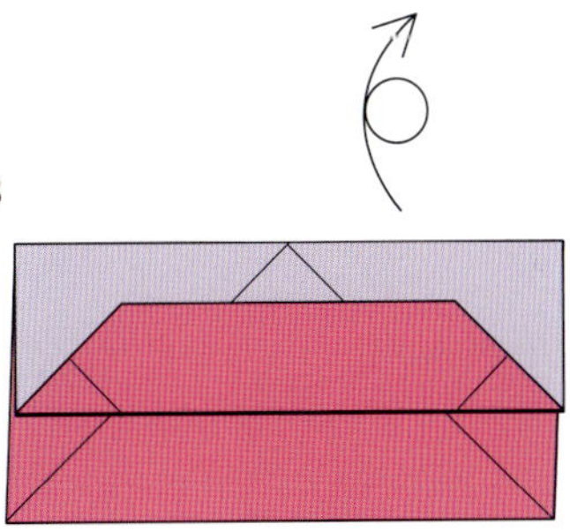

Turn over.

9

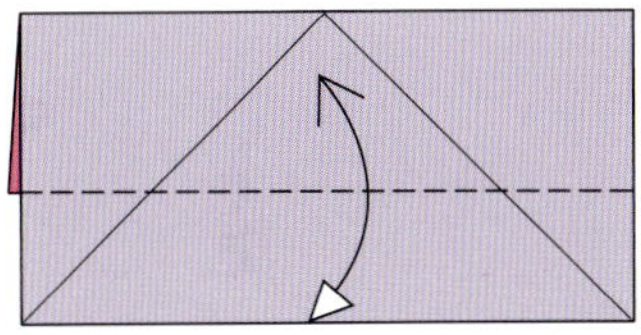

Precrease, aligning with the hidden edge.

10

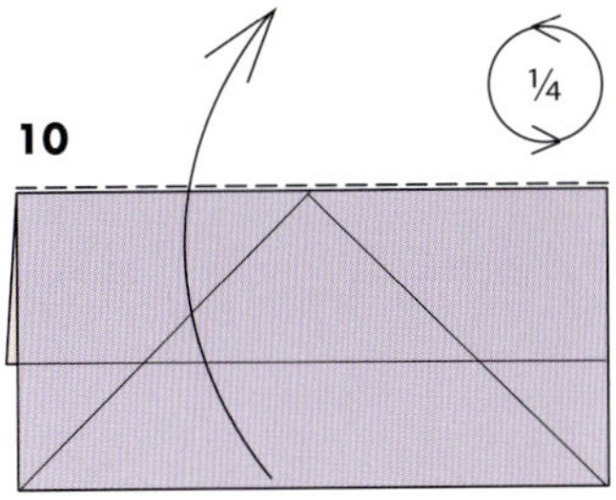

Open out and rotate.

11

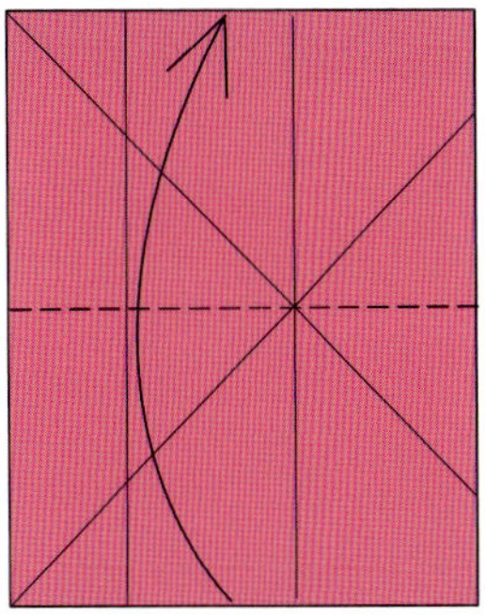

Valley fold in half.

12

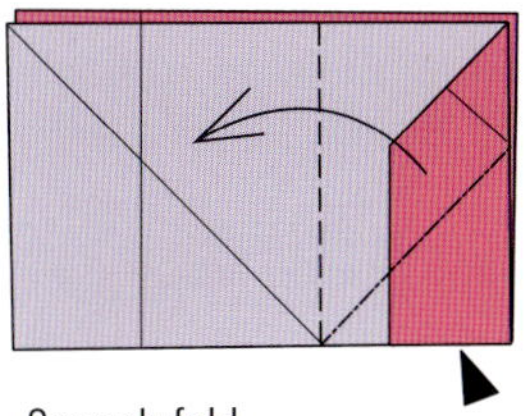

Squash fold.

13

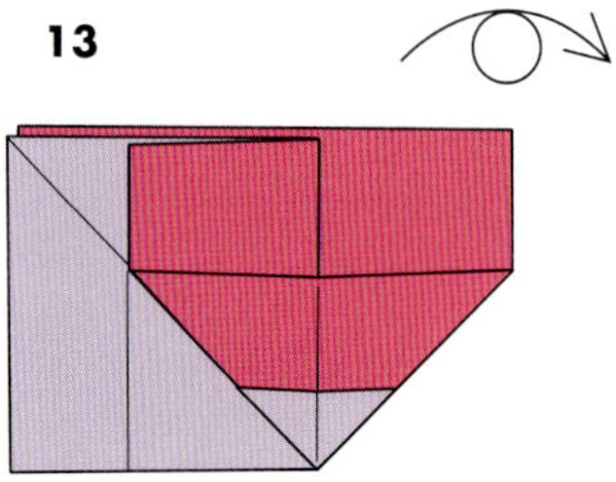

Turn over.

14

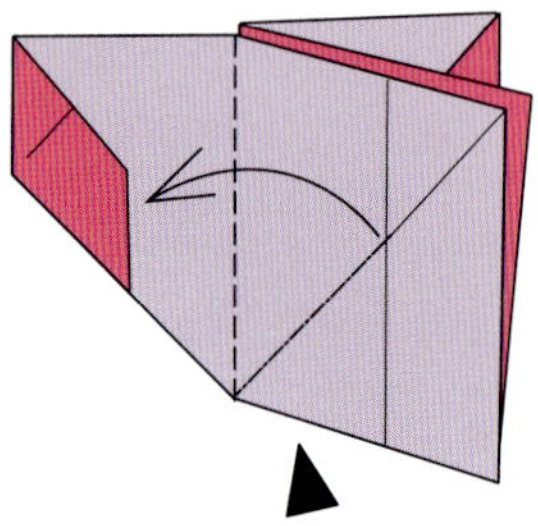

Squash fold, but do not flatten at the top.

15

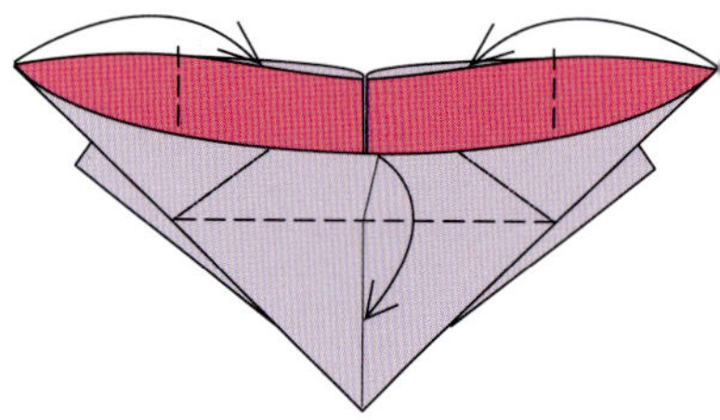

Swivel in the sides to flatten.

16

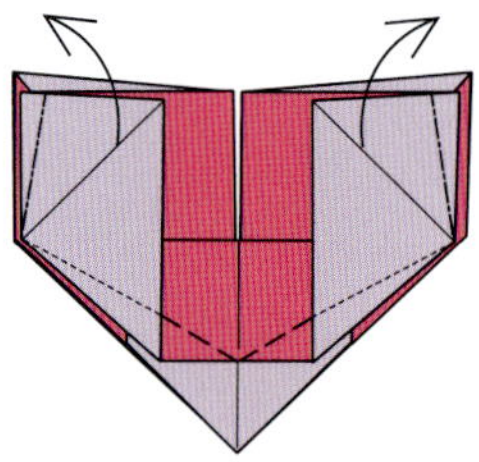

Slide the side edges outward.

17

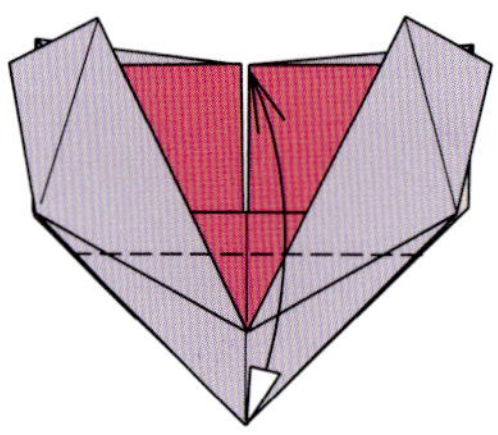

Precrease through all layers.

18

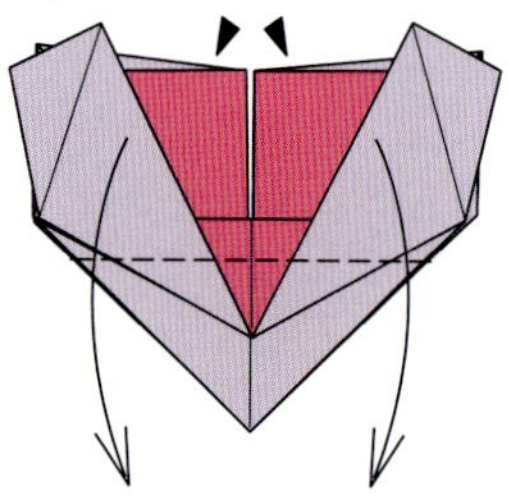

Squash fold the flaps open.

22

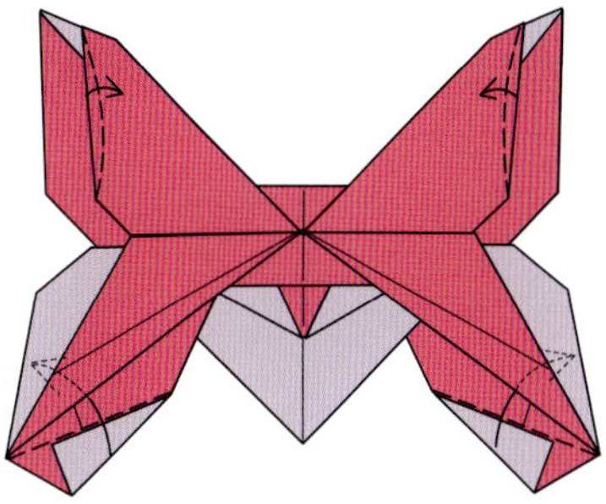

Tuck the lower edges in. Valley fold the top edges with a slightly curved fold. This edge will stick up slightly.

23

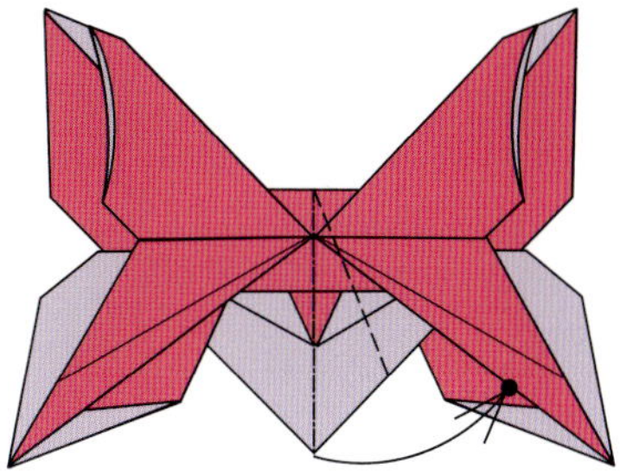

Begin to pleat the middle section, noting the dotted reference point.

21

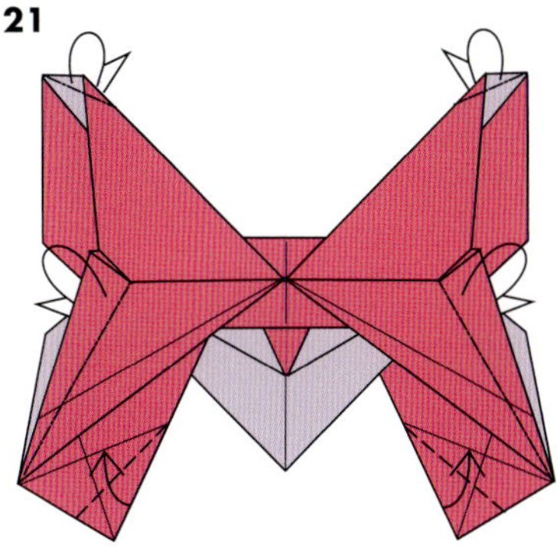

Mountain fold the top edges and the sides. Valley fold the lower edges.

19

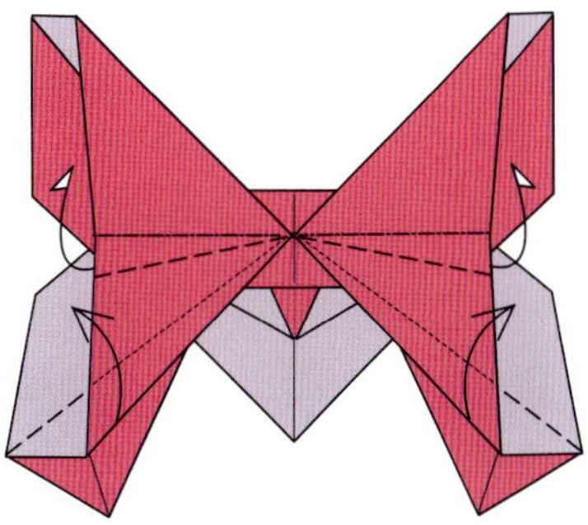

Swivel the top layer at each side.

20

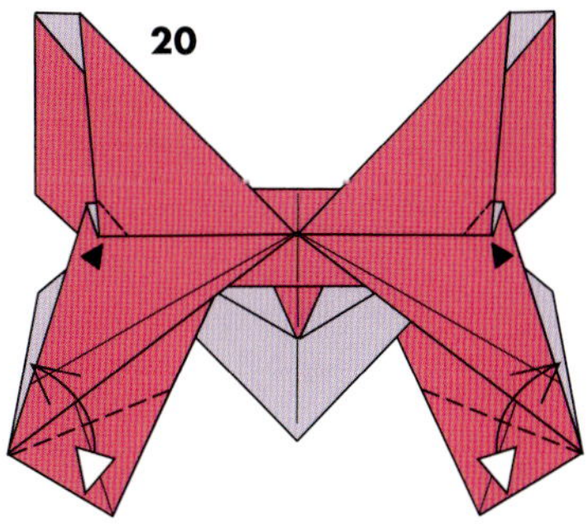

Reverse fold the two corners. Precrease the bottom flaps.

24

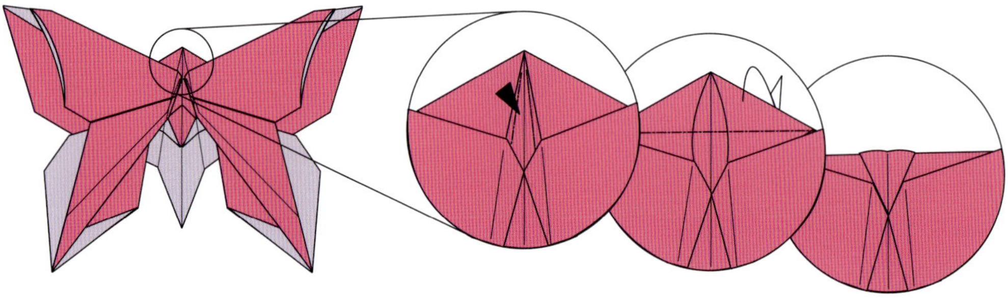

Here the model is opened up slightly. Squash the ridge at the head flat and then mountain fold.

25

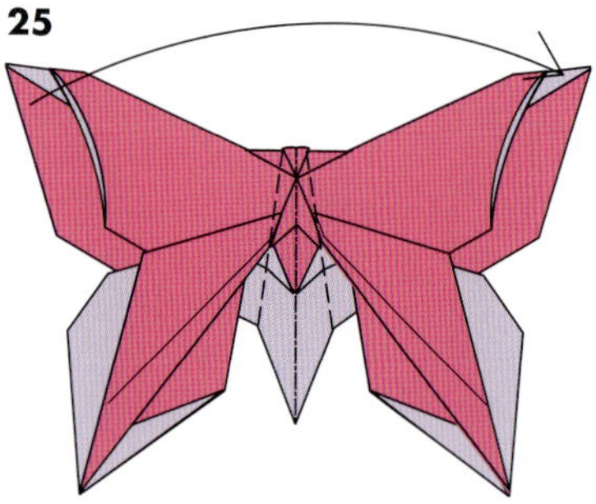

Close the model up.

26

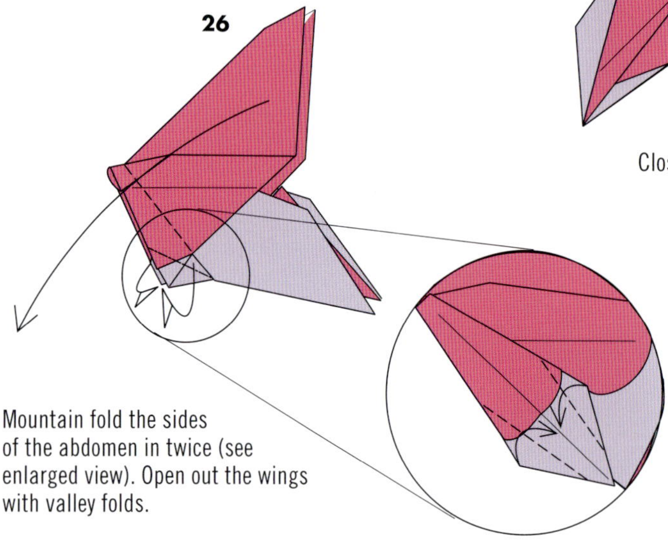

Mountain fold the sides of the abdomen in twice (see enlarged view). Open out the wings with valley folds.

27

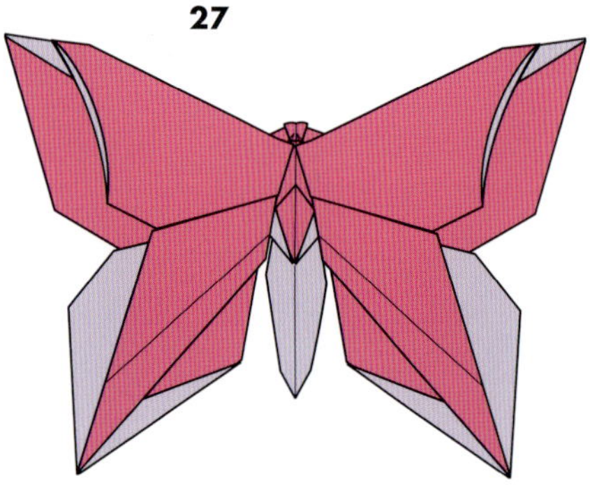

Completed Butterfly for Reiko Tuttle.

Red-Winged Blackbird

Robert J. Lang

Robert's grasp of complex folding techniques is no surprise given what his former career was—see more in his bio on page 153.

video: *youtu.be/XEMA3vIRQNQ*

1

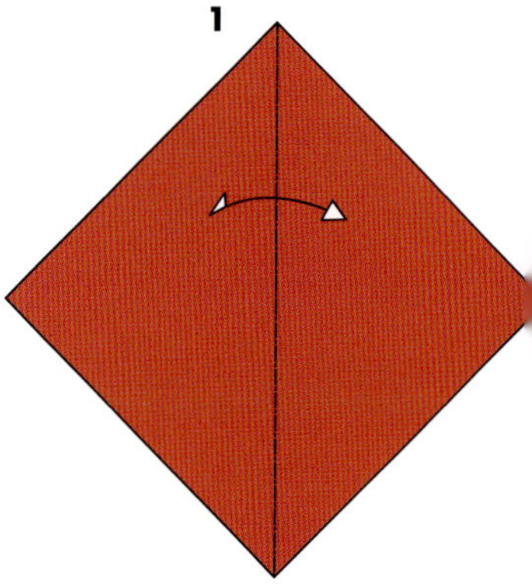

Precrease with a mountain fold.

2

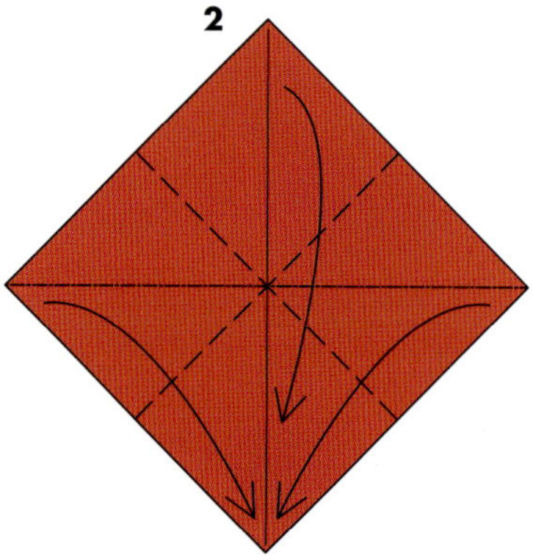

Collapse downward.

3

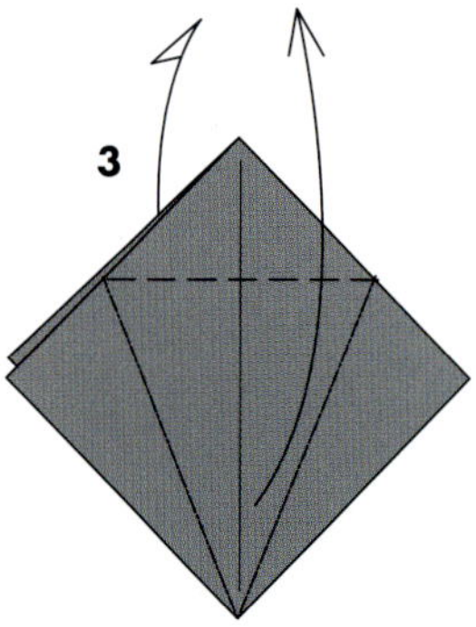

Petal fold both sides.

4

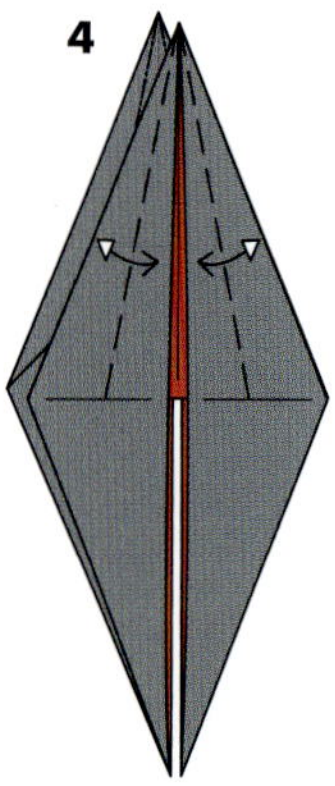

Precrease along the angle bisectors and repeat behind.

5

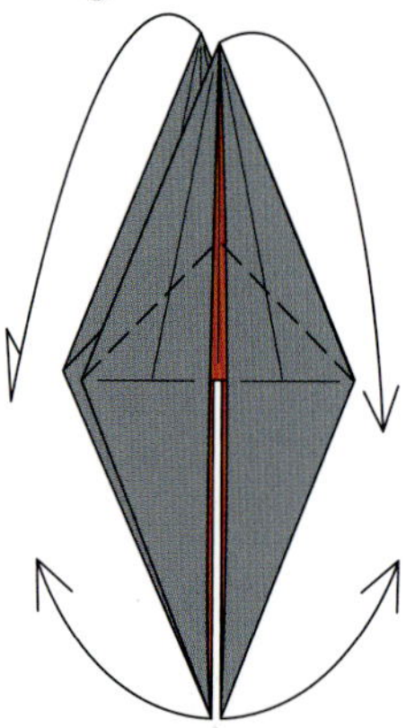

Stretch apart the bottom flaps, allowing the top flaps to come down. The center hidden flap will collapse flat.

6

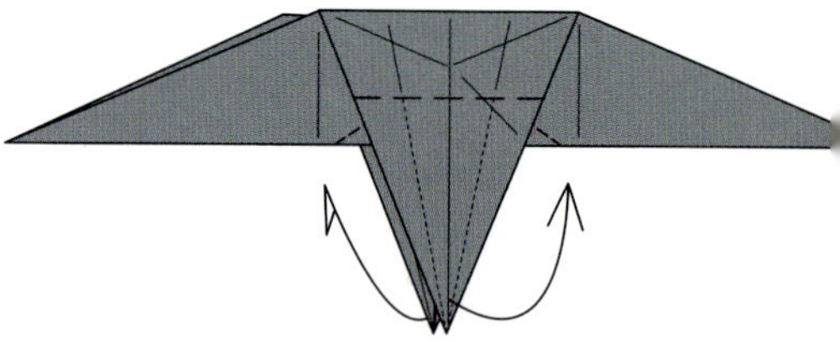

Valley fold the sides up while valley folding the inner layers outward.

7

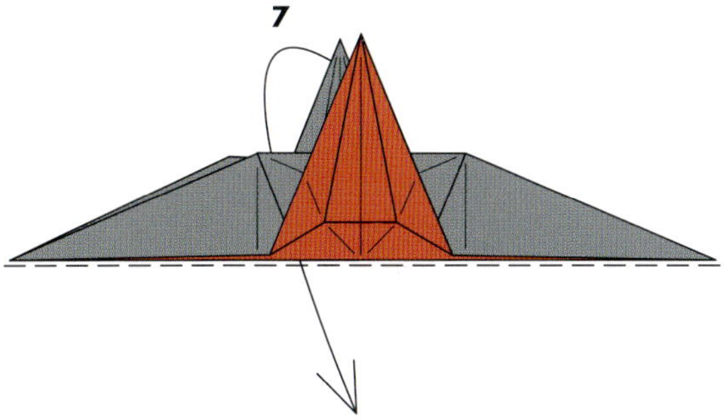

Open out the model along the center.

8

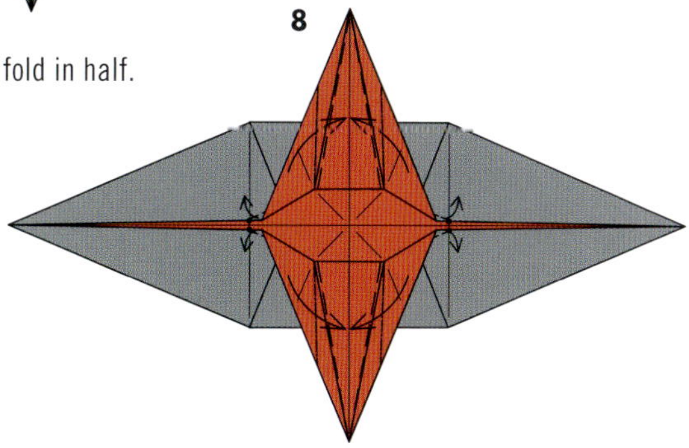

Swivel the top layers inward, noting where the folds hit the dotted creases.

9

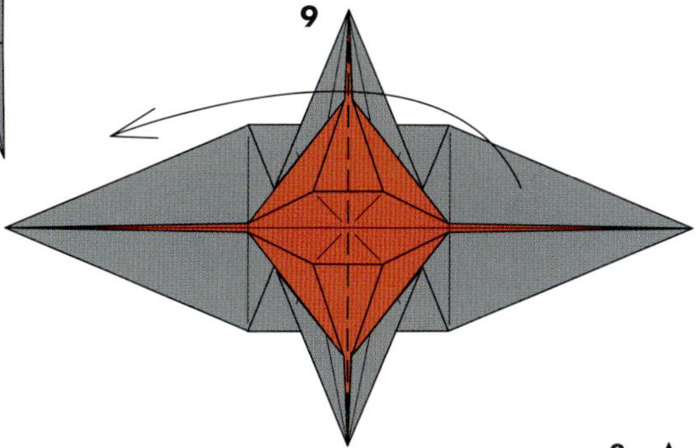

Valley fold in half.

10

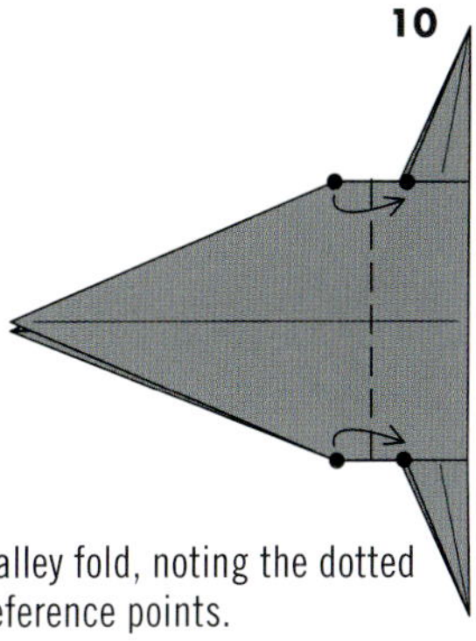

Valley fold, noting the dotted reference points.

11

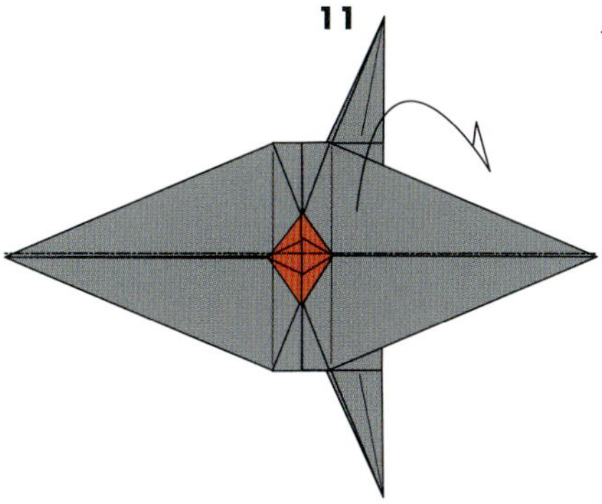

Mountain fold in half.

12

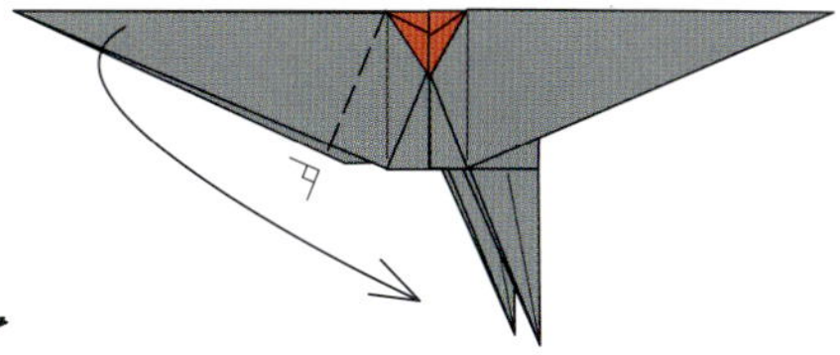

Valley fold.

13

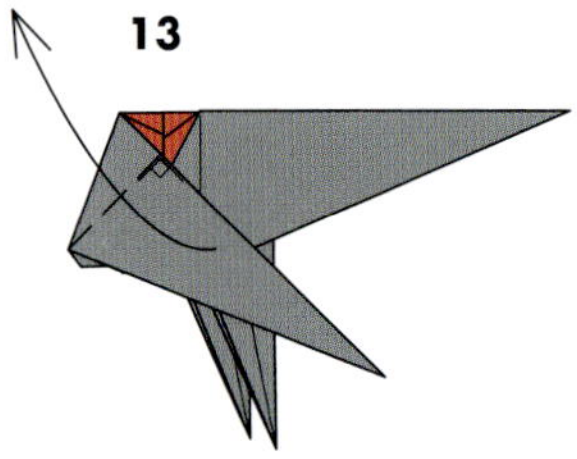

Valley fold up.

14

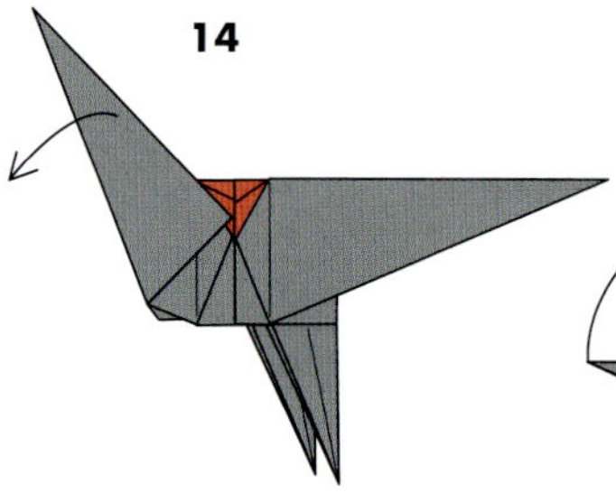

Unfold the pleat.

15

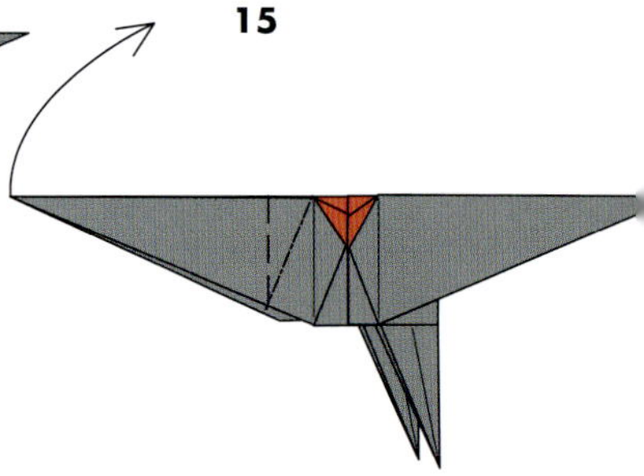

Crimp along the existing creases.

16

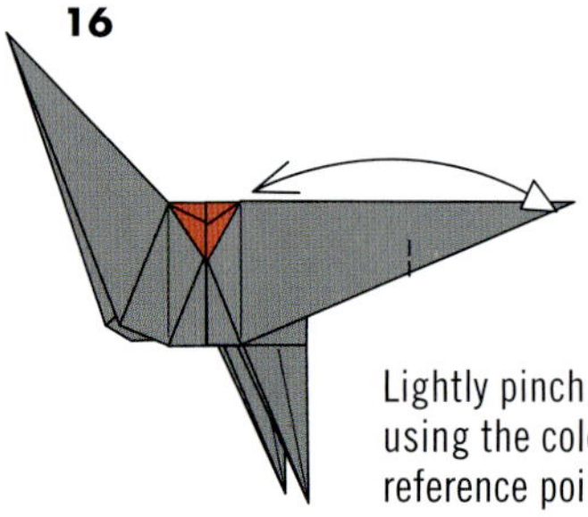

Lightly pinch the lower edge using the colored area as a reference point.

17

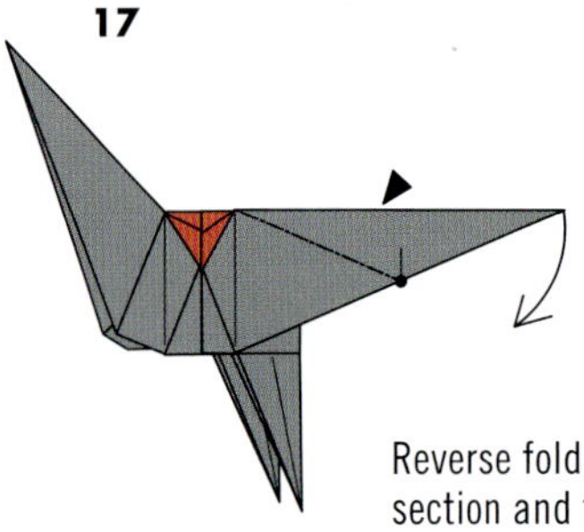

Reverse fold, using both the colored section and the dotted crease as guides.

18

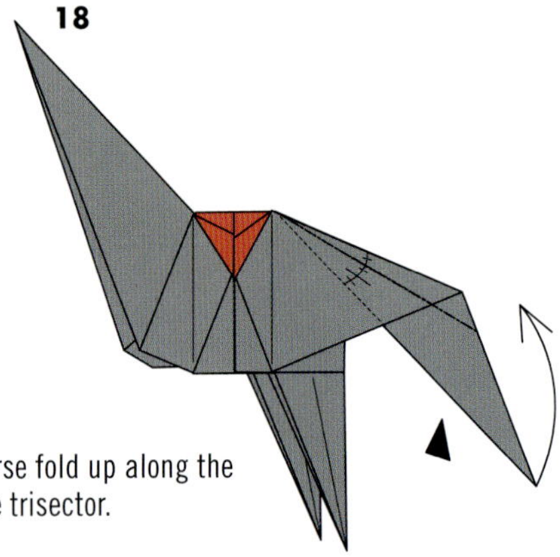

Reverse fold up along the angle trisector.

19

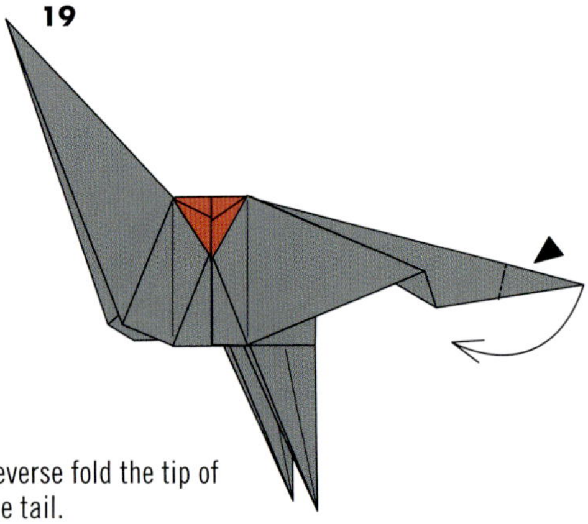

Reverse fold the tip of the tail.

24

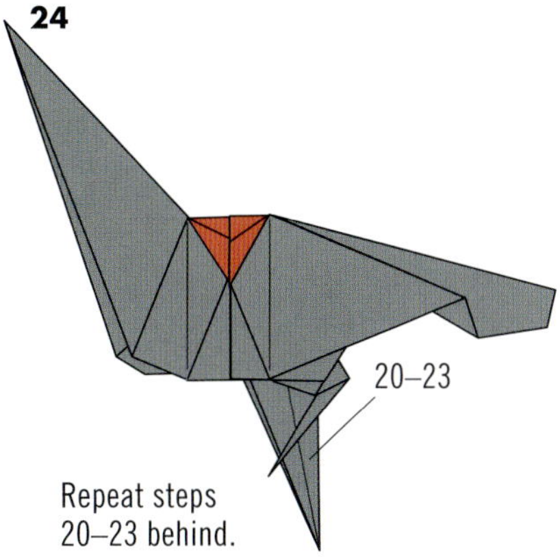

Repeat steps
20–23 behind.

25

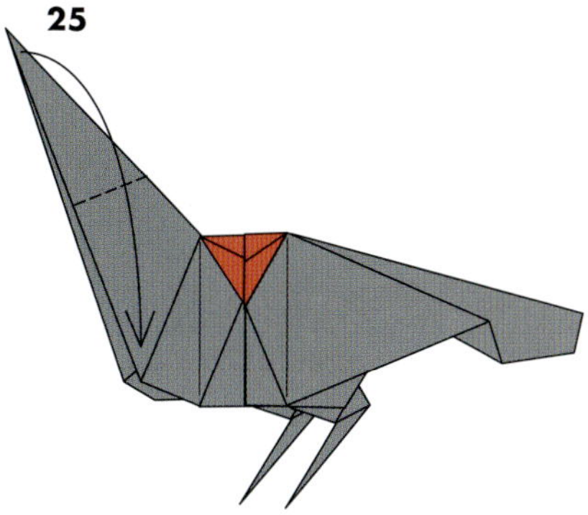

Valley fold halfway.

23

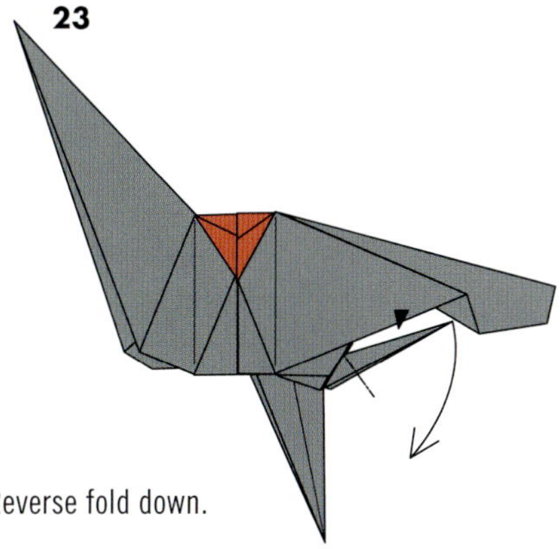

Reverse fold down.

22

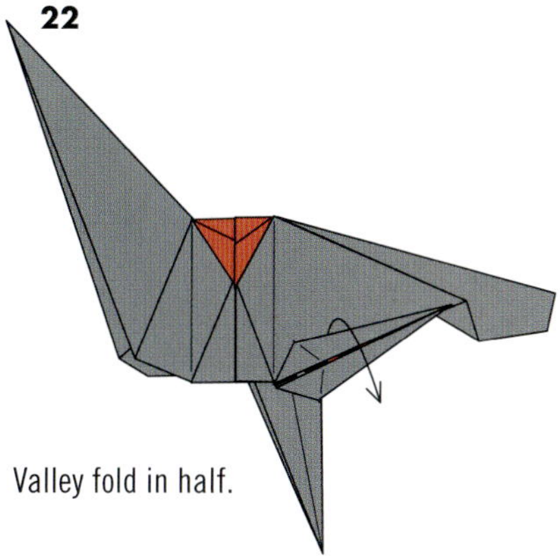

Valley fold in half.

20

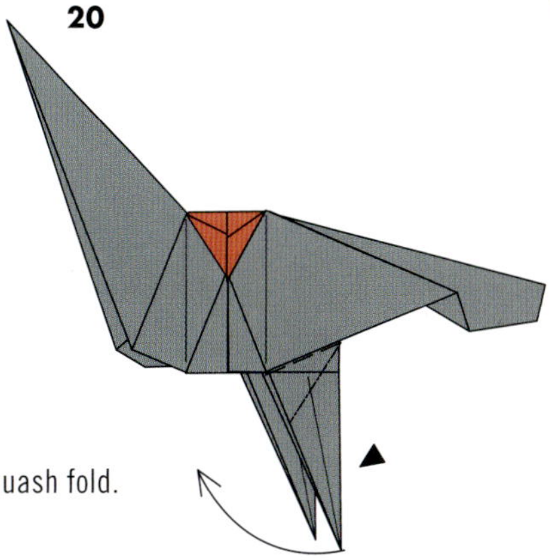

Squash fold.

21

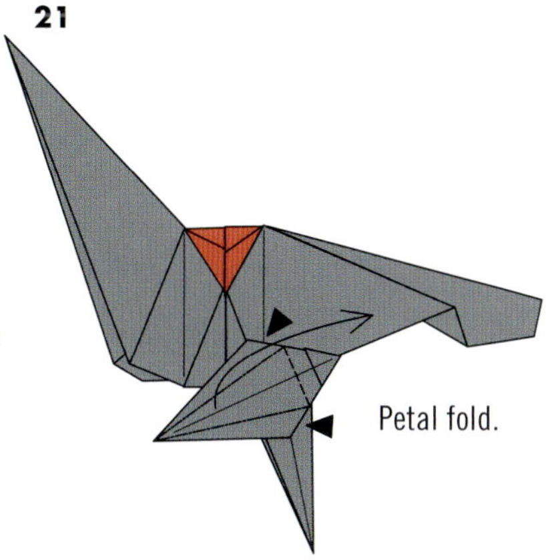

Petal fold.

26

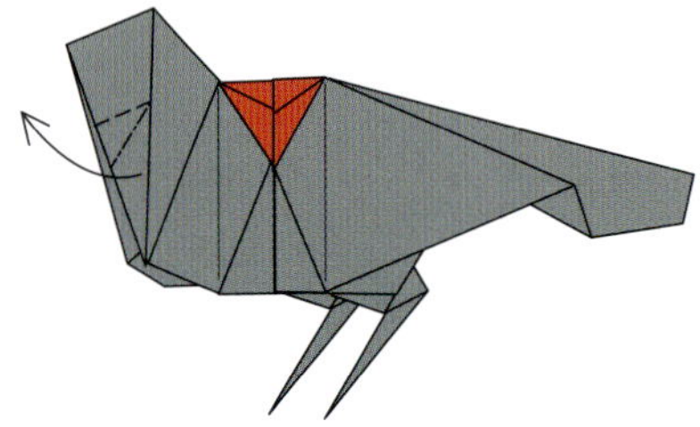

Pleat the flap upward. See the next step for the suggested approximate alignments.

27

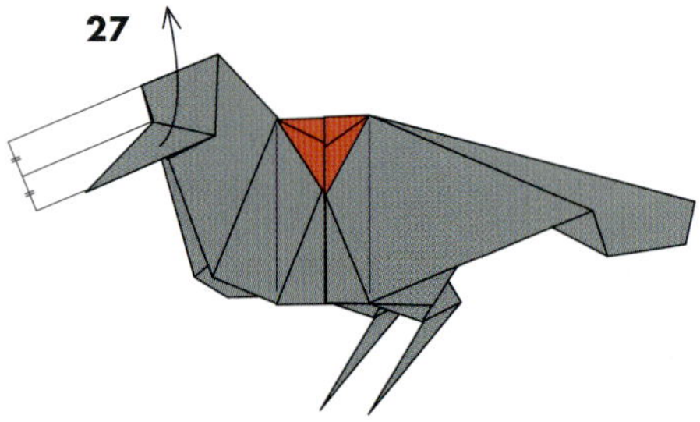

Unfold the pleat.

28

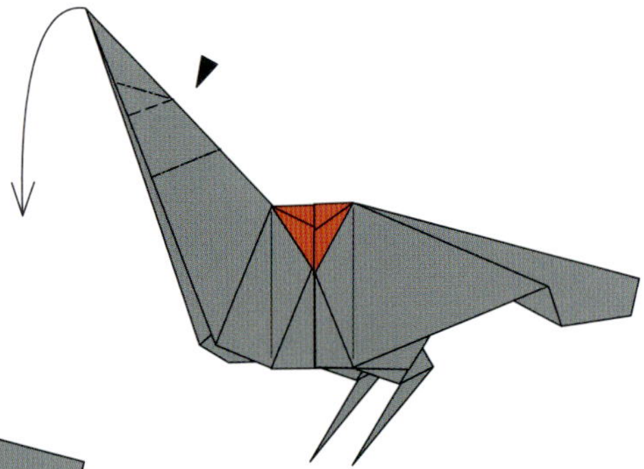

Reverse fold in and out along the existing creases.

29

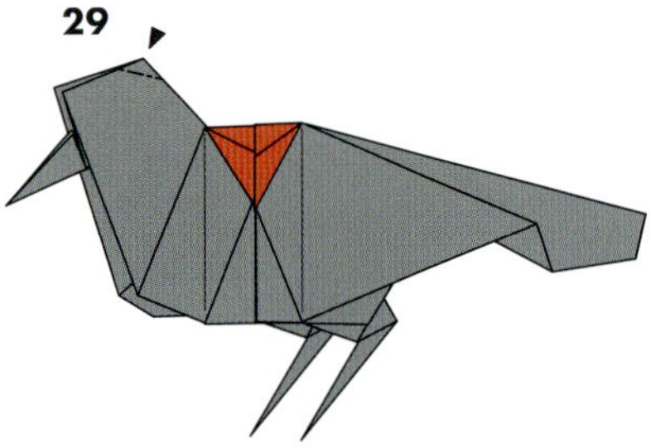

Sink the corner.

30

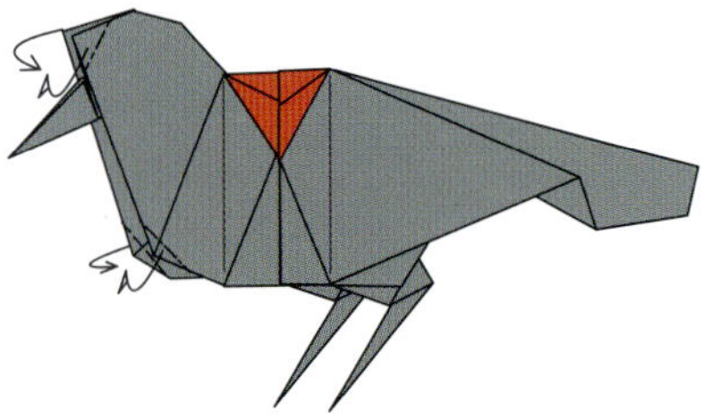

Make two sets of mountain folds to round off the body and the head.

31

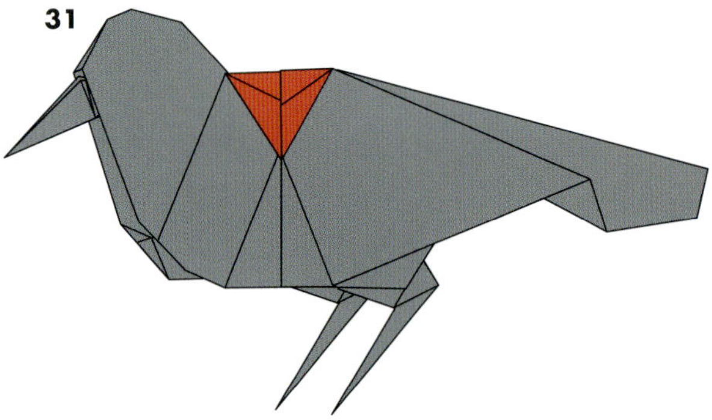

Completed Red-Winged Blackbird.

Cardinal

Robert J. Lang
video: *youtu.be/Cqu5EtOBjxU*

1

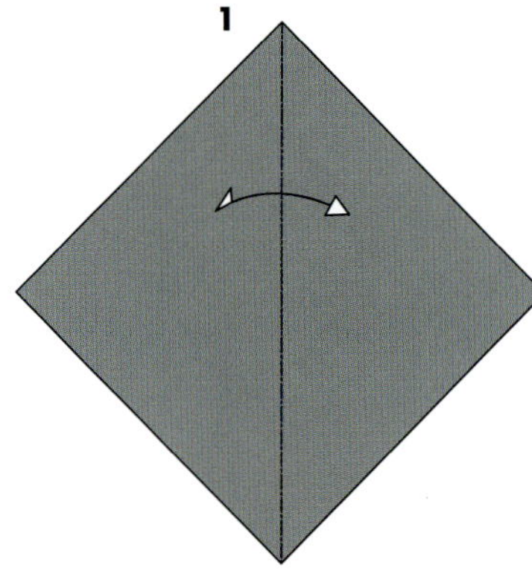

Precrease with a mountain fold.

2

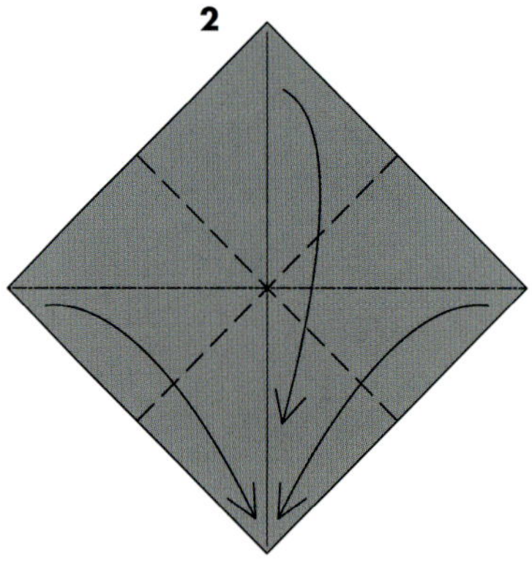

Collapse downward.

3

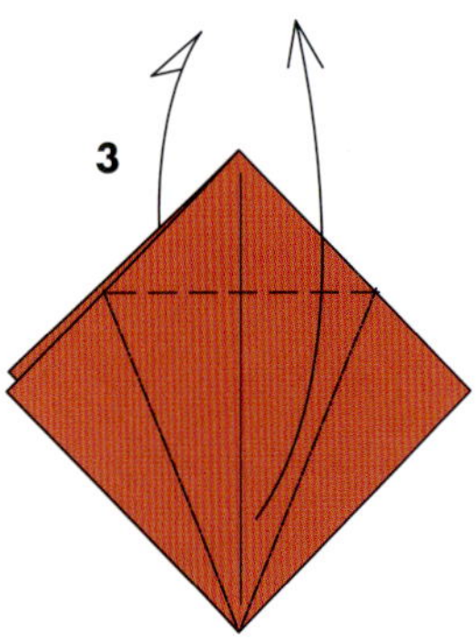

Petal fold both sides.

4

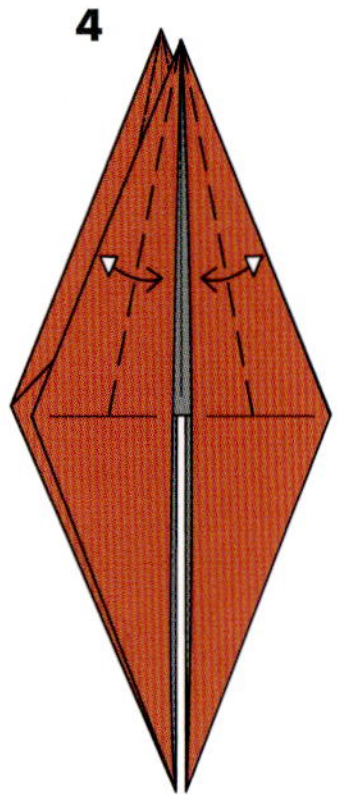

Precrease along the angle bisectors and repeat behind.

5

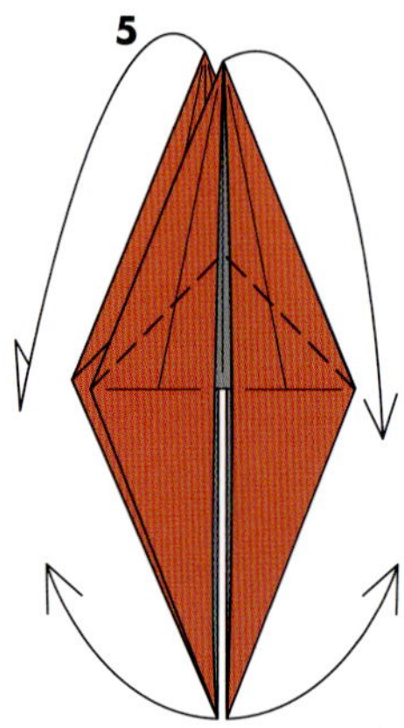

Stretch apart the bottom flaps, allowing the top flaps to come down. The center hidden flap will collapse flat.

10

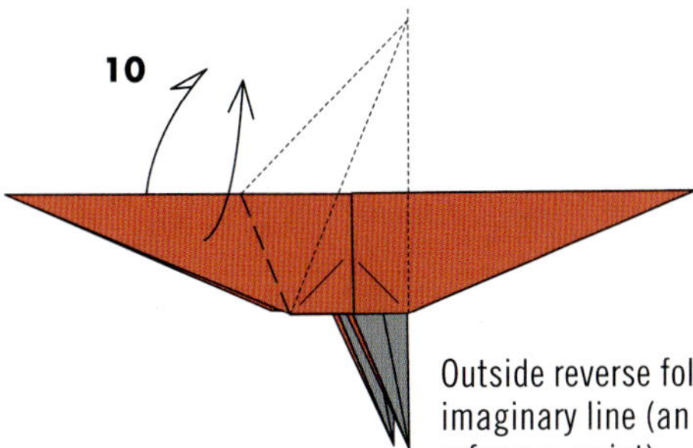

Outside reverse fold toward the imaginary line (an approximate reference point).

11

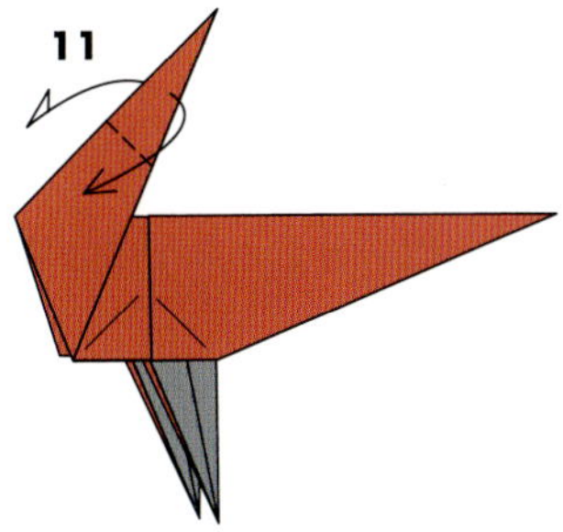

Outside reverse fold, such that the point extends a little bit beyond the body.

9

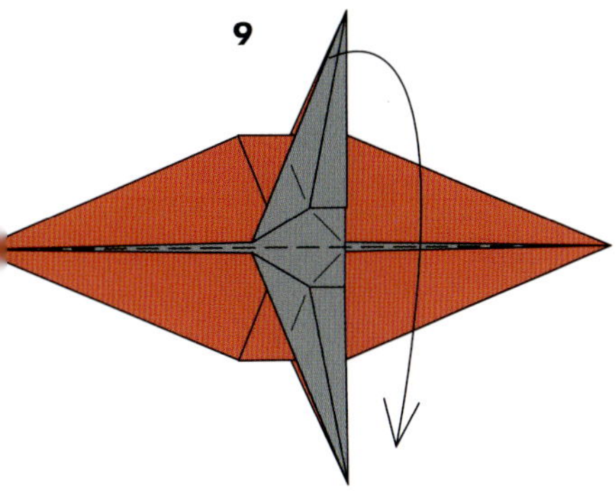

Valley fold in half.

8

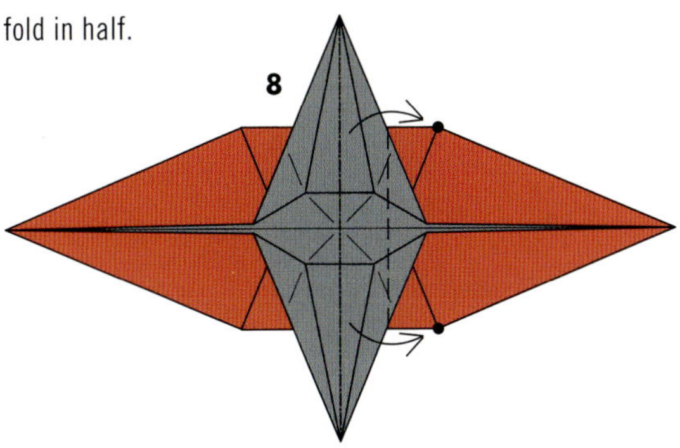

Pleat through all layers.

7

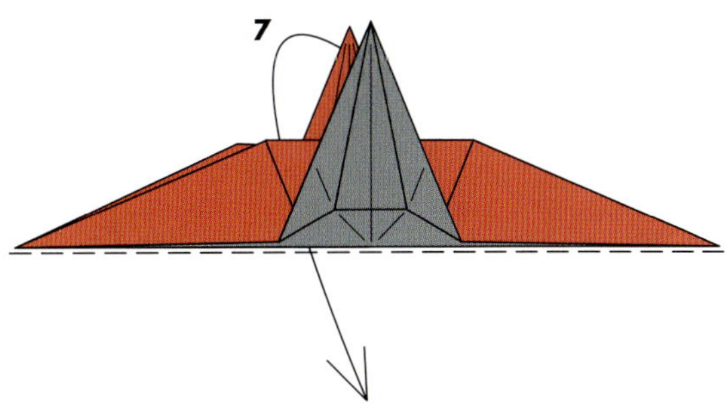

Open out the model along the center.

6

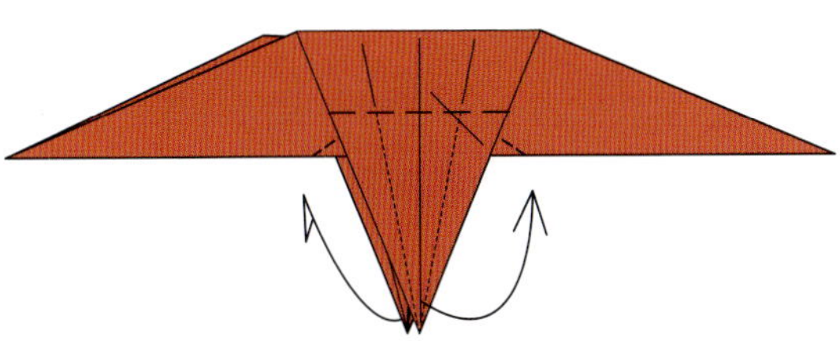

Valley fold the sides up while valley folding the inner layers outward

12

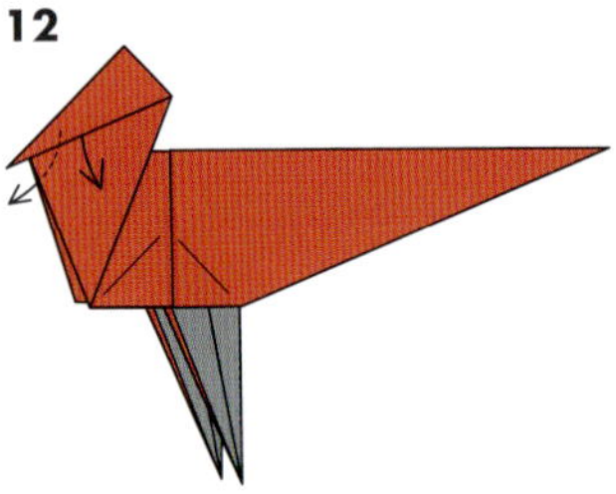

Pull out the inner layers as far as possible.

13

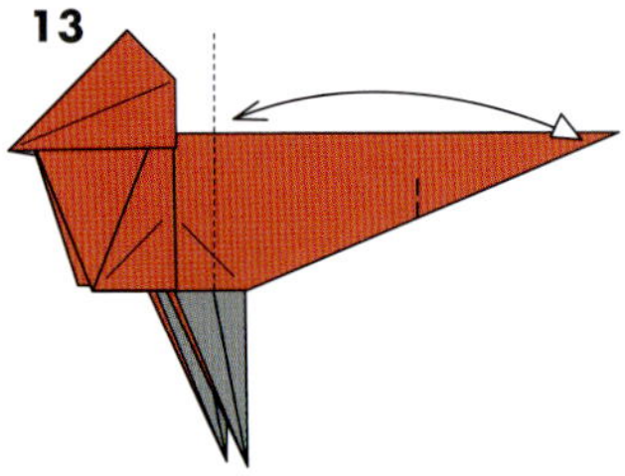

Lightly pinch the lower edge using the imaginary line as a guide (an approximate reference point).

14

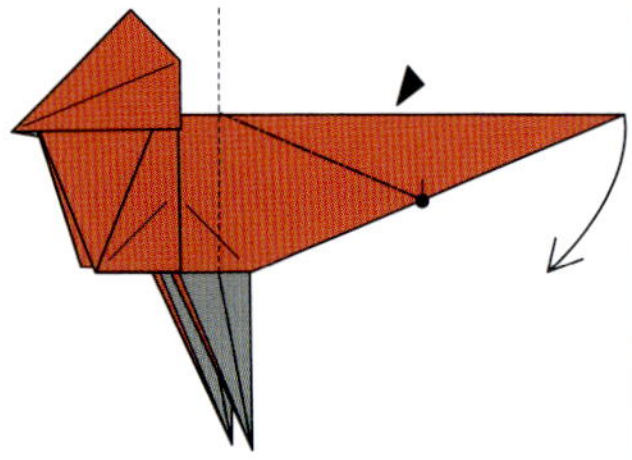

Reverse fold, using both the imaginary line and the dotted crease as guides.

15

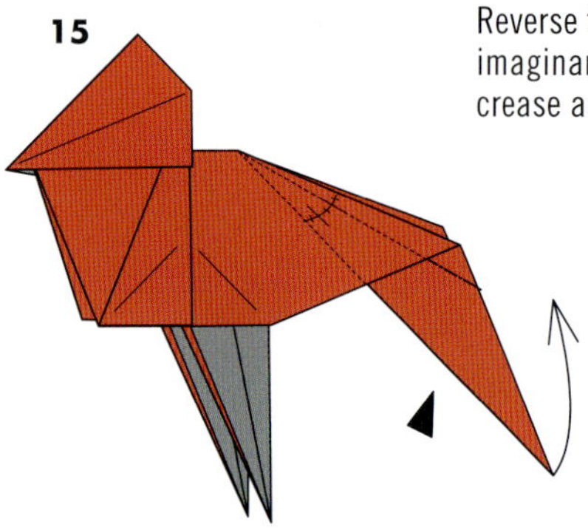

Reverse fold up along the angle trisector.

16

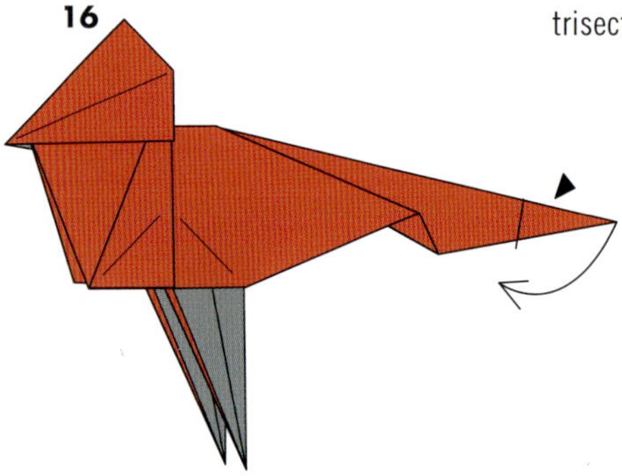

Reverse fold the tip of the tail.

17

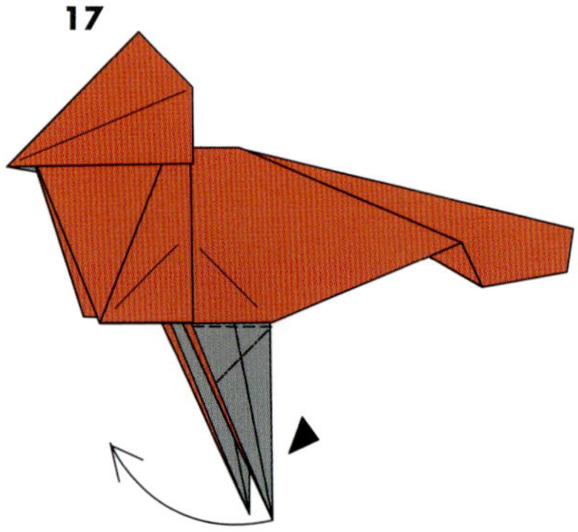

Squash fold.

18

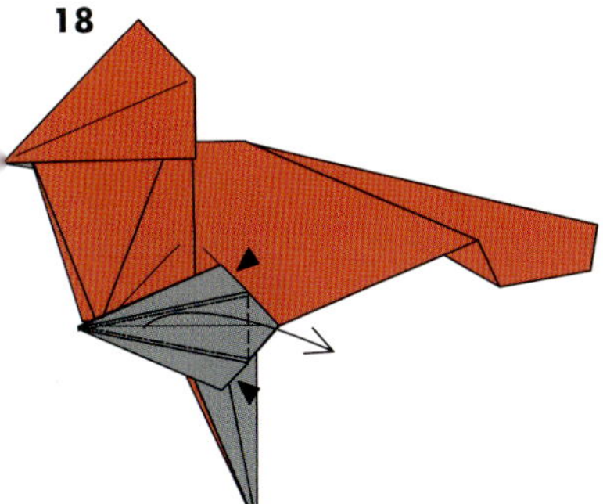

Petal fold.

19

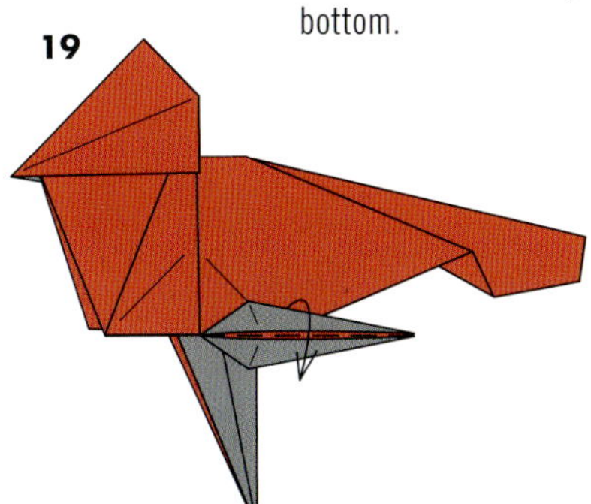

Valley fold in half.

20

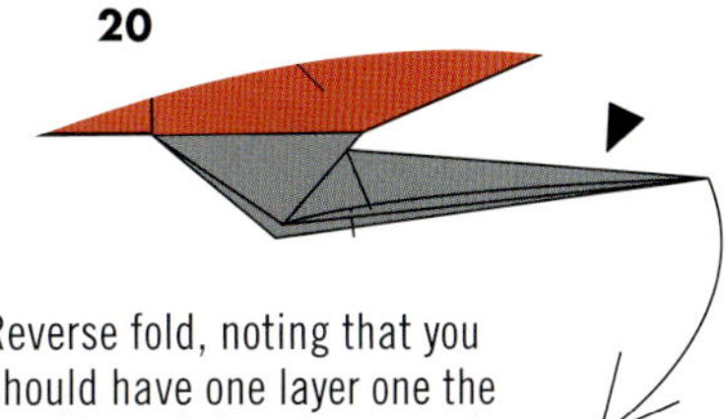

Reverse fold, noting that you should have one layer one the outside and three layers at the bottom.

21

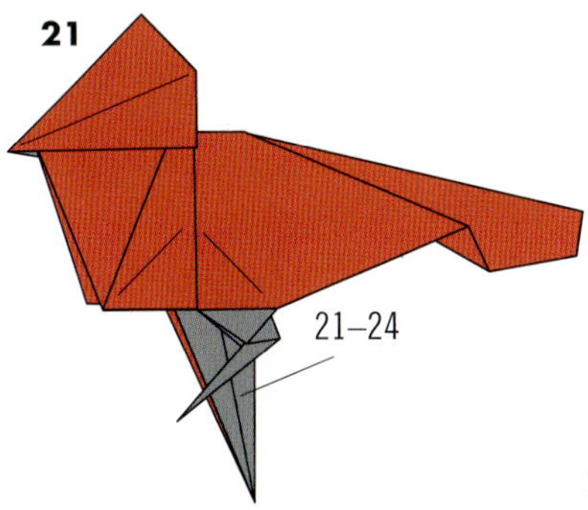

Repeat steps 21–24 behind.

22

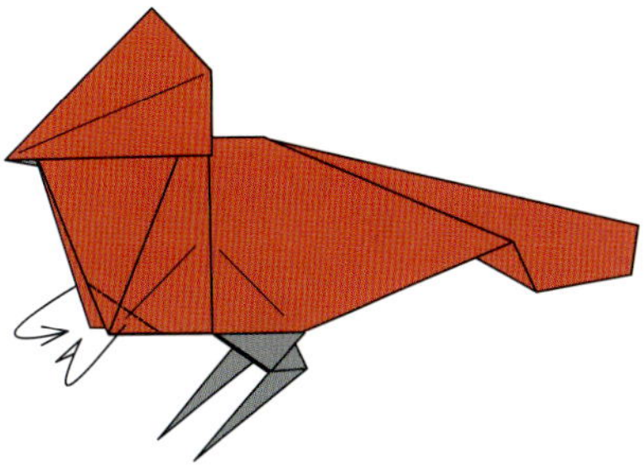

Mountain fold the corners inside.

23

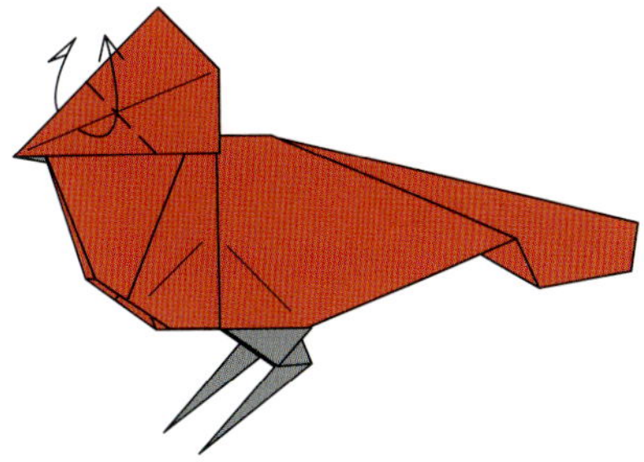

Outside reverse fold.

24

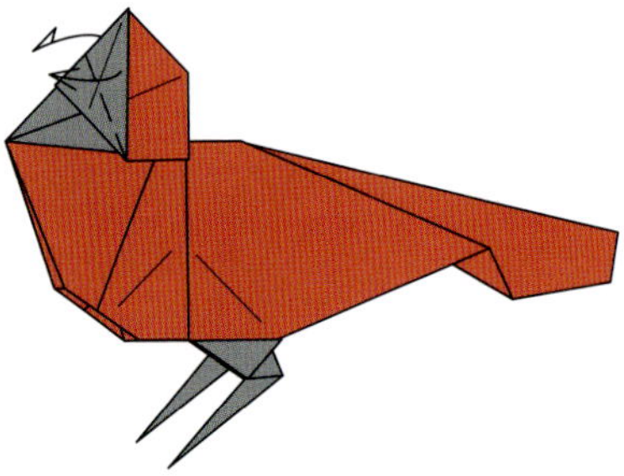

Outside reverse fold.

25

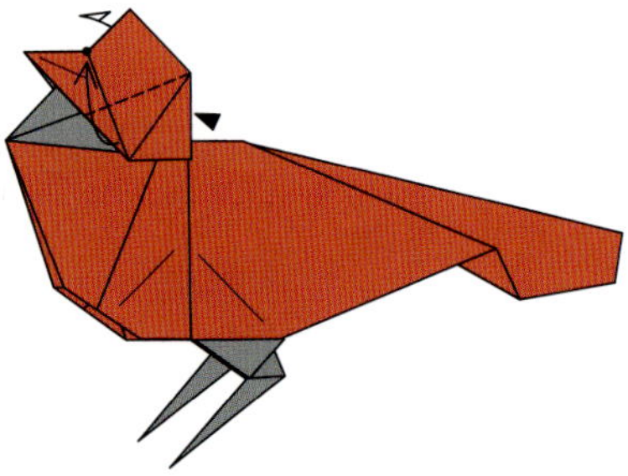

Squash fold both sides.

26

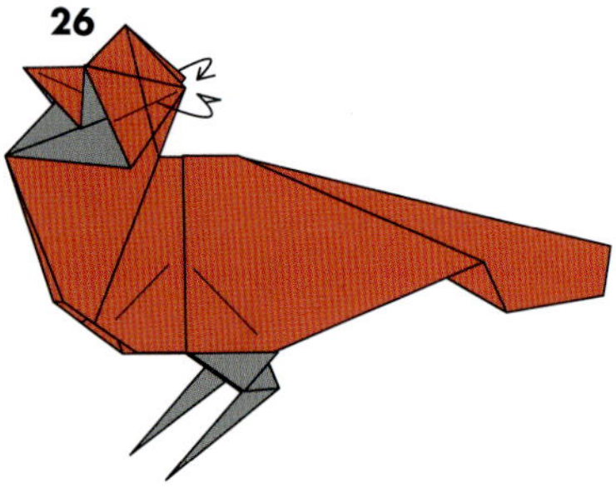

Mountain fold the sides inward.

27

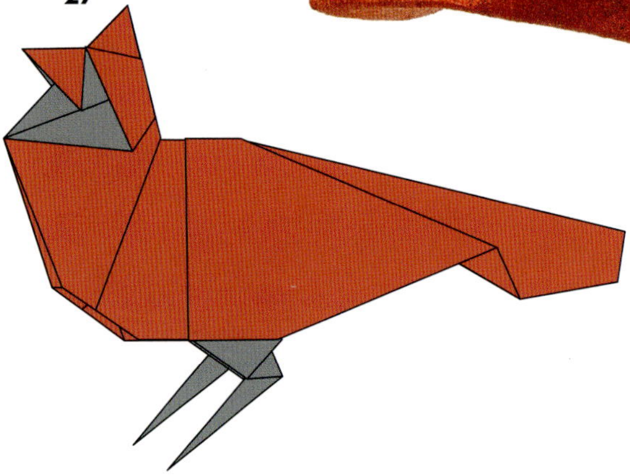

Completed Cardinal.

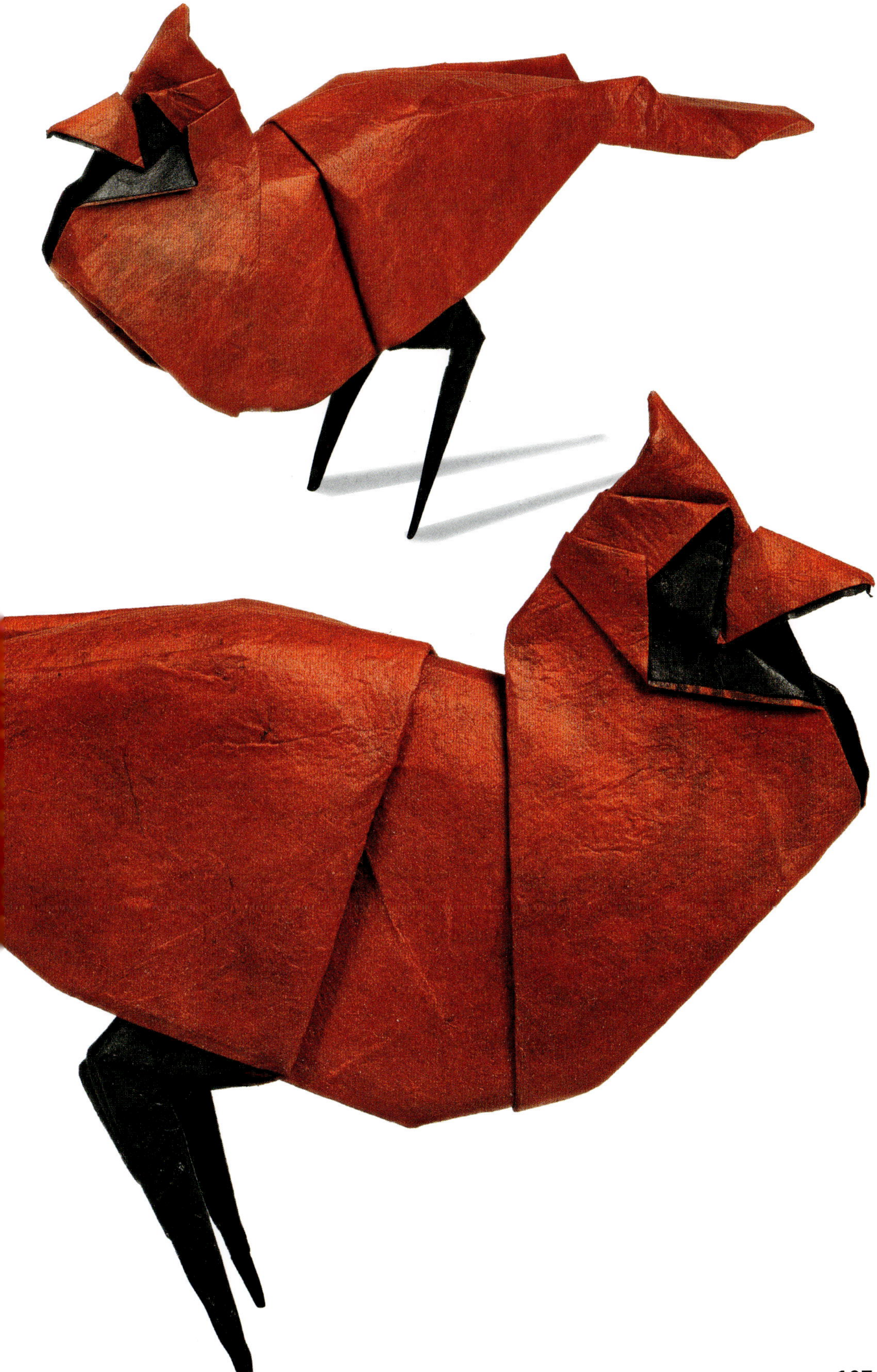

Mother and Child

Bob Neale

Bob Neale is an ordained minister. Check out his bio on page 155 to learn about the connection he sees between origami and religion.

video: *youtu.be/e-p0btm4ndw*

1

Valley fold down a small hem. A quarter inch of a six-inch square wo work well.

2

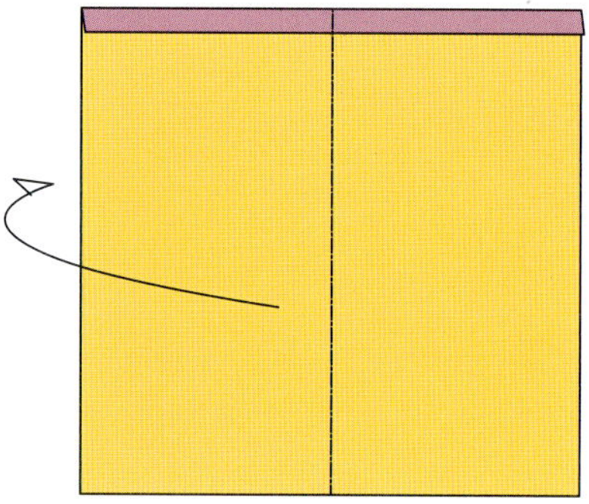

Mountain fold in half.

3

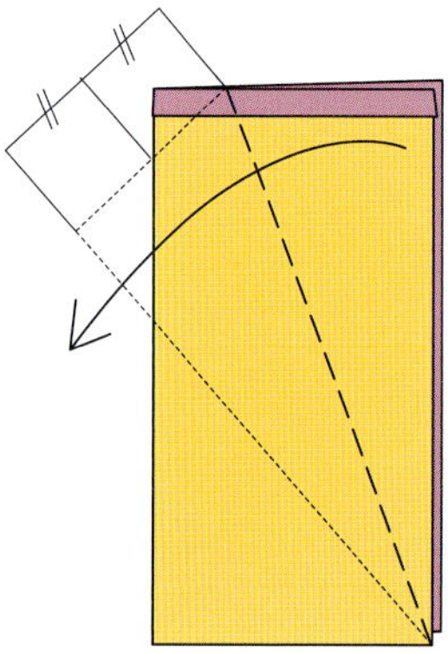

Valley fold, such that the head section hits its midway point.

4

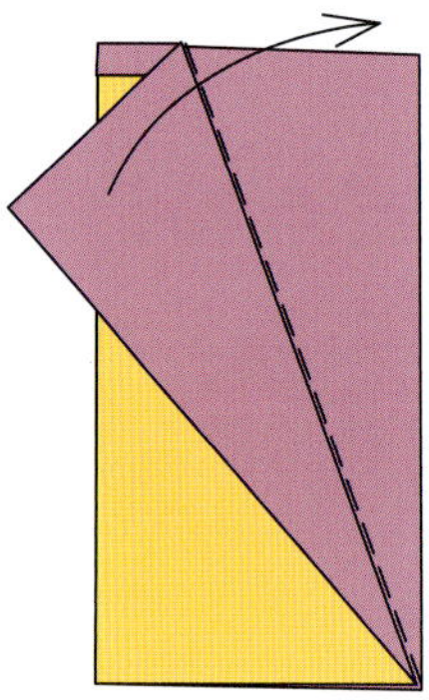

Unfold the last fold.

5

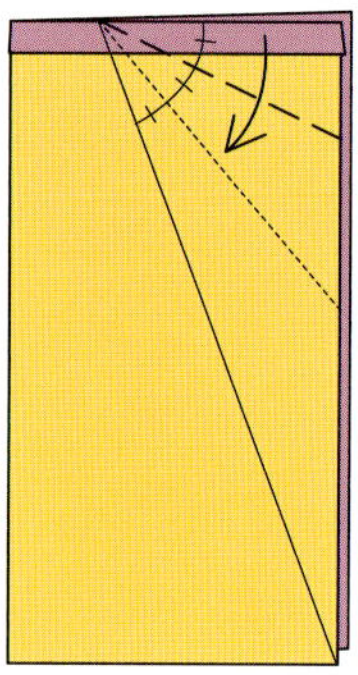

Valley fold in along the indicated angle trisector.

6

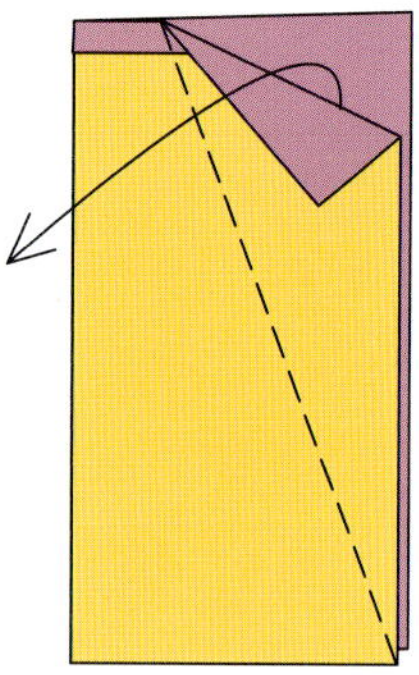

Valley fold along the existing crease.

7

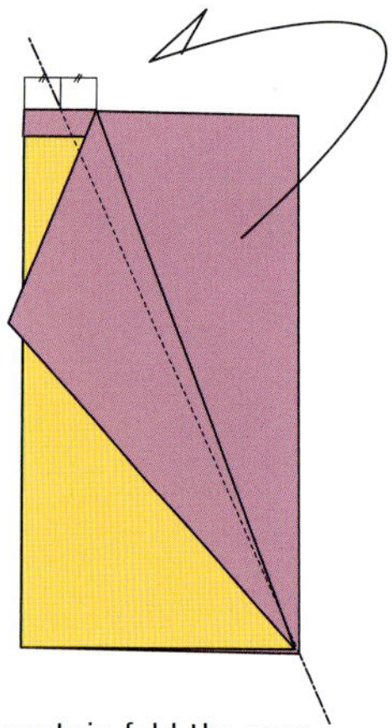

Mountain fold the rear section, noting how the fold starts from the midpoint of the head.

9

Completed Mother and Child.

8

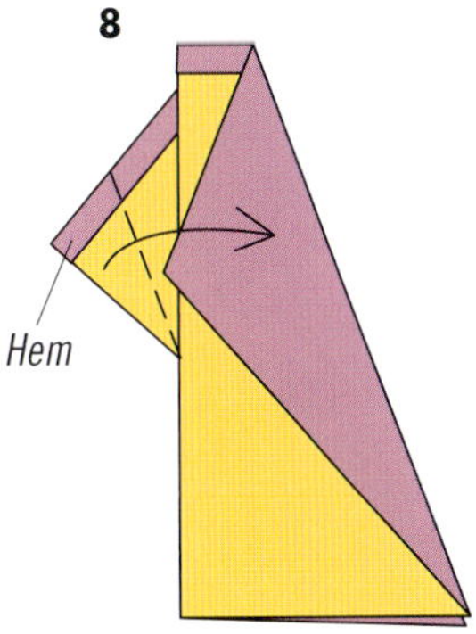

Valley fold the flap over, adjusting the angle so that the indicated hem locks into the arm.

Giant Panda

Bernie Peyton

Find out where Bernie cheers people up with origami on page 152.

video: *youtu.be/OfhPcaYXb90*

1

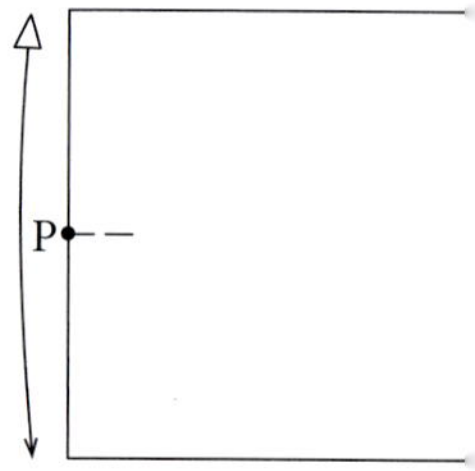

Start with the white side facing up. Valley crease t
midline of the left side at point P.

2

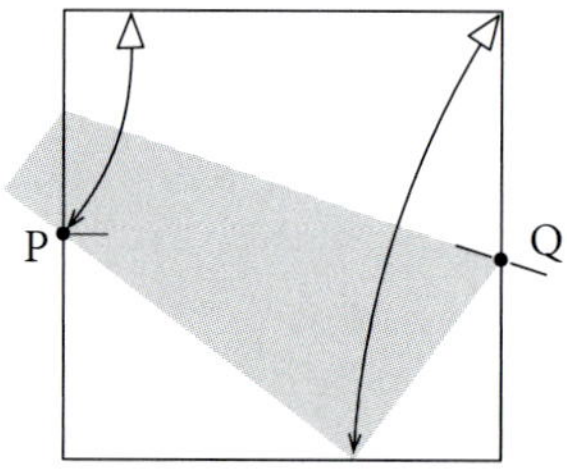

Place the top edge on point P and the top right corner on the bottom edge. Crease the right edge at point Q and unfold.

3

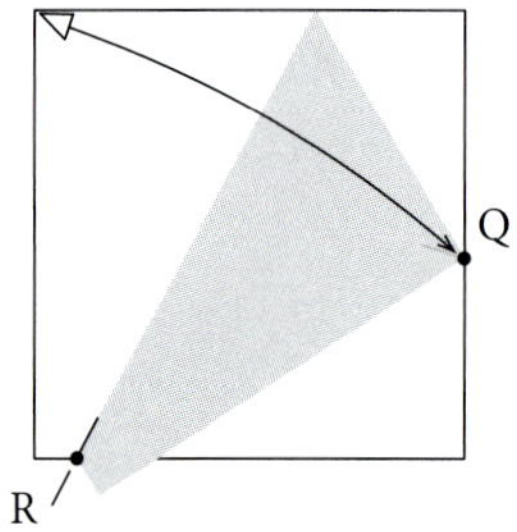

Bring the top left corner to point Q. Crease the bottom edge at point R.

4

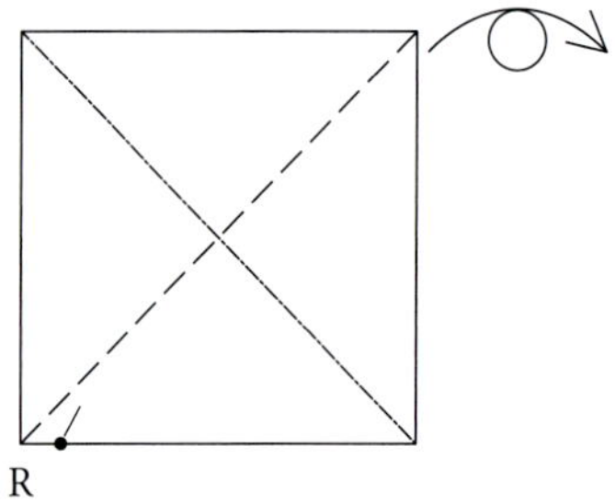

Valley and mountain crease diagonals and turn the model over side-to-side.

5

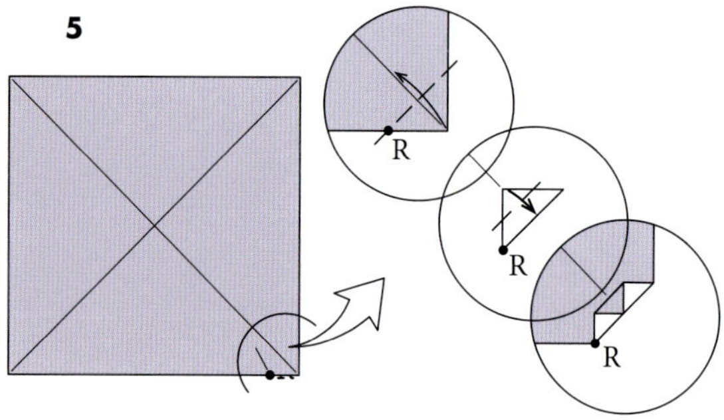

Valley fold a corner through point R and back to the folded edge.

6

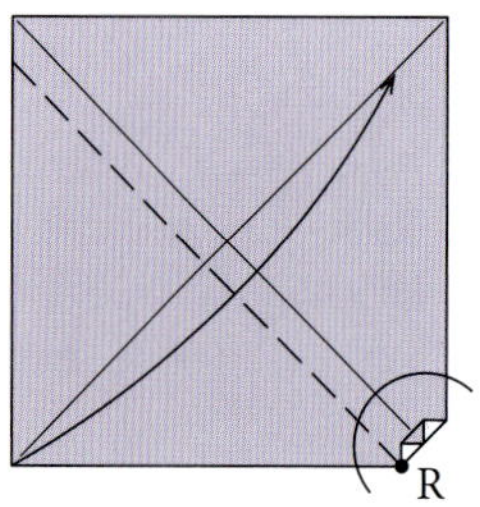

Valley fold through point R.

7

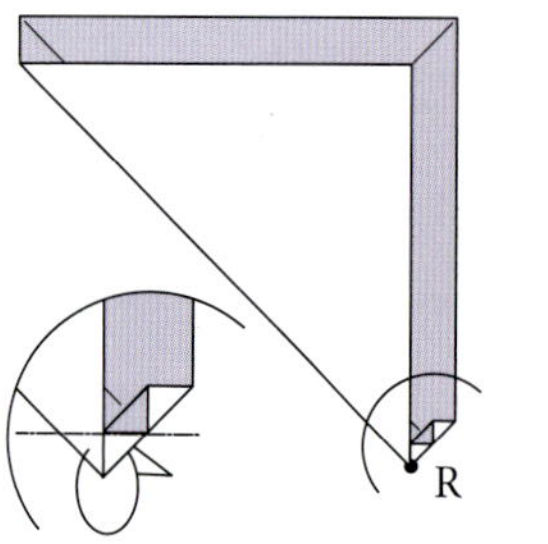

Mountain fold along a raw edge.

8

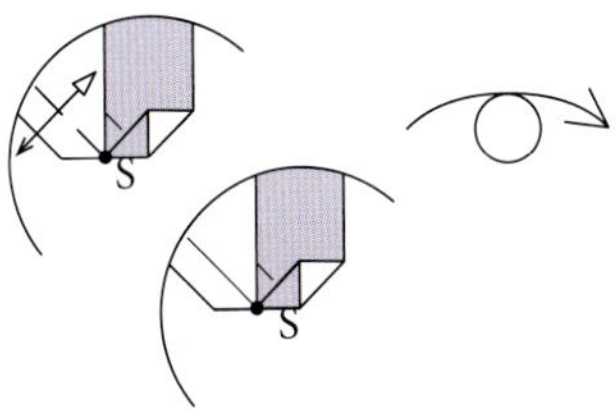

Mark the raw edge at point S with a crease.

9

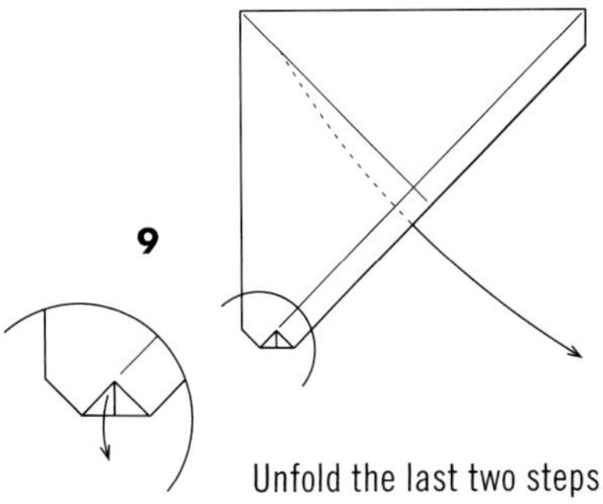

Unfold the last two steps.

10

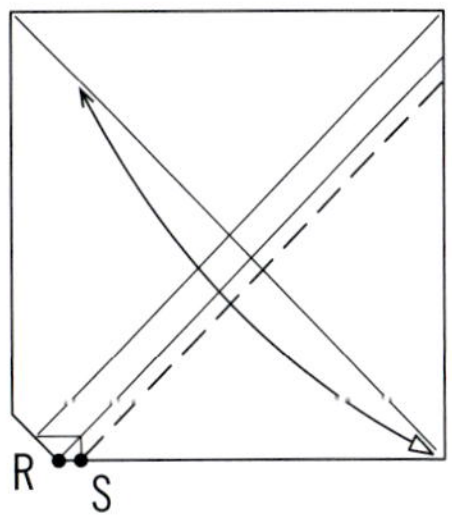

Valley fold and unfold through point S.

11

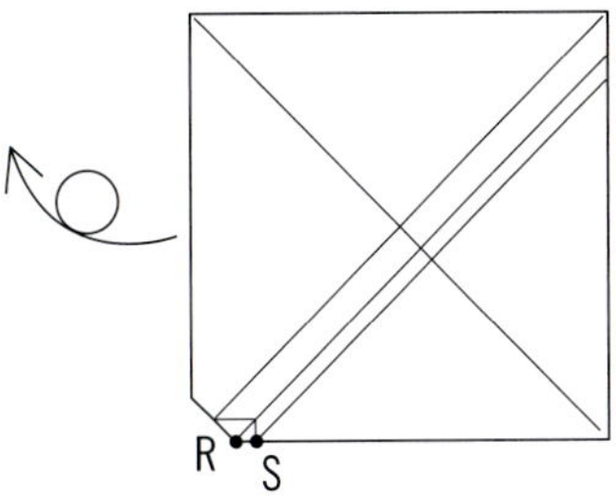

Turn the model over side-to-side.

12

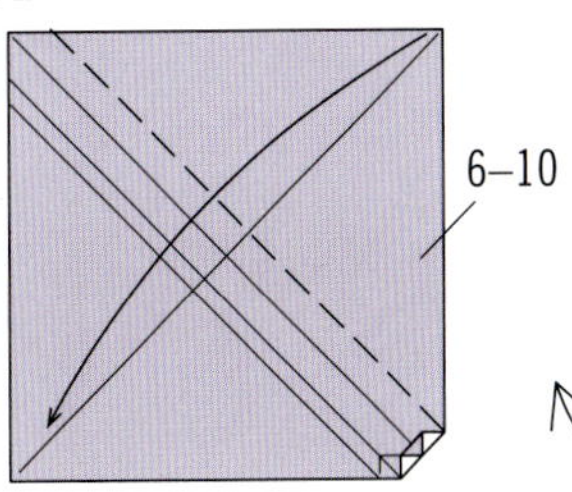

Repeat steps 6–10 on the top right side.

13

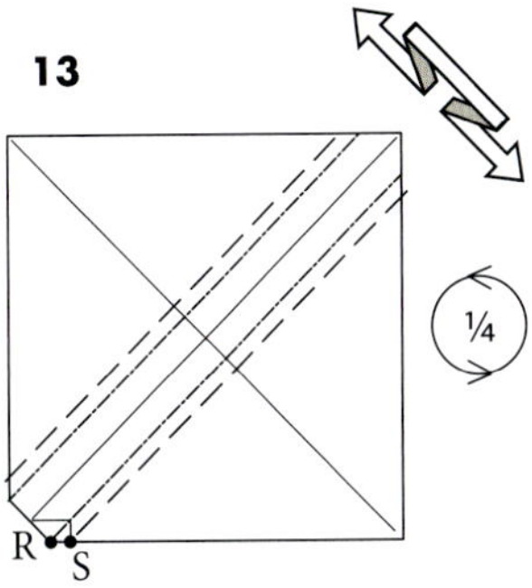

Pleat on existing creases and rotate the model 45 degrees counterclockwise.

14

Mountain fold the top corner behind. Valley fold the lower corners.

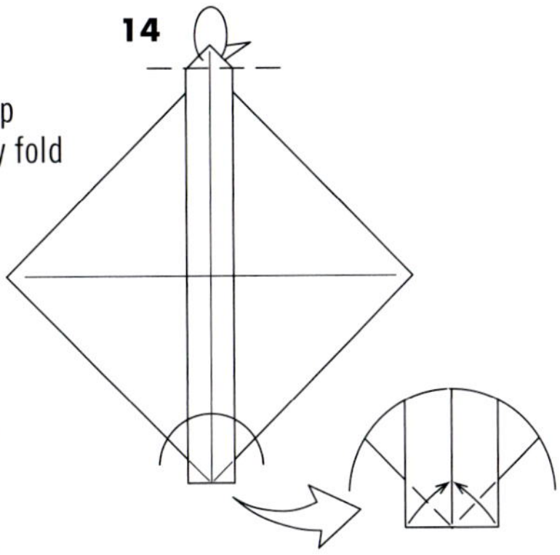

15

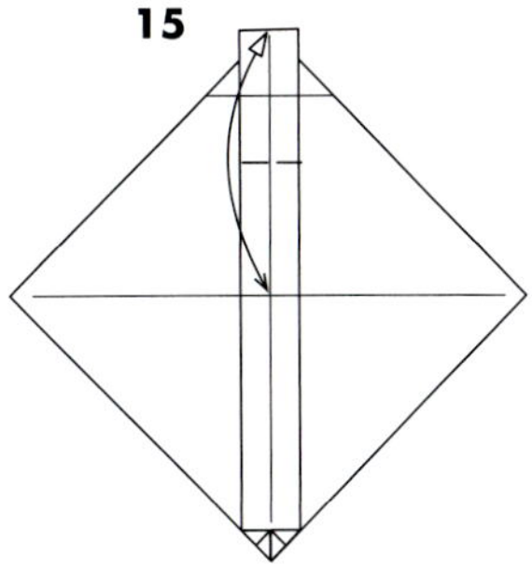

Bisect the midline with a small crease.

16

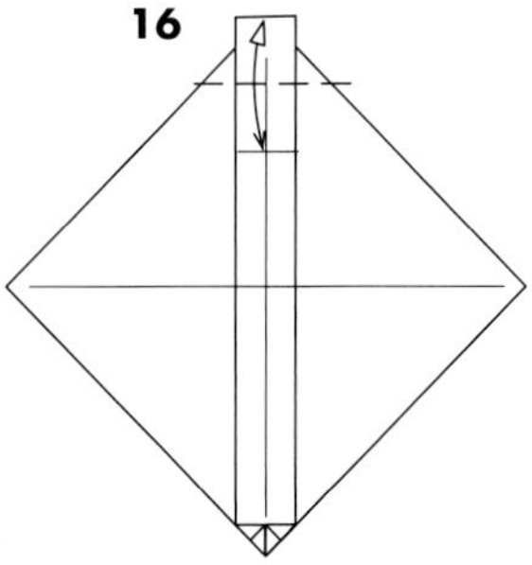

Bisect the distance once more with a valley crease.

17

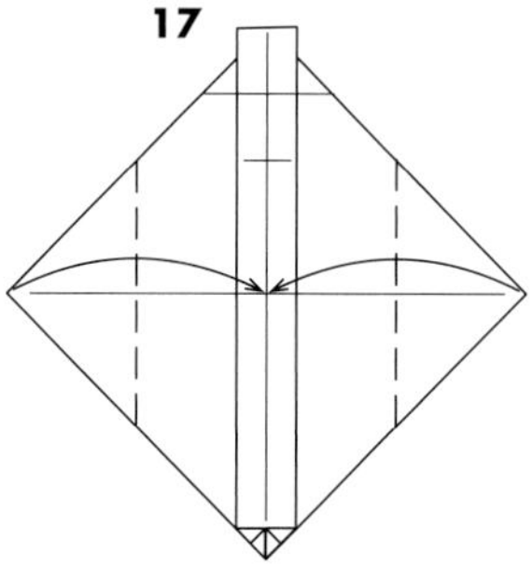

Valley fold the corners to the midline.

18

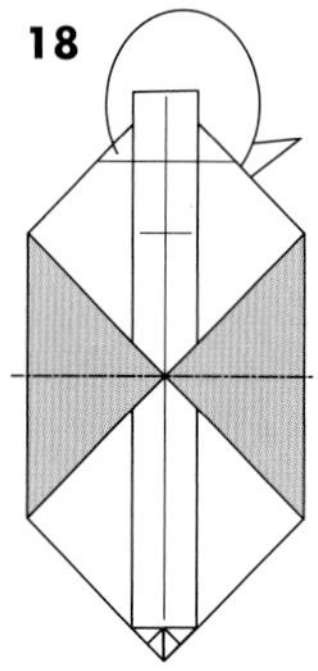

Mountain fold the model in half.

19

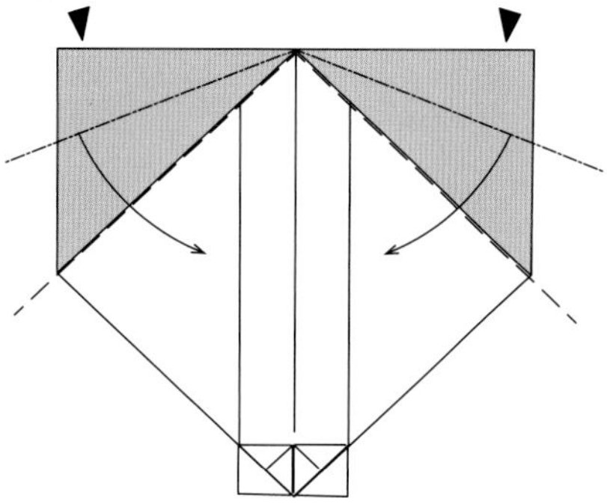

Squash fold.

20

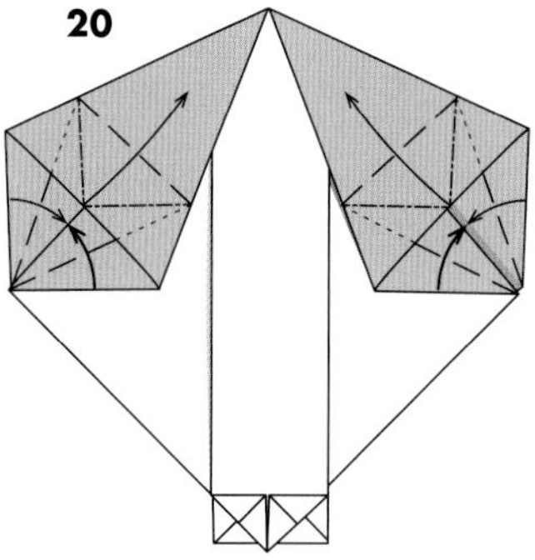

Petal fold the front legs.

21

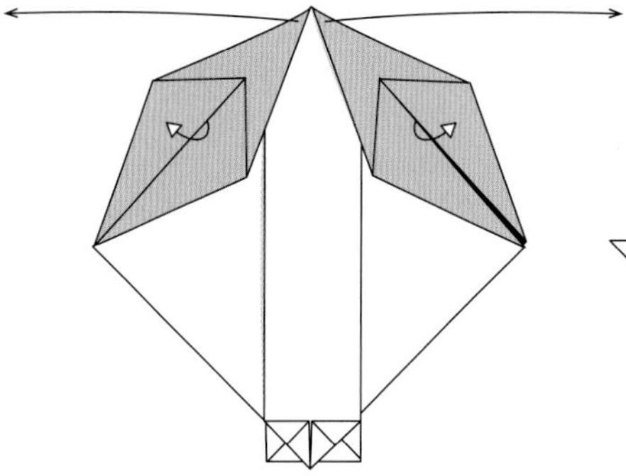

Unfold legs completely.

22

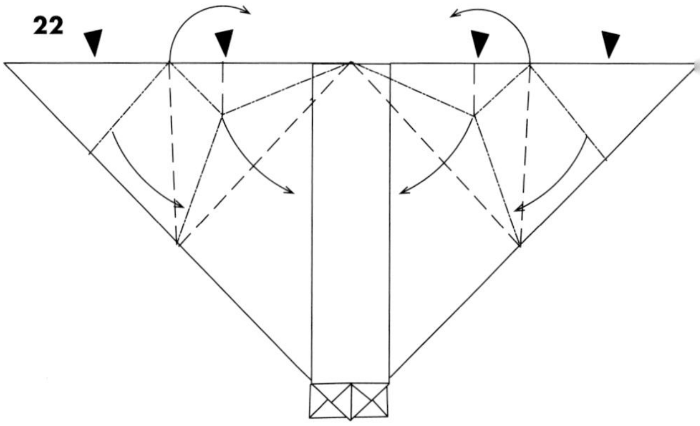

Collapse legs.

25

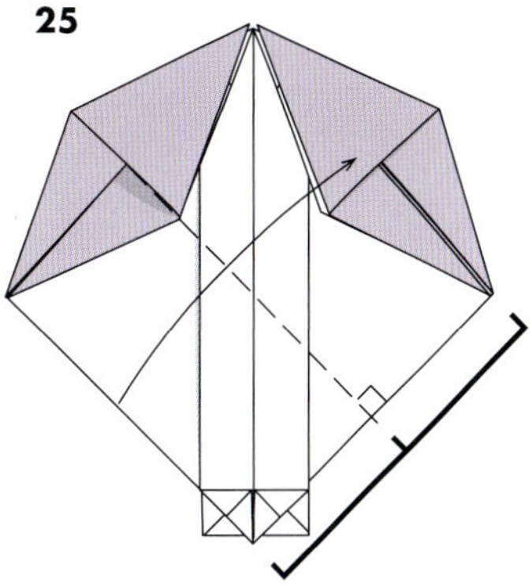

Valley fold an edge up.

26

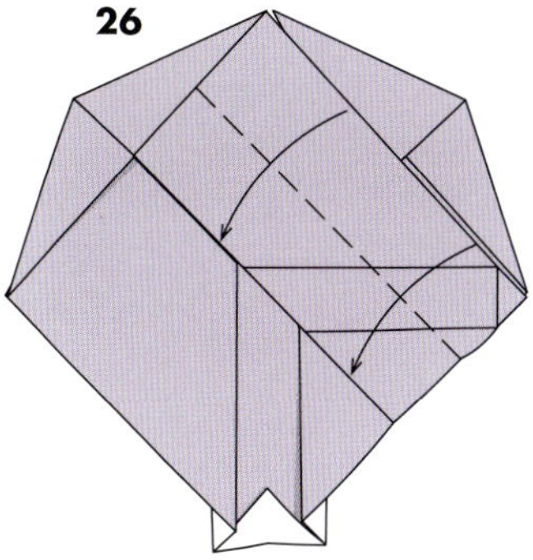

Valley fold the edge back down.

27

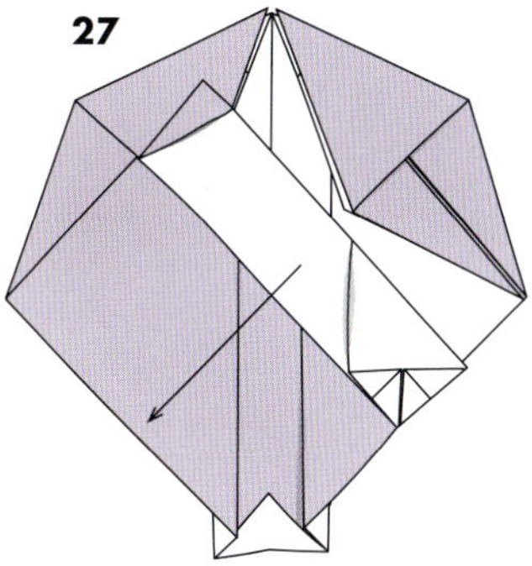

Undo the last two folds.

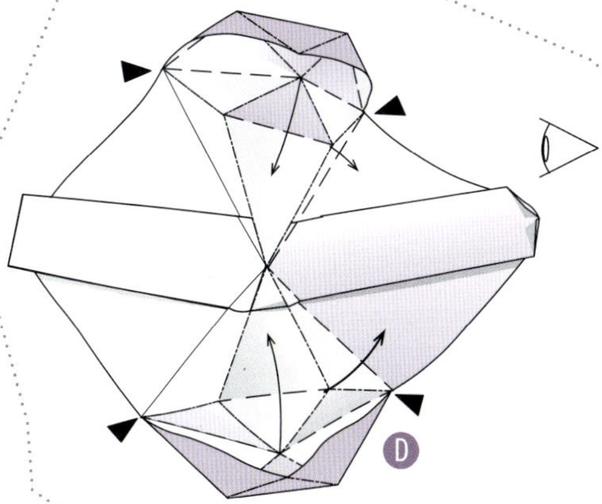

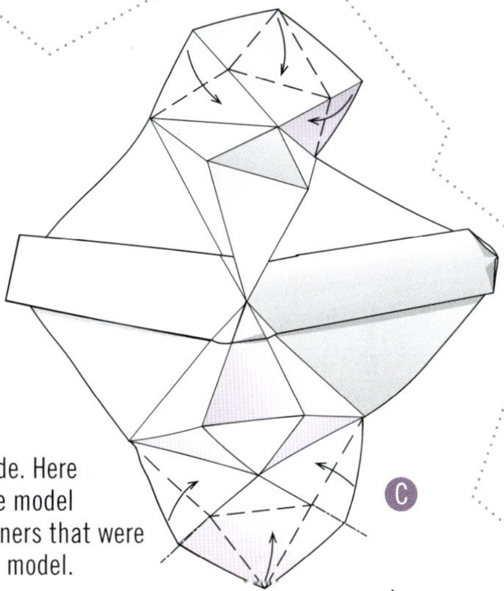

Wrap the top layer to the other side. Here is an easy way to do it. Unfold the model partially. Outside reverse fold corners that were petal folded in step. Collapse the model.

23

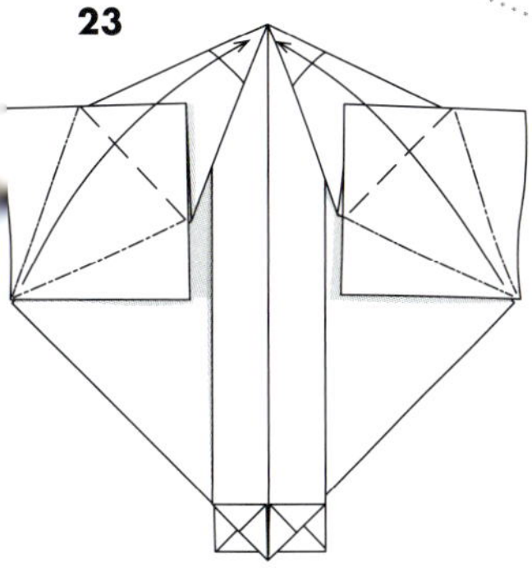

Petal fold.

24

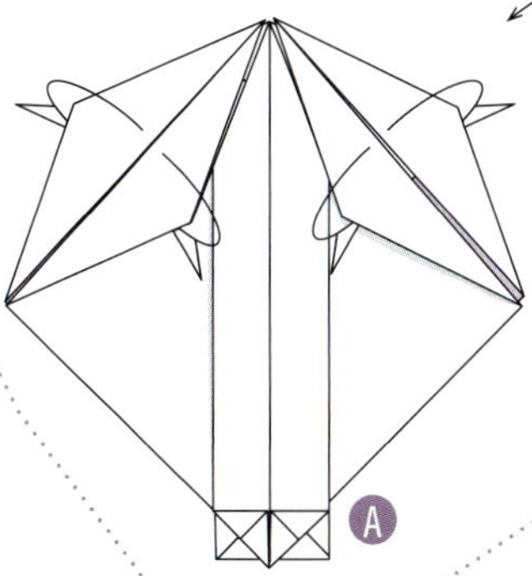

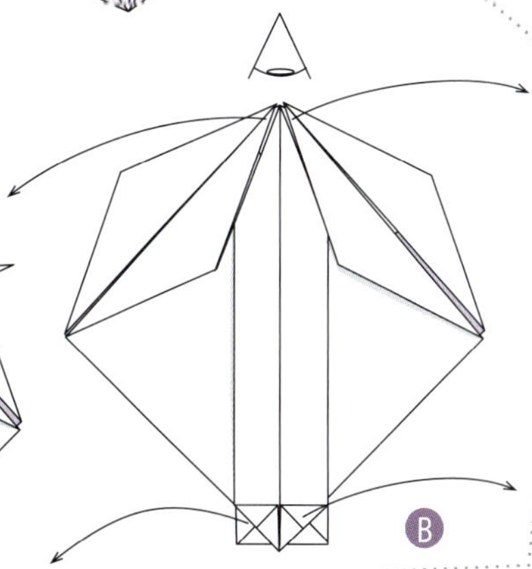

28

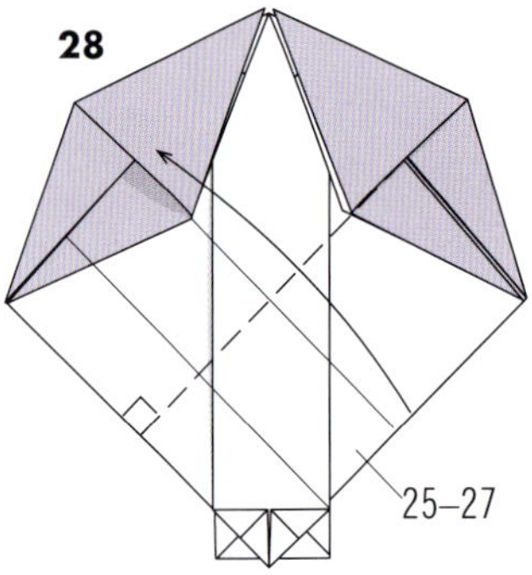

Repeat the last 3 steps on the right side.

29

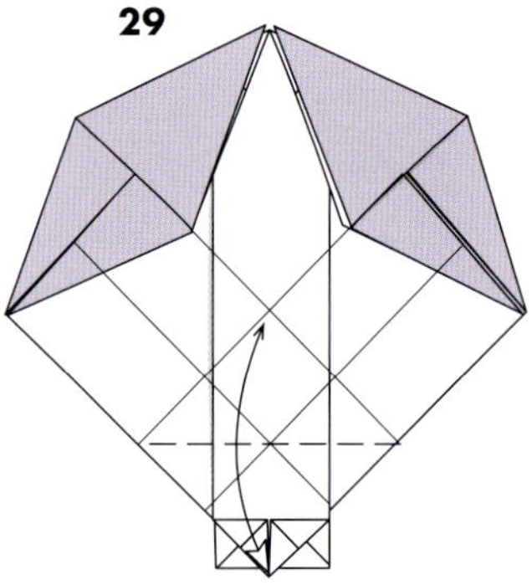

Valley fold and unfold the top layer.

30

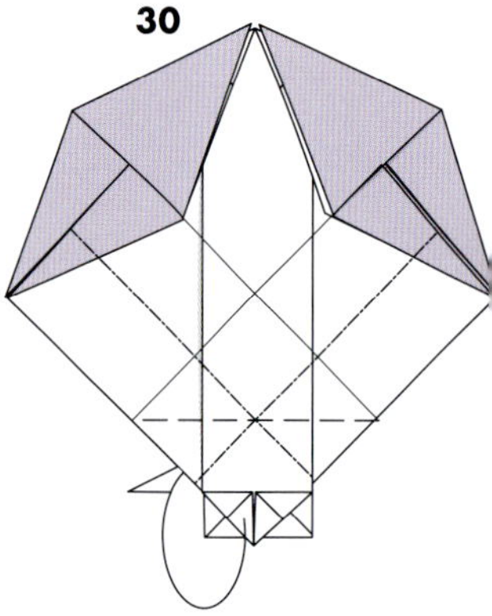

Preliminary fold the top layer (f
the corner under).

31

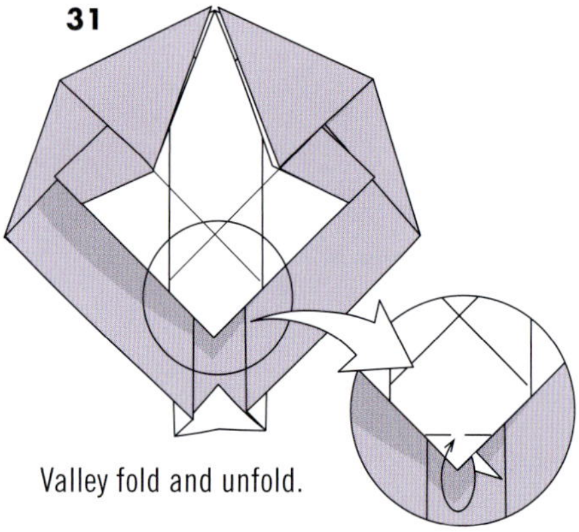

Valley fold and unfold.

32

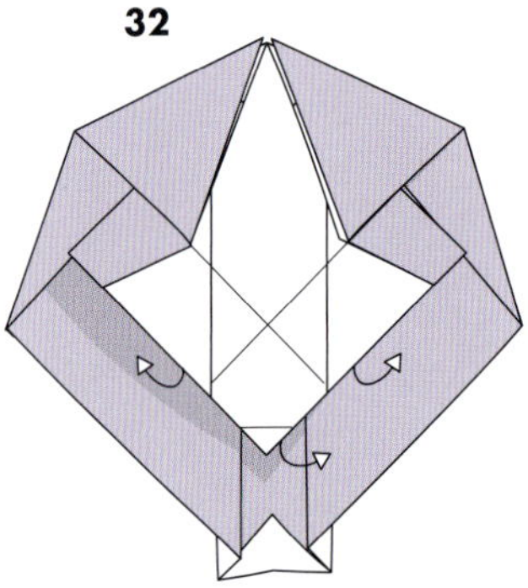

Undo the preliminary fold.

33

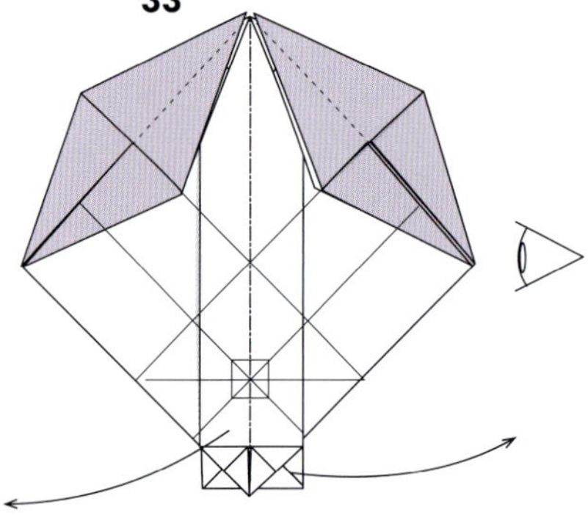

Open the bottom and squash symmetrically.

34

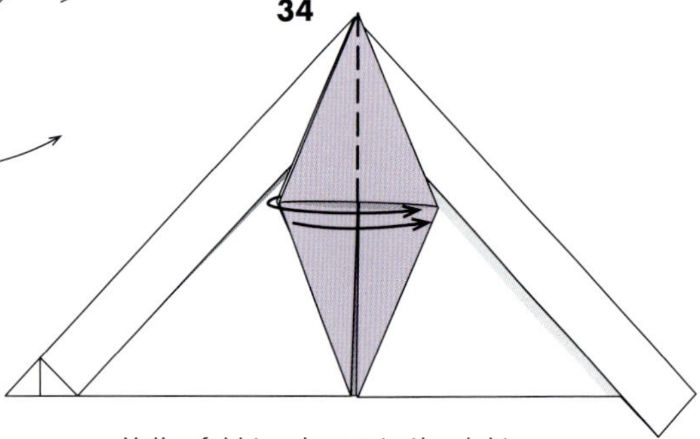

Valley fold two layers to the right.

35

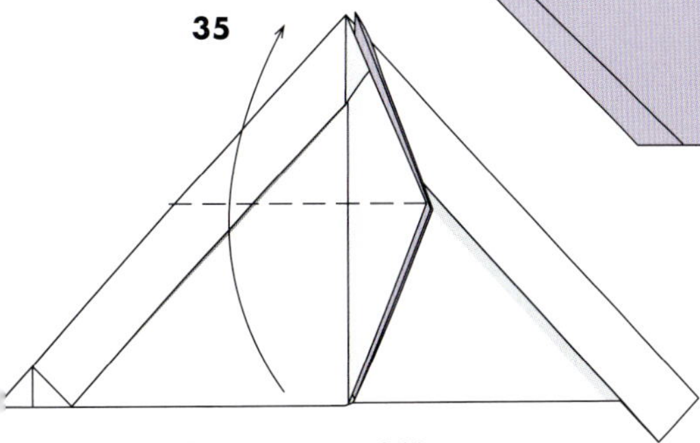

Outside reverse fold.

36

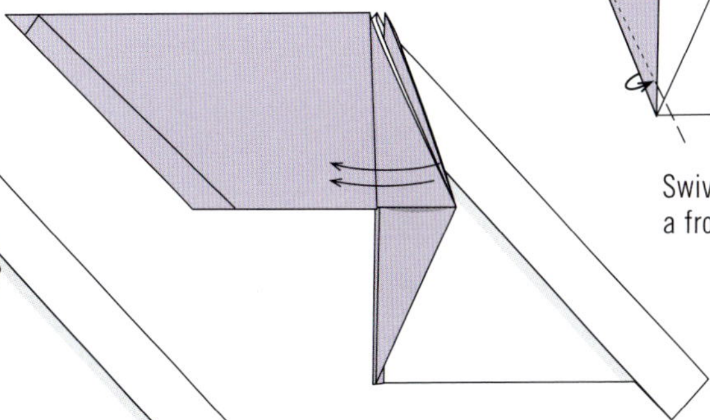

Valley fold two flaps to the left.

37

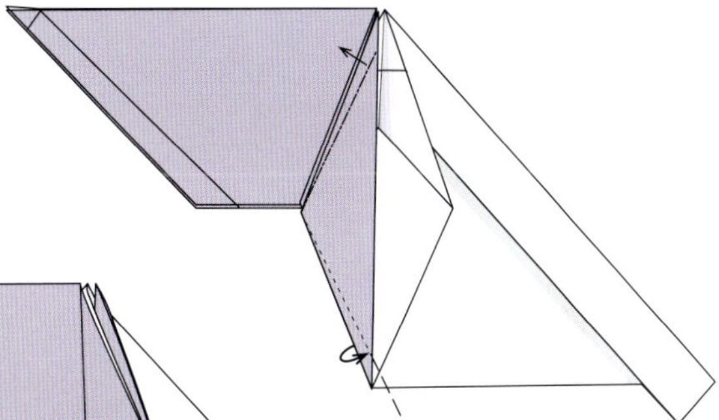

Swivel fold to widen part of a front foot.

38

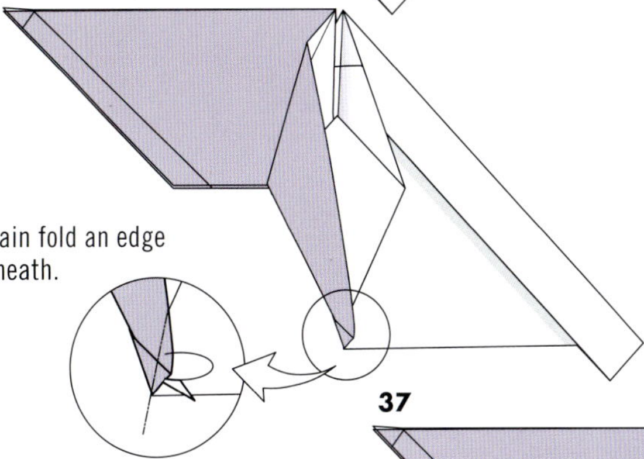

Mountain fold an edge underneath.

39

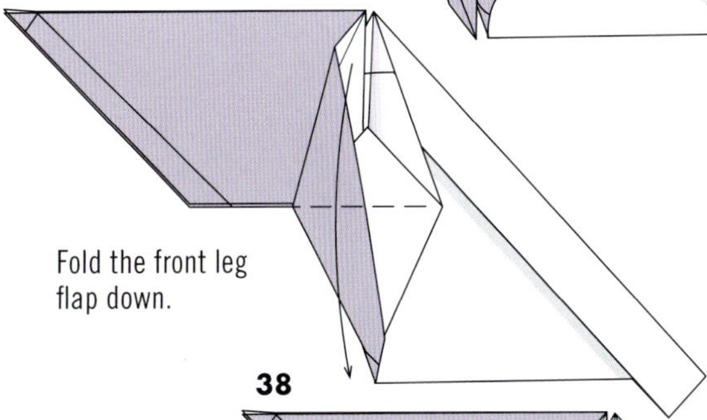

Fold the front leg flap down.

40

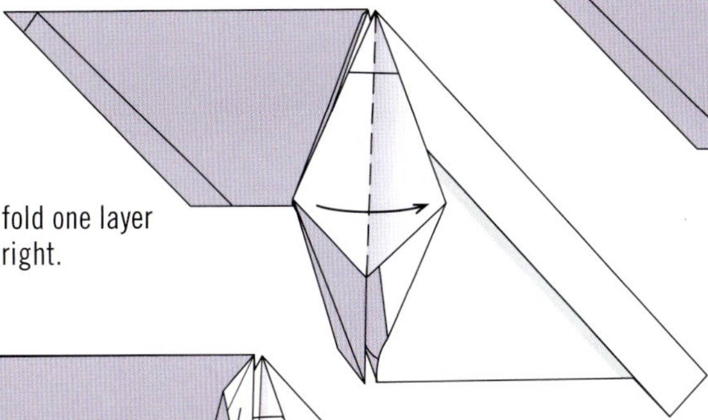

Valley fold one layer to the right.

41

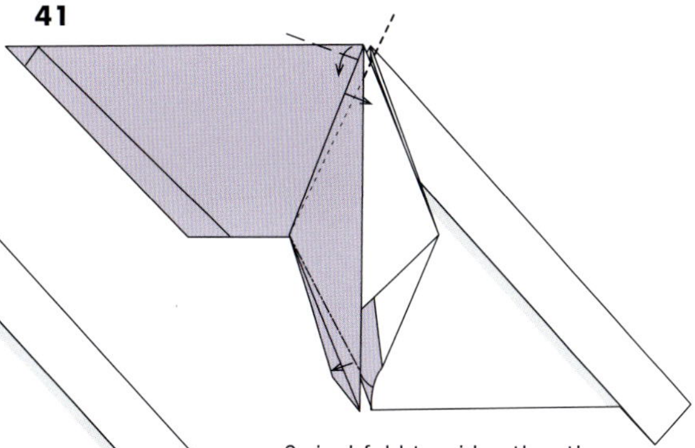

Swivel fold to widen the other half of a front foot.

42

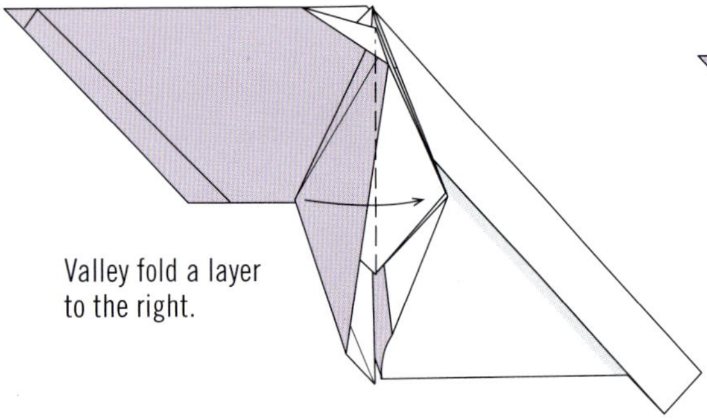

Valley fold a layer to the right.

43

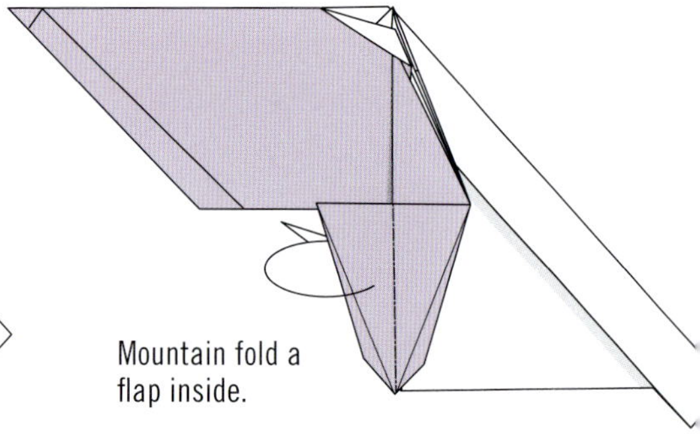

Mountain fold a flap inside.

44

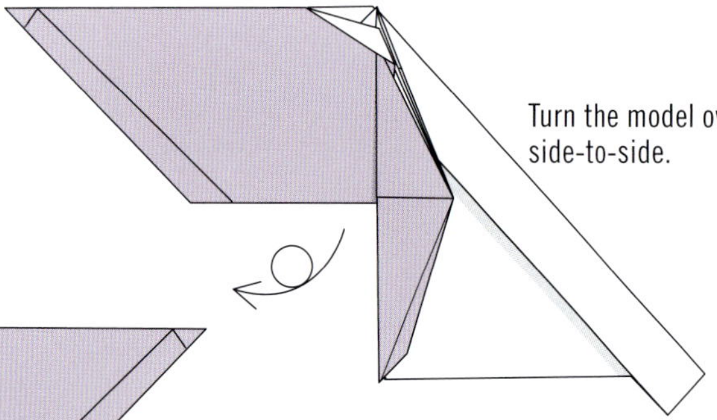

Turn the model over side-to-side.

45

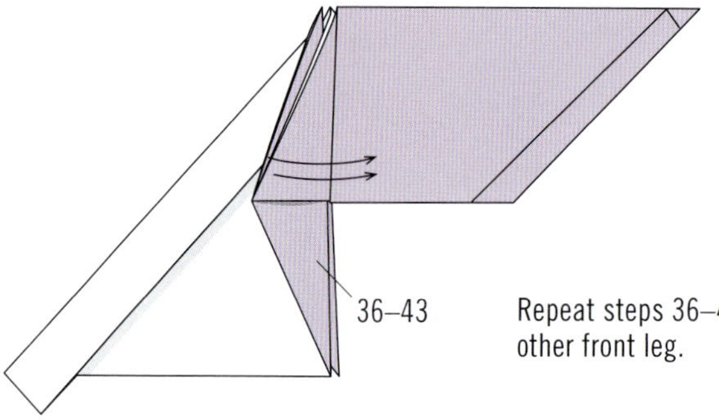

Repeat steps 36–43 on the other front leg.

46

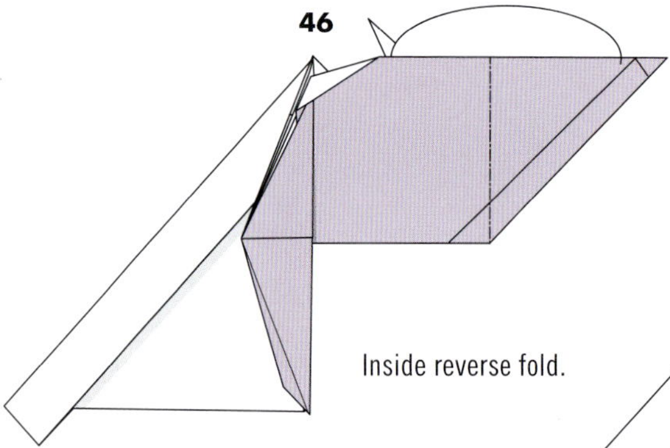

Inside reverse fold.

47

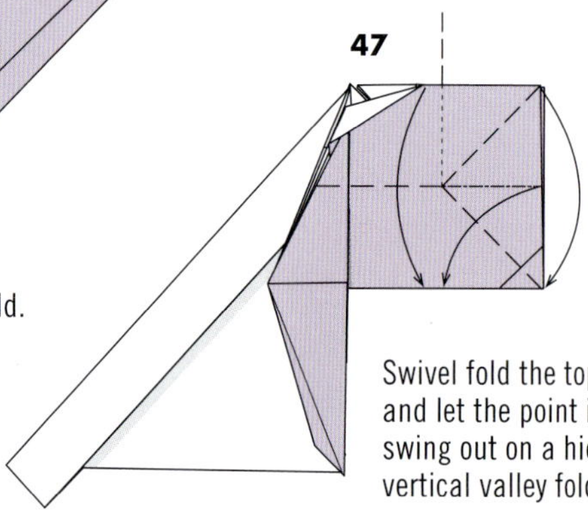

Swivel fold the top layer, and let the point inside swing out on a hidden vertical valley fold.

48

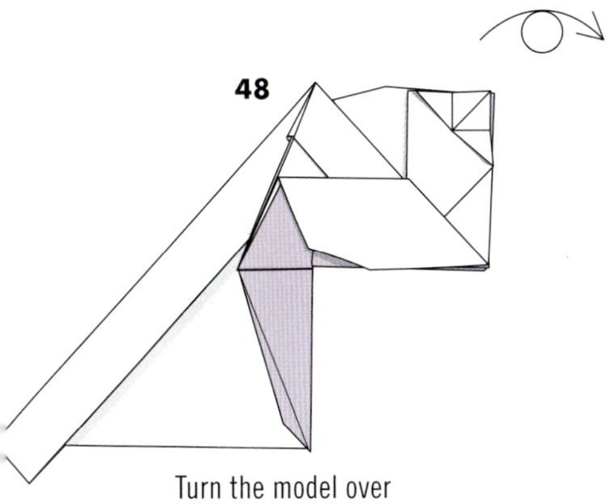

Turn the model over side-to-side.

49

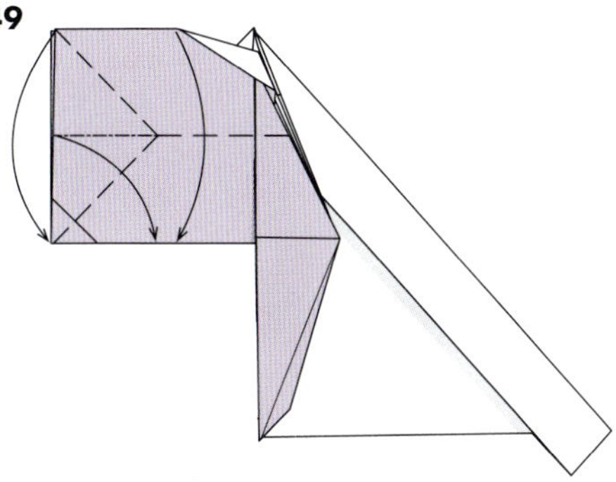

Swivel fold the top layer on this side.

50

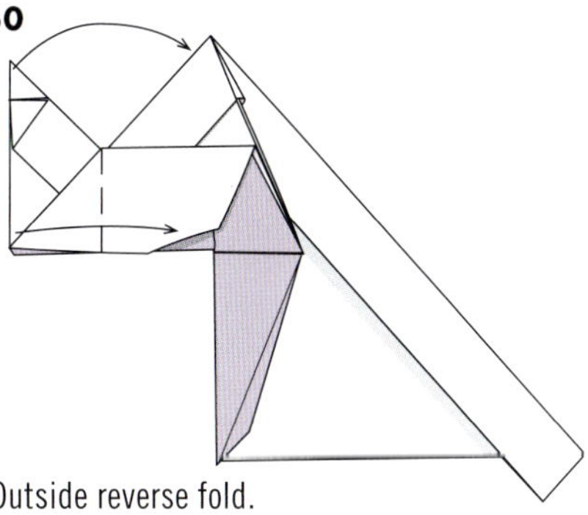

Outside reverse fold.

51

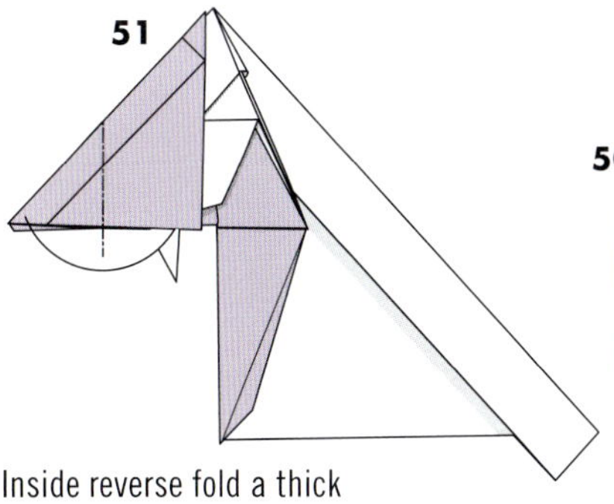

Inside reverse fold a thick point inside.

52

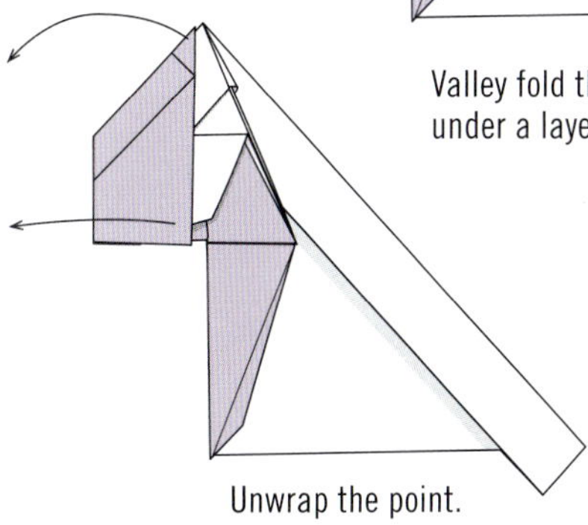

Unwrap the point.

53

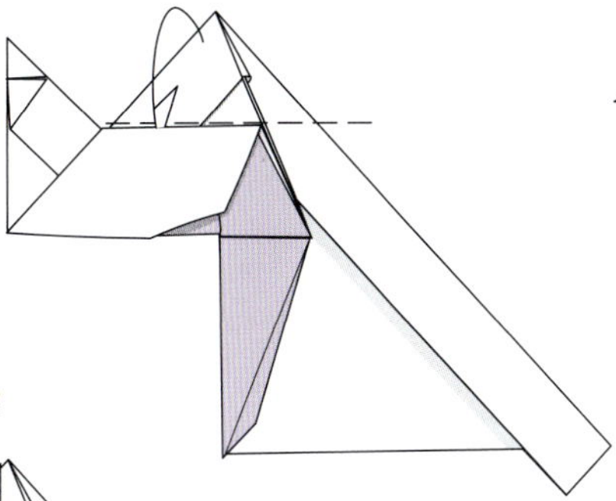

Valley fold the top point under a layer.

54

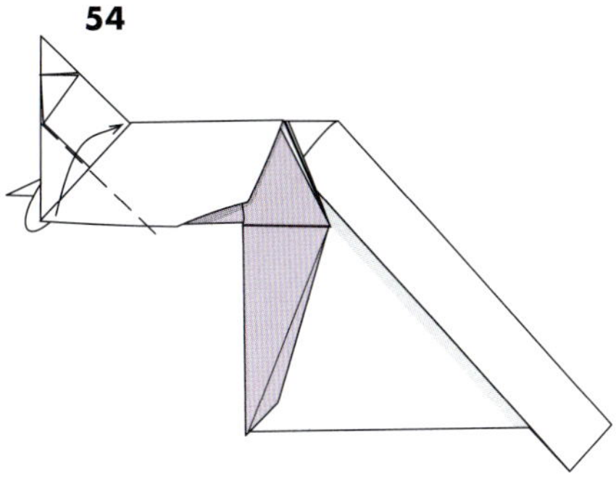

Valley fold corners up on both sides.

55

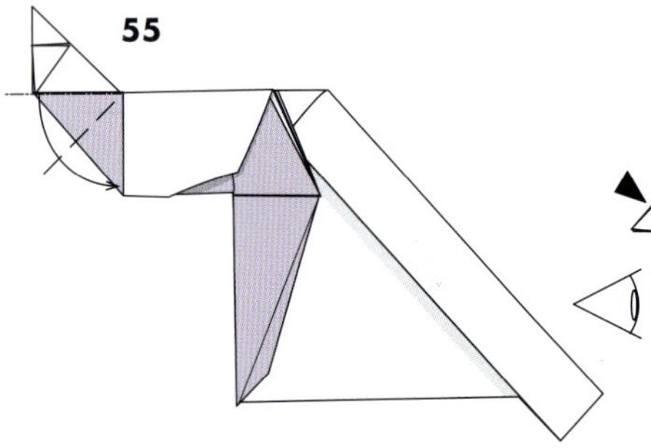

Outside reverse fold the head.

56

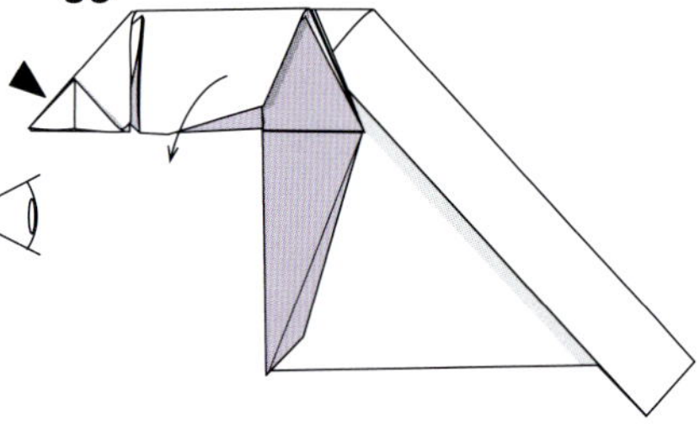

Flatten the head and let the white sides of the neck flare outward. Next view is of the front of the head.

57

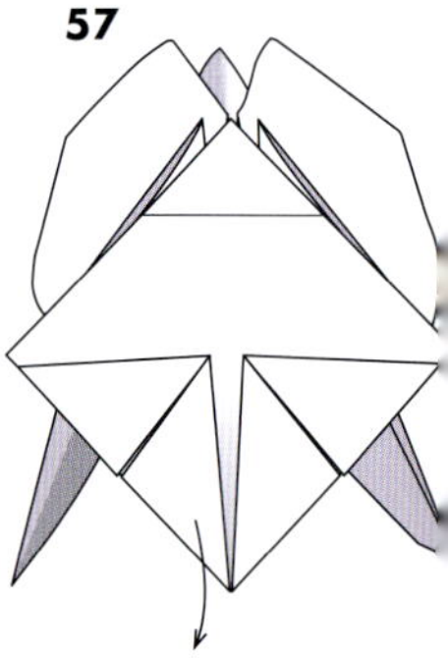

Pull the head out.

58

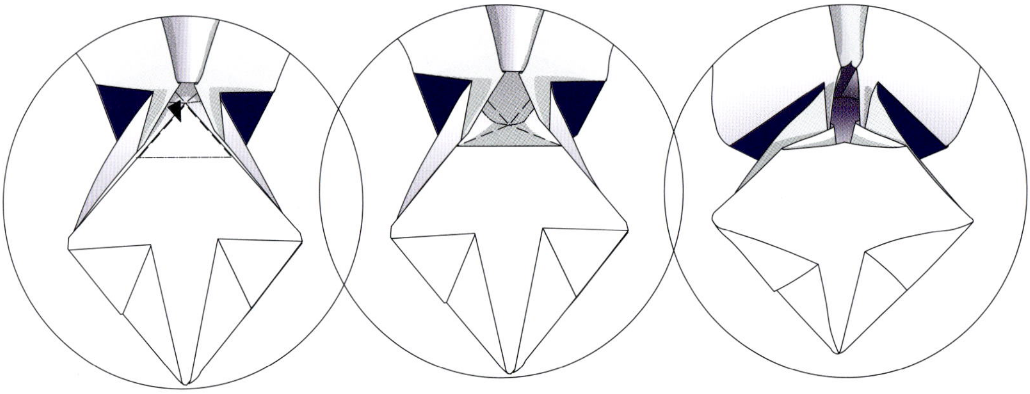

Open-sink the top of the head on the crease of step 31, and then push the head back into place.

59

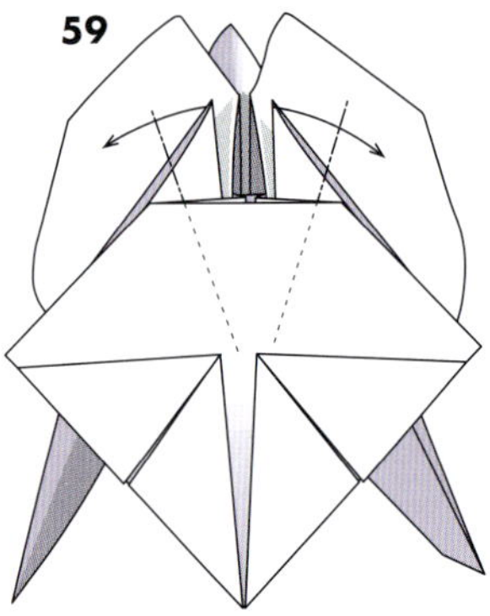

Inside reverse fold the ears.

60

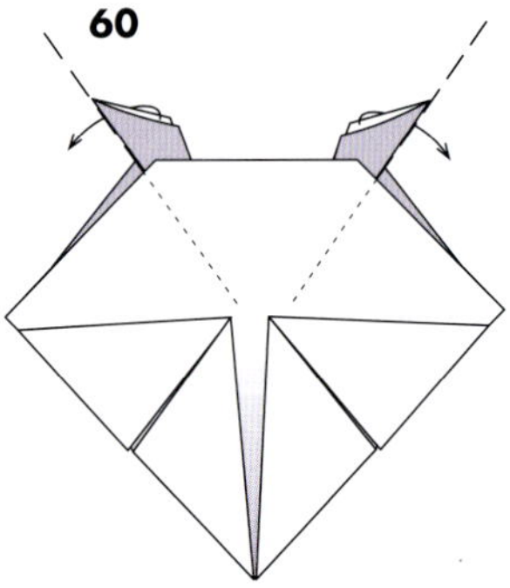

Valley fold the back layer of the ears to open them.

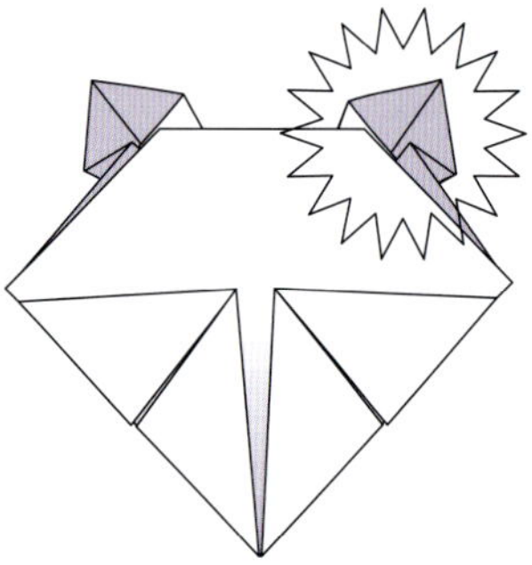

X-Ray view of an optional step.

61

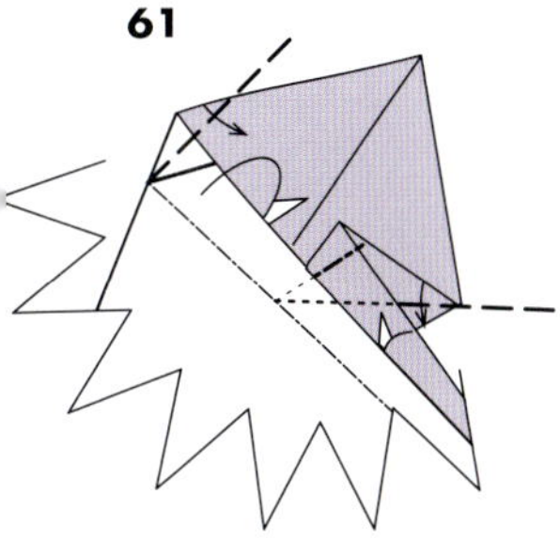

Swivel fold edges of each ear.

62

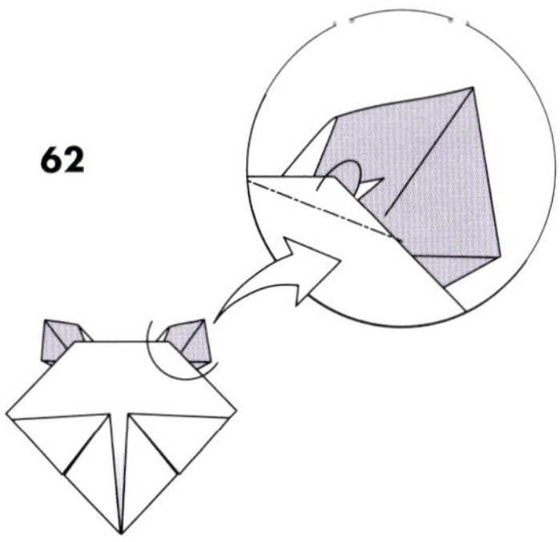

Round the top of the head at each ear with a small mountain fold.

63

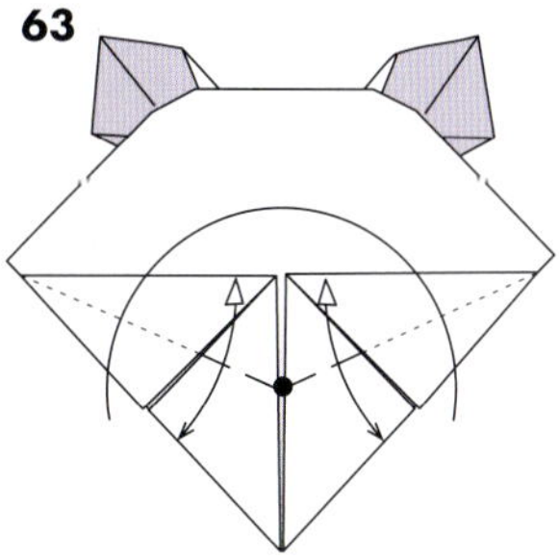

Mark the edges of the eye flaps (dot).

64

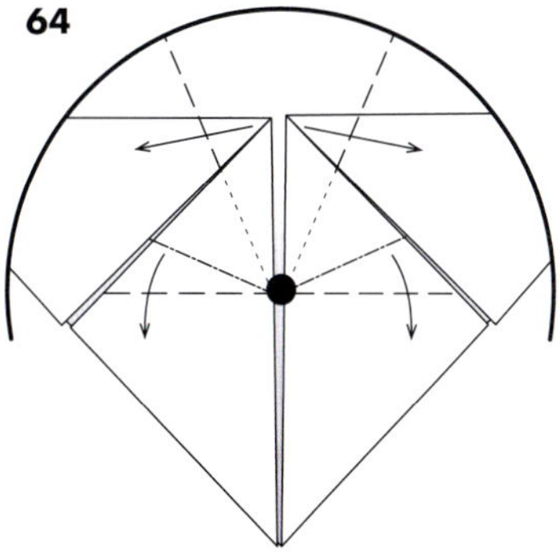

Change the creases of the last step to mountain folds and crimp the eye flaps.

65

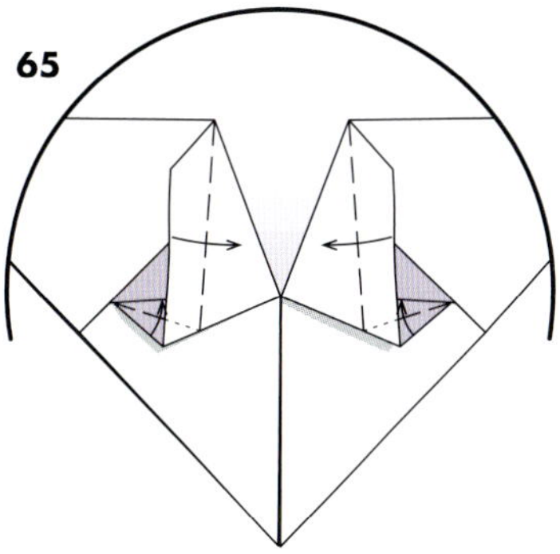

Swivel fold eyes.

66

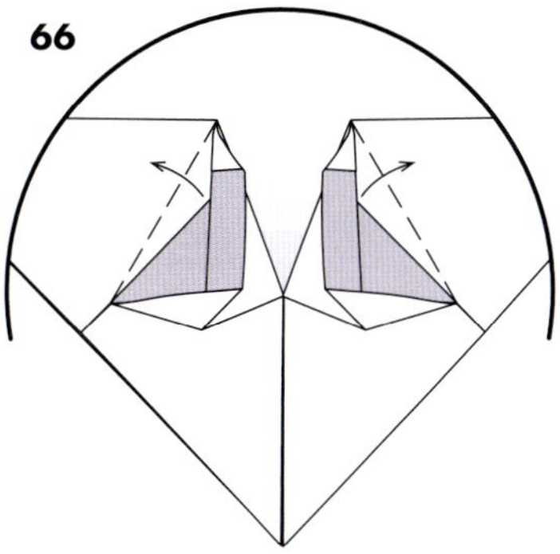

Pull out trapped paper to open the eyes further.

67

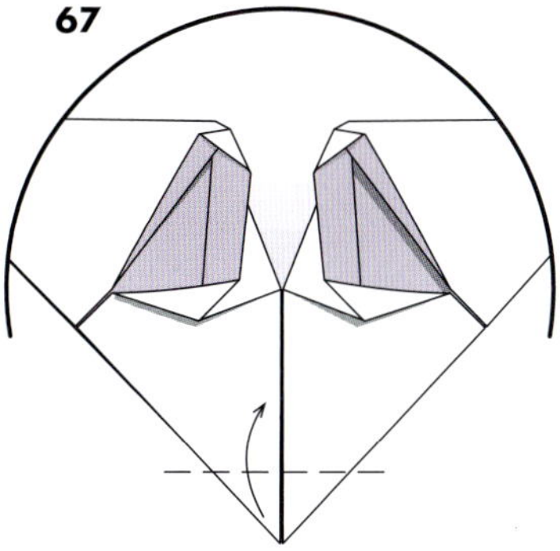

Valley fold the nose up.

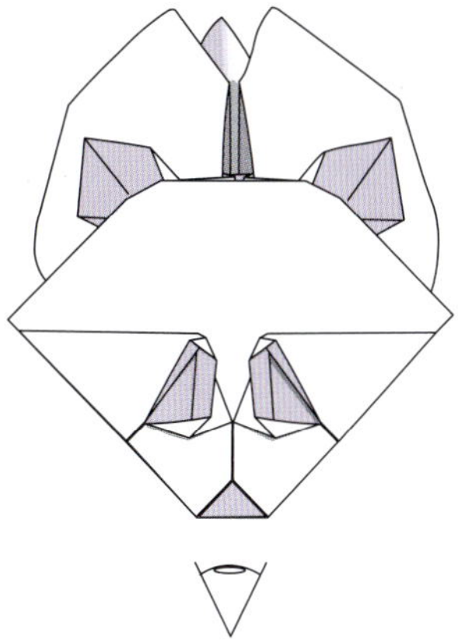

68

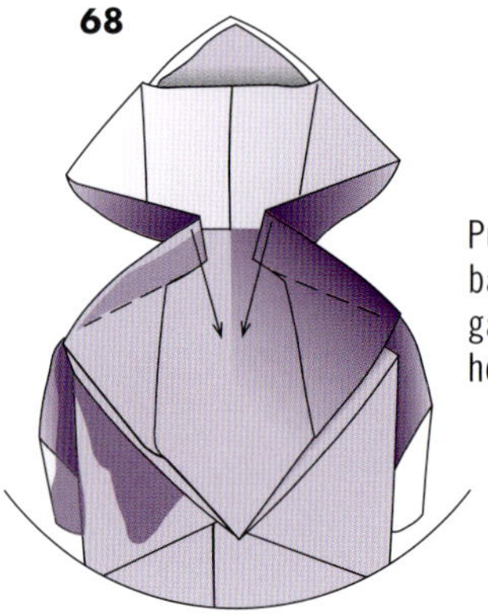

Push the ridges back to close the gap between the head and neck.

69

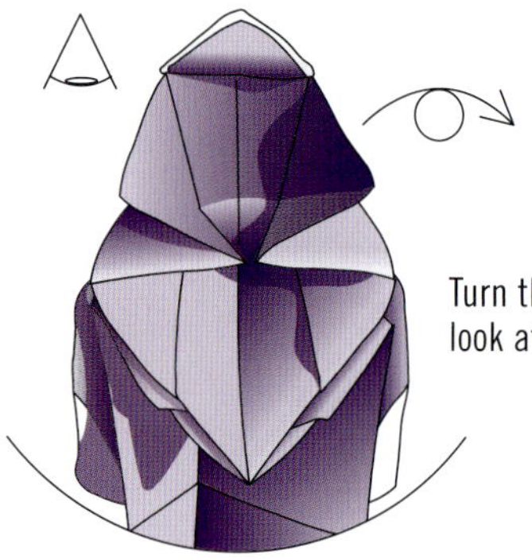

Turn the model to look at the head.

70

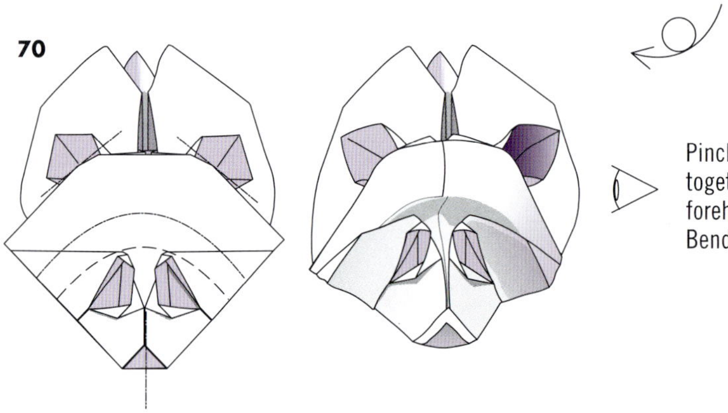

Pinch the sides of the nose together and pleat it into the forehead on curved creases. Bend the ears forward.

71

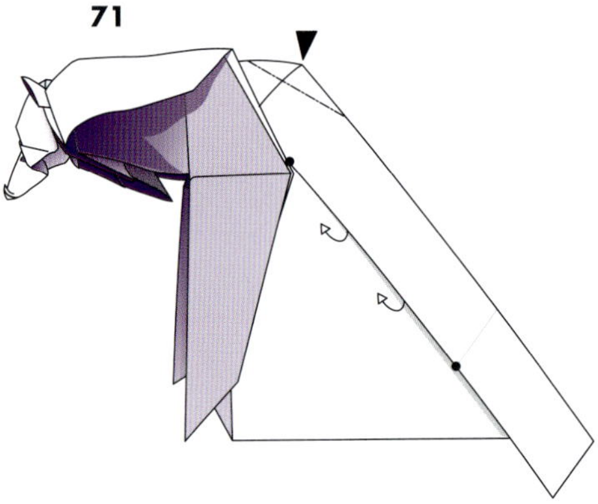

Close-sink a ridge to round the back. Release paper from under the pleats from the front legs to the crease of step 16.

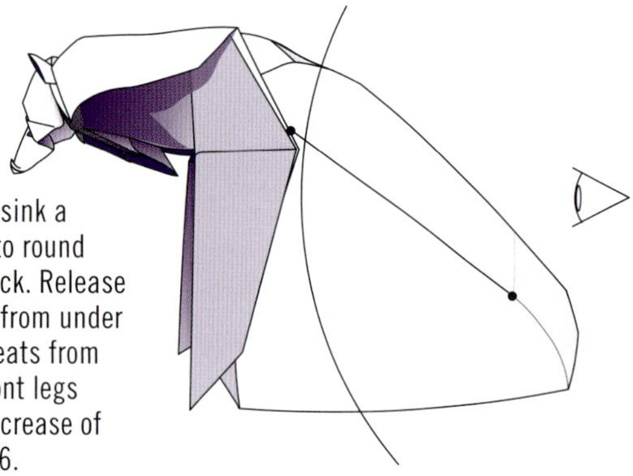

72

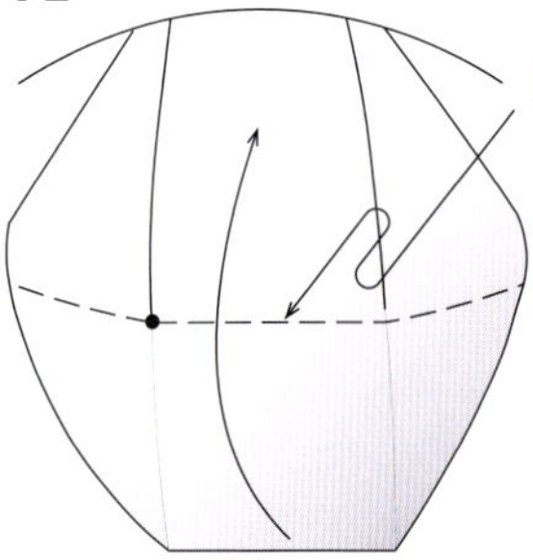

Crease from step 16.

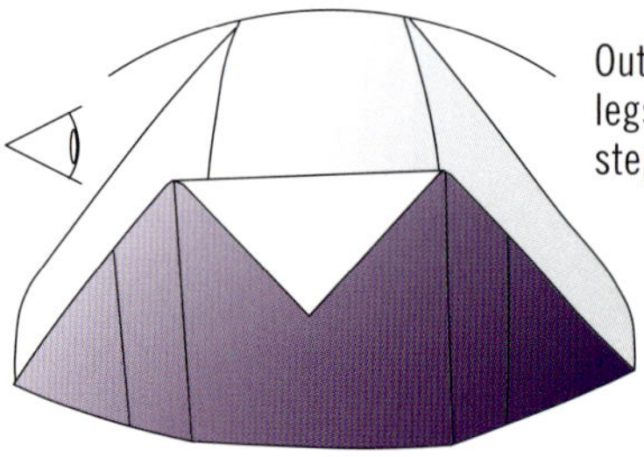

Outside reverse fold "back legs" on the crease of step 16.

77

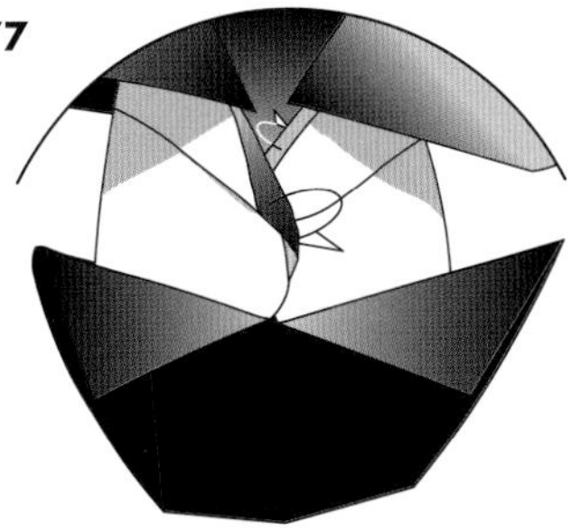

Wrap dark paper edges to the other side.

78

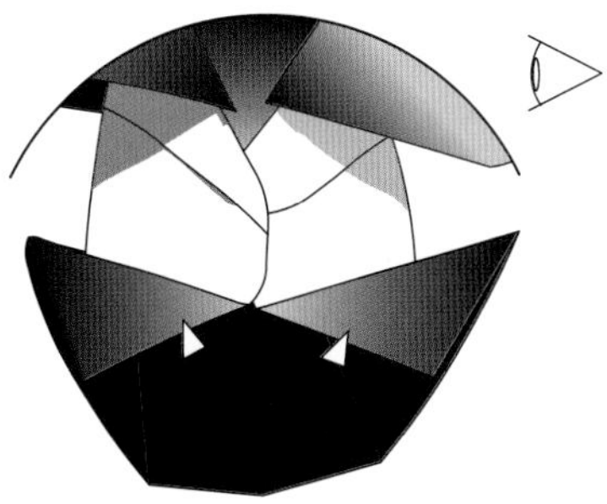

Push the belly flaps into the body cavity and turn the model over.

76

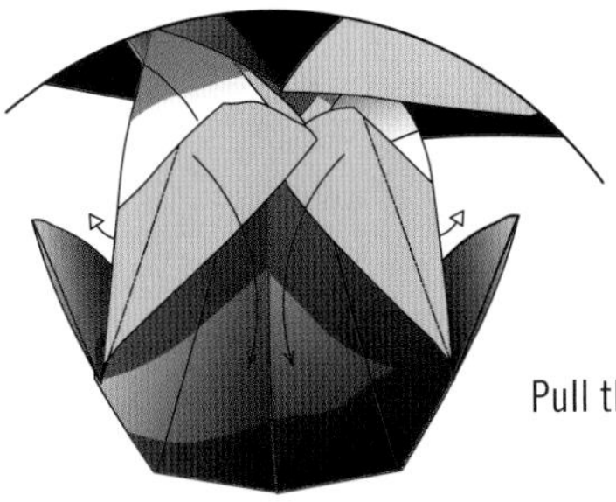

Pull the raw edges on the belly to the rear.

75

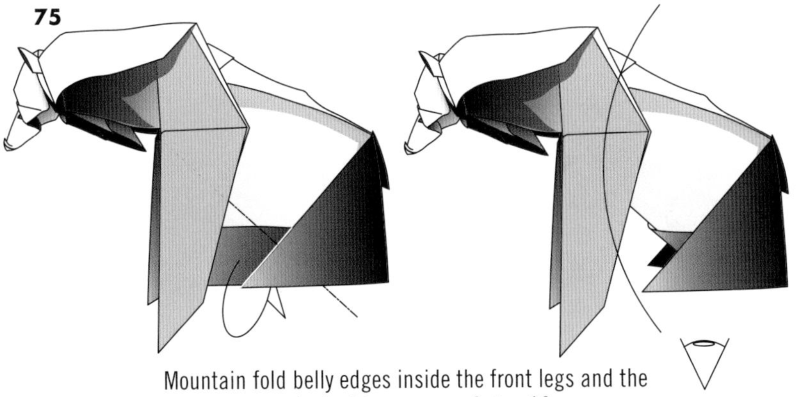

Mountain fold belly edges inside the front legs and the body cavity on both sides. crease of step 16.

73

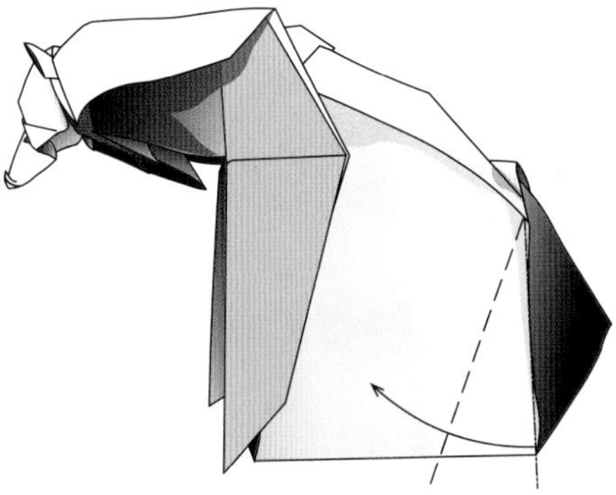

Crimp both back legs.

74

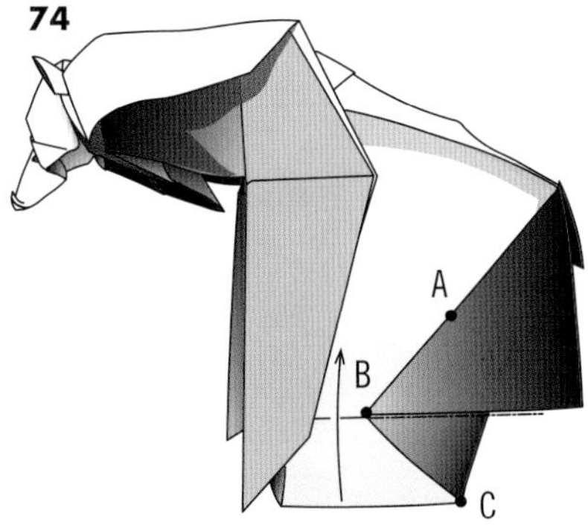

Inside reverse fold edges on both sides. Line-up edge AB with BC.

79

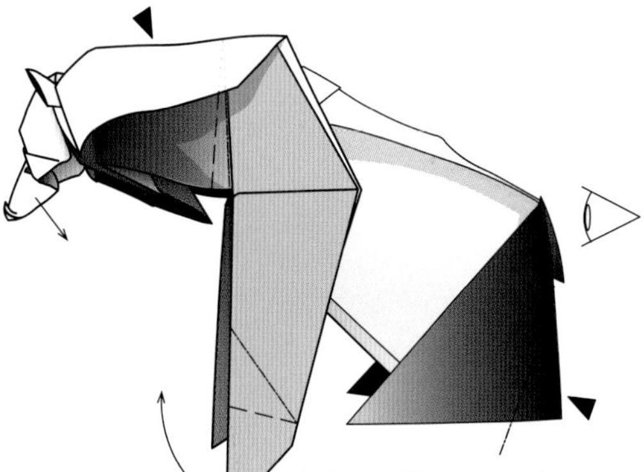

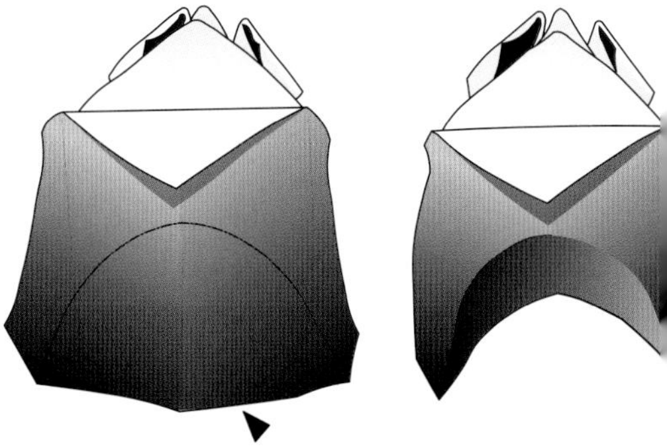

Crimp the neck to lower the head. Inside reverse fold the left front foot. Shape the back legs with a curved mountain crease.

80

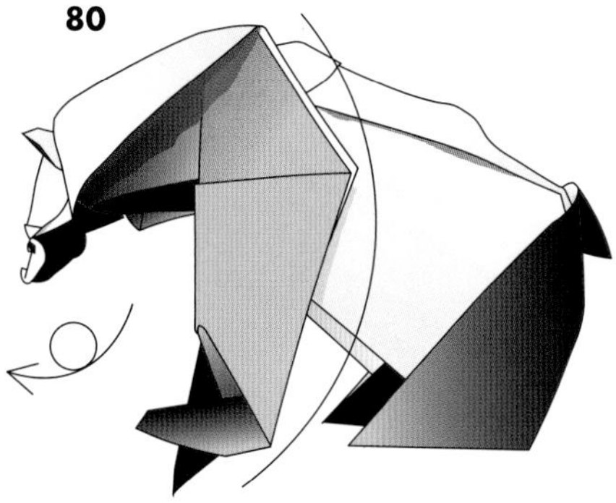

Turn the model over side-to-side.

81

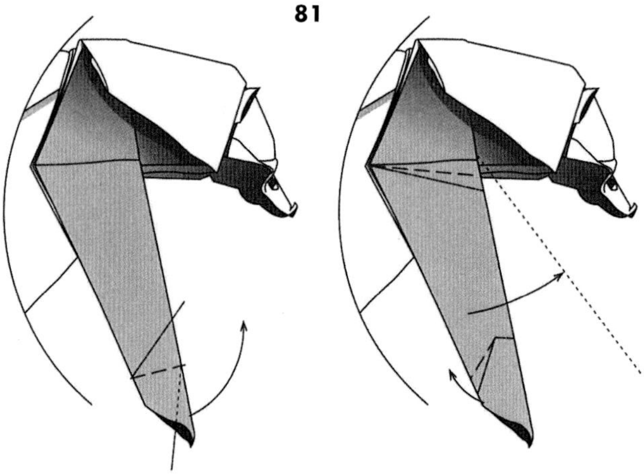

Crimp the right front foot like the left one or . . . crimp the top layer of the right front leg to move it forward and crimp the paw back.

82

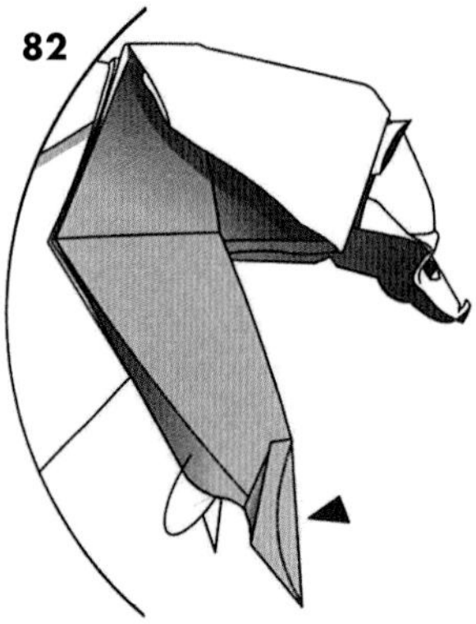

Put excess paper inside the front leg and bend the "toes."

83

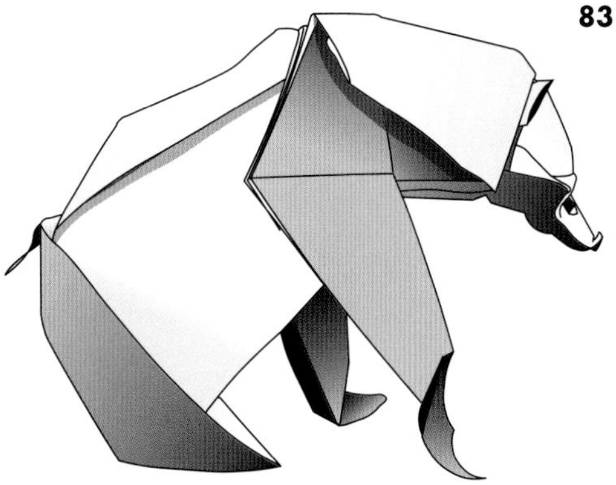

Completed Panda.

Bald Eagle

Fred Rohm

Fred got into origami in the early 1960s. To find out how he advanced the art form, see his bio on page 156.

video: *youtu.be/UCBbtTboEY8*

1

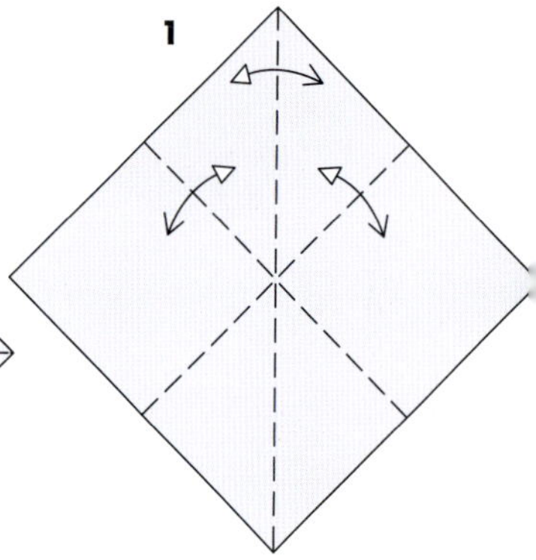

Precrease.

2

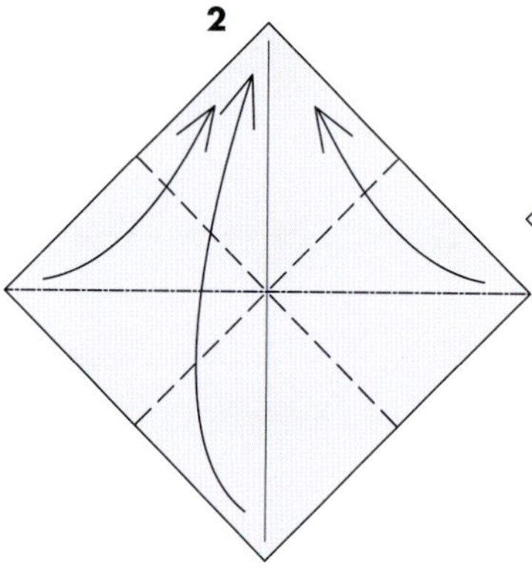

Collapse upward.

3

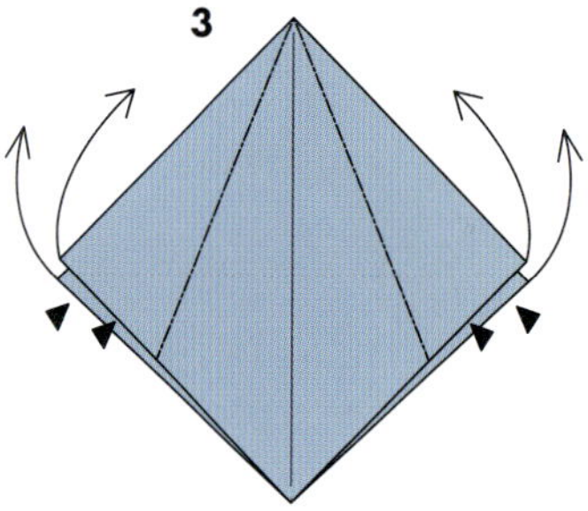

Reverse fold the sides.

4

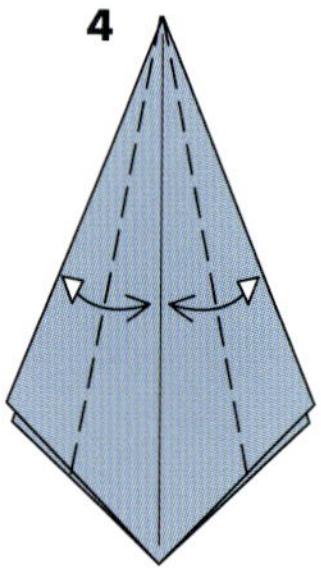

Precrease along the angle bisectors.

5

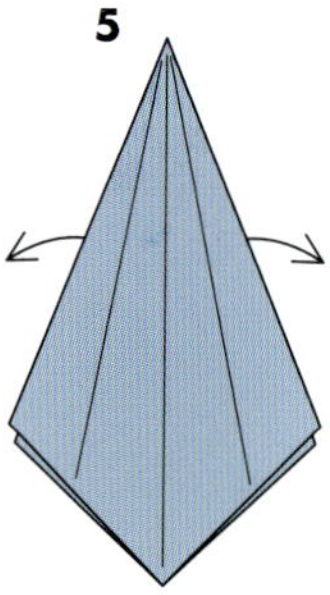

Open out the sides.

6

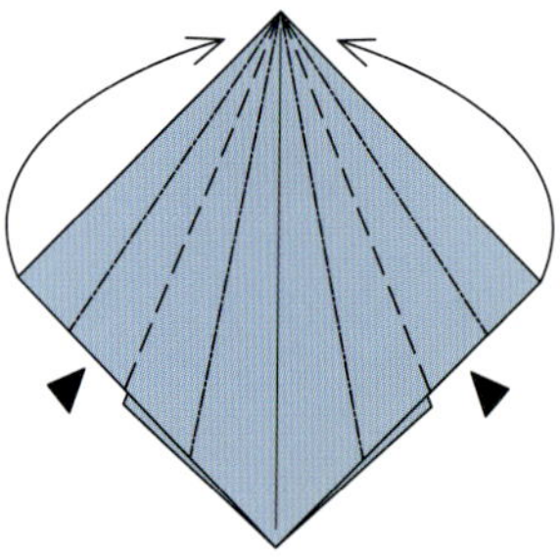

Reverse fold in and out along the existing creases.

7

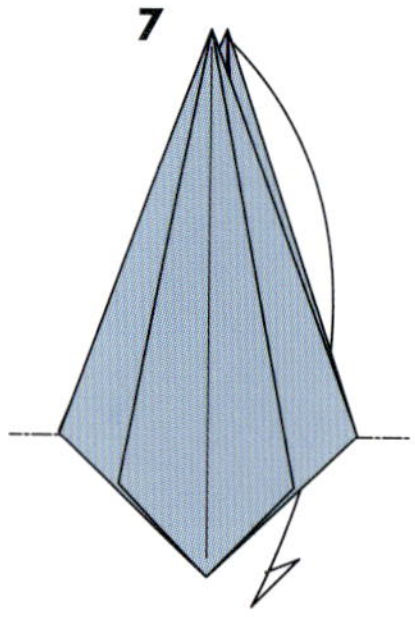

Swing the back flap down.

8

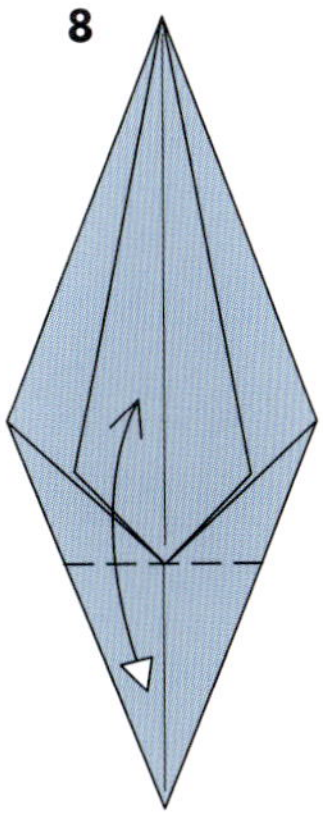

Precrease.

9

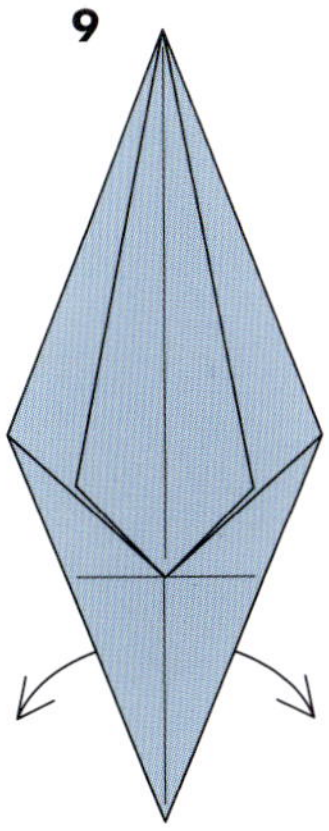

Open out the flap. The model will not lie flat.

10

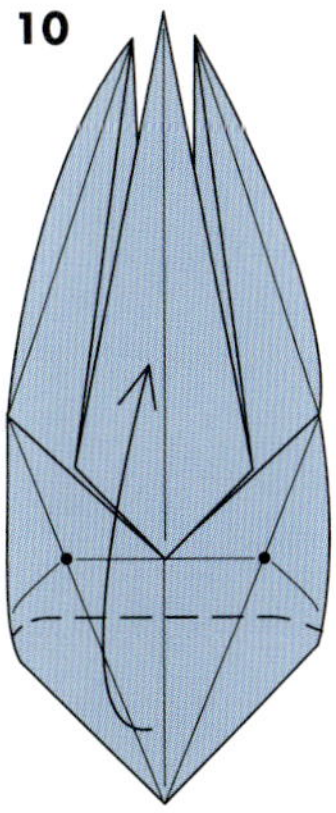

Valley fold up, such that the edges hit the dotted intersections.

11

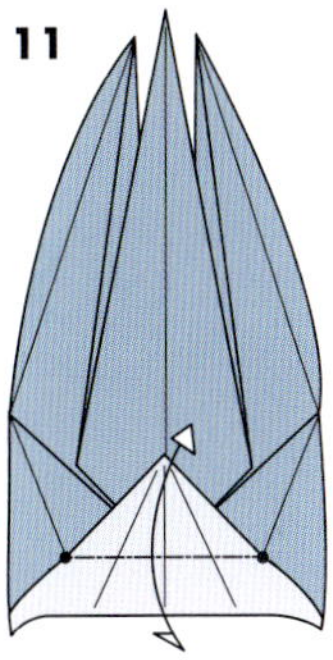

Precrease with a mountain fold.

12

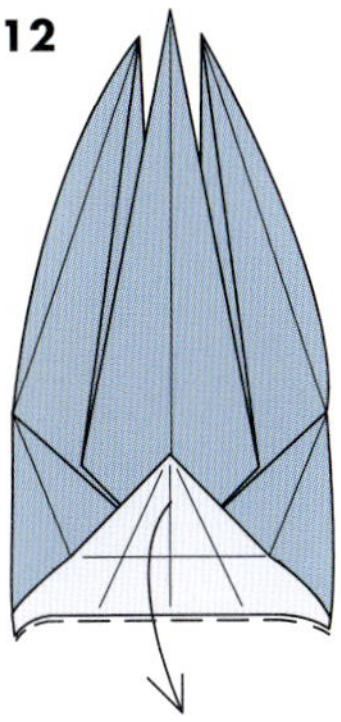

Open out the flap.

13

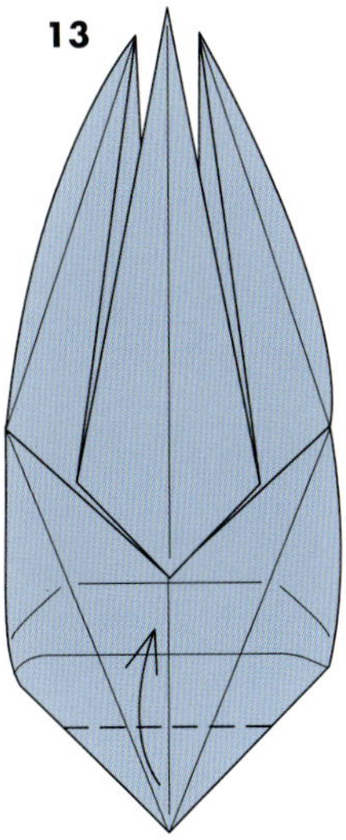

Valley fold along the existing crease.

14

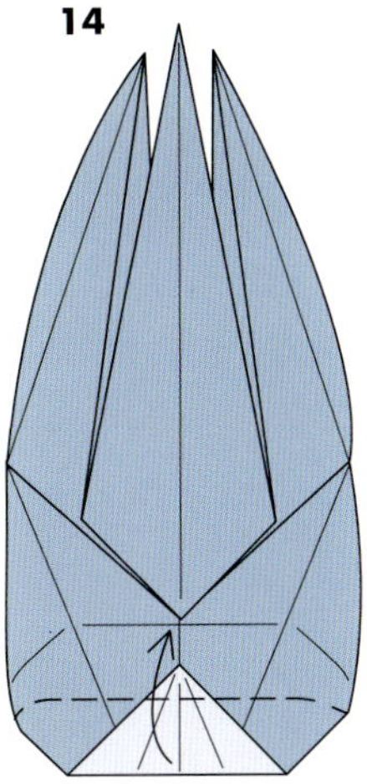

Valley fold up.

15

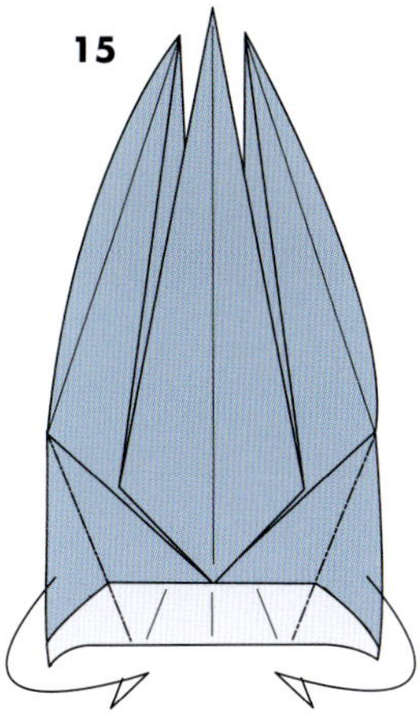

Mountain fold the sides back in.

16

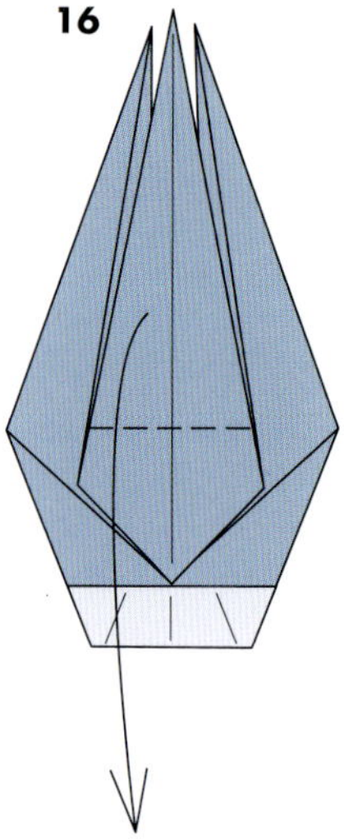

Lightly fold the flap down.

17

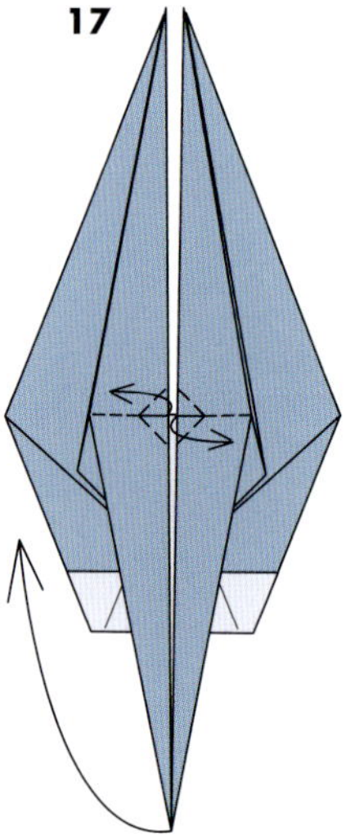

Swing the flap back up while putting in two small reverse folds.

18

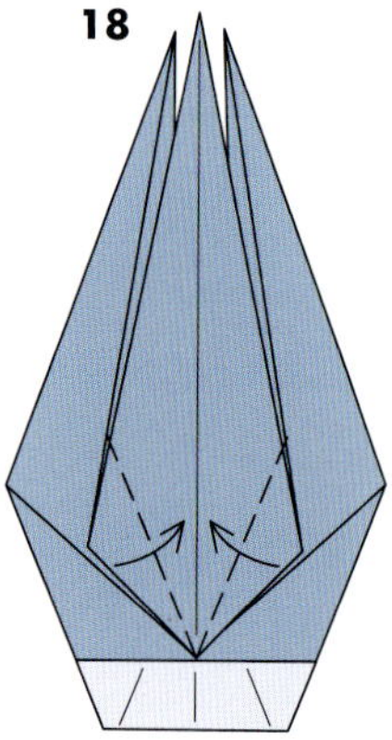

Valley fold the sides in.

19

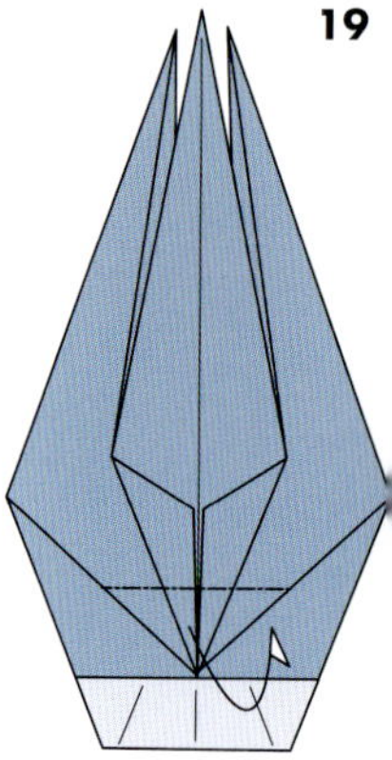

Mountain fold the flap in half.

20

Squash fold, such that summit A hits crease B.

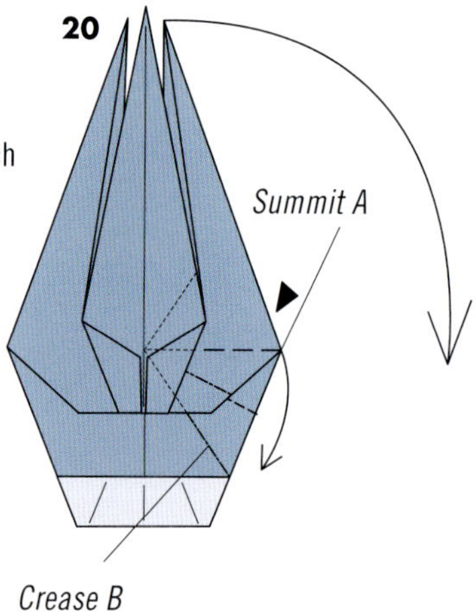

21

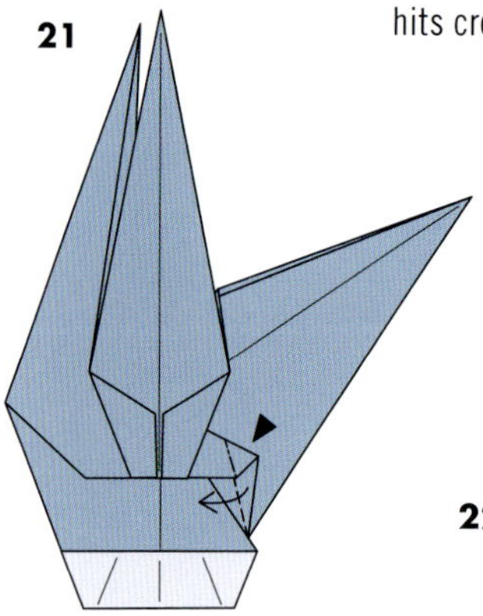

Reverse fold.

22

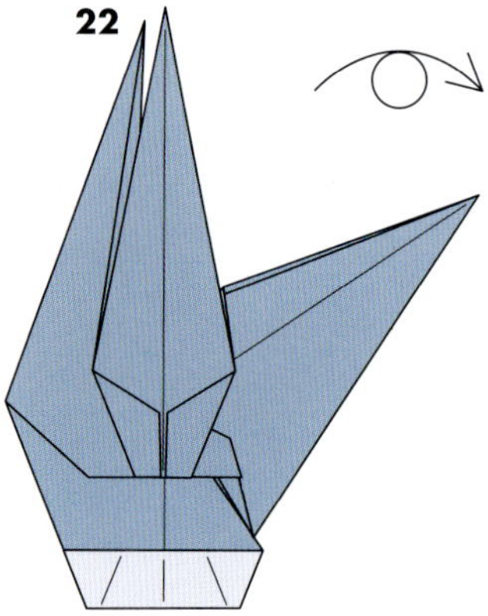

Turn over.

23

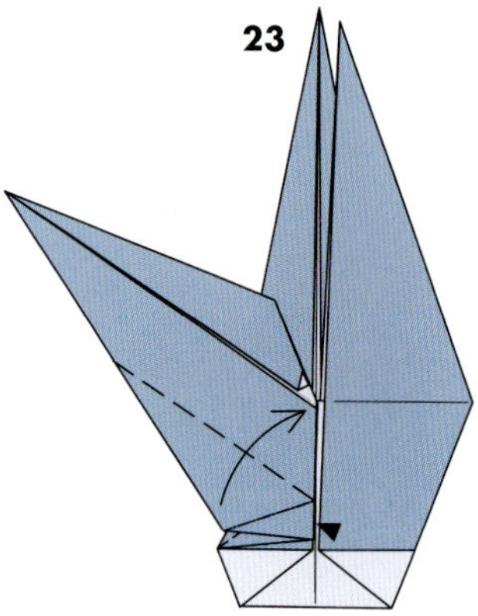

Squash fold.

24

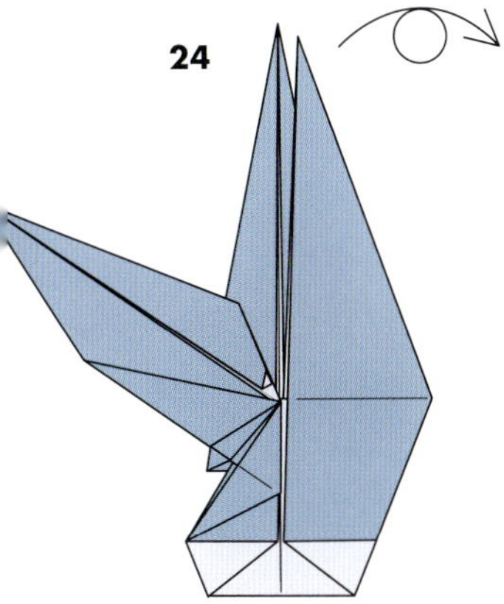

Turn over.

25

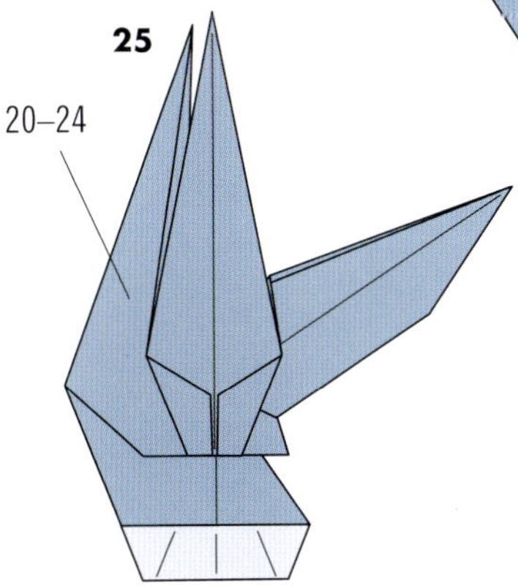

Repeat steps 20–24 in mirror image.

26

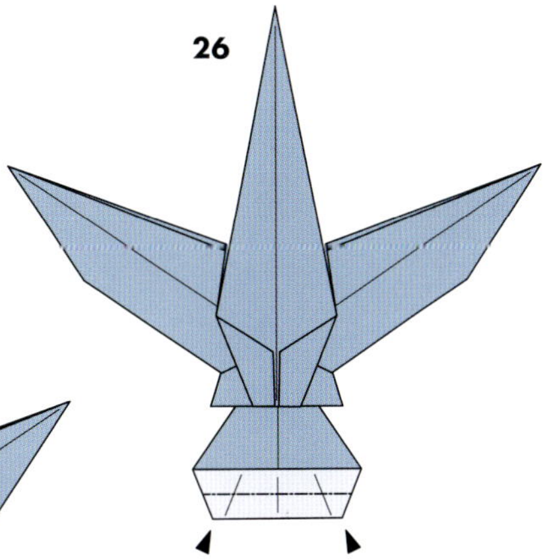

Reverse fold the bottom edge in half.

27

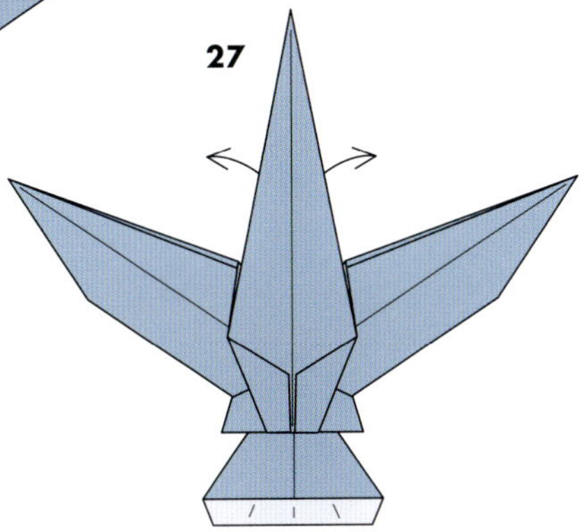

Slide out the side layers until they are straight.

28

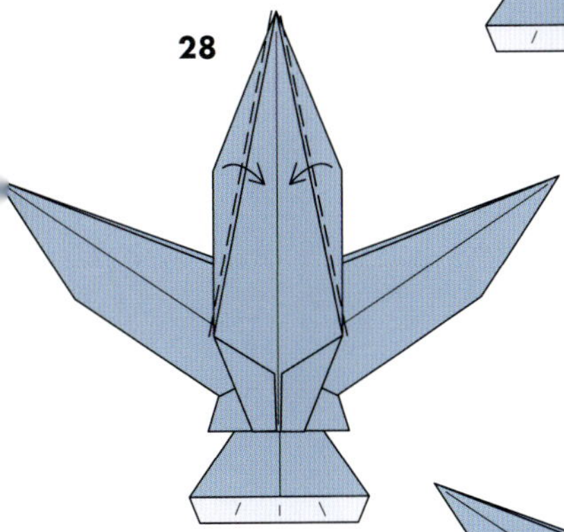

Valley fold the sides inward.

29

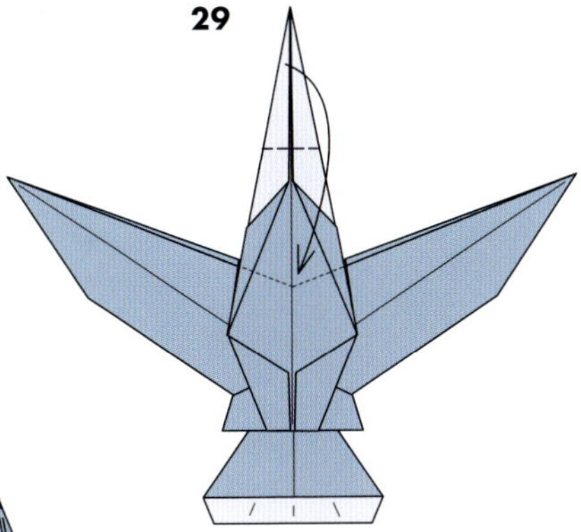

Valley fold toward the (imaginary) approximate reference point.

30

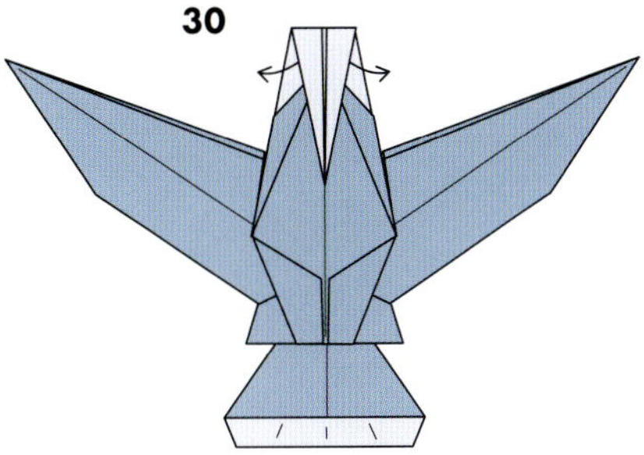

Slide the side layers outward.

31

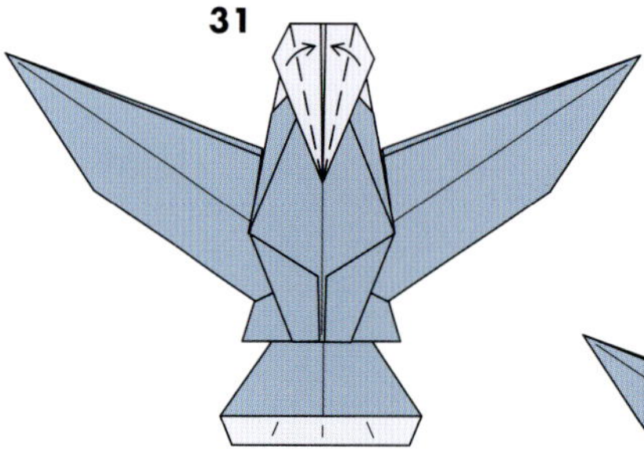

Valley fold the sides inward.

32

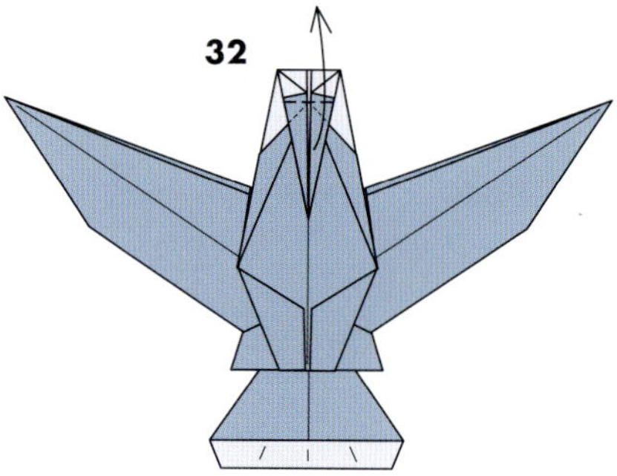

Valley fold up.

33

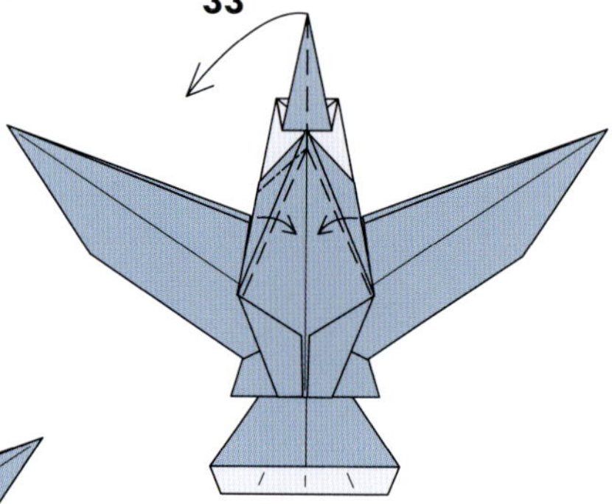

Rabbit ear the flap.

34

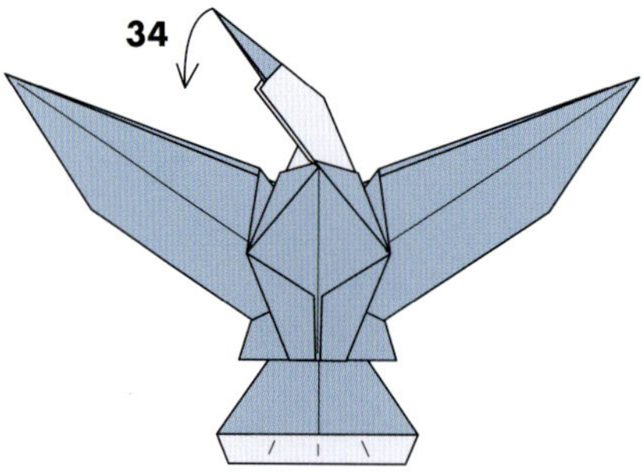

Slide the flap down.

35

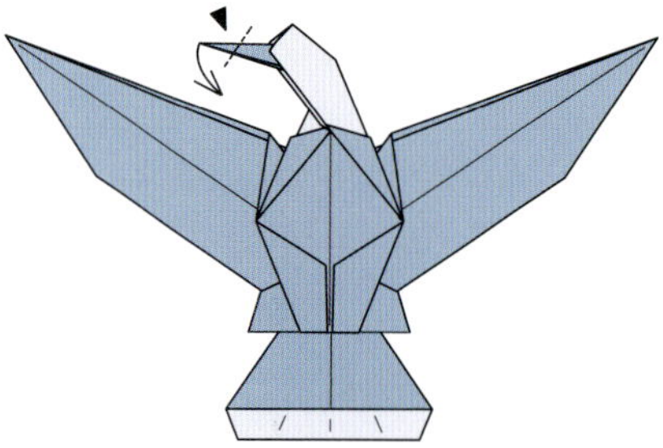

Reverse fold the flap.

36

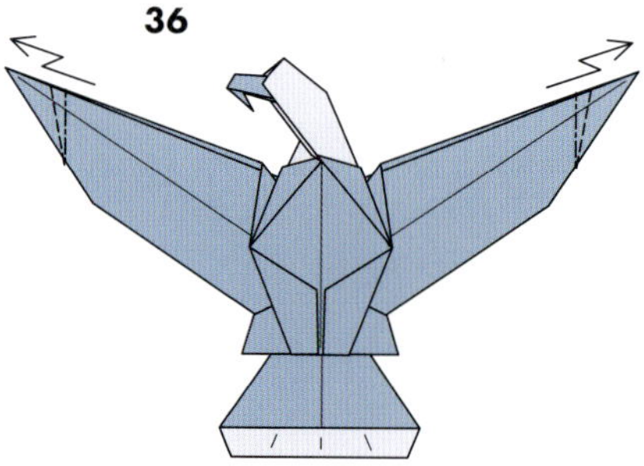

Pleat the tips.

39

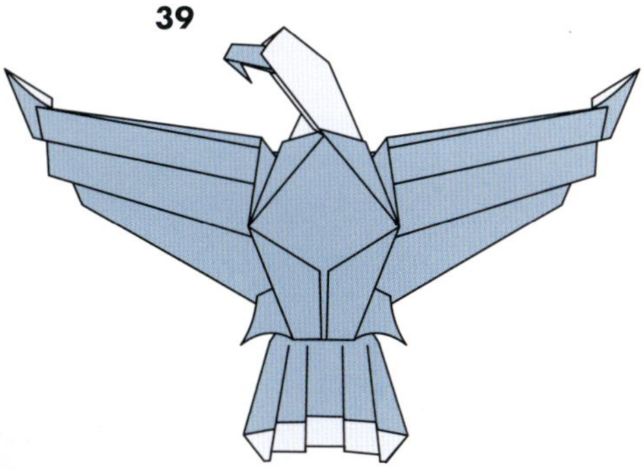

Completed Bald Eagle.

38

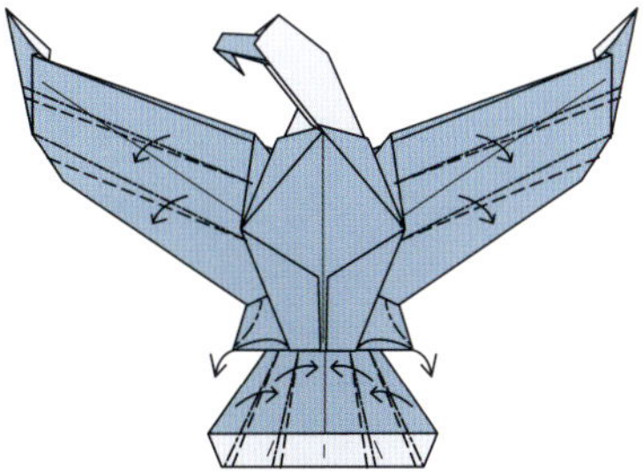

Pleat the tail and wings. Make the feet slightly 3D by pinching them.

37

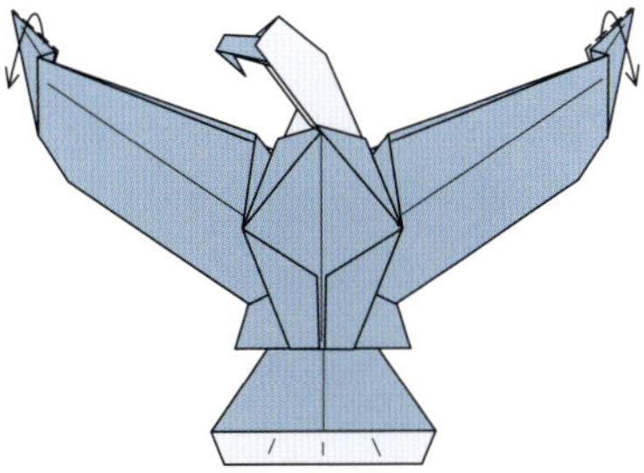

Wrap around a layer at each side.

Time Flies

Jeremy Shafer

See Jeremy's bio on page 158 for how he incorporates origami in his career as an entertainer.

video: *youtu.be/can93ijVnpE*

1

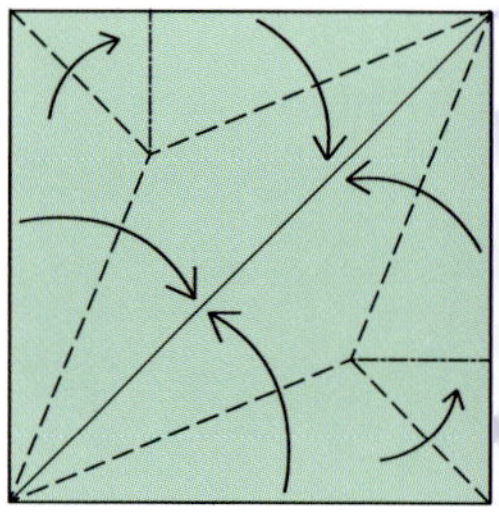

Rabbit ear the sides to form a Fish Base.

2

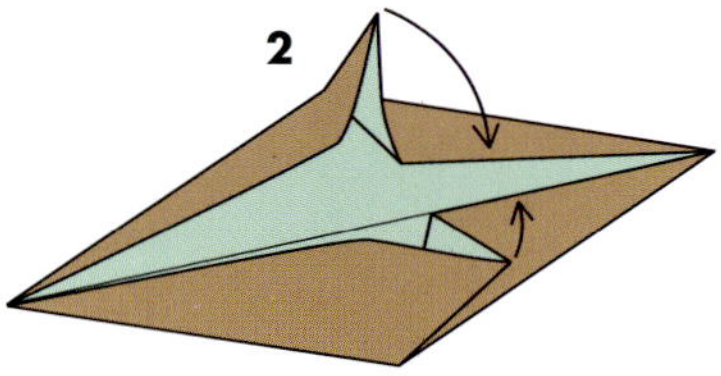

Fish Base in progress.

3

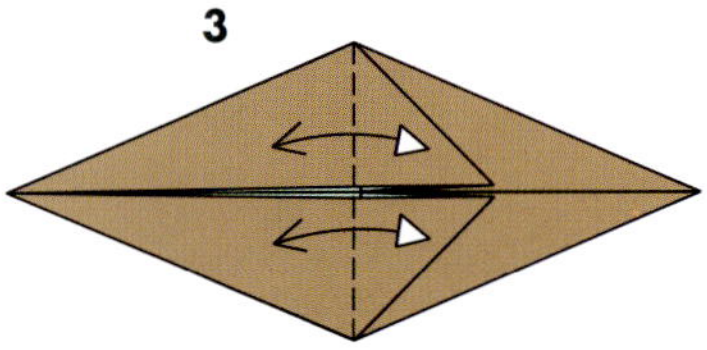

Valley fold the middle flaps to the left side and then swing them back to the right side.

4

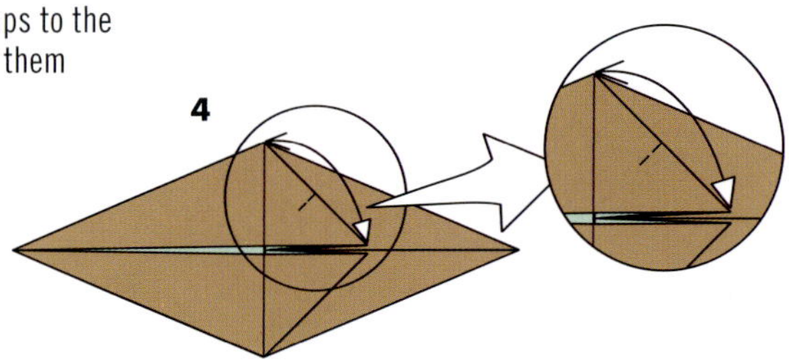

Valley-pinch and unpinch. Enlarged view to the right.

5

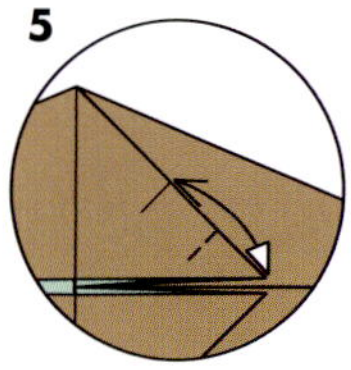

Valley-pinch and unpinch.

6

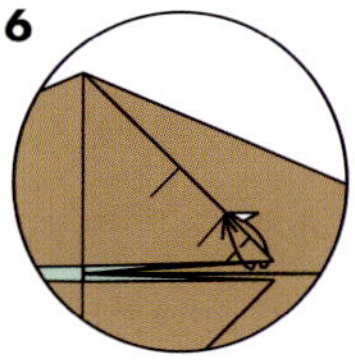

Outside reverse fold to color change the tip.

7

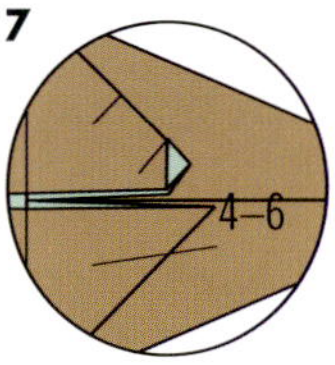

Repeat steps 4–6 on the bottom flap.

8

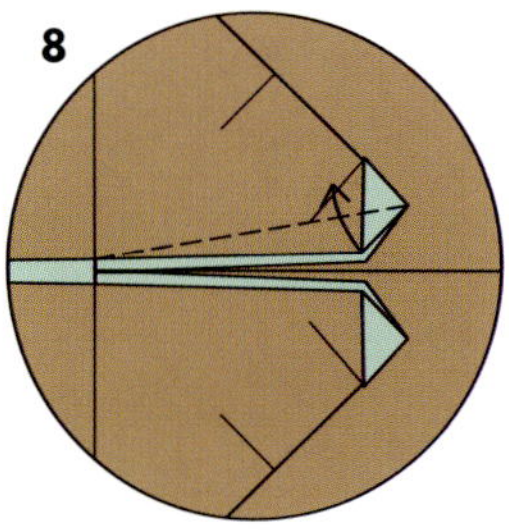

Valley fold.

9

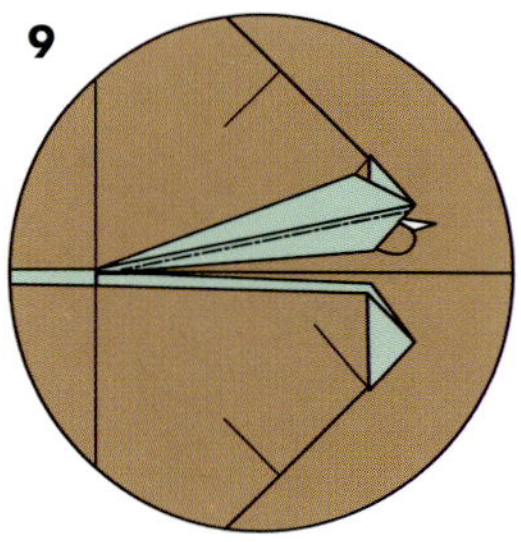

Mountain fold.

10

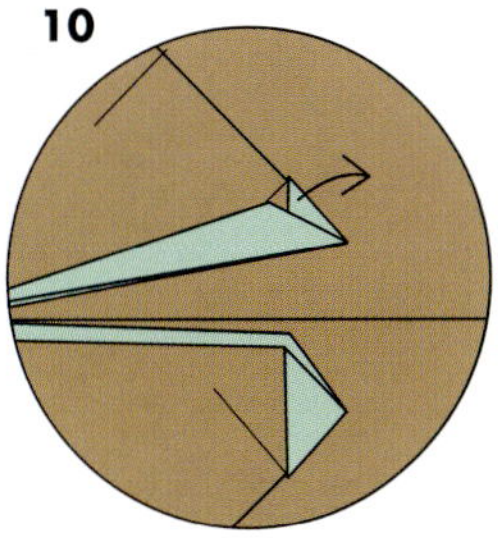

Pull the tip rightward, freeing the trapped layers.

11

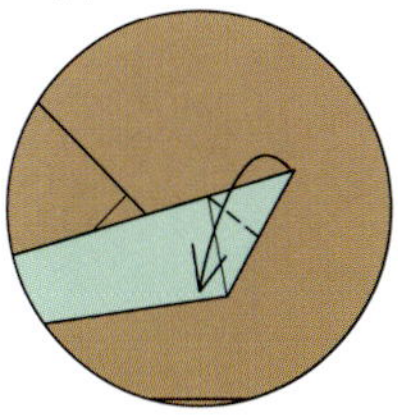

Valley fold to make the hand as symmetrical as possible.

12

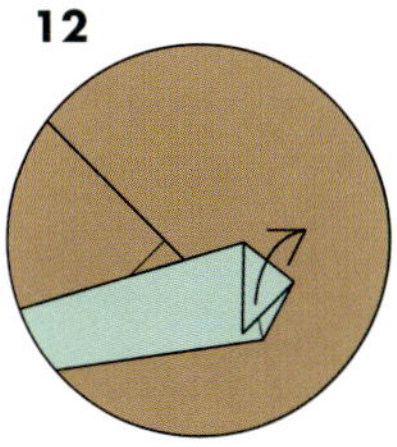

Unfold.

13

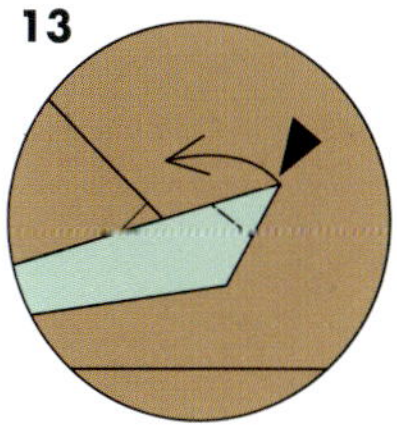

Reverse fold.

14

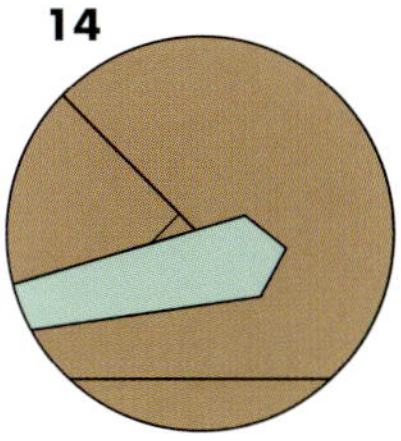

Like this.

15

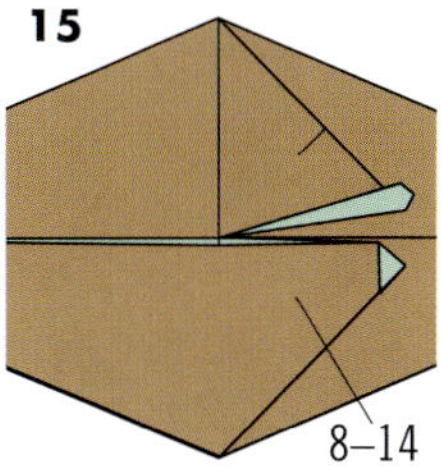

Repeat steps 8–14 on the bottom flap.

16

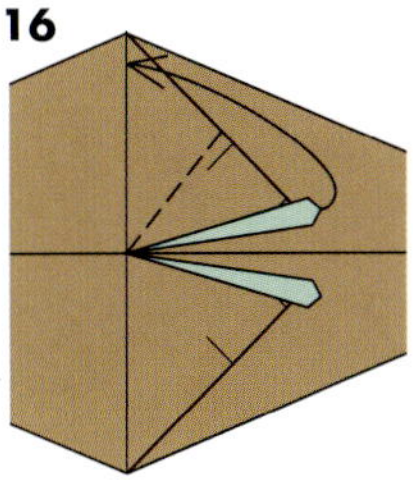

Valley fold point-to-crease.

17

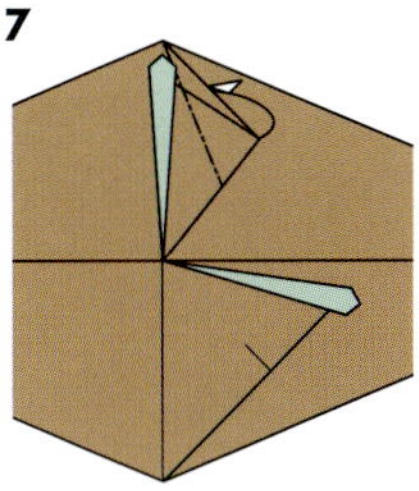

Mountain fold.

18

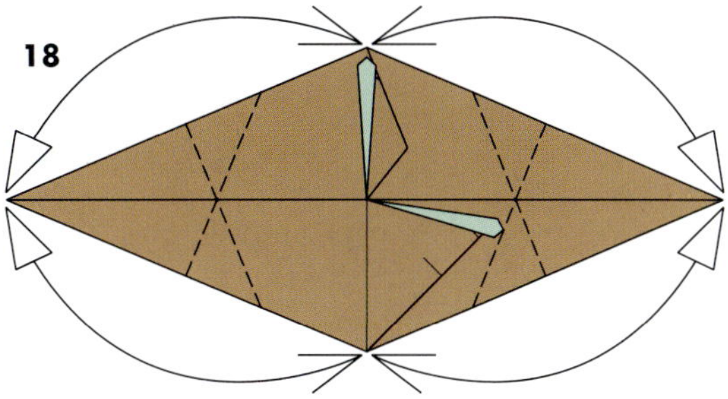

Valley fold and unfold point-to-point.

19

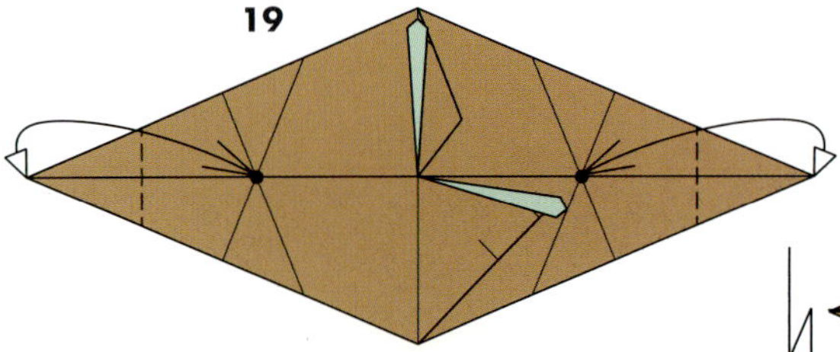

Valley fold to the black dots.

20

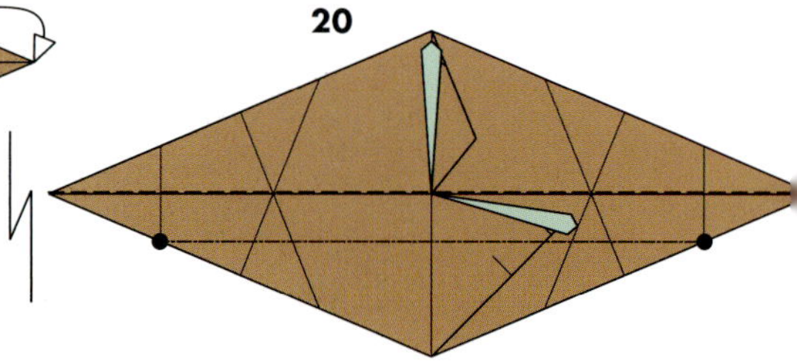

Pleat. The mountain fold goes between the black dots.

21

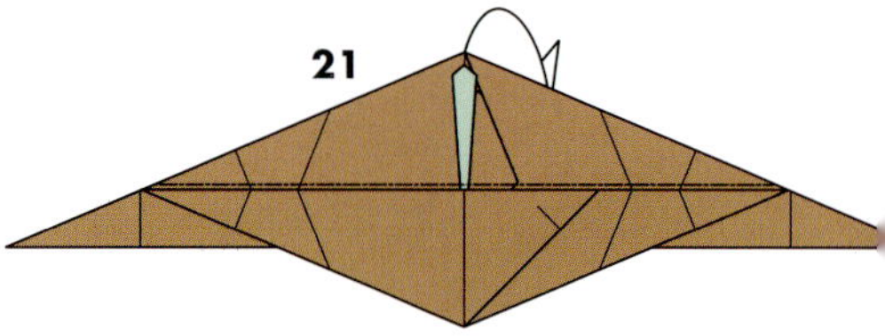

Mountain fold the rear flap.

22

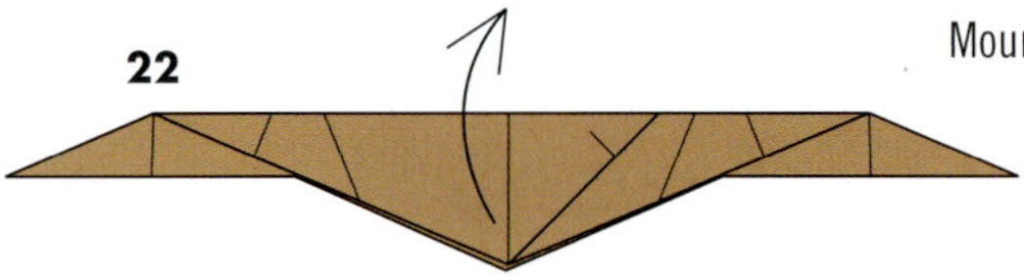

Unfold to step 20.

23

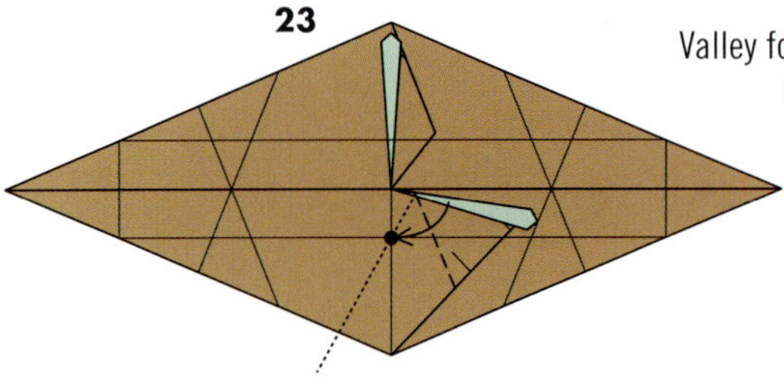

Valley fold so that the clock hand points in the direction of 7 o'clock, and its middle crease touches the black dot.

24

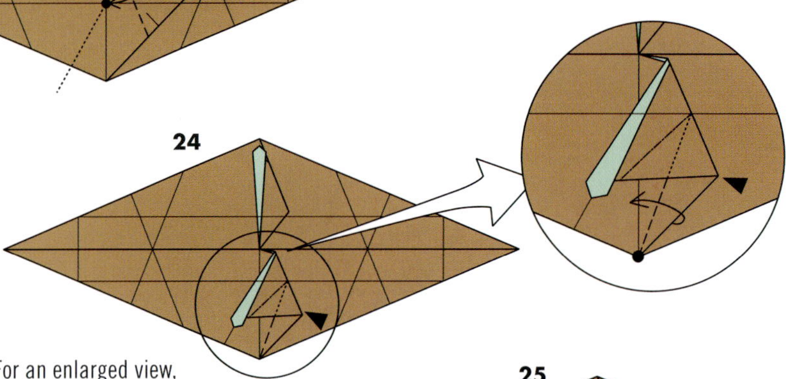

Reverse fold. For an enlarged view, look up to the right.

25

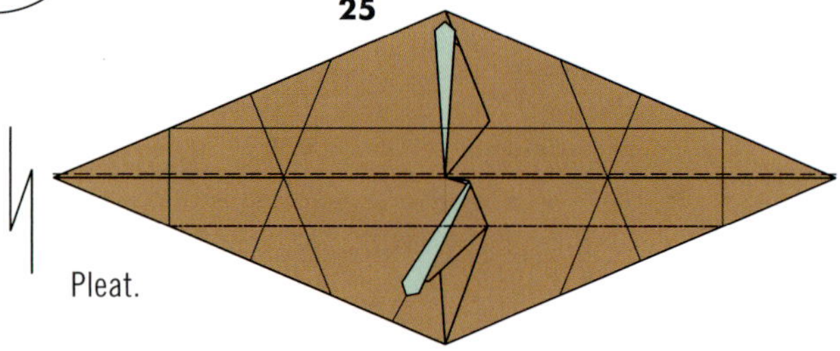

Pleat.

32

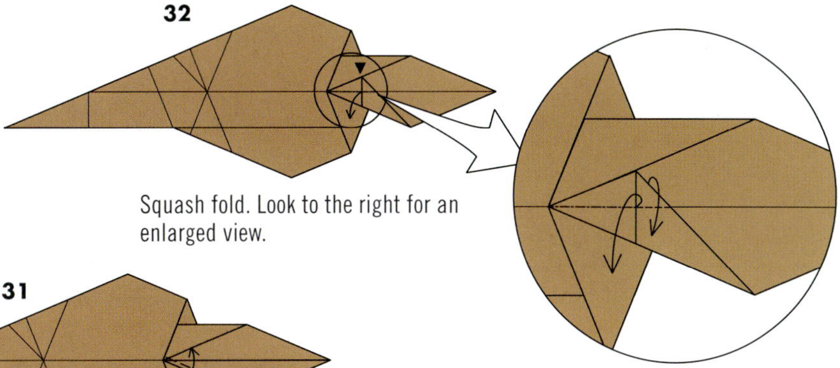

Squash fold. Look to the right for an enlarged view.

31

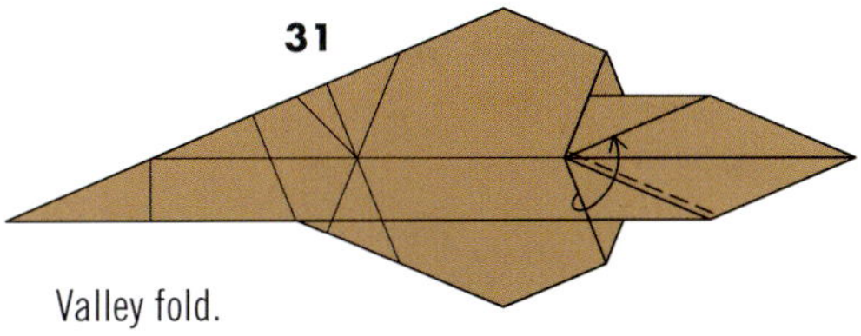

Valley fold.

30

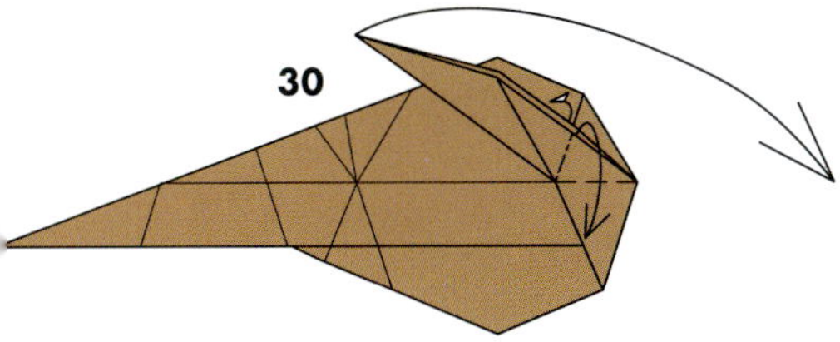

Squash fold the flap rightward.

29

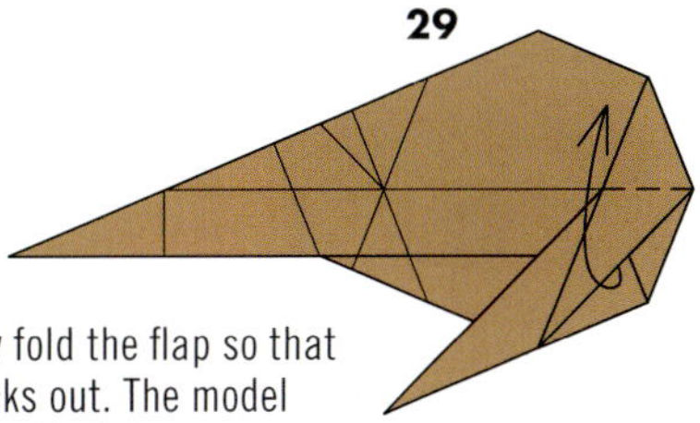

Valley fold the flap so that it sticks out. The model will not lie flat.

28

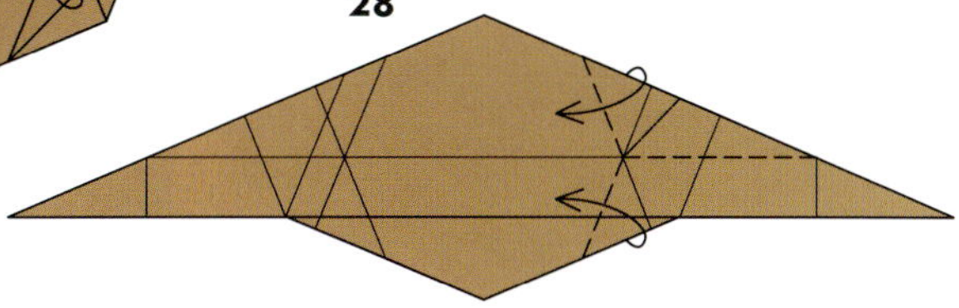

Rabbit ear on existing creases.

27

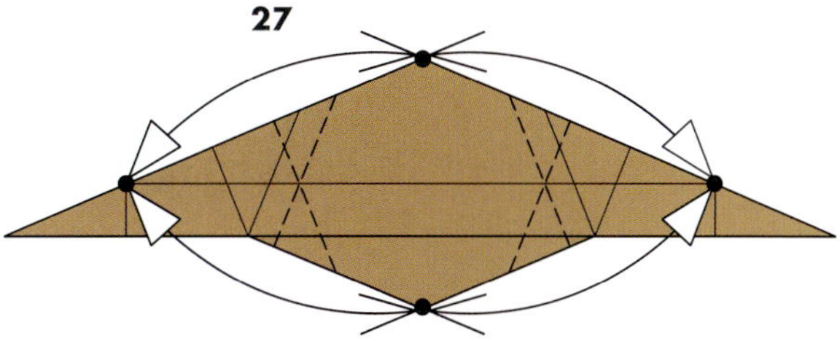

Valley fold and unfold dot-to-dot.

26

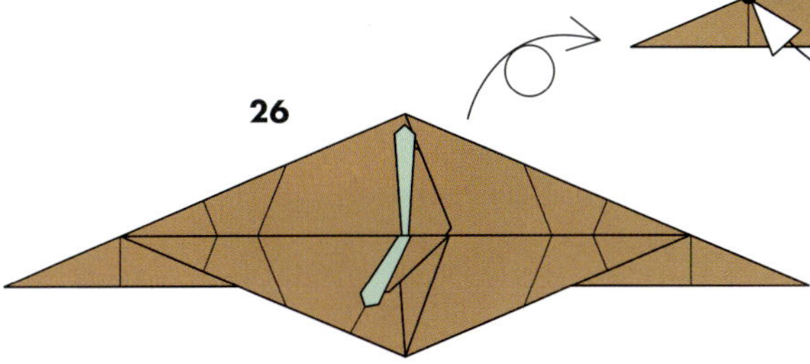

Turn over.

33

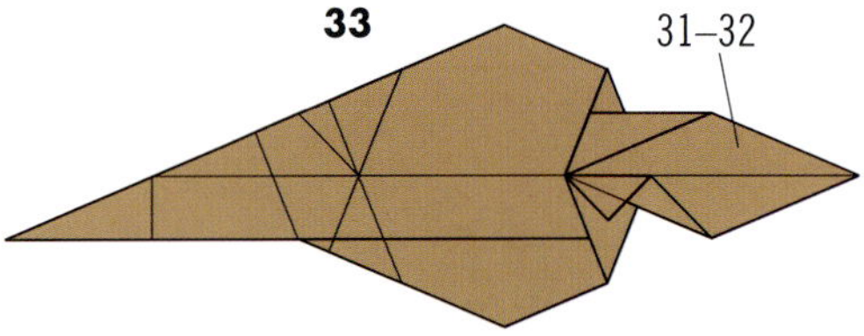

Repeat steps 31 and 32 on the top portion of the flap.

34

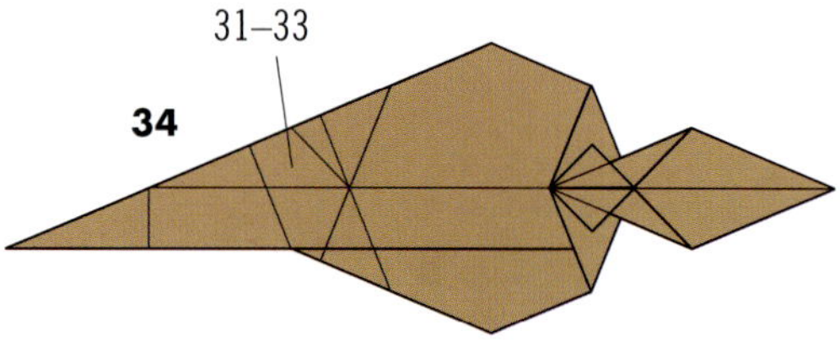

Repeat steps 31–33 on the left side.

35

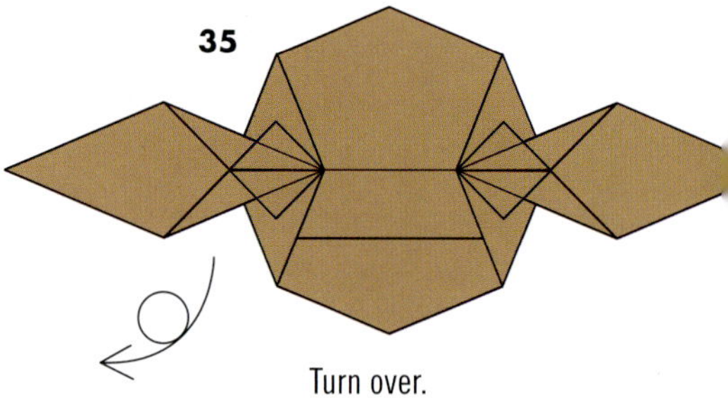

Turn over.

36

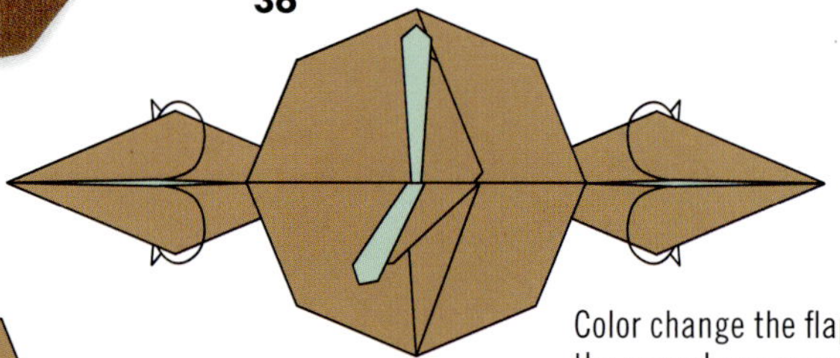

Color change the flaps wrapping the raw edges around to the back. To do this cleanly, you have to partially unfold the model.

37

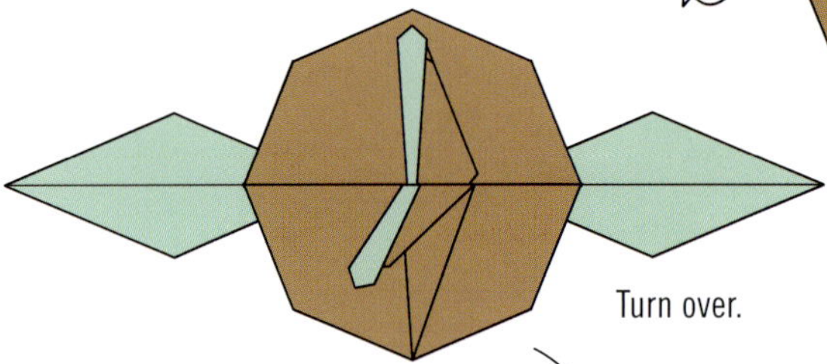

Turn over.

38

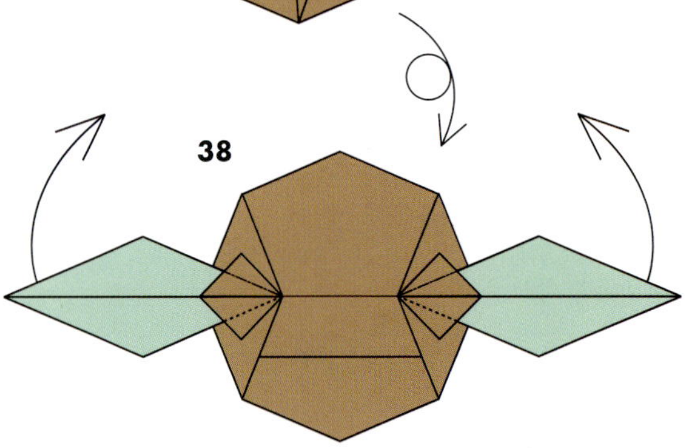

Rotate the white flaps so that they slant upward at 45-degree angles.

39

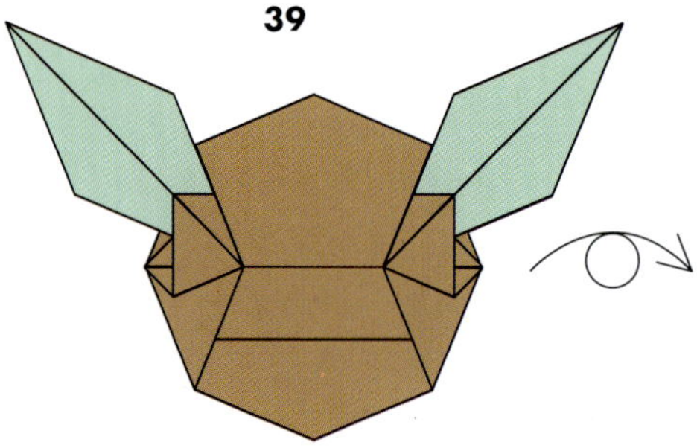

Turn over.

42

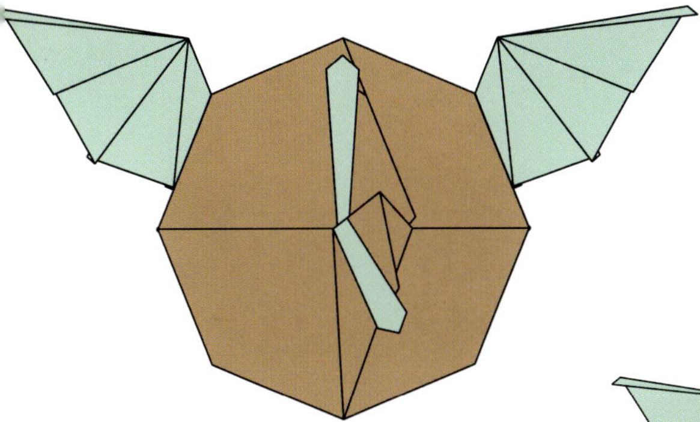

Completed Time Flies.

41

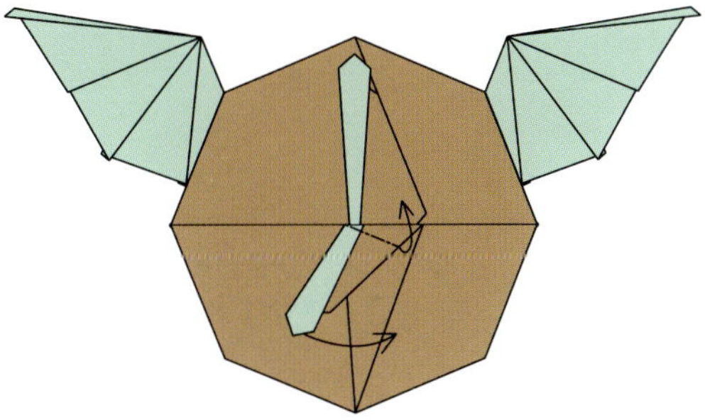

Now it's time to push back time. Rotate the clock arm so that it points in the direction of 5 o'clock. Flatten to form the mountain fold.

40

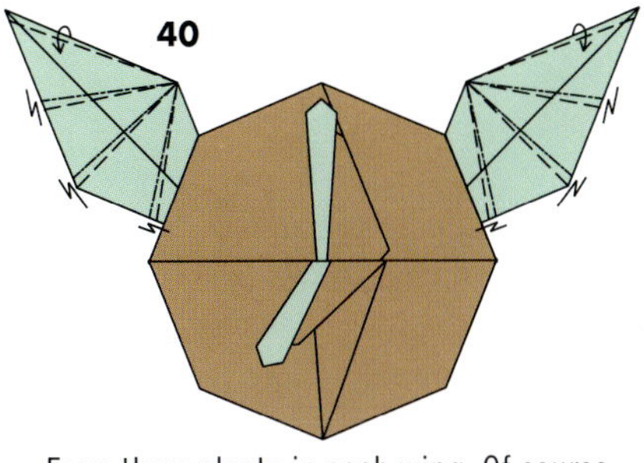

Form three pleats in each wing. Of course you can do more if time permits. Valley fold the top edge.

Luv Bug

John Szinger

John has another, much louder, hobby in addition to origami— *see his bio on page 154 to find out what it is.*

video: *youtu.be/mOsZH8_xLR0*

1

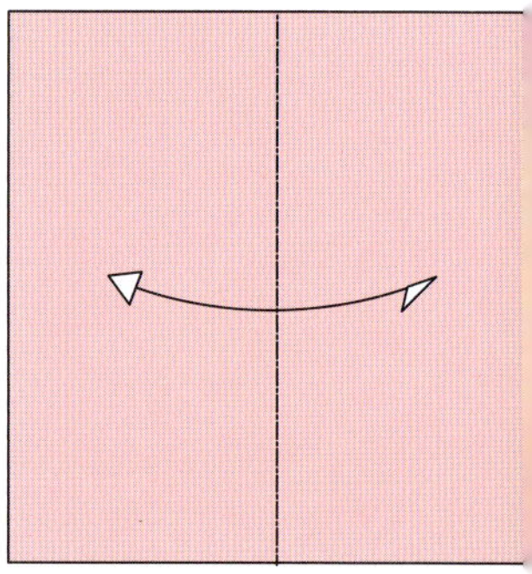

Precrease in half with a mount fold.

2

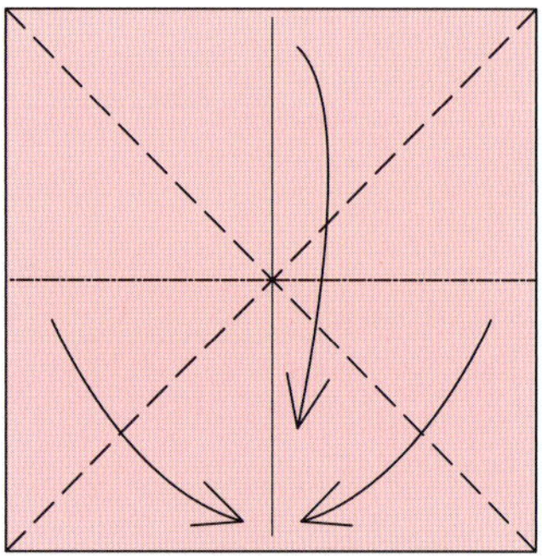

Collapse downward (Waterbomb Base).

3

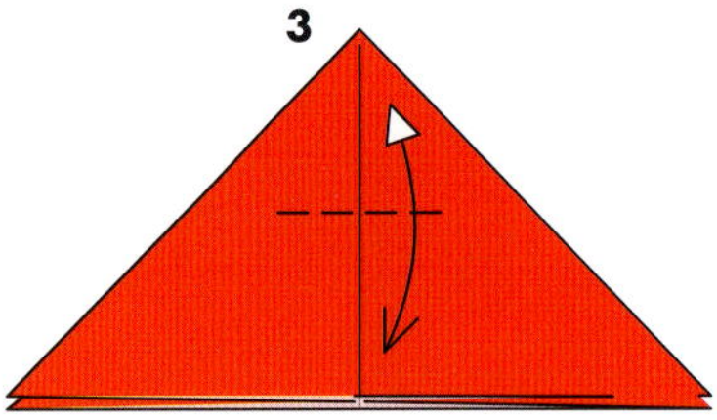

Precrease in half.

4

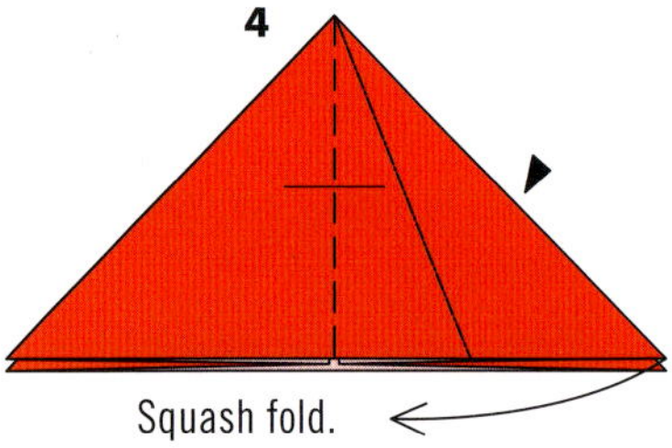

Squash fold.

5

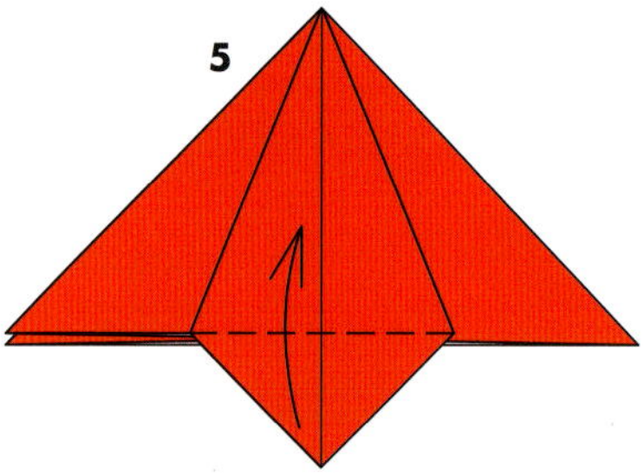

Valley fold up.

6

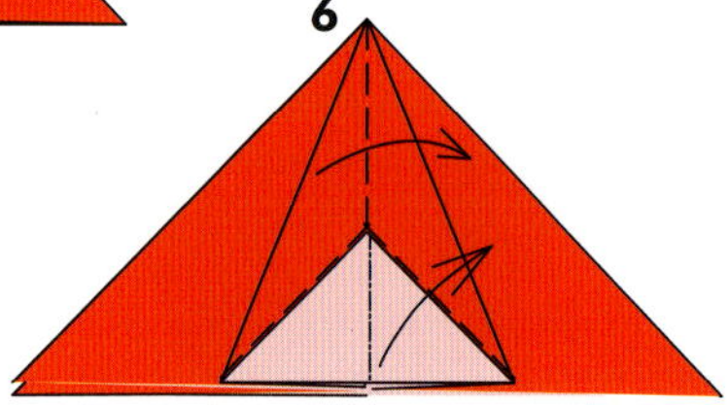

Swing over while incorporating a reverse fold.

7

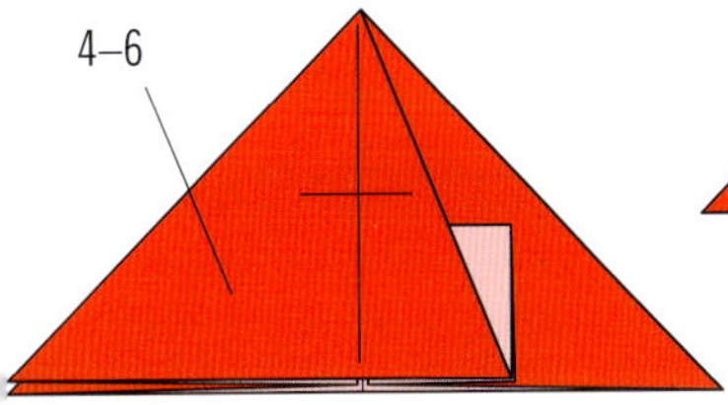

Repeat steps 4–6 in mirror image.

8

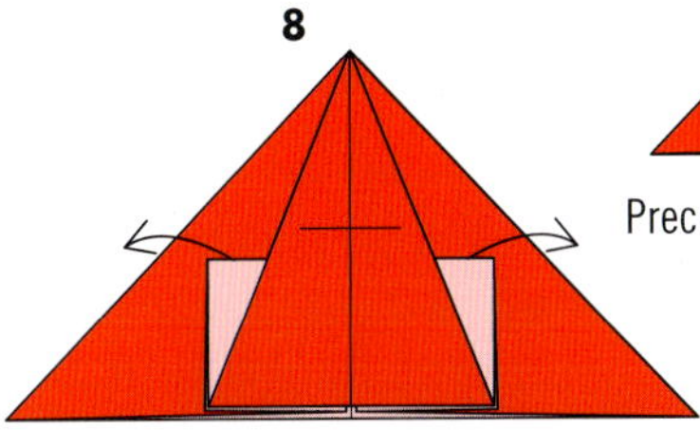

Unwrap a single layer at each side.

9

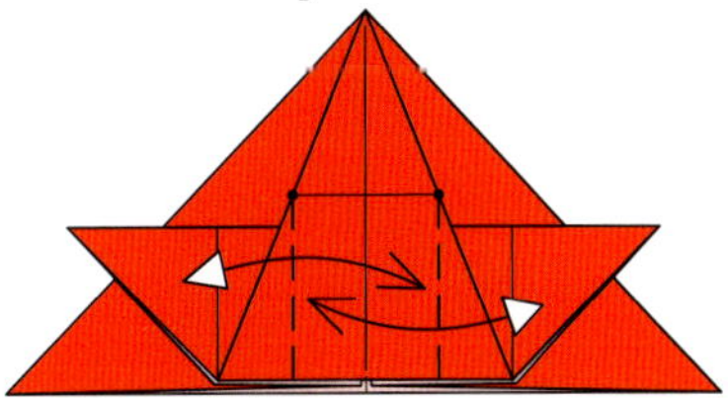

Precrease, noting the dotted intersections.

10

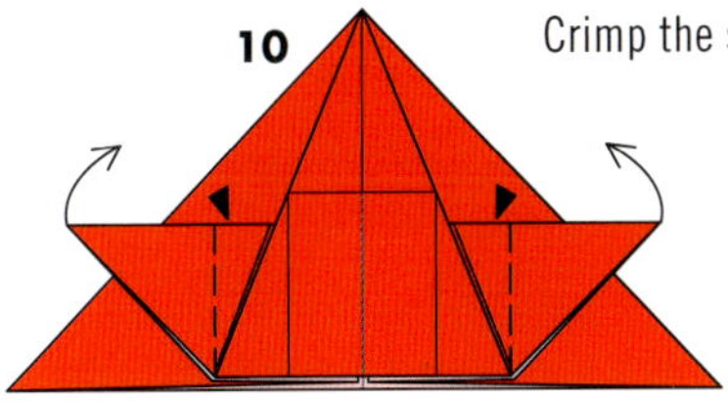

Crimp the sides.

11

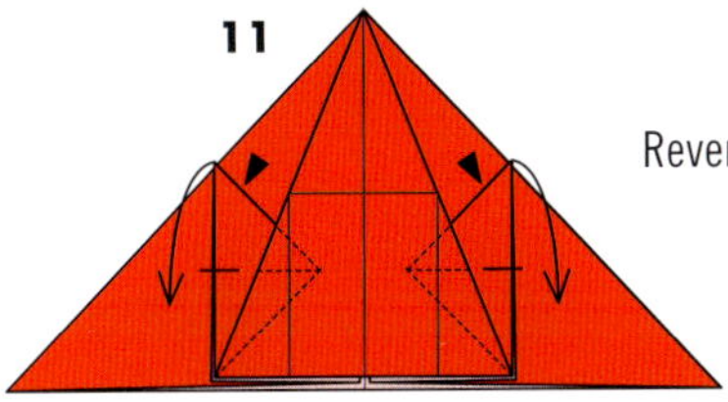

Reverse fold the flaps down.

12

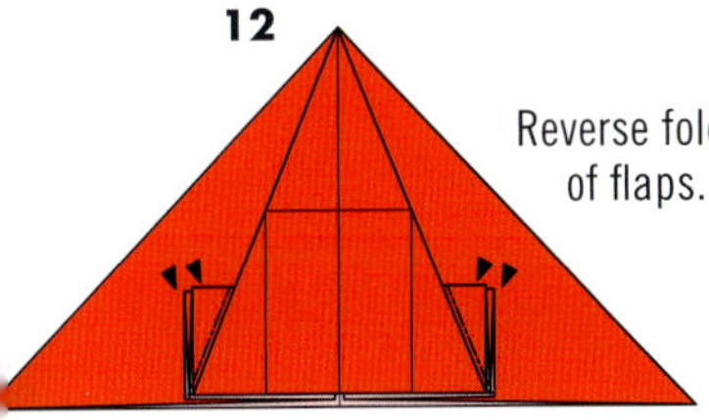

Reverse fold the two sets of flaps.

13

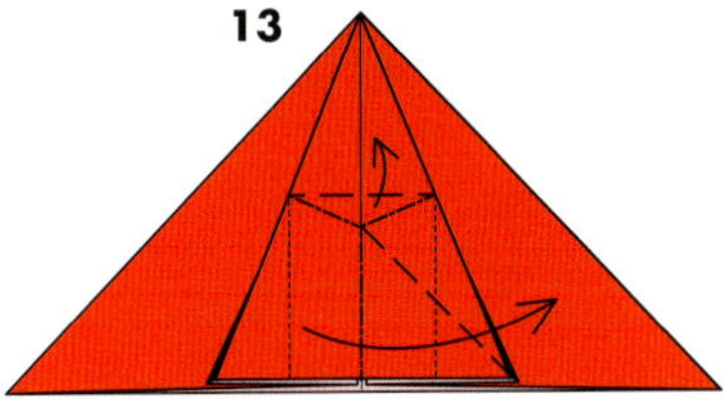

Pull the sides inward, allowing the center portion to swing over to the right.

14

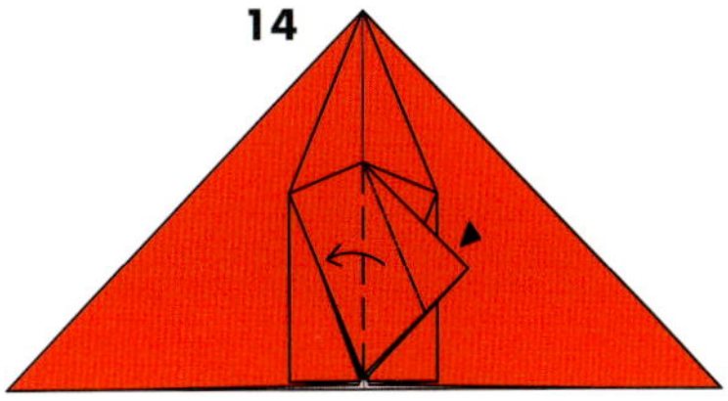

Squash fold.

15

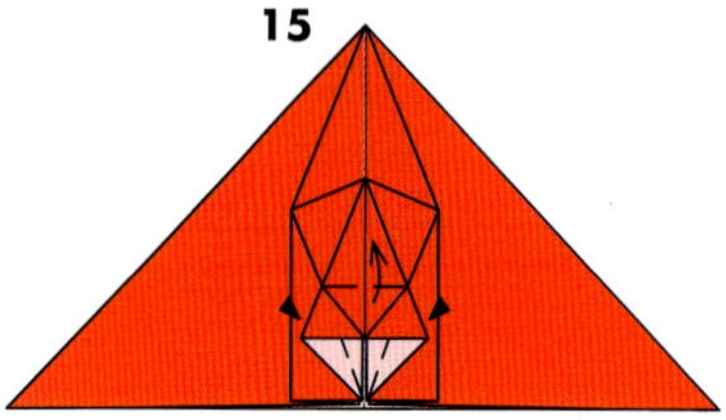

Petal fold the flap.

16

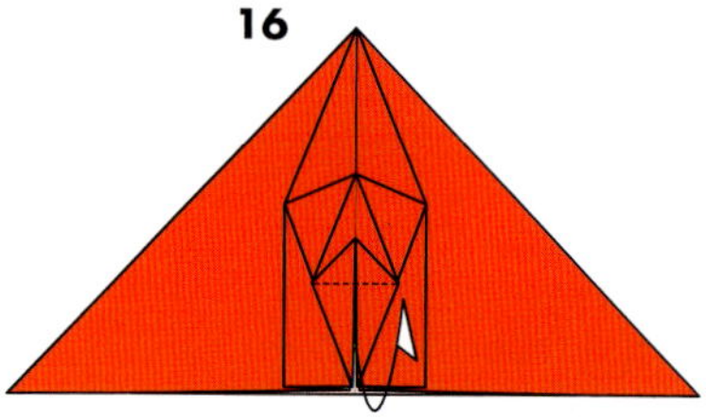

Tuck the flap under.

17

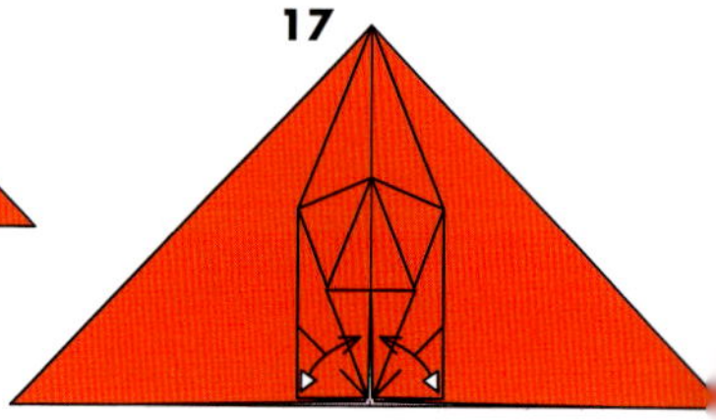

Precrease the side flaps.

18

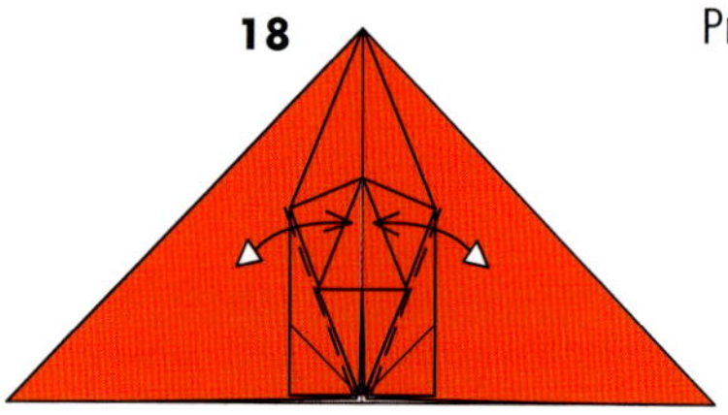

Precrease the flaps again.

19

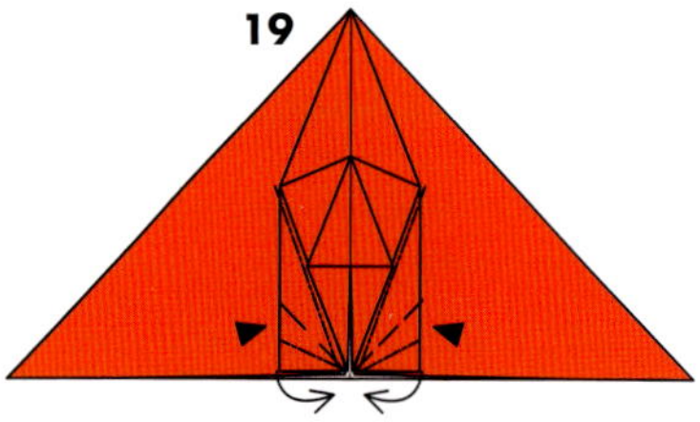

Reverse fold in and out along
the existing creases.

20

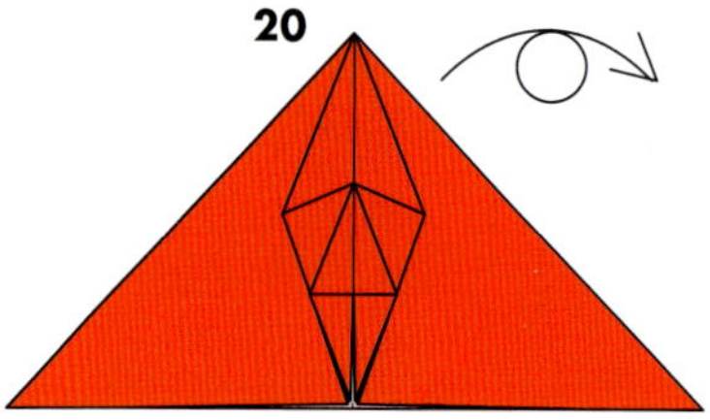

Turn over.

21

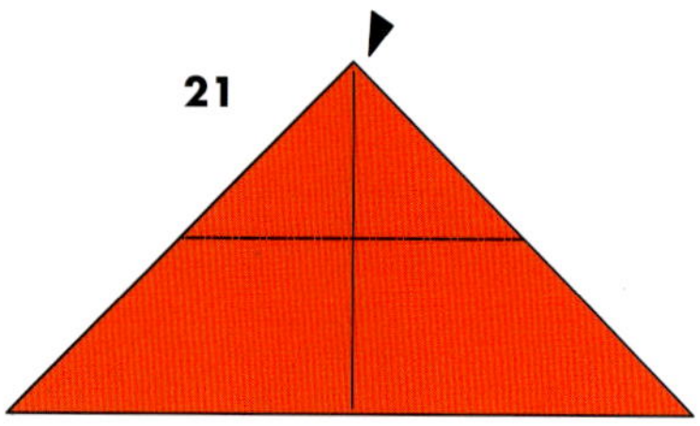

Sink halfway, closed at the surface, and
open at the rear.

22

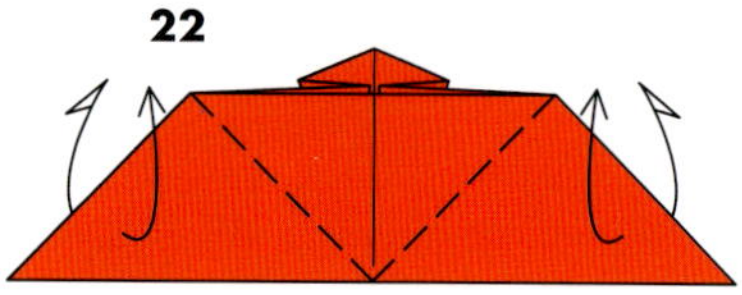

Outside reverse fold the sides.

23

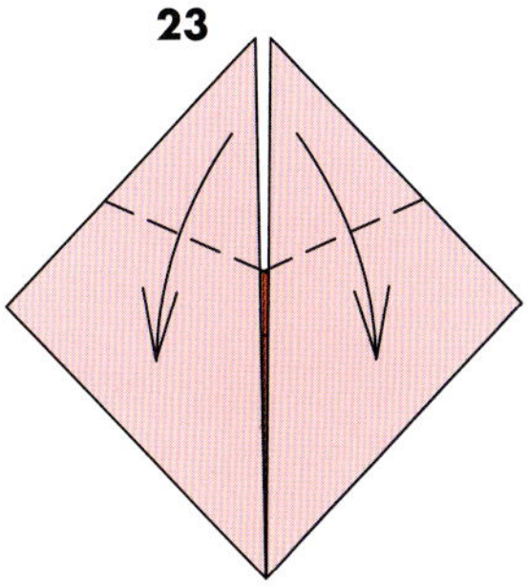

Valley fold the flaps down.

24

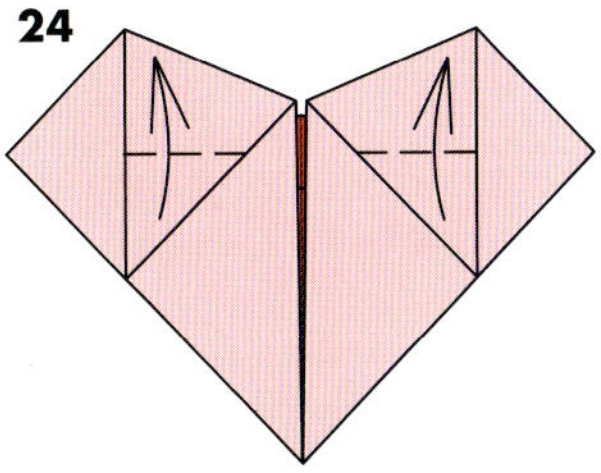

Valley fold the flaps up.

25

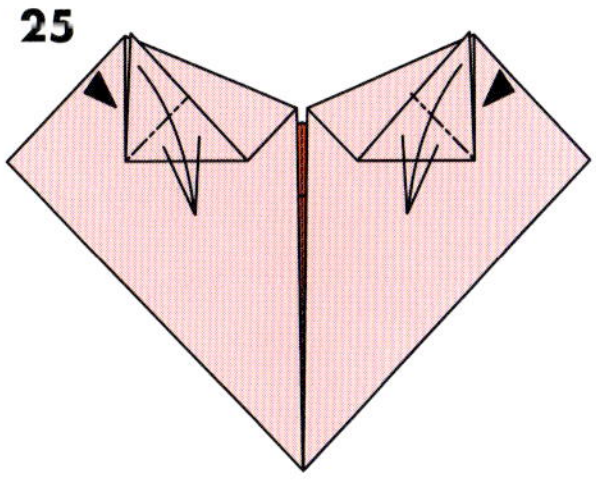

Squash fold the flaps.

26

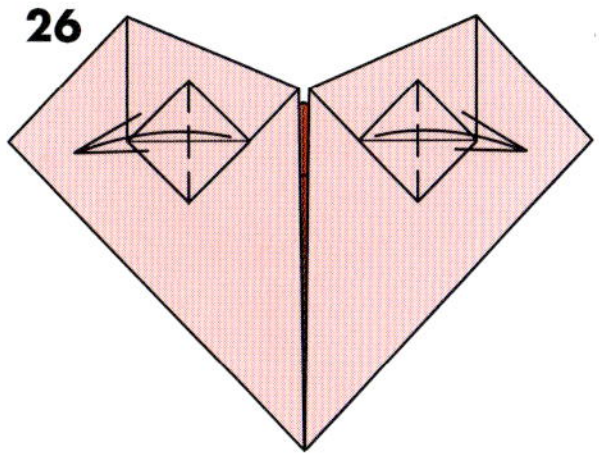

Valley fold the corners outward.

27

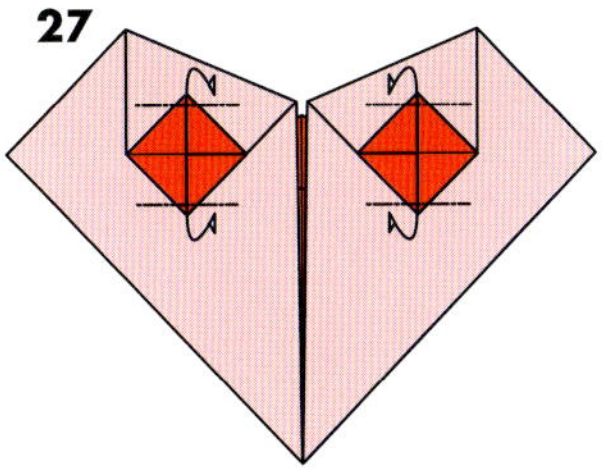

Round off the corners with mountain folds.

28

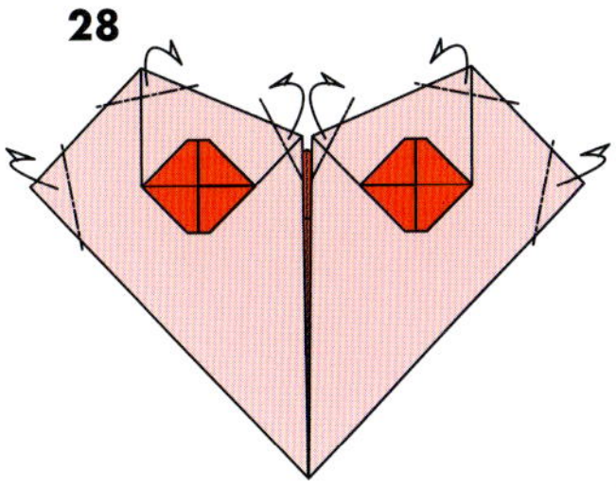

Shape the wings with mountain folds.

29

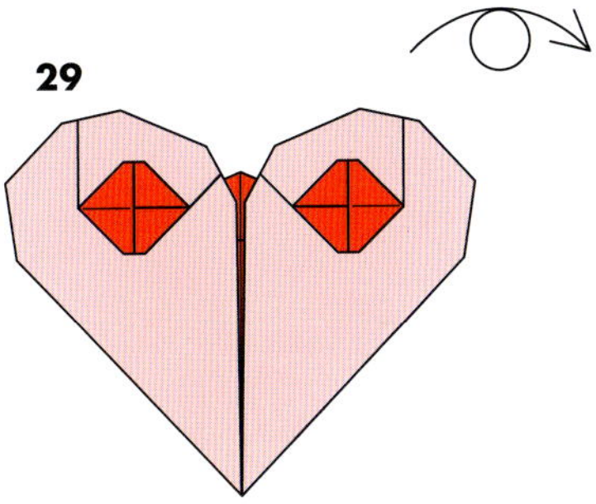

Turn over.

30

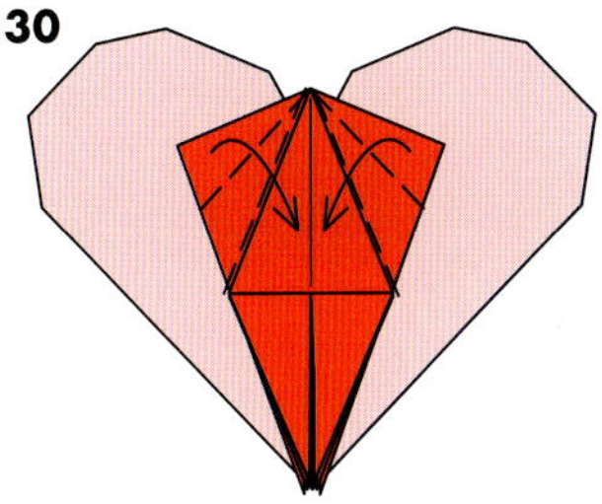

Valley fold the sides in over and over.

31

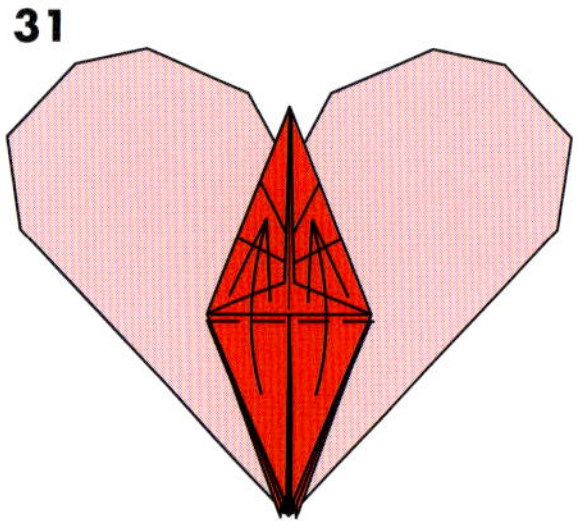

Valley fold a set of flaps up.

32

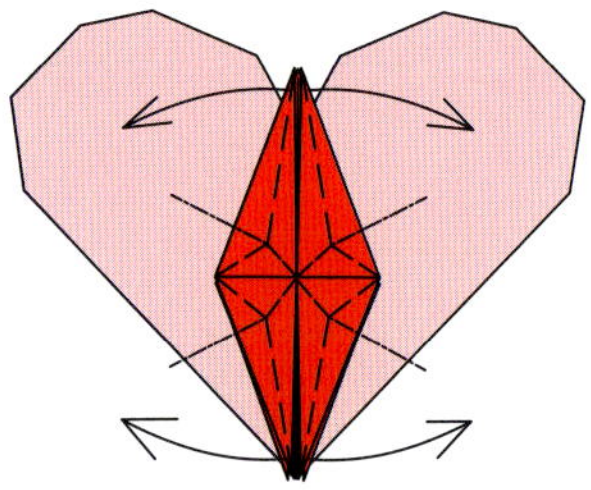

Rabbit ear the top sets of flaps outward.

33

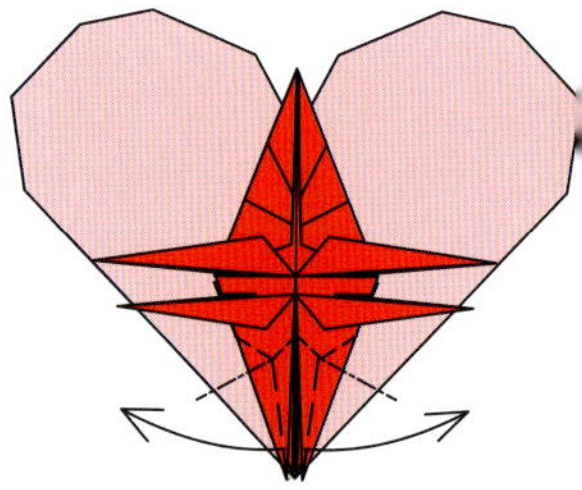

Rabbit ear the bottom set of flaps outward.

34

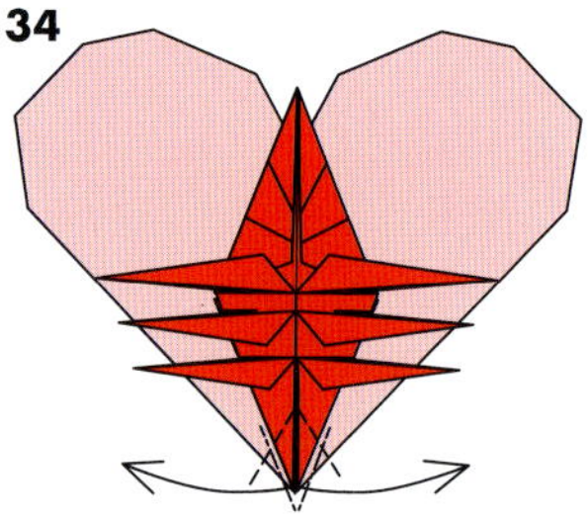

Unwrap a layer at each side to form antennae.

35

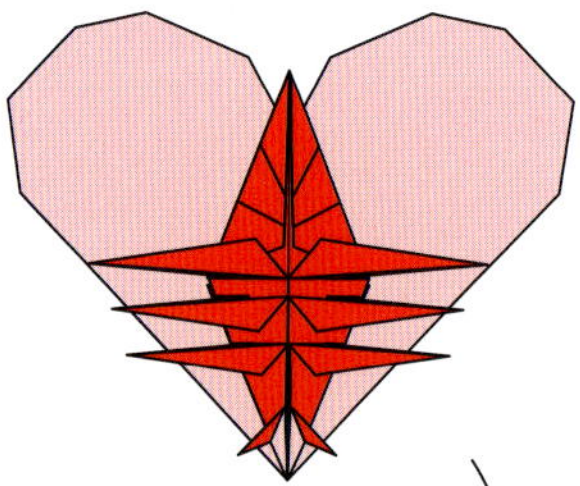

Turn over.

36

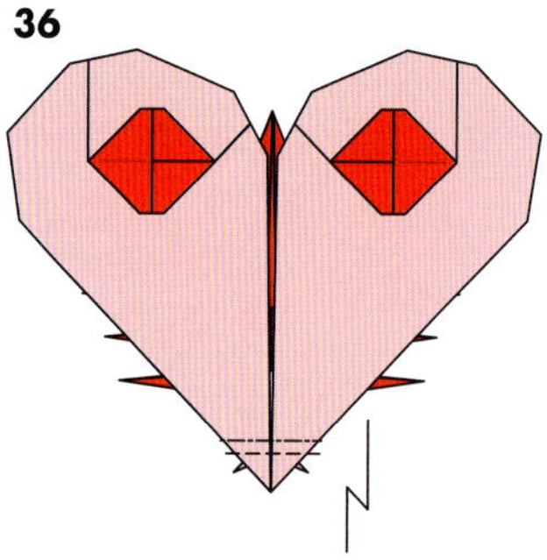

Pleat the bottom and shape and position the wings as desired.

37

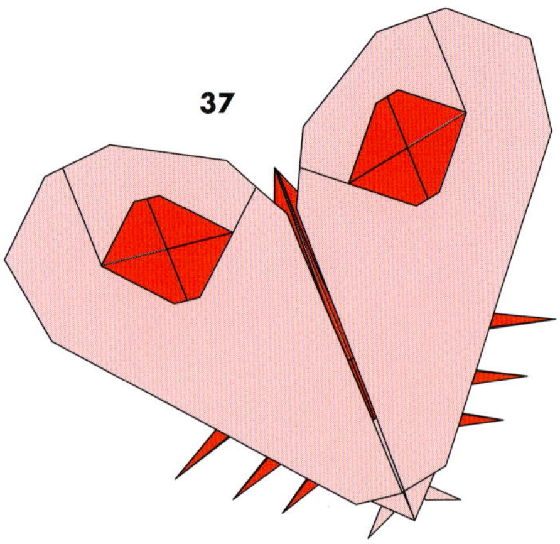

Completed Luv Bug.

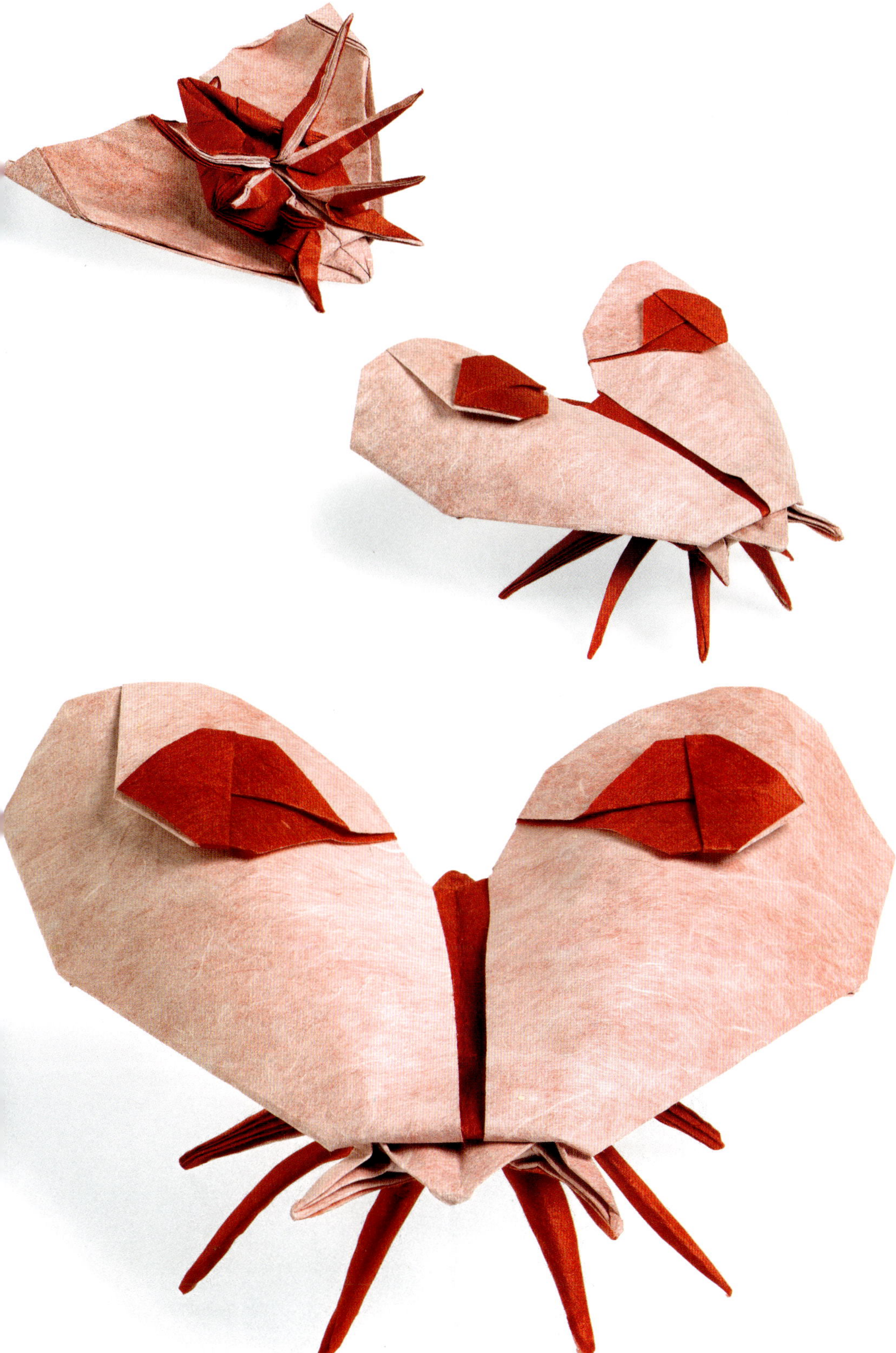

Monk

Stephen Weiss

Stephen's book Wings and Things *taught readers how to fold some pretty interesting forms. Read his bio on page 158 to learn what they were.*

video: *youtu.be/MZJfSA9KkeI*

1

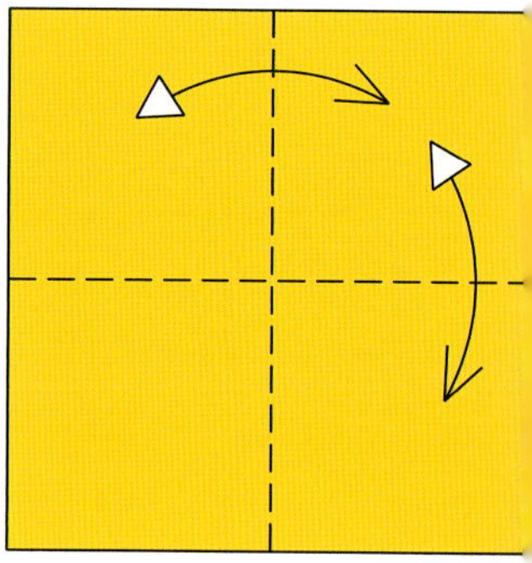

Valley fold in half both ways.

2

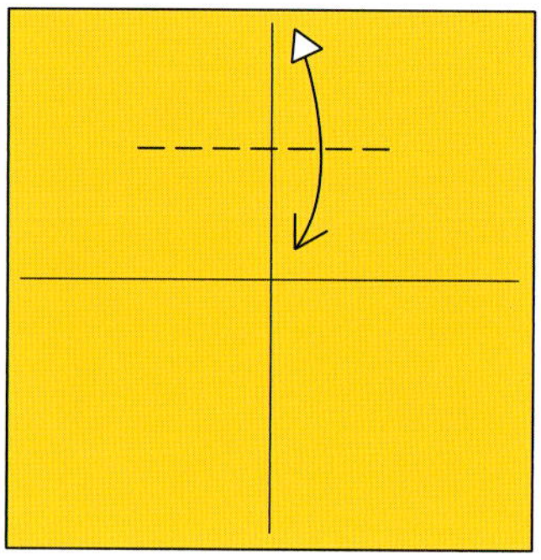

Precrease the upper section in half.

3

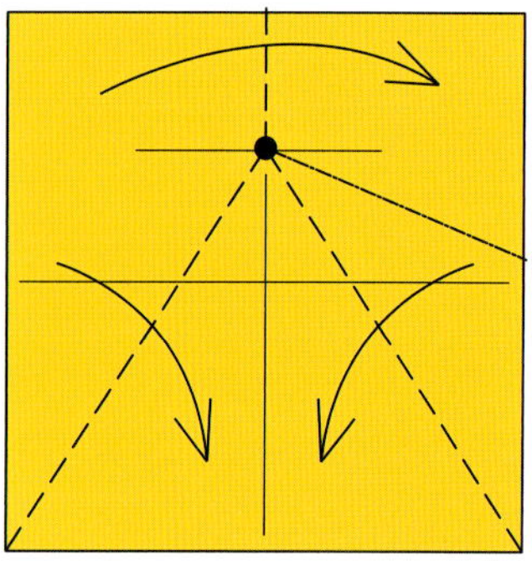

Rabbit ear, noting the dotted intersection.

4

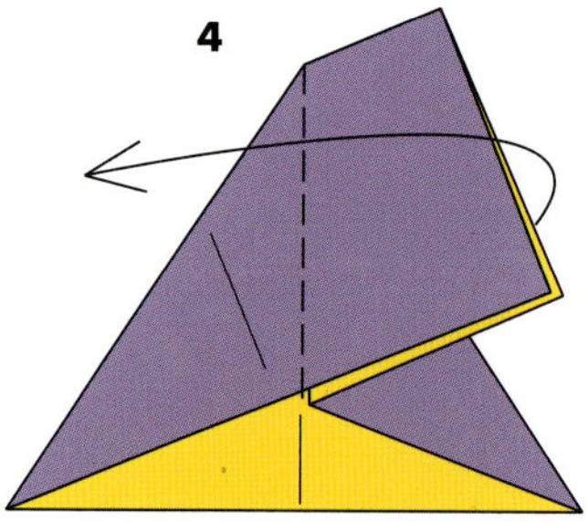

Swing over the center flap.

5

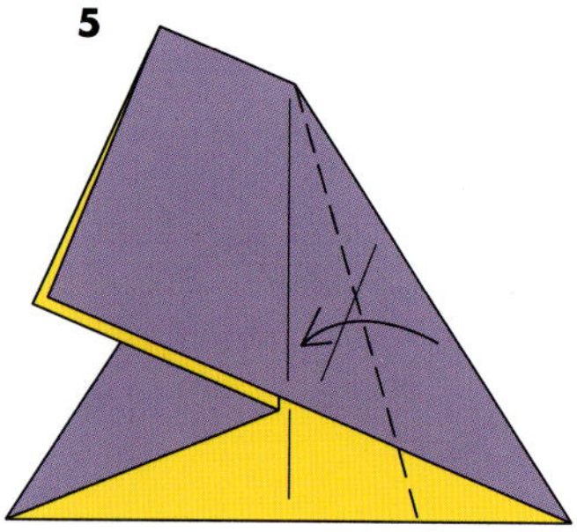

Valley fold toward the center.

9

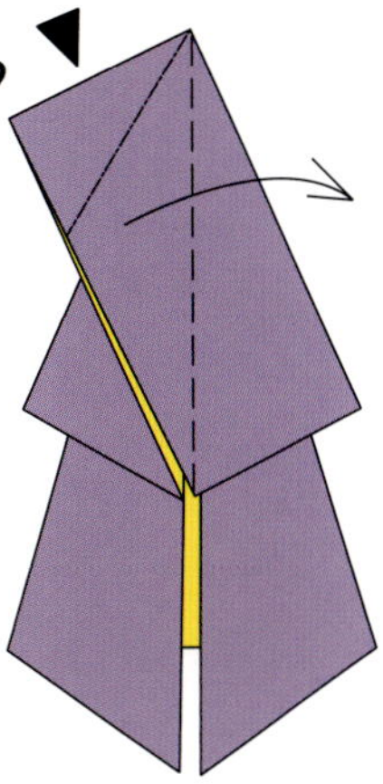

Squash fold the center flap.

10

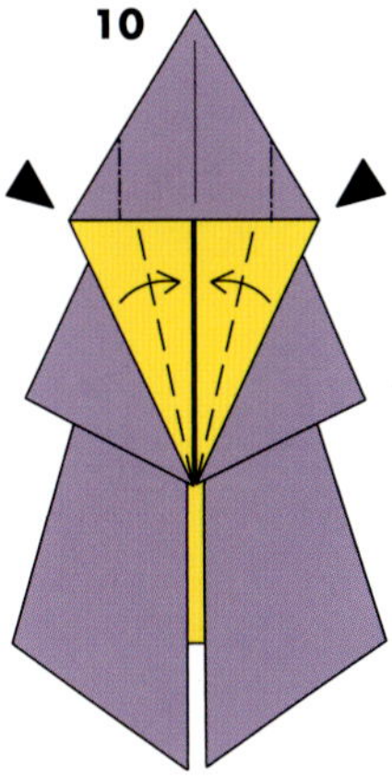

Reverse fold the sides inward.

8

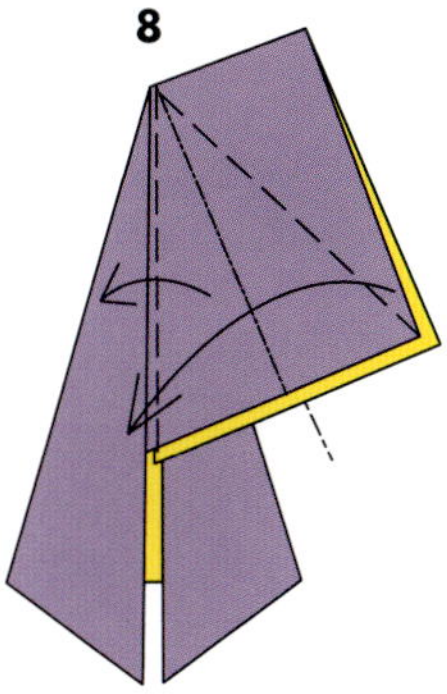

Crimp the center flap over.

7

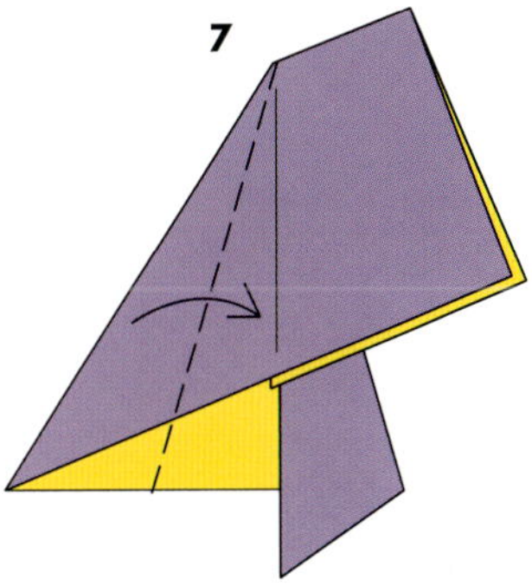

Valley fold toward the center.

6

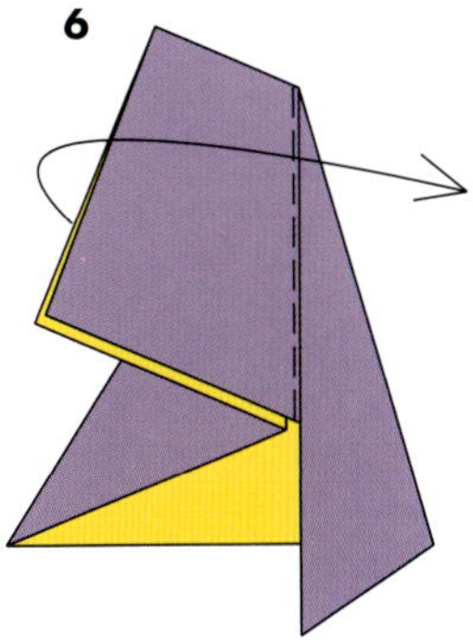

Swing over the center flap.

11

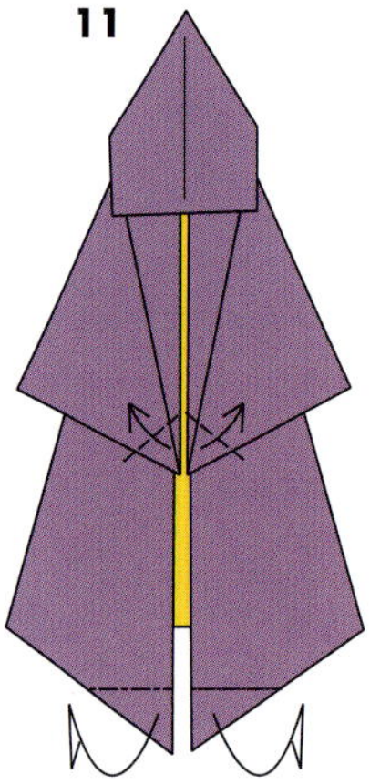

Valley fold the hands and mountain fold the cloak.

12

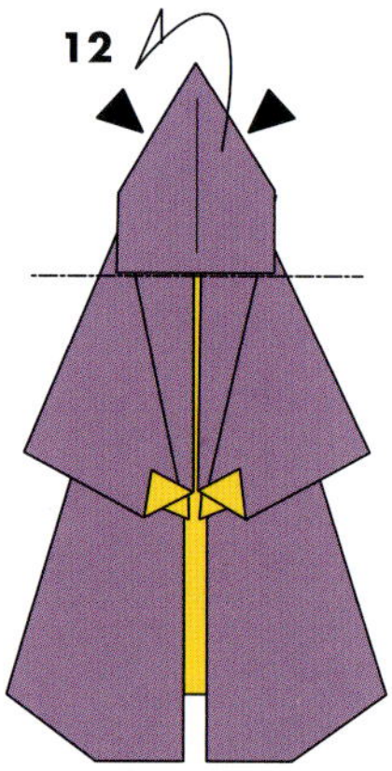

Mountain fold the head section back and open it out.

13

Swivel the shoulder sections back. Round out the model slightly.

14

Completed Monk.

Shamrock/ Four-Leaf Clover

Wensdy Whitehead

Like some of the other origami masters in this book, Wensdy comes from a science background. See her bio on page 157 to learn more.

video: *youtu.be/_fB1iKg80KU*

1

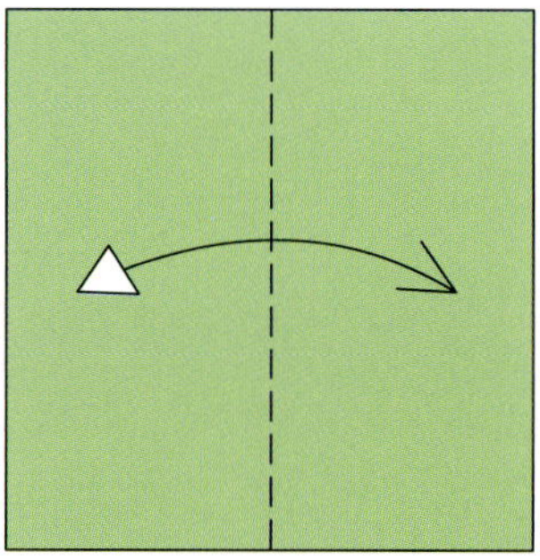

Precrease in half. Turn over.

2

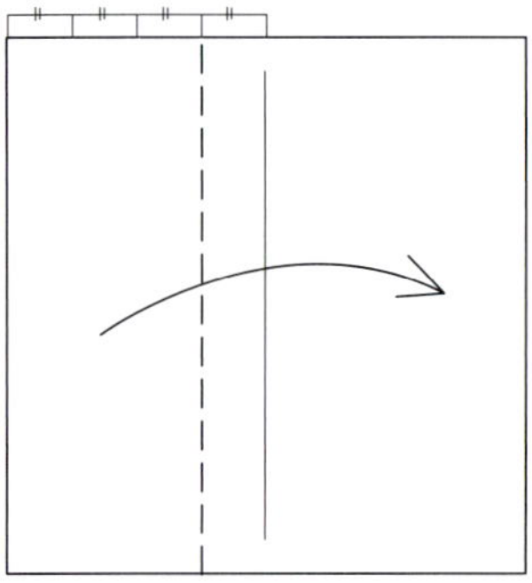

Valley fold over about three-quarters of the left side (an approximate reference point).

3

Turn over.

4

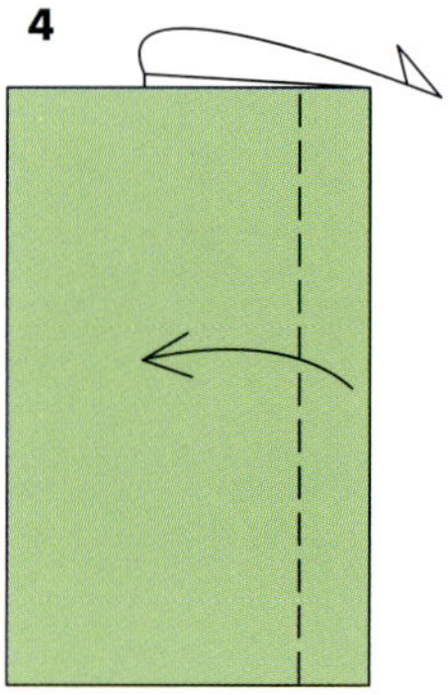

Valley fold along the existing crease, allowing the back flap to flip forward.

5

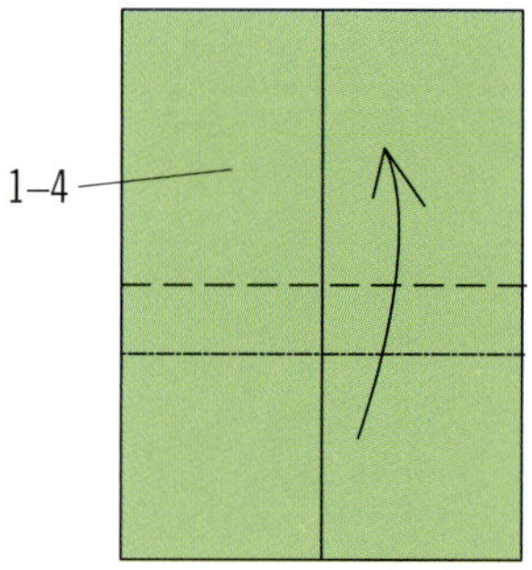

Repeat steps 1–4 vertically, aiming to get a shape that is as close to square as possible. The valley fold lies along the center, and the mountain fold should be at a similar three-quarter mark as used in step 2.

10

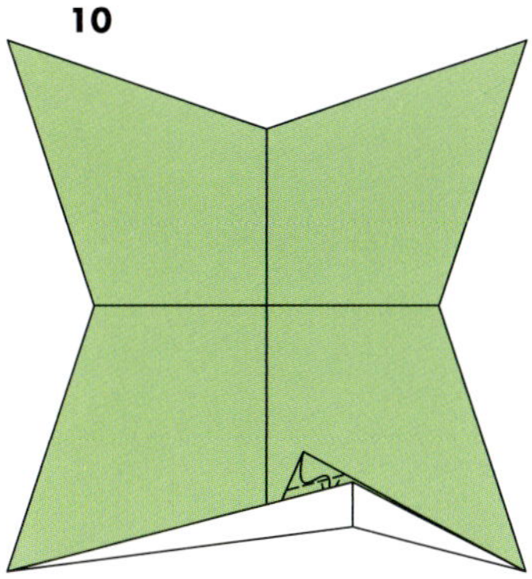

Tuck the protruding corner under the hem.

9

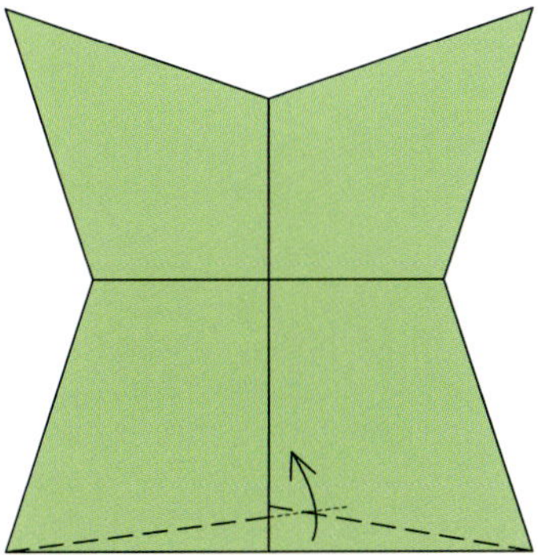

Valley fold the remaining side up, again allowing the center pleat to spread apart. Be sure to keep the outer corners precise.

8

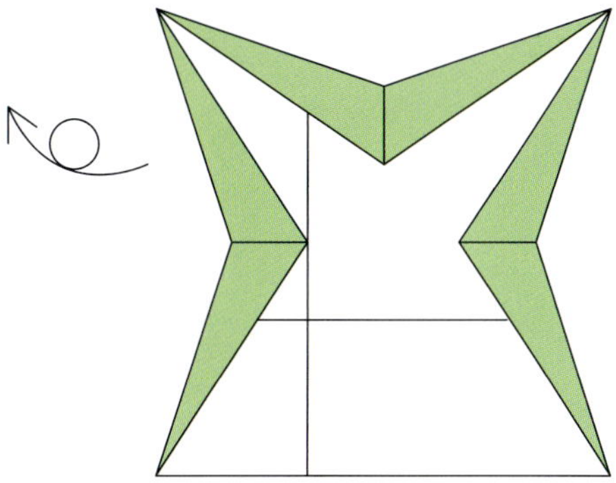

Turn over.

7

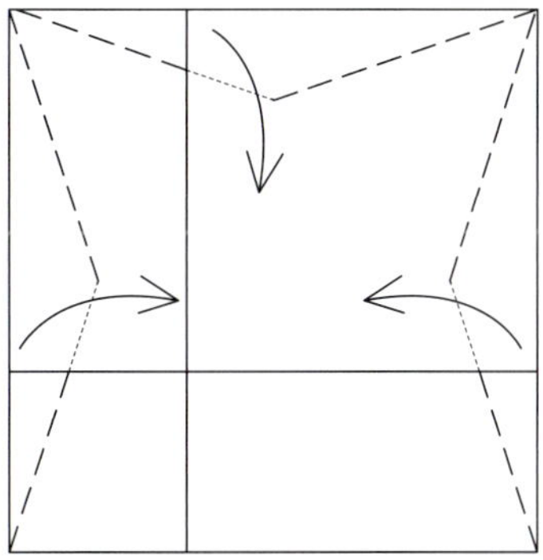

6

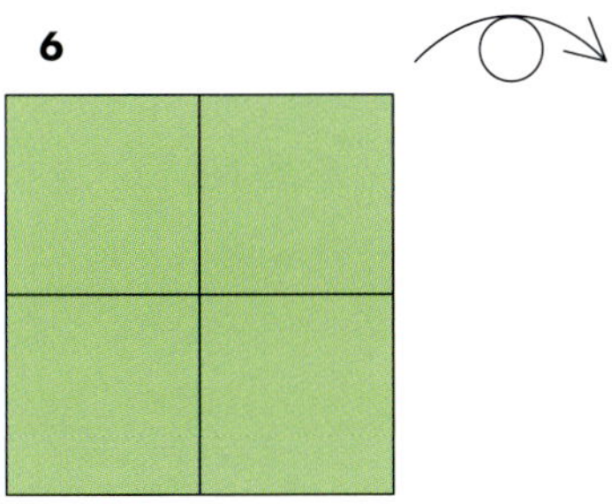

Valley fold the three sides inward, allowing the center pleats to spread apart flat. Try to keep the outer corners precise. Alternatively, for a four-leafed clover, fold all four sides, turn over and skip to step 11.

Turn over.

11

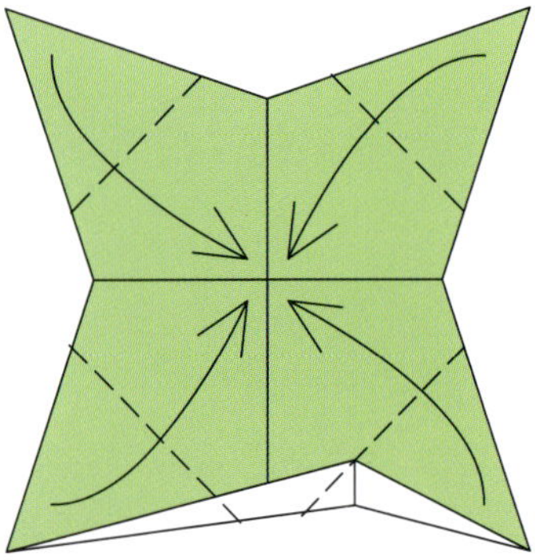

Valley fold the four corners to the center (blintz fold). You can press your leaf flat in a book (just like a real leaf) to make it extra flat.

12

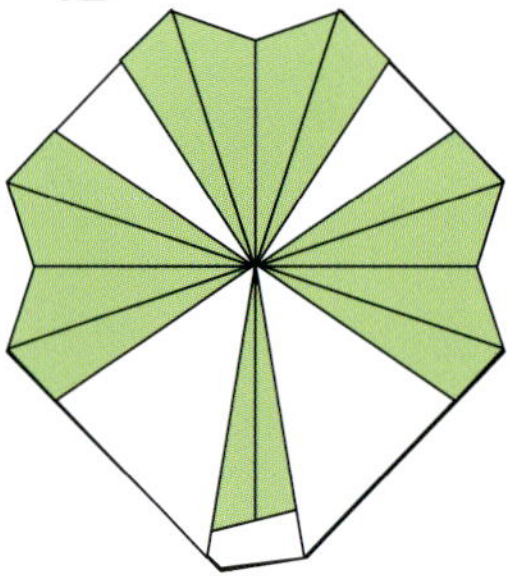

Completed Shamrock.

13

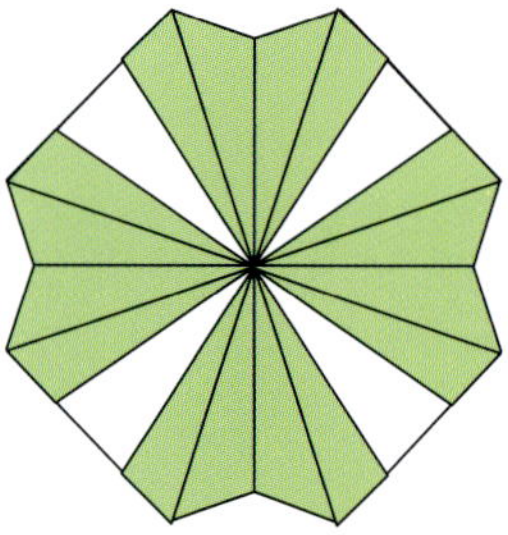

Completed Four-Leafed Clover using the variation described in step 7.

Contributors

Sy Chen

Born in 1961, Sy Chen was introduced to origami by his mother around the age of four. He was fascinated by what a simple piece of paper could do in a few folds. In grade school, he followed instructions from origami books and made up stories for the animals he folded. Among all the designs, an eight-legged crab design eluded him: he was not able to complete it. In Chen's adolescent years, his passion in origami subsided, but in 1989, his interest was rekindled when he stumbled upon an even more impressive crab design by Robert Lang.

The rediscovery inspired him to try his hand at folding more works of origami masters. Gradually, he started to design his own models and found the process to be much more satisfying than following other people's patterns. Chen's work emphasizes an elegant design aesthetic; he typically makes use of both sides of the paper to make sophisticated patterns. He is one of the few origami artists to have successfully created a checkerboard pattern from a single square. Chen is also an expert at designing clever models from dollar bills, which are featured in his second book, *Green Origami Gifts*.

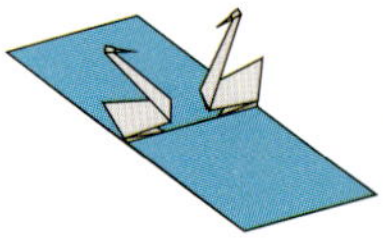

Patricia Crawford

Patricia Crawford (1940–2014) needed an outlet with which to compete against her super-smart brother, and origami worked well with her strong artistic sculpting skills. In the early 1960s she came in contact with what is now known as OrigamiUSA, and was introduced to some of the other origami artists of the time. She was inspired to design origami motels at a remarkably prolific pace. With Fred Rohm as her mentor, her works quickly increased in sophistication, without losing any of their charming qualities. She was able to integrate multiple subjects from a single square, often with stunning results. Robert Harbin of England was a big fan of her works, and heavily featured her origami pieces in his various book compilations. Many of her models have achieved classic status, such as her Unicorn and Full-Rigged Ship. The latter was clearly a favorite subject for Crawford, as she also created remarkably elaborate ship sculptures in the later years of her life. Crawford also mastered geometric models in origami, and some of her final pieces included multicolored stars made with many paper modules. Sadly, Crawford died in 2014. Her fantastic artwork, however, will continue to live on for generations to come.

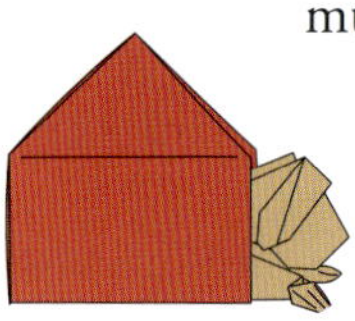

Paul Frasco

Paul Frasco (1979–) is an American origami designer focused on representational and animal designs and was heavily influenced by the modern origami design techniques of Robert Lang and the sculptural techniques of the French origami master Eric Joisel. He began folding traditional designs at a very early age but did not discover the world of advanced origami until much later when he found a copy of Peter Engel's *Origami from Angelfish to Zen*. Frasco worked in a number of sculptural mediums before focusing on origami design. He is an award-winning pumpkin carver and welder, and his original designs have been recognized by companies like Bioware, Rovio, and the Washington Nationals MLB team. His origami work has been featured in public spaces, museums, and galleries around the New York area. In the spirit of some of the artists he admires, Frasco has even invaded public spaces with his large-scale works. Perhaps most impressive, in 2012 he crafted a Dragon Whelp from a single square sheet of paper, 18 ft. x 18 ft., for installation at Stony Brook University's Wang Center for Asian studies. The finished model stood approximately 5 ft. tall. Frasco is noteworthy for being highly skilled at paper preparation. He will use multiple layers of varied colors to achieve a depth and richness rarely seen in origami papers.

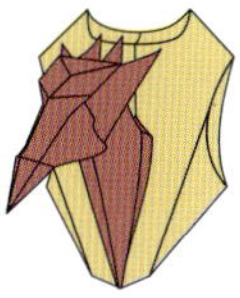

Peter Engel

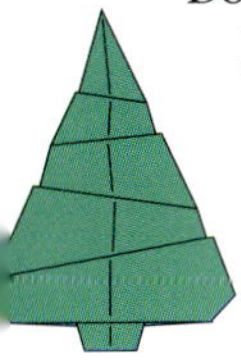

Born in 1959 and raised in New York City, Peter Engel encountered the books of Robert Harbin and Samuel Randlett at the age of 13 and became inspired by the elegance of masters such as Crawford, Cerceda, Rhoads, and Rohm. By the late 1970s, Engel had devised some of the most sophisticated pieces seen at that time. There was a buzz about his first book, *Folding the Universe: Origami from Angelfish to Zen*, released in 1989. This book is now regarded as a classic, largely because of the profound essays contained within; nearly half the book is prose.

Engel drew strong connections between origami and the worlds of nature, mythology, and traditional Japanese arts. Shortly after the book's publication, Engel, who had studied history and philosophy of science at Harvard and architecture at Columbia, took off for India to immerse himself in that country's tradition of sustainable building and craft. It was the beginning of a decade spent living and working in Asia. When Engel reappeared on the origami scene in the late 1990s, in California, his origami design was better than ever, showing more refinement and a newfound influence of indigenous craftsmanship. Engel has since released two more excellent books. He runs an architectural practice in Berkeley and is married with two children.

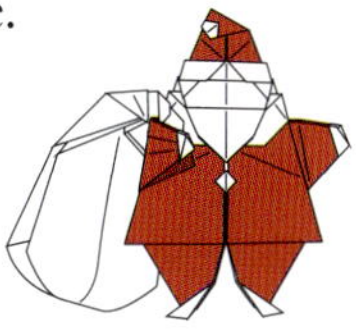

Beth Johnson

Beth Johnson had been folding paper for many years—since she was 8 years old—before she even considered developing her own original works. Necessity was the mother of invention when Beth was trying to make an owl for her niece in 2010. None of the origami owls she knew of fit the look she had in mind, so she tried her hand at developing her own. Beth has since created a few owl varieties, along with dozens of other creations. Perhaps the most unique element of many of Beth's works is how she is able to integrate tessellated patterns into natural forms. Her most famous example is her sheep, which features a coat that pops out through a series of cleverly linked waterbomb bases. She also avoids devising works that are too complex, and her folded examples have a refreshingly clean straightforward look. The popularity of her works has paid off, as her pieces are often featured at origami exhibitions.

Bernie Peyton

Bernie Peyton (1950–) was introduced to origami by his stepfather at age 9 via one of the classic Isao Honda books. He has maintained this interest in paper folding ever since. Bernie's career started in the arts, as a painter and print-maker. In 1976 he made a radical switch to being a wildlife biologist, doing field research on endangered wildlife. He would eventually augment his Harvard degree with a PhD in Zoology from the University of California, Berkley. This was an even bigger switch than his growing up in NYC and moving to California. His scientific background would play a big role in his origami work, as he has become well known for his realistic depiction of bears. Armed with a strong understanding of his subject's proportions, he knows the way the animals he depicts would move. The results he gets often feel very alive. Knowing the rules has enabled Bernie to break the rules, and he often has fun with his subjects, by comically exaggerating features, and even doing things like adding human expressions to plants. His design approach is focused on the final form, and as a result he is no stranger to idiosyncratic folding sequences. Bernie is also an expert on presentation, and has cultivated novel techniques to add depth to his folding papers (chalk dust via a fixative is a successful approach of his), and he creates elaborate dioramas where his pieces interact. Bernie also donates his time by teaching origami to the patients at Children's Hospital and Research Center in Oakland, California. He also served as a board member of OrigamiUSA. Samples of his works can be seen at *berniepeyton.com* as well as in his book *Eco-Origami*.

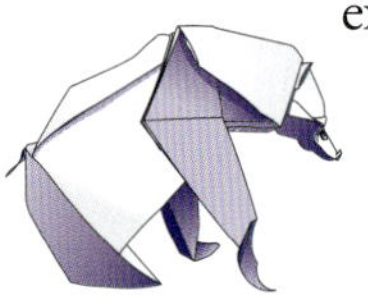

Marc Kirschenbaum

Marc Kirschenbaum (1969–) started folding paper as a form of doodling at the age of 3. At age 10, his origami skills were jump-started when he discovered what is now known as OrigamiUSA. There he was introduced to the works of Neal Elias, whose straightforward design approach he assimilated. He also took to the pure (square paper only, no cuts, no glue) approach that John Montroll championed. Later on, Robert Lang was a big inspiration as well, notably sparking the idea to develop a series of origami musicians. Marc went on to produce books, take part in major origami exhibitions, small and chic SoHo shows, and even a private exhibition at the prestigious National Arts Club. His origami efforts have come full circle, as he is a big contributor with OrigamiUSA. Since the 1990s he has been a managing editor for their publications committee, along with being active as a member of their board of directors.

Robert J. Lang

Robert J. Lang (1961–) would easily make anyone's short list of the most important origami artists. His works have consistently raised the bar for what is possible from folded paper, while displaying a sensitivity and deep understanding of his chosen subjects. His contributions to the origami community have been immense. He has synthesized a wide variety of origami techniques in one of the most influential books in the paper folding domain, *Origami Design Secrets*. He developed a computer program, TreeMaker, that automates several of the algorithms described in that book, allowing its users to draw a stick figure and then have the program generate a crease pattern that can be folded into that stick figure. Effectively speaking, Robert has removed a lot of the heavy lifting needed for a systematic design approach, leaving him freer to focus on the aesthetic nuances of the works he composes. In 2001, he boldly ventured into what few had done before him: he became a full-time origami artist. Always keeping his calendar full, Robert has been a featured artist at numerous exhibitions, shows, and lectures. He also composes privately commissioned works, and his artwork has been used in a number of commercials and advertisements. A sampling of these accomplishments can be seen on his popular web page, *langorigami.com*. In his past life, Robert was a laser physicist with a PhD from Caltech. He still uses his mathematical skills in what can be called applied origami, which is origami applied to technological problems. His contributions in this area include the development of a collapsing method for automobile airbags and of deployment mechanisms for satellite antennas and solar arrays. Robert also manages to carve out time in his busy schedule to contribute to OrigamiUSA. He spent many years serving on the board of directors, and remains an active volunteer. In recent years he has continued to explore the boundaries between origami and technology, harnessing the scoring capabilities of a laser cutter to create curved folds and polyhedral forms that would be impractical to create by conventional means. Not content to rest on his laurels, Robert continues to break new ground in origami techniques and approaches.

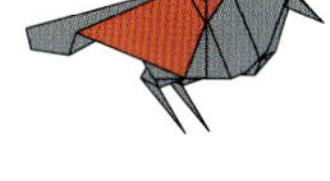

John Szinger

John Szinger, born in the late 1960s, was introduced to origami while in first grade, and quickly went from folding paper airplanes to conquering the models in the most advanced origami books at the time; John Montroll's works certainly left a lasting impression on John, and strongly influenced his future paper folding excursions. Other interests took over as he got older, and as an accomplished saxophonist, he would be found fronting various rock and jazz bands. When he had his first child, he needed a much quieter creative outlet, and his interest in origami was rekindled. He attended an OrigamiUSA convention, and was inspired by how much the art form had developed. While at an origami design class held by Marc Kirschenbaum, John came up with his first deliberate design. Many design efforts later, he now has a few books under his belt, and has been part of several major origami exhibits. His origami style combines realistic, 3D representations with a sculptural elegance and clarity. He is known for his animals, spaceships, and geometric forms including single-sheet polyhedra and tessellations. You can see his work at *zingorigami.com*.

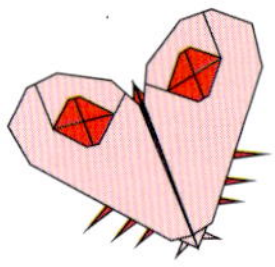

Michael LaFosse

Michael LaFosse is a true ambassador of origami. As a teenager, he was captivated by Leland Stowe's 1970 *Readers' Digest* article about Akira Yoshizawa, whose distinctive look inspired Michael to moisten and fold grocery bags, and then to learn to make his own papers. Michael began sharing this passion by teaching in local schools and clubs. He met fellow biologist Richard Alexander in 1988, and together they pioneered origami video lessons, and have since authored more than 70 publications. When Michael went full time, they opened Origamido Studio to teach, sell art, publish, design installations, collaborate with other artists, and make custom papers. Origamido® papers are sought out by folding artists worldwide.

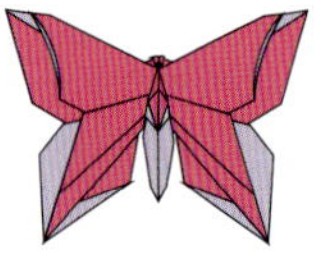

Michael has been in major exhibitions of origami art including the "Carrousel du Louvre" in Paris; "Masters of Origami" in Salzburg; and "Origami Now!" at the Peabody Essex Museum in Salem, Massachusetts. Michael has continued Yoshizawa's tradition of folding artwork that feels alive by suggesting a wide range of features by gently coaxing a seemingly plain paper flap. His biology training boosts his understanding of anatomy and behavior, and this helps his artwork seem realistic.

Bob Neale

Bob Neale (1929–) began folding paper in 1958, which he discovered through his interest in magic. He developed his first original design the following year. As a prolific artist, he was already able to have enough pieces for the first major American origami exhibition held that same year at the Cooper Union Museum in NYC. Bob's works often feature clever, yet accessible folding sequences. He has developed a wide array of charming action models, and many of his dollar bill folds have attained classic status. His square-based models have been popular as well. For instance, his Dragon has been used as a starting point for dragon models by a handful of other artists. One of his books, *Folding Money Fooling,* is noteworthy in the way he integrated his magician patter with his original designs. Aside from his books on origami, Bob has written books on magic and on religion. The latter should come as no surprise, as Bob is an ordained minister in the United Church of Christ. To him, origami, magic, and religion are all exercises in imagination. Origami has been a means of expression for Bob, which are frequently presented with social, political, and philosophical meanings.

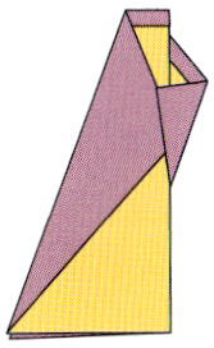

Neal Elias

Neal Elias (1921–2005) is one of the few origami artists to have a technique named after him. The elements of the Elias Stretch were explored by other artists prior, but no one else had cultivated this process to the heights that Neal had. Neal came to folding paper through his interest in magic, and was soon introduced to fellow folder Fred Rohm. By the late 1960s Neal started experimenting with folding structures that consisted of appendages coaxed from fan-like pleats. He devised systematic approaches to stretching these pleats into a wide range of configurations. Within a few years he was developing highly detailed models, often with multiple subjects from the same sheet of paper. He would often come up with creative names for his pieces. Why call a model "Guitarist Sitting on a Bench" when you can have an evocative title like "Andres Segovia?" Incredibly, while maintaining such high design standards, he was remarkably prolific with hundreds of pieces to his name. Neal kept meticulous records of all of these works, diagramming them in a special shorthand. He was a pioneer of what we now call crease patterns. More importantly, he also documented the works of other great origami artists of the time; without his notes, many masterpieces would have been lost forever.

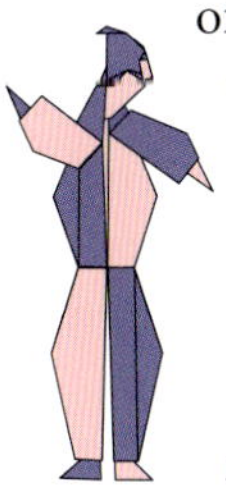

Gay Merrill Gross

Gay Merrill Gross remembers her fascination at age 6, with the colorful paper forms displayed on shelves and furniture tops, at the home of her older cousin. At age 9, Gay was excited to try origami for herself by following the instructions in a book she received as a gift. Unfortunately, this particular book had poorly crafted instructions for simplistic, uninspiring models that hardly seemed worth the effort. She might have given up had she not found much better books in the library. But her frustration with the first book planted the seed to try to make learning origami more fun and accessible.

In 1979, in her mid-twenties, Gay began attending monthly folding meetings at what is now known as OrigamiUSA in New York City. At the suggestion of cofounder Michael Shall, she also began helping the organization's founder, Lillian Oppenheimer, with her extensive collection of origami books and models. These origami mentors inspired and encouraged her to teach origami professionally. She was a pioneer of origami storytelling, integrating fun tales with folding sequences to make the models easier to remember. Gay also developed her own original versions of origami designs, which are typified by being easy to fold and teach, and are often whimsical. In 1989, Alice Gray, another OrigamiUSA cofounder, recommended Gross to a publisher looking for an author for a book on fun and interesting ways to use origami. Gay is now the author of 11 books. Her publications are often at the top of lists for first-time folders and anyone interested in using origami in creative ways. Through her books and workshops, she loves to share the joy and creative inspiration she receives from this magical art that requires nothing more than a simple sheet of paper.

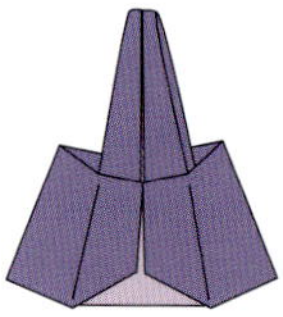

Fred Rohm

Fred Rohm (1907–1991) turned to origami in the early 1960s as a way to keep his fingers busy after quitting smoking. He was already familiar with paper-folding concepts through his strong interest in magic and from some traditional models he was introduced to as a kid. He soon struck up a running correspondence with fellow folder Neal Elias, and the two of them would push each other to new technical heights. Fred's personality was such that he would not give up until a problem was solved, and this perseverance helped him successfully tackle the origami design challenges that were posed in the origami community. Some challenges were self-imposed, like the series of stars he developed toward the end of his folding career. He was very proud to have developed a clever way of making a star with a hole in its center without cutting. While most origami designers at the time would use a traditional base as a starting point, Fred was one of the first to radically venture outside that comfort zone. He did not want to be confined to the structures that were already developed. As many of his works have attained classic status, they are sure to be enjoyed for generations to come.

Wensdy Whitehead

Wensdy Whitehead (1971–) began folding at age 4, two years before she ever heard the word "origami." Her mother started her off with a couple of traditional models, and by age 9 she was off hunting for origami books to feed her creative appetite. After college, Wensdy became active in the origami community by becoming a regular at local origami groups and national conventions. These became the platform to showcase her own original pieces. The more she created, the more she felt compelled to create her own works so she could have something original to share. Her folding sequences are typically both clever and accessible, and she has a knack for choosing interesting subject matter. Notable series include entire words and phrases created just through folding single sheets, and she went through a phase of integrating heart shapes onto traditional models and her existing works to give them new meaning. Wensdy has also had much success exploiting the geometries of dollar bills, and even created a book on the subject, *Election Money Folds 2012*. As a skilled folder, Wensdy has taken part in a few major origami exhibitions, including "Origami Now!" at the Peabody Essex Museum near Boston. She graduated from Cornell University with a Bachelor of Science degree in computer science, which she practices when she is not folding paper. This education affects how she approaches origami design; she thinks about folding algorithms much more than about geometric allocation of paper.

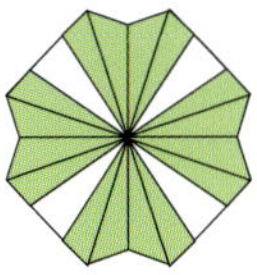

Jason Ku

Jason Ku (1986–) has been folding since the age of 5, having been introduced to a traditional model through his maternal grandmother. He was captivated enough by origami to start designing his own works in high school. Jason's works evolved quickly in their complexity and sophistication, although more recently he has made an effort to develop pieces that are more accessible. In 2005, he was the recipient of the prestigious Yoshino fund, making him the special guest at the Tanteidan convention in Tokyo, Japan. In that same year, as a student at MIT, he joined the school's origami club and served as president for seven years. His most noteworthy achievement in that capacity was initiating an annual origami convention at MIT. Jason also joined the OrigamiUSA board of directors, and cultivated and managed their online publication, *The Fold*. His works have found their way into a variety of origami books and have also been regularly featured at origami exhibitions around the world.

Jeremy Shafer

Jeremy Shafer stands out from his origami peers in the way he has turned paper folding into performance art. As a professional entertainer (he is a world-class juggler and unicyclist) he has integrated many of his action models into his routine. The first of his three books, *Origami to Astonish and Amuse,* was aptly titled. Working with fellow origami artist Chris Palmer, he has developed pleated structures that can easily expand and contract, called "flashers." To further spread his entertainment reach, Jeremy has developed a YouTube channel, *jeremyshaferorigami*. You can even hear some of his piano playing as the background music.

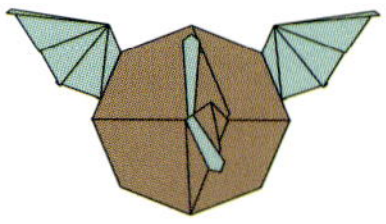

Stephen Weiss

Stephen Weiss (1948–) was exposed to maybe 8 or 10 traditional models from age 8 to 13, but started creating original origami pieces in the late 1970s. He is very sensitive to the form of his subjects, most of which tend to be animals, and will often try different approaches and adjustments to obtain the best results, and sometimes spend years perfecting his pieces (although others may be mostly finalized in a few days). This meticulous attention to detail is especially apparent in his dollar bill folds, where the patterns on the dollar can often be used to represent features, for example, eyes, of the subject. His dollar bill models rank among the most popular in the genre. Stephen also took an interesting turn in the 1980s with his book *Wings and Things* that showcased his flying origami pieces. Unlike most paper airplane books at the time, his models were all from single uncut squares, and often took novel forms (for instance a flying nun). He is also half responsible for the classic *Origami Zoo,* which he coauthored with Robert Lang. Weiss's works have also been featured in origami exhibitions around the world.